Disability Services
in Higher Education

KIRSTEN T. BEHLING, EILEEN H. BELLEMORE, LISA B. BIBEAU, ANDREW S. CIOFFI, AND BRIDGET A. MCNAMEE

Disability Services in Higher Education

An Insider's Guide

ILLUSTRATED BY ANDREW S. CIOFFI

TEMPLE UNIVERSITY PRESS
Philadelphia • *Rome* • *Tokyo*

TEMPLE UNIVERSITY PRESS
Philadelphia, Pennsylvania 19122
tupress.temple.edu

Copyright © 2023 by Temple University—Of The Commonwealth System of Higher Education
All rights reserved
Published 2023

Library of Congress Cataloging-in-Publication Data

Names: Behling, Kirsten (Kirsten T.) author. | Bellemore, Eileen H., 1970– author. | Bibeau, Lisa B., 1972– author. | Cioffi, Andrew S., 1982– author, illustrator. | McNamee, Bridget A., 1980– author.
Title: Disability services in higher education : an insider's guide / Kirsten T. Behling, Eileen H. Bellemore, Lisa B. Bibeau, Andrew S. Cioffi, and Bridget A. McNamee ; illustrated by Andrew S. Cioffi.
Description: Philadelphia : Temple University Press, 2023. | Includes bibliographical references and index. | Summary: "This book serves as an introduction to and point of reference for stakeholders in the field of disability services in higher education"— Provided by publisher.
Identifiers: LCCN 2022056206 (print) | LCCN 2022056207 (ebook) | ISBN 9781439923450 (cloth) | ISBN 9781439923467 (paperback) | ISBN 9781439923474 (pdf)
Subjects: LCSH: College students with disabilities—Services for—United States. | People with disabilities—Education (Higher)—United States. | Student affairs services—United States—Administration.
Classification: LCC LC4818.38 .B45 2023 (print) | LCC LC4818.38 (ebook) | DDC 371.9/0474—dc23/eng/20230313
LC record available at https://lccn.loc.gov/2022056206
LC ebook record available at https://lccn.loc.gov/2022056207

Printed in the United States of America

9 8 7 6 5 4 3 2 1

Contents

Supplemental Job Aids — vii
Acknowledgments — ix
Meet the Authors — xi

Part I: Introduction
1 Introduction to Disability Services in Higher Education — 3

Part II: Disability Services in Higher Education
2 Disability as a Social Construct — 11
3 Disability Services in Higher Education: An Overview — 33
4 The Day-to-Day Operations of a Disability Services Office — 50

Part III: The Interactive Process
5 The Transition from High School to Postsecondary — 79
6 Establishing Disability in Higher Education — 94
7 Determining Reasonable Accommodations — 115

8	Accommodations	142
9	Assistive Technology and Auxiliary Aids	156
10	Case Management	181
11	Roles and Responsibilities of Faculty	199

Part IV: Compliance

| 12 | How Legal Cases Influence Our Work | 217 |
| 13 | Distinguishing between Policies, Processes, and Procedures | 231 |

Part V: Inclusion by Design

14	Access to the Built Environment	249
15	Access to the Digital Environment	264
16	Universal Design as an Access Option	284
17	Collaboration across Campus and Beyond	304

Part VI: Conclusion

| 18 | In Summary | 317 |

| References | 323 |
| Index | 333 |

Supplemental Job Aids

Disability services professionals (DSPs) are often on the lookout for tools and resources to simplify our work, whether by improving processes, communicating more effectively, refining policies, or training stakeholders, among other things. We thought it would be helpful to share some materials we use in our day-to-day practices. In the online repository at https://scholarshare.temple.edu/handle/20.500.12613/8373, you will find cost-free, customizable job aids to inspire, copy, or revise. They are listed here along with the chapters in which their content is based.

Chapter 3:
    Event Accessibility Checklist

Chapter 4:
    Examples of Job Descriptions
    Sampling of Interview and Evaluation Questions
    Onboarding Checklist
    DSO Overview Training
    Verifying Accommodations Process and Sample Letter

Chapter 5:
    Questions to Ask the Disability Office

Chapter 6:
    Documentation Review Form
    Student Intake Form

Chapter 7:
  Sample Accommodation Letter (Accommodations Grouped by Category)
  Sample Accommodation Letter (Accommodations with Descriptions)
Chapter 8:
  Attendance Accommodation Agreement
  Assistance Animal Request Intake Form
  Emotional Support Animal Agreement
Chapter 9:
  Assistive Technology Evaluation Form
  Equipment Agreement Option 1
  Equipment Agreement Option 2
  Alternative Course Material Request Form
  Faculty Resource: Working with Disability-Related Interpreters
Chapter 10:
  Differentiating between Intake, Service Coordination, and Case Records and Reports
  Intake Interview Questions
  Case Management Communication Tools
  Campus Resources
Chapter 11:
  Roles and Responsibilities of Faculty
  Managing Student Attendance/Absences: Attendance Guidance for Faculty
Chapter 12:
  Helpful Resources
Chapter 13:
  Tips from an ADA Compliance Office and Key Terms and Definitions
  When to Write a Policy
  Policy Topics and Associated Processes and Procedures
  Example of a Reasonable Accommodation Policy
Chapter 14:
  Barrier Report Form
  Campus Accessibility Map
Chapter 15:
  Example of a Captioning Policy
  Statement of Accessibility on All Web Pages and Web-Based Applications
Chapter 16:
  Best Practices for Ensuring Accessibility in Online Courses: A Checklist
Chapter 17:
  Collaboration Meeting Agenda

Acknowledgments

We came together through a shared desire for professional development and forged friendships as board members of the New England Association on Higher Education and Disability (AHEAD). Over the years, we sought advice and consolation from each other, and from those conversations, the idea for this book was conceived. Engagement with our professional disability services (DS) communities has been the bedrock of our success. We are grateful to the following groups for their contributions to this book:

Our trainers and colleagues at the Postsecondary Disability Training Institute (PTI) and AHEAD who have generously shared their wisdom and experience through quality programming and rich discussions.

The Disabled Student Services in Higher Education (DSSHE) listserv network for its collective expertise, humor, and eagerness to share successes and setbacks.

The Disability Services Office (DSO) teams at our respective institutions that share the trials and tribulations of our daily work and push the envelope toward a barrier-free educational experience with dignity and respect.

The staff, faculty, and administration who walk with us in championing universally designed environments and share an unyielding commitment to supporting disabled students.

Students with disabilities (SWDs): Through their lived experiences, they have been *our* teachers. It is their stories that have inspired us to think creatively and practically in bending the arc toward full and equal access. They have been the catalyst for change and are the reason we wrote this book.

Meet the Authors

If you are like us, you might be reading this introduction and asking, Who are these so-called experts? Why should I believe them? These are fair questions. We wanted to take a minute to introduce ourselves through our personal narratives. Collectively, we have over seventy years of experience in the field and have worked at various types of institutions of higher education (IHEs). Each IHE has provided us with unique experiences from which to draw and share. Much like our DS colleagues, the pathways leading us to DS work are as varied as your colleagues' pathways. Later in the book, we share some basic demographics of those in the field to further highlight these differences. But for the moment, meet your authors.

Kirsten Behling

I grew up in a small town in New Hampshire. When I say small, I mean my kindergarten class was three students, and my elementary school had three classrooms. My little sister went to the same schoolhouse, but she spent her days isolated in a corner. She had a significant learning disability. As we grew, I watched my parents take her from diagnostic tester to diagnostic provider, public school to private school, and have countless arguments with teachers and towns on how best to educate her.

Watching my sibling's experience was difficult. Watching it without knowing what to do was really difficult. After seeing my sister and parents struggle to figure out what her future looked like, I decided to focus my education on trying to help. I began my DS career writing and managing grants through the U.S. Department of Education's Office of Postsecondary Education. Our goal was to empower faculty to be more inclusive. But often, faculty members would tell me there was an office to work with *those* students. Which students? *Those* students, they would say. Those were the offices I wanted to work in, then. I figured I could help disabled students while teaching faculty be better instructors.

I have worked in DSOs at four different institutions throughout my career, most recently at Tufts University in Massachusetts. I have consulted and worked with countless other IHEs across the country around universal design for learning (UDL), reflective practice, and conducting DSO audits of other institutions. And at each institution, despite the fact that no two look or even function alike, there is a deep and sincere desire of those doing DS work to ensure equal access for all. It is a profession I am proud to be a part of.

Eileen Bellemore

My interest in educational psychology was crystallized early in my high school years. My mother, a middle school educator, invited me to help in her classroom on days I did not have school. That's where I met Michael, a student with the hyperactive/impulsive type of ADHD for whom my mother had a soft spot. While Michael was thrown out of most classrooms, he thrived in hers. She designed her classroom to meet his needs and nurture his strengths. Unlike others, she recognized Michael was bright, creative, and sweet, yet deeply misunderstood. That experience ignited my passion for inclusive pedagogy.

After graduating with an advanced degree in educational psychology, I spent twenty-five years in education. Much of that time was serving K–12 as a school psychologist, 504 coordinator, and special education team chairperson.

There was no single, defining moment that precipitated my departure from K–12 for higher education, but rather a growing disenchantment with the fact that the laws in place to protect disabled students are not fully or even adequately funded by the federal government. Resource limitations meant that disabled students did not get the high-quality services they deserved. As a special education chairperson, I had the authority to commit district funds but faced pressure from administration not to. I often struggled to find balance between being a fierce student advocate and a fiscally conservative administrator. Time after time, the ethical balance tipped toward student support. It was time to move on.

My educational and experiential background proved to be a perfect fit for subsequent roles as a DSP in higher education. For a little more than a decade, I led single-person offices across three small, private colleges. I have since left higher education for a role as an accommodations consultant with the Association of American Medical Colleges (AAMC). I am grateful the work allows me to remain connected to my DS roots and colleagues.

I often wonder what became of Michael—whether people took the time to appreciate his talents, whether his teachers thought about inclusive design, and whether he was successful. At the core of my professional ethos is ensuring that students like Michael have every opportunity to realize their potential and feel they belong.

Lisa Bibeau

The law and how it relates to social justice issues first became an interest of mine before I left high school. Entering college, I thought it would be my path, but I took an education course and was hooked. I switched majors and got my undergraduate and graduate degrees in general and special education. In graduate school, I was hired to work specifically with athletes with learning disabilities. A new program was started to support student-athletes with disabilities, and I was the first hired into this position working with the men's basketball team. When I attended my graduate program, the men's basketball team at my university, became the center of attention. They were ranked nationally and became my work's primary, exclusive focus. I believe the national attention, and the teams schedule, allowed me to focus on a more inclusive model, and I became the academic support for all team members.

This was the accidental way I found my passion for working with students in higher education. It was a ride watching students succeed at incredible levels academically while finding themselves in the final four of the NCAA tournament. The team was embroiled in a scandal, and the professional position offered to me upon graduation was eliminated.

In July of that year, I found myself looking for teaching jobs and was offered a position teaching seventh-grade special education on a team of superstar teachers. We began to plan together and soon were teaching inclusively taught students while practicing true co-teaching. I loved my three years teaching middle school, but my true passion was still in higher education.

I was able move to an entirely different part of the country and start my career as an assistant director at the University of North Carolina at Greensboro. I spent three years there only to find my heart was still in New England, so I moved into my job at Salem State University, where I have spent the past nineteen years.

Equitable access to education is built around understanding the civil rights legislation providing equal access to students at the higher education level.

I found myself doing work that marries my interests in young adulthood with my desire to work in higher education.

Andrew Cioffi

I must have been one of those rare kids who always loved school. I did not really know what I wanted to be when I grew up until high school. I have a clear memory of the day, in the third grade, when I came to the sudden realization that school was important. Somewhere along the way, I got the idea that it is probably a good career if you can make a living helping people.

In high school, I had this one teacher, the archetypal biology teacher, who really sparked my passion for science. His curiosity was infectious, and the way he taught (with passion and gusto) had a lasting impact. That was it. I wanted to be a scientist.

I came to Suffolk University against the advice of a few teachers. It was "just a law school," after all. But I found a small, welcoming environment brimming with talent and dedicated professors, not to mention a well-established biology program. It ended up being a perfect fit. After my first semester, I decided to try my hand at tutoring. I had done well as a student and saw tutoring as a way to make some money and keep myself sharp for grad school admissions tests. I soon realized that it was not just science that piqued my interest—it was *teaching* science I had fallen in love with.

During my time at the learning center, I got more and more involved in educational programming and, eventually, educational consulting. When it came time to apply for grad school, I made the hard decision to go with my gut and pursue education. My formal graduate training was related to curriculum and instruction, but I knew that student services were where my heart lay. I never really considered that to be an option.

I was drawn to my first professional role in the field because it was in line with what I knew at the time. I was an assistant director for a learning center at a small college outside of Boston. What I did not expect was that part of my job would be to serve as academic advisor to students with disabilities in a specialized cohort program. I had learned quite a bit about learning disabilities before, but this was my first experience *really* working with students with a wide range of disabilities. Over the next few years, I developed my passion and skills for working with students, as well as learning the tech side of accessibility. It was time to transition to a role in a dedicated DSO. I was able to return to my alma mater, Suffolk University, in the role of assistant director, where I currently serve in the role of director of disability services. My first supervisor in the field of DS was Kirsten, my dear colleague and coauthor of this book. Twelve years later, here we are . . .

Bridget McNamee

I grew up with parents in civil service who modeled kindness and inclusivity, and I was always drawn to helping professions.

After graduating from college, I began working as an assistant teacher in a suburban Boston public school system. Working with preschool-aged children on the autism spectrum while obtaining my master's degree in special education set me on a path of working in two suburban and urban public school systems with students with disabilities of all ages. The opportunity to participate in a grant-funded initiative related to accessible curriculum introduced me to the world of accessibility services in higher education, and fourteen years ago I made the transition from secondary education to the postsecondary realm.

The work, while always challenging, has increased in complexity over the years. When I first started, it was all about learning disabilities and curriculum access. With the increase in higher education enrollment of students with autism spectrum disorder and major mental health and physical health diagnoses, and an overall increase of disabilities represented on campus, the work touches every aspect of the college experience from transportation and parking to living, dining, learning, socializing, and feeling connection and belonging. I did not anticipate needing to know how to retrofit a locker with a Bluetooth unlocking mechanism for a student with a physical disability or how to create tactile graphs for engineering calculus with pipe cleaners for a student with a visual impairment, but here we are! It is the opportunity to constantly learn from students, stretch my skills as a professional (although I still do not understand engineering calculus), and contribute to creating an inclusive and welcoming environment that energizes me.

My most recent career move brought me to the employment space as an accommodations advisor in the business sector. While legal and compliance requirements and the environment are different, the work is surprisingly similar. I have found that the employment space could learn a lot from the work done by IHEs, and my background has prepared me well for this career phase.

Disability Services
in Higher Education

Part I

Introduction

1

Introduction to Disability Services in Higher Education

Disability: A status, not a condition. A difference, not a defect. An identity, not a label.

Disability means many different things to many different people. The Americans with Disabilities Act (ADA) defines disability as physical and mental conditions that limit major life activities. That law is intended to protect against discrimination as a civil right. Yet nothing in the ADA supports the perception that disability is part of the "norm," part of human diversity.

How would you define disability? Perhaps you would start by making associations to physical or mental conditions, to people you know or stories you have heard, to notions of access and opportunity, or to adjustments in daily life you experience or observe. If you are reading this text, there is a good chance you interact with disabled students and have a working definition that resonates with you both personally and professionally. Perhaps you are reading this to broaden your definition or to rewrite it entirely.

The legal definition of disability begins with establishing limitations. The word itself, "disability" (dis + ability), suggests a reduced capacity for achievement. We know that that does not tell the whole story of the millions of disabled individuals. The truth is that 26 percent (one in four) of adults in the United States report having a disability (CDC 2020). Disability can be transient. It is one of the few facets of diversity that can change over the course of a lifetime. Disability is intersectional, crossing boundaries of race, color, religion, sex, gender, national origin, age, or other protected statuses. Disability is a natural aspect of the human condition. It intersects with all major life activities. But under what conditions are limitations exacerbated? In what contexts does our legal achievement fall short? It has been roughly a half century since the civil rights of disabled individuals were first recognized by law, and we are still struggling to answer these questions. Before moving forward, let us step back for a brief review of relevant legislation.

The foundation of educational legislation around access for individuals with disabilities became reality in the late twentieth century. Many advocates for students with disabilities (SWDs) would agree that the Rehabilitation Act of 1973 was the first piece of legislation to provide individuals with disabilities equitable access to postsecondary institutions. The legislation stipulates that if an institution receives federal funding, it cannot deny otherwise qualified students from participating in and benefiting from its services due to a disability (U.S. Department of Education 2018a). This fundamental legislation requires postsecondary institutions receiving federal funds to provide nondiscriminatory and equal access to people with disabilities, including access to facilities and programming.

While many see Section 504 of the Rehabilitation Act as foundational to postsecondary educational equity, it only addresses areas of nondiscrimination for institutions receiving federal funding. In 1990, the ADA extended the protections offered by Section 504. With the passage of this legislation, an extension was made for protections to public accommodation, telecommunications, transportation and service, and programming by the state and local governments (U.S. Department of Justice Civil Rights Division 2013). The ADA is divided into codes and titles, the most relevant to higher education being Titles II and III. Title II applies to governmental institutions that include public higher education. Title III covers private higher education under the area of public accommodation.

The ADA was amended on January 1, 2009, to clarify who is considered as having a disability (U.S. Department of Education 2020b). Specifically, the Americans with Disabilities Amendments Act (ADAAA) altered the manner in which disability was interpreted, expanded the list of covered major life activities, and established a more inclusive interpretation of the term "substantially limits." The amended law made it easier for disabled individuals to establish protection and qualify for accommodations. Without a doubt, the expanded list of major life activities—including learning, concentrating, thinking, and reading—established a basis for more students to be afforded the academic adjustments and auxiliary aids and services necessary for equal opportunity to participate in a school's program. The significant changes brought about by the ADAAA expanded the numbers of eligible college-bound students and higher education's obligation to provide access.

College SWDs are protected against discrimination and entitled to access to accommodations and resources, yet many still face enormous barriers to access and inclusion. The laws may have broadened the definition of disability, but they have not changed the narrative. Today's college students have grown up with the ADA and Section 504. Still, they report challenges navigating a multitude of institutional, environmental, and attitudinal barriers. SWD college completion rates lag 17 percent behind the rates of those without disabilities (PNPI 2021). What factors contribute to this discrepancy? Consider the resources not readily available to SWDs, the amount of extra work required to get their needs met, and the burden they must assume to demonstrate they belong.

As disability services professionals (DSPs), we recognize that there is a difference between the letter of the law and its intent. We understand that compliance is the floor by which justice is served, not the ceiling. In the disability services (DS) field, we aim for the ceiling—environments that are dignity focused, barrier free, and inclusive of all. Despite our institutions' inherent differences in campus size and location, capital and human resources, and professional level and background, DSPs are philosophically united in advancing campus culture and amplifying the conversation about the value of disability diversity.

Disability access and inclusion is an institutional responsibility. Many of our institutions' mission statements proclaim commitment to fostering cultures of equity, inclusion, access, and dignity for all. Often, we are the ones driving that mission. Since our work extends to every corner of our campuses and beyond, we are the agents of change rallying our leaders and campus partners to join us in building an inclusive culture. We are the educators elevating community awareness and knowledge of best practices. Our sustained commitment drives us to monitor compliance, shape policies, enhance culture, and advocate for resources to honor the mission.

One of the most powerful barriers to inclusion is attitudinal. The language we use can itself be a barrier. So, in writing about disability and language conventions—identity-first or person-first—we opted against a "one size fits all" approach. We respect the Association on Higher Education and Disability's (AHEAD) position of adopting identity-first language and agree that the implications of doing so embrace personal authenticity while shunning negative connotations of disability. At the same time, we honor the highly personal preferences of how people want to be identified and defined, so our writing uses a mix of both conventions. More on language is discussed in Chapter 2.

This book serves two functions: (1) to provide an overview of the day-to-day responsibilities of a DSP through an examination of relevant literature, case law, and narrative on established practices, and (2) to offer resources that current professionals can modify for use in their day-to-day practice. The overview takes a wide stance on how college students with all types of disabilities are supported. It serves as a comprehensive text for those in the field to learn about and navigate the nuances of their professions, including disability evaluation, accommodation decisions, management of a disability services office (DSO), advocating for resources, and collaborating both within and outside of the institution of higher education (IHE). Through an online repository at https://scholarshare.temple.edu/handle/20.500.12613/8373, we offer a wealth of supplemental resources to complement chapter learnings and guide work. These cost-free, customizable materials—checklists, forms, interview questions, policy statements, and other helpful resources—have been curated or developed by the authors and represent examples of what we use in our day-to-day practice.

This practitioner-friendly book helps newcomers and seasoned professionals explore and evaluate practices in the field. While there are numerous professional development opportunities, we recognize that time and funding often work against us. Our inspiration for writing this book emerged from our investment in supporting the needs of stakeholders who call on us to provide guidance, share resources, and discuss trends. We provide a wealth of resources and insights, culled from years of experience by frontline professionals working in a wide variety of educational settings, on navigating the complexities of this ever-evolving field and building a roadmap for better serving the needs of students, colleagues, community, and institution.

Utilizing research, reflective exercises, helpful tips, personal anecdotes, and best practices, this book is an essential resource through which we weave judicial precedent within a social justice framework to shape policies, procedures, and services.

As the student body in higher education is becoming more diverse than ever (Villarreal 2022), equity and inclusion efforts have become institutional imperatives. Disability should be fully integrated into broader diversity conversations with the recognition that many students embrace intersectional identities. We explore organizational structure and a continuum of service delivery models. Recognizing the sweeping legal, philosophical, and logistic shift that occurs between K–12 and postsecondary education, our review of relevant laws and preparatory practices serves as a primer to facilitate that transition.

Next, we offer a practical framework for establishing disability through a deliberative and interactive process—and for the use of professional judgment in determining eligibility for accommodations. Highlighting the important distinction between access and accommodation, we explore the latter in terms of barrier removal across curricular and cocurricular environments. The importance of assistive and emerging technologies in fostering inclusivity and independence is reviewed. While efforts to create more inclusive environments are a shared responsibility, in our role as DSPs, we play a vital role in creating more welcoming environments, increasing equity in services and programs, and collaborating with campus partners. Integral to furthering this mission is facilitating practices and pedagogies to reach the broadest range of students. Our work with faculty is both educational and supportive. Through training on accommodation implementation and inclusive teaching methods, faculty awareness of disability-related needs and pedagogical impacts are enhanced.

As the value of higher education continues to be called into question, postgraduate success is an increasingly important metric for students considering higher education. Given the discouraging employment rates of disabled individuals, we should be mindful of connecting students with employers, organizations, and agencies looking to diversify their workforce by hiring SWDs. Student participation in experiential learning opportunities such as internships, cooperative work experiences, or practicums is an impactful factor in students securing gainful employment. Even though these experiences often happen outside the boundaries of our campuses, we have a role in ensuring access.

Through discussion of case law and prevailing campus practices, we look at policy and procedure-related considerations for all aspects of campus accessibility. Sample policy statements, illustrative examples, and model forms complement these discussions.

Our focus on inclusion through design delves into the standards for built and digital environments. The design of spaces has the power to include or exclude. Commitment from campus partners at every level of the institution is required to ensure our environments are safe, accessible, and inclusive.

With remote, hybrid, and tech-enhanced learning on track to become permanent modes for course delivery in higher education, we examine existing web accessibility standards in easy-to-understand language. Because universal design underpins an environment where people feel they belong, we flesh out the universal design framework in a variety of applications.

Finally, we hope this book not only facilitates knowledge of the DS world but also catalyzes conversations about advancing access and inclusion. Reading professional listservs, attending DS trainings, and chatting with colleagues, you will find varying approaches to office operations, documentation practices, eligibility determination, policy interpretation, etcetera. Wide-ranging and sometimes colorful feedback from our peers illuminates the spectrum of our professional philosophies. Some lean toward policy enforcement, others toward social justice. The richness and diversity of these discussions challenge us to adapt and evolve. Few folks outside of DSOs really know what we do, the challenges we face, and the complexities of our role. DSPs are a small but mighty few, disability advocates for all.

We believe this book will resonate with a broad audience, some chapters more than others. Table 1.1 is a roadmap of this text designed to direct your focus to chapters most relevant to your work.

TABLE 1.1 A ROADMAP TO THIS TEXT	New or Prospective DSPs (0–2 Years of Experience)	Seasoned DSPs (2+ Years of Experience)	High School Educators, Counselors, College Consultants	Faculty	Institutional Partners
Part I: Introduction					
Chapter 1: Introduction to Disability Services in Higher Education	x	x	x	x	x
Part II: Disability Services in Higher Education					
Chapter 2: Disability as a Social Construct	x	x	x	x	x
Chapter 3: Disability Services in Higher Education: An Overview	x	x	x		x
Chapter 4: The Day-to-Day Operations of a Disability Services Office				x	x
Part III: The Interactive Process					
Chapter 5: The Transition from High School to Postsecondary			x	x	x
Chapter 6: Establishing Disability in Higher Education	x	x	x		x
Chapter 7: Determining Reasonable Accommodations	x	x	x	x	x
Chapter 8: Accommodations	x	x	x	x	x
Chapter 9: Assistive Technology and Auxiliary Aids			x	x	x
Chapter 10: Case Management					x
Chapter 11: Roles and Responsibilities of Faculty	x	x		x	x
Part IV: Compliance					
Chapter 12: How Legal Cases Influence Our Work				x	x
Chapter 13: Distinguishing between Policies, Processes, and Procedures	x			x	x
Part V: Inclusion by Design					
Chapter 14: Access to the Built Environment	x			x	x
Chapter 15: Access to the Digital Environment	x	x		x	x
Chapter 16: Universal Design as an Access Option	x	x		x	x
Chapter 17: Collaboration across Campus and Beyond	x	x		x	x
Part VI: Conclusion					
Chapter 18: In Summary				x	x

Part II

Disability Services in Higher Education

2

Disability as a Social Construct

Disability is, first and foremost, a personal journey. Disability is also a social construct, and it can mean many things to different people, whether they identify as having a disability or not. Disability can mean a lifetime of both personal and shared experiences of opportunities, barriers, compliments, empathy, sympathy, stigma, understanding, acceptance, exclusion, and, hopefully, inclusion. The types of disabilities that exist are as varied as the individuals who experience them. This text is geared toward DSPs who work in IHE settings. It is, however, primarily about people. In this chapter, we explore the identity development of a person with a disability on an individual and societal scale, as well as models of understanding and engaging disability, disability culture, social justice, and, ultimately, disability as diversity.

▶ Guiding Questions

1. *What did the ADA establish in terms of disability rights?*
2. *How important is the language we use in our personal and professional lives?*
3. *Why do stigmas related to disability persist?*
4. *What is the difference between equity and equality as they pertain to DS in higher education?*

Disability as Diversity, Defined

Every person has a unique set of abilities; it is a large part of what makes someone the individual they are. The types and varieties of abilities that a person can have are boundless. Institutions of higher learning can be rich and diverse environments where people can access a world of opportunity. This opportunity is created, in large part, from a wealth of talent, thinking, and learning that enables the progression of ability. But where does disability fit in all this?

The word "ability" itself can be defined in a neutral way, without implying rank or comparison. Simply put, an ability is a thing that can be achieved—certain knowledge or an attainable skill. Broad examples include domain knowledge, learning, analytical thinking, creativity, organization, communication skills, and technical skills (Spacey 2018). The more common way to define ability, however, centers on the power, innate or acquired, to do or achieve these things. This definition brings concepts such as potential and aptitude into the equation. It also establishes that there can be strengths, weaknesses, and, by extension, comparisons.

Our working definition of disability (covered in detail in Chapter 6) is a "physical or mental impairment that substantially limits one or more major life activity" (U.S. Department of Justice Civil Rights Division 2013). When we consider that major life activities—standing, walking, seeing, hearing, reading, breathing, etcetera—are abilities, we can surmise that a person with a disability is, by definition, less able.

But it's so much more complicated than that, isn't it?

In fact, letting the above statement define whether a person is less able is reductive and, as we explore in this chapter, potentially damaging on individual, institutional, and societal levels. Hal Lasko, who was legally blind, painted beautiful and award-winning paintings. Django Reinhardt, dubbed "three-fingered-lightning," is considered one of the most accomplished guitarists and jazz composers of all time. Sudha Chandran became one of the most celebrated classical dancers in India after sustaining an accident early in her career that resulted in a right leg amputation. Who gets to decide whether we call someone blind or a painter? Are we to assume that a person with impaired dexterity cannot master an instrument? Is it okay to say that a person is a talented dancer "for someone who only has one leg"? On the other hand, does it tell the complete story to let their achievements stand alone?

Perception

There is often a dissection of identity traits when regarding an individual. With this type of perceiving, comparison abounds. Comparing, in and of itself, is not a negative exercise. It is, after all, fundamental to establishing disability status and determining reasonable accommodations. It underlies the concept of person perception, the process by which we form impressions (Cherry 2019). Forming impressions takes place subconsciously, is largely subjective, and happens almost instantaneously. According to Cherry, "this allows us to make snap judgments and decisions, but [it] can also lead to biased or stereotyped perceptions of people." Biases and stereotypes are common phenomena experienced by individuals with disabilities.

Social Categorization

One outcome of person perception is social categorization (Cherry 2019). Freeman and Johnson (2016) support that these types of "initial social perceptions are, in fact, hardly 'initial'" and are centered, in part, on social constructs "harbored within perceivers." Their work supports, however, that these outcomes are "malleable to higher-order social cognition." The notion that we can change the way we perceive and socially categorize individuals underscores the importance of our work as advocates and agents of change. In this way, the role of the DSP extends far beyond the provision of accommodations.

"Able" is a complicated and nuanced construct, one that is given far greater meaning than evaluation of a singular capability. It can refer to potential, which can be granular (i.e., the potential to learn a skill or complete a task) or broad (i.e., the potential to be part of a group or to take part in a given venture). A person who is able *can*. It can also imply a capacity to succeed—a person who is able *will*. Assumptions that a person with a disability cannot or will not, however, are unfounded and categorically untrue.

With social categorization, snap judgments on whether a person is able are two-tailed. That is, some people might have the initial impression that a person is either able or not able. Two-tailed tests can be nuanced as well, deeming a person more able or less able. Visual perception plays an important role in this type of social categorization. The fact is, however, that most disabilities are not readily visible. Of the disabilities of millions of Americans, "96% of them are unseen" (Morgan 2020). Formed impressions about people with disabilities are, at the very least, unreliable.

Disability is not as simple. The ADA definition of disability, with subsequent guidance from the Department of Justice (DOJ), is intended to be broad. There is no list of qualifying conditions, and qualifying conditions do not necessarily dictate specific major life functions (even if there are common themes). Conditions affect individuals in different ways, and a person's collective abilities and experiences can shape the outcome. We are seeing new conditions and new effects on major life activities on a regular basis—as well as new ways of adapting and responding. Resulting disabilities from the

COVID-19 pandemic are prime examples. Disability is unique to the individual and is definitely a unique aspect of a person's identity and diversity. And like other diversifying traits, no single archetype can represent the breadth of diversity within a group. Therefore, our core responsibility as DSPs is to conduct individual assessments.

From a DSO's perspective, a disability may mean that an individual has ability in a specific area that is different enough from most people in the general population to warrant an adjustment. One of the most common requests for adjustment we receive relates to the time it takes to complete an exam. Some students request this adjustment because it takes them longer to read or process information; some do because of distractions they encounter in class. Others might request an extension because it takes longer to navigate an exam document with assistive technology (AT) or to work with an exam proctor. These examples speak to individual factors but are not indicative of a student's ability to successfully complete the exam. In this way, the term "disability" can be misleading. In fact, as we explore in Chapter 3, a lot of DSOs are rethinking their name.

Diversity, Defined

We have established that disability is a characteristic of diversity. We have also established that there is broad diversity among the types of disabilities that people experience, as well as the ways in which people experience impacts to major life activities. There is broad diversity among individuals within the population of those who have a disability, and a person's disability can interact with other attributes in limitless ways. We know that diversity can mean differences, variations, or even nuances, but it is important for DSPs to acknowledge how diversity is defined as a practice.

The Global Diversity Practice defines diversity as

> any dimension that can be used to differentiate groups and people from one another. In a nutshell, it's about empowering people by respecting and appreciating what makes them different, in terms of age, gender, ethnicity, religion, disability, sexual orientation, education, and national origin.
>
> Diversity allows for the exploration of these differences in a safe, positive, and nurturing environment. It means understanding one another by surpassing simple tolerance to ensure people truly value their differences. This allows us both to embrace and also to celebrate the rich dimensions of diversity contained within each individual and place positive value on diversity in the community. (Global Diversity Practice 2018)

This definition describes diversity as an active process and matter of practice rather than just as recognition and appreciation of differences. Including disability in this definition is critical, and there are growing efforts to expand awareness and advocacy of disability as a matter of diversity.

The Global Diversity Practice defines inclusion as

> an organizational effort and practices in which different groups or individuals having different backgrounds are culturally and socially accepted and welcomed, and equally treated. Inclusion is a sense of belonging. Inclusive cultures make people feel respected and valued for who they are as an individual or group. People feel a level of supportive energy and commitment from others so that they can do their best at work. (Global Diversity Practice 2018)

Diversity and inclusion practices are becoming more and more prevalent at IHEs—and rightfully so. Colleges and universities are dedicating resources to these efforts, including recruitment and retention practices for underrepresented students, staff, and faculty. Offices dedicated to diversity and inclusion provide individual student and group support, programming for students, and community education and service (both on and off campus). There appears to be little data on the inclusion of disability in these efforts, but anecdotally, we know there are gaps. As SWDs are historically underrepresented, it is safe to say that more work in this area is needed.

Occasionally, our campuses call on DSPs to lead this charge. In other cases, we need to advocate to be at the table. Campus efforts that relate to physical infrastructure, curriculum and instruction, student service implementation, information and technology, communications, marketing, and so on must include active representation of community members with disabilities. One of the core philosophies of universal design (which we explore in Chapter 16) is that if you design for the margins, you meet the needs of the rest. SWDs are kept in the margins, quite simply, by lack of awareness.

Persons with Disabilities

By the Numbers

According to the Centers for Disease Control and Prevention (CDC), as of 2020, there are sixty-one million Americans (26 percent, or one in four) living with a disability (CDC 2020). The World Health Organization (WHO) estimates nearly one billion people worldwide have a disability (WHO 2021). These numbers are "dramatically increasing . . . due to demographic trends and increases in chronic health conditions, among other causes" (WHO 2021).

According to the National Center for Education Statistics' (NCES) survey of postsecondary students, 19–20 percent of undergraduate students in the United States report having a disability, with 10–12 percent of postbaccalaureate students reporting the same (U.S. Department of Education 2019b). These numbers represent students from the 2015–2016 academic year. The NCES report from 2013 states that approximately 11 percent of undergraduate students from the 2011–2012 academic year reported having a disability (Zeisler 2016), suggesting an 80 percent increase in students reporting a disability after four years. We expect this upward trend to continue.

Transience and Intersectionality

Setting aside prevalence and root causes, we can learn a lot from a sociological perspective. First, disability can be transient—that is to say, it can come and go. As we explore in Chapter 6, not all injuries qualify as disabilities, but some do, as do a vast number of acquired medical conditions that are not innate or congenital. This invariably means we will have different SWDs at our institutions all the time. When we work with faculty, one of our common talking points is that, given the numbers, they surely have SWDs in their classes, whether the SWDs identify or not. We also share that this might change. The concept of transience is a critical part of diversity awareness and inclusion on our campuses and should be incorporated into campus planning and community education efforts.

Ability is intersectional; it connects with all other identities and social categorizations (NCCJ n.d.). The concept of intersectionality originated during the women's rights movement during the late nineteenth and early twentieth centuries. It was used to challenge the notion that the movement only applied to white women. Women's liberation needed also apply to black women.

> Today, intersectionality is used to address identities beyond race and gender. These identities include but certainly aren't limited to: class, religion, sexual orientation, age, ability and ethnicity. People who do social justice work have come to realize that talking about people in a multifaceted way, instead of focusing solely on one aspect, produces a much more open and safe environment! (NCCJ n.d.)

Research on disability and gender shows that women have a higher prevalence of disability than men. "There is also a lack of research on individuals who are transgender and genderqueer as research on the intersection between disability and gender assumes a gender binary" (Medlyn 2017).

Disability does not have equal impacts across all social categorizations. The CDC reports that disability is more common among women, older adults, and minorities (CDC 2019). Data from the CDC shows that American Indian and Alaskan Native adults have a higher prevalence (three in ten) than the national average, while Native Hawaiian/Pacific Islander (one in six), Hispanic (one in six), and Asian adults (one in ten) show lower prevalence of disability. The numbers show that one in five white adults have a disability, as do one in four black adults.

Race is not the only intersecting social categorization. One study suggests that adjusting for socioeconomic factors reduces disparity in prevalence (Goyat, Vyas, and Sambamoorthi 2015). Additionally, numerous studies cite that the intersection of poverty and disability increases prevalence. The National Disability Institute's report *Financial Inequality: Disability, Race, and Poverty in America* cites that "poverty causes disability . . . disability causes poverty," and "race is linked to poverty and disability in America" (Goodman et al. 2019). The CDC, as well as other sources, shows significant differences of prevalence between urban and noncore (rural) counties. Adults living in noncore counties, for instance, are 9 percent more likely to report having a disability.

Although varied from institution to institution, IHEs are diverse places. Diversity in every social categorization can and will be represented. The same is true for SWDs. While it is not possible (or expected) for the DSP to be an expert on diversity and inclusion, awareness and intentional practices are becoming more essential to the role every semester. Listening to and engaging students, understanding their identities and experiences, cultivating campus partnerships, initiating conversations, advocating, championing, and creating opportunities have become core competencies. These are not only ways of building rapport with students but ways of raising awareness, steps toward creating an inclusive educational experience that is beneficial for all.

Language

Before we look at individual and cultural identities related to disability, let us explore the nature of the language we use when interacting with and referencing people with disabilities. Having a way to address students respectfully is important. Doing so in a way that directly acknowledges a student's disability can take some consideration—and a little background knowledge of your student and commonly accepted practices.

Using language that identifies a student's disability has two immediate outcomes. The first is that it identifies the student as having a disability. This outcome is obvious, but there is an important distinction to make. A student owns the right to disclose their disability. We need to be aware of this, and of who we are speaking with, prior to using any disability-inclusive language so as not to out the student as having a disability. The second outcome of using disability-inclusive language is dictating that social categorization. This is often a necessary step, especially when communicating about eligibility, advocating with and for students, and engaging in community education. Because of these outcomes, there are a number of considerations for determining the right practices, and there are many implications for getting it right. Would it not be easier just to refer to someone as a "student"?

It is complicated. Avoiding disability-specific language is contrary to inclusion. The goals of inclusion are awareness, acceptance, and enrichment. Not including ability devalues individuals' identities, negates the benefit that diverse abilities can have on a variety of social groups, and is, quite simply, not good practice. However, there will be instances when a student does not wish to identify as having a disability. It is their choice, and we have moral (and legal) obligations to protect that choice. The best thing to do is to ask the student their preference.

When we do use disability-inclusive language, there are two major approaches. We can communicate about people with disabilities using either person-first or identity-first language. Person-first language means referring to someone as "a student with a learning disability" or "a person who has ADHD." This type of language identifies the person before the condition. Identity-first reverses the order and introduces the way the person identifies first. Examples include referring to someone as "a Deaf student" or "an autistic student."

Person-First and Identity-First Language

Person-first language intends to minimize defining individuals by diagnoses, implying a separation between the person and the physical or mental condition in terms of identity and social categorization. This choice can be considerate of conditions that may be culturally stigmatized as impairments, such as diabetes, cancer, dyslexia, etcetera, or conditions that have been historically marginalized, such as mental health conditions or intellectual disability. However, disability as a social categorization is much more complicated.

Some noted exceptions to the preference for person-first language that DSPs have adopted come from the direct guidance of disability communities. The two predominant examples are "Deaf" and "autistic."

The National Association of the Deaf (NAD) includes the following quote by Carol Padden and Tom Humphries in their guidance on Deaf community and culture:

> We use the lowercase deaf when referring to the audiological condition of not hearing, and the uppercase Deaf when referring to a particular group of deaf people who share a language—American Sign

> Language (ASL)—and a culture. The members of this group have inherited their sign language, use it as a primary means of communication among themselves, and hold a set of beliefs about themselves and their connection to the larger society. We distinguish them from, for example, those who find themselves losing their hearing because of illness, trauma or age; although these people share the condition of not hearing, they do not have access to the knowledge, beliefs, and practices that make up the culture of Deaf people. (NAD 2019)

From this knowledge and guidance from the Deaf community, some DSPs tend to favor the identity-first language of "Deaf student" over the person-first alternative of "student who is Deaf." However, while this is a general guideline, the NAD highlights individual choice.

> How people "label" or identify themselves is personal and may reflect identification with the deaf and hard of hearing community, the degree to which they can hear, or the relative age of onset. For example, some people identify themselves as "late-deafened," indicating that they became deaf later in life. Other people identify themselves as "deaf-blind," which usually indicates that they are deaf or hard of hearing and also have some degree of vision loss. Some people believe that the term "people with hearing loss" is inclusive and efficient. However, some people who were born deaf or hard of hearing do not think of themselves as having lost their hearing. Over the years, the most commonly accepted terms have come to be "deaf," "Deaf," and "hard of hearing." (NAD 2019)

In a 2020 editorial response, Vivanti addresses the question of person-first or identity-first language for individuals with a diagnosis of autism. He writes that

> the person-first approach has been challenged by self-advocates with autism (e.g., Sinclair 1999) as well as scholars (e.g., Gernsbacher 2017) on the grounds of two complementary arguments; (a) autism is a central, identity-defining feature that cannot be separated from the individual, and (b) the use of person-first language might perpetuate stigmatizing views, as desirable attributes are normally expressed through pronouns preceding nouns (e.g., "a smart child"), and alternative linguistic constructions might suggest undesirable attributes. (Vivanti 2019)

For communities such as Deaf and autistic, Vivanti (2019) confirms that person-first language separates the person from the diagnosis, and in doing so, runs the risk of perpetuating the stigma that the diagnosis is inherently negative.

While support for identity-first language within certain communities is growing, in 2021, AHEAD (AHEAD 2021b) announced a shift from person-first to identity-first language in the organization's communication, information, and materials.

Ultimately, in the current environment, the answer may be a bit easier than it would appear. Quite simply, it depends. It would do a disservice to students and the profession to choose one framework over another and strictly adhere to it. The above examples highlight cases where both person-first and identity-first language are appropriate. Even within those examples, there is variability. The key is that an individual owns their identity and the language associated with how they identify. As DSPs, it is not our place to decide how an individual views their own disability or how they want to be represented. We can, however, engage students in conversations about their identity. There will be times when we use person-first language and times when we use identity-first language. There will be times when we do not use any identifying language. There will also be times when we make mistakes. Our best possible practice is to make decisions informed by student preferences.

Neutral Language

While the use of person-first and identity-first language is fluid, the need for neutral language is firm. The general rule is to "not use language that portrays the person as passive or suggests a lack of something: *victim, invalid, defective*" (ADA National Network 2019). Some terminology can suggest that a person with a disability is "less than" or that there is a norm against which the person is negatively compared.

Neutral language supports the notion that disability is not a negative term from a societal perspective. Terms like "victim" or "sufferer" can elicit sympathy or pity and perpetuate stigma. Regardless of intention, they can lead to discrimination. The suggested practice is to focus on the individual or their identity and not on an impact or impairment.

"The" and Other Words to Avoid

Expanding on neutral language, there are specific terms we should never use as DSPs or members of a civilized society. Our ultimate goals are diversity and inclusion built on an understanding that individuals have unique experiences and abilities. In most cases, we avoid painting with broad strokes. "The" terms, such as "the disabled," "the learning disabled," and "the handicapped" are no longer acceptable. The major exceptions to this rule include instances where categorization is defined by community culture and shared experiences, such as "the Deaf" and "the blind." These categorizations are used and embraced by individual communities.

Terms that focus on impairment are no longer accepted. "Choosing language that emphasizes what people can do instead of what they can't do is empowering" (ADA National Network 2019). Terms such as "wheelchair-bound" or "confined to a wheelchair" not only focus on impairment, but also suggest passivity. Referring to a person as a "wheelchair user" reflects ability and an active role. Terms such as "schizophrenic" perpetuate negative stereotypes. Instead, opt for something like a "person who has schizophrenia."

These considerations apply to the ways we refer to individuals who do not have a disability. Terms such as "able-bodied" and "able-minded" perpetuate the stereotype that individuals without a disability have more power. Even the term "normal" implies that having a disability is "not normal" and that disability means something is wrong. All social categorizations have derogatory language associated with them. Terms that were once widely used (some as recently as within the past few decades), such as "hearing-impaired," "r*****ed," and "m**get," are considered offensive.

A number of terms and idioms that are ingrained in our culture are insensitive, perpetuate stigma and negative stereotypes, and should not be used. The term "crazy" might be used to describe an extremely busy or difficult day at work. This implies that a mental health condition is inherently bad and could have similar connotations for a person with a mental health condition. Some terms are condescending. Avoid using terms like "brave," "trooper," "superhuman," or "courageous." These terms imply less ability or that some accomplishments are not typical of individuals with disabilities.

Language is complicated and difficult. Some of the language we use requires education and takes practice. Incorrect use of language is also prevalent. As DSPs, we owe it to students and our campus communities to own a role in the process of inclusion. This role may, at times, mean modeling proper language. At other times, it may mean confronting improper use of language, which can be done in educational ways. There is great diversity within the social categorization of disability. Respecting proper language is a good first step in respecting individuals' experiences and identities. The best intention we can have is to treat people with disabilities the way they deserve to be treated: as people.

Personal Histories

Every individual with a disability has a unique story to tell. Experiences differ greatly from disability to disability, but no two individuals with the same diagnosis will experience their diagnosis in exactly the same way. There are certainly shared experiences, which are a major factor in establishing disability cultures and subcultures. Students' experiences are shaped by many factors. Both internal and external factors affect how a student views their disability, and, ultimately, how they identify as having a disability.

The first and most prominent internal factor relates to how the physical or mental condition itself impacts the person. Some impacts are positive; some are negative. While we embrace the term "disability" as a civil right, an eligibility status, a social categorization, an identity, and a point of pride, it is undeniable that there can be negative impacts of a physical or mental condition or its pathology. Some conditions cause, or are caused by, experiences such as physical or emotional discomfort, pain, or trauma. In some cases, these experiences cause additional physical or mental conditions rising to the level of disability. Individuals vary greatly in how they internalize these experiences. Individual responses, coupled with other internal and external factors, can play a positive or negative role in identity development.

Higher order internal factors also affect an individual's disability experience. People differ in their personal views and beliefs, and a spectrum of attributes and abilities shapes one's personal history. Innate attributes such as temperament and other personality traits play a role in how an individual experiences their disability. Other such attributes include coping mechanisms and learned skills. Perhaps some of the most important internal factors are simply past experiences. A person as a unique individual possesses exceptional abilities that may have been shaped by personal history. These can include factors such as the diagnostic process, kind and quality of care, efficacy of interventions, and so on. Beyond these factors, family environment, family and cultural acceptance, socioeconomic factors, and social interaction (in person and online) play a major role.

Experiences like acceptance and inclusion have just as much effect on students' histories as being marginalized or excluded. Some students experience positive social interactions; some experience bullying. Some experience achievements, and others may experience setbacks. There are social rewards and stigmas, open doors and barriers, and successes and failures, and there is almost always a mix of both sides. These experiences are as much a part of a student's disability as any major life activity or accommodation. The diversity these experiences add to our institutions is nothing short of astounding.

The fact is that the student sitting in front of us to request accommodations brings a wealth of knowledge, ideas, and emotions about who they are and what they have experienced. When we engage students in their personal histories, we find that so much of their stories are written in school. Our first interactions typically revolve around determining eligibility and granting or denying accommodation requests, and much of the story we collect relates to an academic and accommodation history. Students have a much richer story to tell. We can and do work with students at all stages of identity development. Students need their stories and their voices to be heard. As DSPs, we can play an active role in this process, facilitate a successful transition to higher education, and nurture positive identity development. In this way, our role moves beyond accommodation interactions toward student development and advocacy, making us active partners in the inclusion process.

Identity Development

An individual's identity development is a lifelong process and unique journey. Furthermore, the higher education experience is a time when many students work to understand their identity, separate from their families, and begin to navigate their experiences on their own. Identity development as it relates to disability is intimately connected to an individual's personal history.

> Each person will have a different answer, story, or way of understanding their disability. This is one way of beginning to understand an individual's disability identity, which is a unique aspect of identity that includes a person's sense of self as a person with a disability, as well as their connection to the disability community. (Forber-Pratt et al. 2020)

The Model of Social and Psychosocial Disability Identity Development, as developed by Forber-Pratt et al. (2020), includes four statuses to understanding disability identity development. Those four statuses are as follows:

Acceptance Status
- Become disabled and/or born with disability
- Person accepts own disability
- Close friends and family are accepting of the disability

Relationship Status
- Person meets others like herself/himself [sic]
- Engages in conversation with these individuals
- Learns about the ways of the group

Adoption Status
- Adopts the shared values of the group

Engagement Status
- Become a role model for others

- Help those who may be in other statuses
- Give back to the disability community

Progression through these four stages happens in a few ways. Sometimes the progression is natural, occurring as personal stories are written and affected by any of the factors we explored above. Sometimes positive progression takes place by happenstance, a product of a supporting environment (home, school, social circles, etc.). Sometimes interventions are required. Provision of care can result in achievement of a status as a byproduct, or intentional programming can be designed to address individual stages.

Some individuals achieve every stage, and some do not. As DSPs, we can learn a lot about students by exploring their progression through these four stages. There are conventional things we can glean, such as the student's comfort level with seeking accommodations. A student's identity may also tell us about how they transition to college, self-advocate, make use of accommodations, etcetera. Here, we can "meet a student where they are" and provide either direct support or resource referrals to foster positive identity development.

Social Constructs of Disability

The way we frame disability as a social construct has a direct impact on the success or failure of our inclusion efforts. From a disability studies perspective, there have been two predominant constructs in the way clinicians, scholars, case managers, educators, and DSPs refer to and interact with the categorization of disability. These are the medical and social models of disability. There are other models for constructing disability, but DSPs—in solidarity with those clinicians, scholars, educators—have adopted the social model.

> The medical model examines disability as resulting from a health condition. This model, which includes language and perspective, establishes that an individual has an impairment and suggests that the impairment and consequential limitations must be addressed on the individual level for the person to be able to overcome barriers, participate in daily life activities, and function in society. Ultimately, it means that a person is "disabled," and in this use of the term, it means that something is "wrong." The medical model is perhaps the most common way people without a disability refer to individuals with disabilities. (Disabled World 2010)
>
> Prominent critics [of the medical model] have included disability scholars and self-advocates, who attacked the so-called "medical model"

and espoused an alternative "social model," which characterizes disability as the product of an unaccommodating and oppressive society, rather than an individual and medical problem. (Hogan 2019)

The social model of disability establishes that disability is a difference. Barriers to access are not a problem of the individual but a problem of the environment or society. This model wholly supports the way we have defined disability so far. Disability is a status, defined where a physical or mental condition intersects with barriers. "If barriers are removed, a person may still have an impairment but they would not be disabled" (Open Learn Create).

The DS profession is based on interaction and intervention. As accommodation providers, we work with the student to determine eligibility for reasonable accommodations. We are not clinicians. What we provide is flexibility, resources, and services to reduce or eliminate barriers. We now know that it is the barriers themselves that are disabling, and those are our appropriate targets. A person who uses a wheelchair is not excluded from an inaccessible building because of their medical condition but because there is no ramp. Table 2.1 further outlines the differences between the medical model and social model.

Social model thinking has major implications for creating inclusion on our campuses. As we have established, SWDs have incredibly diverse personal histories. The medical model for disability is outdated for our purposes, as it fosters exclusion. Fully including SWDs in every campus opportunity, in addition to designing opportunities for all abilities, allows for many more voices, ideas, and life experiences to be shared, enriching the educational experience of our entire campus.

TABLE 2.1   MEDICAL MODEL VS. SOCIAL MODEL

Medical Model	Social Model
Person is faulty	Person is valued
Diagnosis	Strengths and needs defined by self and others
Labeling	Identify barriers and develop solutions
Impairment becomes focus of attention	Outcome-based program designed
Assessment, monitoring, programs of therapy imposed	Resources are made available to 'ordinary services'
Segregation and alternative services	Training for parents and professionals
Ordinary needs put on hold	Relationships nurtured
Reentry if normal enough OR permanent exclusion	Diversity welcomed, person is included
Society remains unchanged	Society evolves

Source: Mason, Micheline, and Richard Reiser, 1994.

It is important to note that these constructs are ways of thinking, engaging, and referring. Our work is nuanced and extends far beyond evaluating requests and transactions related to accommodations. As we discuss later in this text, we, as DSPs, need to advocate across all institutional lines. This advocacy means working daily with faculty, staff, and administrators who are not experts in these areas and may not have their own well-defined construct. Providing contrast between the social and medical models might be a quick way to close gaps, but we can often find better routes to fostering allies. Some of the viewpoints presented below may directly align with institutional priorities and our associates who are charged with orchestrating them. For instance, access and inclusion efforts may have a positive impact on students' retention. Sometimes it helps for DSPs to understand the politics of an institution—knowing that higher education is a business—and speak the right language.

Equity Matters

Discrimination

Disability, like many other social categorizations, is subject to frequent inequality. Discrimination and issues of access for people with disabilities is unfortunately common and can exist in a number of forms. There are four common types of discrimination that impact the disability community in education and employment settings. Those are direct discrimination, indirect discrimination, failure to make reasonable adjustments, and harassment. (Workplace Fairness 2022)

Direct discrimination occurs when a person with a disability is treated as less than their peers without disabilities or other individuals with disabilities. Direct discrimination may be intentional or unintentional. In this type of discrimination, a person is excluded from educational programs, housing or meal plan offerings, athletics, provision of goods or services, study abroad, internships and employment, cocurricular activities, and so on based on disability.

Purposeful discrimination can and does exist. It can happen on any level and at any intersection between students and institutions. While there are laws in place that prevent IHEs from making admissions decisions based on disability status, discrimination can happen. Take, for instance, a scenario where a Deaf student requests an ASL interpreter for a campus tour and interview. There can be considerable cost associated with the provision of those services for the duration of a student's enrollment. If that cost in any way influences a decision, it constitutes direct and intentional discrimination and is a violation of the law. Consider a scenario with a student program that involves traveling to an away game to support an athletics team, with transportation provided by the institution. If the vans used to transport students are not accessible, a student who uses a wheelchair would be excluded. Though this might not be an intentional exclusion, it is still a form of direct discrimination.

Indirect discrimination in higher education often involves marketing and communications materials or course content. Take, for instance, a scenario where a faculty member finds a magazine article on their morning commute that happens to be applicable to their course. The faculty member takes pictures of the article with their phone and posts it to the class's learning management system (LMS) page so they can discuss it in the morning's lecture. A picture of text would not be accessible to text-to-speech or screen reader technology, and a blind student or a student who has a learning disability would not be able to access the content. Or consider a scenario where commencement programs are printed for families and guests for the day of the ceremony, and large print or electronic formats are not available. These would constitute examples of indirect discrimination.

Failure to make reasonable adjustments is perhaps the most common type of discrimination at the postsecondary education level. This type of discrimination might be intentional or unintentional. It takes place when a reasonable request is denied, or a granted accommodation is not implemented. Take, for instance, a scenario where a student with a medical condition that requires a highly restrictive diet is denied their request to be removed from the requirement to purchase a meal plan. There are, of course, a number of potential variables, but failure to accommodate might constitute discrimination. Consider a scenario where a student who has a learning disability is granted an accommodation to record their classes, but the professor in their world language class does not allow it. Like the example above, there are several potential variables, but failure to implement the accommodation might constitute discrimination. We explore a considerable number of examples throughout this text, discussing ways to review variables, make informed decisions, and respond appropriately.

"Harassment occurs when someone treats, taunts, or antagonizes you in a way that makes you feel humiliated or offended" (Workplace Fairness 2022). Harassment is, unfortunately, common for SWDs. Some examples might include direct targeting, but any number of other bias incidents can occur. Take, for instance, a scenario where a student requests to use their extended time on exams accommodation, and the faculty member says something to the effect of "this exam is easy, you should be able to do it without your accommodation." Whether the granted accommodation is provided or not, this comment might constitute discrimination. At a number of institutions,

DSOs are located in close proximity to other success service offices, so it is not uncommon for students to be seen entering or engaging with the DSO. A student saying to a peer "I didn't know *you* went *there*" or "you don't seem disabled to me" could be examples of interactions that constitute harassment.

One particular type of discrimination that pertains to disability is ableism. Ableism can be defined as

> A set of beliefs or practices that devalue and discriminate against people with physical, intellectual, or psychiatric disabilities and often rests on the assumption that disabled people need to be "fixed" in one form or the other. (Smith n.d.)

Ableism may inform viewpoints that lead to the types of discrimination and harassment above, as well as other bias incidents such as macroaggressions. We have covered the concept of ableism quite a bit in this chapter already. It is essentially the viewpoint that "able" is the norm and "disabled" is less than. Terms such as "able-bodied" and "able-minded" and comparison against those for people with disabilities are prime examples of ableist thinking. Ableism asserts that certain abilities are required for normal functioning—the ability to hear, concentrate, read print, and maintain eye contact are some examples. On our campuses, we see ableism most often manifested when people do not actively consider SWDs. The above example of commencement materials, for instance, or selecting a venue for an event without considering accessibility are the results of ableism. We will explore multiple avenues and mechanisms for eliminating ableism—redefining "normal," using neutral identity language, and implementing universal design—throughout this text.

Discrimination is a direct threat to inclusion on our campuses. One way we address and combat this threat is by including disability in our institutions' social justice initiatives. Race and gender are at the forefront of most institutions' social justice stances and initiatives; as a similarly marginalized social categorization, disability should also be in the conversation.

Social Justice

Social justice assumes advocacy, awareness, and activism working toward equal rights. There are four major goals of social justice: human rights, access, participation, and equity (Soken-Huberty 2020). While these goals and their individual objectives align among all social justice movements, some objectives under each outcome are uniquely defined as they pertain to disability.

One underlying theme in this chapter is that sometimes disability is marginalized because it simply "wasn't on the radar." Disability is not often included in the literature pertaining to social justice, and it is not always included in diversity and inclusion efforts. Human rights are a given, and we would be hard pressed to find people working in higher education who do not agree that human rights apply to people with disabilities. The challenge is that "persons with disabilities have, however, remained largely 'invisible,' often excluded in the rights debate and denied from enjoying and exercising the full range of human rights" (United Nations n.d.). Our offices have the power to address this issue, at least within our own institutions. Core components of our role as DSPs include assisting students in the process of enjoying equal rights and, at times, addressing human rights violations. Providing community education on equal rights as they pertain to people with disabilities must also be considered.

Access is of particular interest in the world of DS. One meaning of the word "access" deals with the ability to enter and participate. Having all opportunities available to all students, regardless of social categorization, should be a defining philosophy of our institutions. Access as it relates to disability takes on specialized meaning. Our places of public accommodation must be physically accessible, which means implementing facilities such as ramps, elevators, braille-embossed signage, wayfinding, and so on. The ADA provides strict guidelines for public and private entities to follow. The new frontier for access for DS in higher education relates to accessibility of electronic and information technologies. We explore the concept of accessibility in depth later in this text, but one of our guiding principles should be expanding the definition of "access" from "available to all" to "usable by all."

Participation as it relates to social justice means more than just access to opportunities. Individuals with disabilities should be allowed and encouraged to play an active role in defining community standards and shaping learning opportunities. If student focus groups are recruited, SWDs should be included. When designing programs, people with disabilities, or their representatives and/or advocates, should be consulted. DSPs may often be called on to participate in this way, but we have a responsibility to seek opportunities to advocate. This means cultivating allies and inviting ourselves to the table.

Equity is one of the most important concepts related to disability as a civil right. We use the terms "equal rights" and "equal opportunity" when framing access and accommodations. We move toward equal rights and opportunity by seeking equity for students. Equality means providing everyone the same path to equal access. But "fair" does not mean that everyone gets the same. "Fair" means that everyone gets what they need. Take exam time, for instance. Providing equality would negate the concept of a reasonable adjustment. Some students can read a test question and begin to process their response; others read a test question and need to process the question before they can respond. This translates into less time to complete the assessment. Accommodating would provide the second student with more time, which is not equal but equitable and not advantageous. Figure 2.1 is a common representation of equality versus equity.

The Americans with Disabilities Act (ADA)

Nondiscrimination as a human right was formalized in the United States for people with disabilities with the passage of the ADA in 1990. The Rehabilitation Act of 1973 provided similar coverage but was specific to places where federal moneys are received. The ADA mandates nondiscrimination in employment settings (Title I), state and local government (Title II, which covers public colleges and universities), places of public accommodation (Title III, which covers private colleges and universities), telecommunications (Title IV), and provides additional coverages, such as protection against retaliation (Title IV).

The ADA provides a framework for the DS profession. While it does not, in and of itself, ensure that everyone's rights are realized, it provides a clear

Figure 2.1 Equality vs. Equity (Interaction Institute for Social Change. Artist: Angus Maguire)

statement and process—and perhaps most importantly, it provides recourse. It is our mandate and our authority. It defines disability as a status and not a condition. It demands equal opportunity, recognizes diverse ability, and paves the way for inclusion.

> Enactment of the ADA reflects deeply held American ideals that treasure the contributions that individuals can make when free from arbitrary, unjust, or outmoded societal attitudes and practices that prevent the realization of their potential. The ADA reflects a recognition that the surest path to America's continued vitality, strength and vibrancy is through the full realization of the contributions of all of its citizens. (University of Texas at Austin 2013)

In Summary

Disability is a complicated and often misunderstood experience. It is an identity that intersects with all facets of a person's life. Disability can affect any and all individuals and influence cultures and communities. There are rules and regulations that protect the rights of individuals with disabilities, and there are moral and ethical obligations to include all persons, provide access, advocate, and amplify voices. Our campus communities and society as a whole benefit from engaging in the discussion of ability. Designing educational opportunities and providing access to physical and intellectual domains benefits all.

There are barriers to access and inclusion, and our jobs are far from done, but overcoming them is a humanistic endeavor. Disability is not a condition; it is a positive identity. Identifying as a person with a disability can be both challenging and rewarding. Actively including individuals with disabilities, fostering potential and ability, embracing disability culture, and creating opportunity enriches our campuses. It is also the right thing to do. Disability is diversity—our ultimate goal transcends accommodation and strives for inclusion.

▶ Reflective Exercise

At Harcourt College, a small, private four—year college, there has been a dramatic increase in accommodation requests from students with mental health-related disabilities. Professor Sampson, a full-time, tenured faculty member in the humanities department, has been teaching at Harcourt for nearly twenty years. Professor Sampson is known to be strict but fair. A student in her race, politics, and culture course, a seminar for first-year humanities majors, disclosed to Professor Sampson that they have diagnoses of anxiety and depression prior to requesting accommodations through the DSO, communicating that they may need flexibility with deadlines. Professor Sampson responded by saying, "Everyone gets sad sometimes. All of the due dates are listed on the syllabus well in advance of the due dates. It's your responsibility as a college student to be planning ahead." The student reports this to you during an intake appointment after a second professor referred them to meet with you. Consider ways that you may respond when the student shares this information. Outline the steps you may take when the student asks for assistance with advocating to Professor Sampson.

3

Disability Services in Higher Education

An Overview

This chapter is a tour through the different types of DSOs at IHEs. DSOs vary from campus to campus in terms of physical location, location within the hierarchy of the university, number of staff members, and overall responsibilities. DSOs are like snowflakes: no two are alike. This chapter also looks at the roles of DSPs in higher education programs designed specifically for SWDs.

▶ Guiding Questions

1. *What are the different structures of a DSO in higher education?*
2. *Does a DSO's placement in terms of organizational chart and physical office location impact its work with students?*
3. *How does the size of a DSO affect the work it is responsible for?*
4. *Does the name of the office really matter?*
5. *Are DSOs responsible for accommodating students in specialized programs?*

No two DSOs are alike. No matter the type of IHE (public vs. private, two-year vs. four-year, residential vs. nonresidential, liberal vs. professional, profit vs. nonprofit), the likelihood that a DSO is in the same physical location within the university and has the same number of staff, the same responsibilities, the same resources and even the same name is low. There are reasons for these differences: the structural makeup of each institution is different (even among state schools); the number of resources varies; the date of the establishment of a DSO (if one even formally exists) is inconsistent; the knowledge base of different types of disabilities and the needs of higher education SWDs is wide. In part, the flexibility DSPs have is due to the lack of a federally mandated blueprint for higher education around the provision of DS.

Higher education must provide services to SWDs under the ADAAA, but other than saying that we must provide services, the government does not issue a "how to" guide. DSOs are on their own. The lack of federal guidance requires many DSPs to cultivate best practices and specific strategies from a variety of resources: AHEAD, national and local conferences and listservs, court case decisions and Office for Civil Rights (OCR) settlements, and one-on-one conversations with others in the field. These information resources can be helpful, but they require a DSP to know what to ask and to filter the potential flurry of responses. Higher education is unique in the field of education. Unlike educators in preschool, elementary, middle, and secondary schools, as well as those in the field of psychology and social work, DSPs are not required to have any formal training or licensure to work with students. Most of us do not have an advanced degree strictly associated with our roles. In fact, of the five authors of this book, only three of us have an undergraduate degree associated with education.

This is not to say DSPs are not qualified to work in this field. Many enter the profession with clinical, rehabilitation, and legal backgrounds. Yet to be well versed in the field requires professional development. Professional degree programming for DS is now available through a handful of formalized graduate degree programs. For DSPs already immersed in the field and perhaps feeling overwhelmed by its intricacies, this book is designed to help navigate those nuances.

Several different factors common to DSOs can make them unique. These factors can be lumped into seven categories:

1. Location (hierarchal and physical) of the office
2. Name of the office—what the name says about a campus's embracement of disability
3. Role and number of staff members
4. Responsibilities assigned to the office
5. Central versus decentralized models of support
6. Satellite campuses both nationally and internationally
7. Fee-for-service disability support programs

These factors are woven in throughout this book, and this chapter closely looks at each category.

Location (Hierarchical and Physical)

When we discuss location, we are discussing two different aspects: the location of the office within the hierarchy of the institution and the physical location of the office. Let us focus first on the hierarchical location. The location or "ownership" of the DSO in an institution may affect who the office serves (i.e., students, employees, visitors) and how it functions within the larger collegiate picture.

Hierarchical Location

Just as type of DSO is not consistent across intuitions, neither are the divisions of student or academic affairs. Typically, a division of student affairs is a student support–driven group of professionals responsible for enhancing the growth of students outside the classroom. Offices within the division might include orientation, residence life, student activities, diversity services, athletics, veterans affairs, Greek life, health services, career services, and the dean of students. Again, remember that this list is not exclusionary and will vary from university to university.

DSOs under the academic affairs title may be grouped with the learning center, advising, international programs, the library, and in some cases faculty development offices. Finally, several IHEs have placed DSOs within a specific department, namely the counseling center, a diversity center, or an academic department like psychology, counseling, or social work.

Where the DSO is located within the hierarchy of an institution may affect how the office is run and what its mission is. DSOs located within a student affairs division tend to have a more student-centered, holistic approach. Their focus is on ensuring that students have the services they need

---

In her role as DSP, Kirsten has worked both on the student affairs and academic affairs side of the house. Interestingly, at both institutions she began underneath student affairs. She was easily able to form collaborative relationships with the dean of students office, residential life, student activities, counseling and health services, athletics, and others. Built-in divisional meetings allowed her to not only share information related to the support she was offering to SWDs—and understand what her colleagues were doing to promote the nonacademic experiences of students—but also to push the topic of access when other departments were planning events, revisioning processes, or considering new avenues for students. The value of these informal relationships was immense.

In both institutions, the reporting structure switch to academic affairs was the result of a higher-level reorganization. Upper-level administrators moved on, creating opportunity for university leadership to rethink reporting structures and divisions. The DSO was malleable across both divisions. At one institution, the move to the academic side of the house also reflected the merge between the DSO and the tutoring center. It was thought that because these two offices were becoming one, it made the most sense to put them under one leadership. The presence of the tutoring center aligned more with the mission of the academic side of the house and less with the work of the student affairs side. Despite the switch, because Kirsten had already established a relationship with colleagues associated with the student affairs division, the move offered more symbolism than functional change.

A technical institution we worked with housed its DSO within the counseling center under the division of student affairs. The placement of the DSO was not intentional; it "just made sense" when the ADA was signed into law. While it is not the most common structure, there are many benefits to having a close collaboration between DS and mental health counseling. There is so much overlap between disability and mental health, especially in the last ten to fifteen years. Some may have the knee-jerk reaction that this structure reinforces the medical model or that it may deter students from connecting with DS because of the stigmas attached to mental health. Rather, the DSO experienced the opposite effect by taking a holistic approach to student support under the umbrella of wellness. Eliminating the runaround for students, providing opportunities for counseling and disability staff to learn from one another, and treating access and mental health as the cornerstones of well-being initiatives shaped the university's attitude about what it truly means to be well and set up for success.

for a positive college experience outside the classroom. Offices located within an academic affairs division tend to focus on the academic experience of a student. Does the student have what they need to be successful in the classroom? This might include helping the student with referrals to tutoring, advising, and role-playing conversations with faculty.

DSPs in the academic affairs division usually have smoother access to faculty and academic deans when working with students than those based in the student affairs division. This point is especially poignant when DSPs offer professional development to their institution. If the DSP is based in the academic affairs division, they may attract more faculty to access and inclusion-based workshops than if within the student affairs division. They may also have more credibility in the eyes of faculty, academic department chairs, deans, and provost when working one-on-one with a faculty member around a specific student need. The myth that DSPs are more in tune with faculty needs if they belong to the academic side of the house is just that—a myth. But in this profession, there can be a need to play up myths from time to time to advance a student's experience.

DSPs situated in the student affairs division often have a better relationship with offices staffed to support students on campus outside of the classroom. DSOs in this division are usually called on for their expertise in ensuring that events are accessible (convocation, commencement, and community performances), residence halls are welcoming, and the campus is physically accessible.

In other situations, the DSO is independent of the division that governs it and lives autonomously. This situation also has its benefits and challenges. It is beneficial because it allows DSPs the freedom to create an environment that is welcoming and independent of others. It is challenging because DSPs must work harder to first create that welcoming environment, then make sure faculty, staff, and students know about it, and finally increase communication with offices and departments from which they are physically separated.

As college administrations change and new leaders join institutions, the hierarchical location of a DSO may change. At least two of the authors have switched divisions within their institution for these reasons. Switching divisions can be beneficial if relationships in the previous division have already been established. The most effective DSOs observe and respect their hierarchical placement but reach across divisions and into various departments as needed to advocate for students.

Physical Location

The physical location of a DSO also varies across institutions. The topic of location is often discussed among DSPs at conferences. Many believe that the physical location of the office is directly related to the institution's philosophy of SWDs (which can admittedly be outdated). A handful of IHEs still locate their DSOs in basements or areas that are not well traveled.

These institutions justify the locations as being the only accessible choice or as offering students a degree of privacy when seeking out services. Out-of-the-way locations are akin to older K–12 special education models in which SWDs were pulled out of general education classrooms and sent to special education offices in out-of-the-way locations. Even if these are the only accessible locations on a campus, the message being sent to SWDs and all those who support them is undeniably archaic.

Recently, many DSOs have been housed near or in spaces with high student traffic, like the library, student union, or academic support center. Institutions that have made this choice theorize that the proximity to high traffic student areas (for any student) make the DSO more visible, encourage natural cross-programming opportunities, and encourage those who may need support to seek out services. Situating a DSO within one of the university-wide resources has the effect of reducing stigma associated with the accommodation process. An added benefit of a central location is the ease in which DS staffs can form collaborative relationships between offices in close proximity, increase awareness of the types of supports available to SWDs, and collaborate collectively on general campus initiatives aimed at increasing access for all. It is not uncommon for a DSP to physically walk a student to another office and guide them through asking for targeted support. Finally, faculty are more likely to be aware of the DSO if it is situated within a space where other resources they might frequent are located. This choice increases not only awareness of the office but also understanding that a DSO is one more resource in the list of university resources available to all students.

If the office is located within another office (the dean's office, an academic department, or counseling services), it is imperative for the DSP to make known where they are located and how they differ from other services being offered in the same physical space. Being placed within these offices has its advantages and disadvantages. On the one side, there is the ability to easily refer students to resources located within the space if needed. On the other side, a student may choose not to seek out services because of the stigma associated with a counseling center (consider the medical model of DS); many do not have any need to go to a particular academic department or may associate the dean's office with conduct and emergencies only. The effort then is to focus on reducing the stigma of these offices, increasing general awareness and carving out the DSO's own identity.

Interestingly, there has been a grassroots movement in recent years by some DSPs to embed their office within the diversity office or center. If we look at disability as a form of diversity, we place value on a student's disability as one more characteristic of who they are in the long line of what makes them unique individuals. It is an effort to further move away from viewing disability as a medical issue and place it in the realm of a social justice matter. Institutions that have placed the DSO within the diversity and inclusion office report an increased ability to provide campus programs focusing on disability awareness in higher education.

What's in a Name?

There is ongoing discussion and debate among DSPs as to what the DSO should be called. Should the name highlight disability, access, or both? As perspectives on disability have evolved and shifted over time to social or social justice frameworks, so too has the language we use. In efforts to be more inclusive, some DSOs moved away from using "disability" in their name in favor of terms such as "access" or "accessibility." One impetus for this change centers around the negative stigma associated with disability, potentially creating a barrier for students seeking support. Rebranding toward "access" has also been prompted by an intentional shift in focus from a disabled individual's needs—a viewpoint rooted in the medical model—to an environment proving inaccessible.

Proponents of maintaining "disability" in the title argue that doing so promotes positive views of disability by putting the term front and center. They intend to show that disability, like other aspects of diversity, is a valued aspect of the human condition, and not one to be hidden or excluded. Others note that using "disability" in the name helps people know where to seek assistance. When considering a name change, it is essential to seek input from institutional stakeholders, including students, to ensure messaging reflects campus culture and what makes sense for your office.

Who Works in a DSO? What Is Their Role?

When thinking of a DSO, most think of a person or group of people who, in an ideal situation, are responsible for meeting with students, determining if they qualify for accommodations, and providing those accommodations. Maybe from time to time the DSP is also able to do a bit of disability awareness programming, provide staff and employee accommodations, offer faculty trainings around best practices, and in some cases oversee ADA compliance. These tasks are often associated with DSOs, but the degree to which the professionals in the office can and do fulfill these tasks varies from institution to institution, and even within institutions (different schools, satellite campuses, and online environments) themselves.

If an IHE receives any federal funding, then it must have at least one person on campus who handles the needs of SWDs to be compliant with the ADAAA. At minimum, an institution needs one professional staff member who is familiar with the laws and understands the accommodation process. It is not illegal for them to wear multiple hats, nor is there any written law as to how many students one individual can support. As long as each IHE has someone whose role it is to support SWDs, it is in compliance. How is it determined how many professionals are needed at each institution? The answer usually comes down to resources and, in some cases, the institutional value of supporting SWDs.

Quantifying the need for staff by number of students seeking support and available financial resources is a straightforward calculation. How many SWDs have identified as needing services? What types of services do they need? What is the cost of those services to the institution? And how transactional does the institution want the process to be (a quick meeting to determine accommodations or a more hands-on, check-in approach)? A general rule of thumb is that the ratio of DS providers to students should be no more than 1:200.

Two hundred students with different needs may seem overwhelming, but it is highly unlikely that that same person will be actively working with each student all the time. Most of the work centers around first-year students and those with high needs. First-year students need to be oriented to the university through an intake process. These are the students a DSP is educating about the higher education process, helping to set expectations and goals, and walking through how to enact each approved accommodation. Typically, by the time they get into their second year, students are just renewing their accommodations and understand how to use them. High-need students—students who have complex disabilities and need multifaceted accommodations (sign language interpretation, room relocation, brailled or electronic texts, etc.)—also absorb a lot of DS staff time.

Depending on comfort level with accommodation use, a typical active caseload of two hundred registered students should be closer to 1:75. If the ratio exceeds 1:200 or the institution has a number of high-need students enrolled, then ethically the institution should provide additional support to the DSO. The nature of that support may vary from providing an administrative assistant to handle accommodation logistics to hiring a specialist (whether disability or technology based depending on the need of the institution) to removing any other "hats" the DSP is wearing so that they may focus on this role solely.

Table 3.1 provides a list of the more common job titles of DSPs and a summary of their roles. Often, professionals who do the same thing have more than one title for their position, or the title varies from institution to institution. We have tried to be conscious of that, focusing on the most common titles only.

How is it determined which of these professionals are needed in an institution? The answer is tied to financial resources, student need, and compliance. If an institution can meet compliance of the ADA with minimum personnel, it might. Many institutions meeting minimal need are retroactively approaching DS. They are responding to the immediate need of their

TABLE 3.1 COMMON TITLES IN DSOs

Title	Description
Director	This person is usually in charge of running the office. They may see students, depending on the support they have. They typically spend time educating others in the institution's community about what the office does and how the office can support faculty, staff, and students. They manage the budget and oversee office staff if applicable.
Associate Director/ Assistant Director	This professional typically sees students, may assist the director with outreach, and may oversee other staff within the office if applicable. They may also be assigned to special tasks such as working with student groups or managing AT or interpreters.
ADA/504 Coordinator	Often, this person serves a similar function to a learning specialist or service coordinator, seeing students, determining accommodations, and administering those accommodations. ADA coordinators may be independent of the disability service office—their primary responsibility is to oversee the institution's compliance with the ADA. They frequently play an important role in policy development both for the DSO and the institution. Finally, they are often the last stop in a grievance complaint, hearing the complaint, researching the case, and determining a final outcome.
Specialist (Disability, Accessibility, Learning)	These folks are hired to work with SWDs from start to finish. They may meet with prospective students, conduct intakes with new students, and help current students navigate their college experience with accommodations.
Assistive/Adaptive Coordinator/ Specialist	These professionals are usually hired to support students and their technology-related needs. In some cases, these professionals have access to an assistive/adaptive lab that they manage, and in others their role is to work with a student after initial intake to determine what AT they need.
Advisor/Academic Counselor	This professional may work with students from intake through the accommodation process, but they may also serve as academic advisor throughout a student's college experience. This model is not common; most DSPs work closely with their advising office, but in some instances, it is believed that a DSP will be able to support a student in course choice better than a general advisor.
Counselor/ Psychologist	These professionals may wear two hats. They may work as counselors, but because of their background administering and interpreting diagnostic testing, they may be deemed most appropriate to work with SWDs and determine what accommodations the students need.
Interpreters	This position may include sign language or CART interpreters who are hired on a full-time, part-time, or hourly basis to interpret for students in and out of the classroom.

(continued)

TABLE 3.1 COMMON TITLES IN DSOs *(continued)*	
Title	Description
Professors	Some professors serve as DSPs, and some DSPs teach classes. The distinction here is their primary role. In most situations it is the latter, but in some smaller schools, faculty, particularly in education or psychology, are also the DSPs for the institution.
Dean/Vice President	These professionals are typically deans and vice presidents first, and DSPs by default. They oversee student affairs or a tutoring center and due to a lack of need or resources also review accommodations.
Administrative Staff	Administrative staff support the needs of DSPs. They may also support other offices and/or support the DSO in an expanded manner (overseeing test proctoring or accommodation letter pickup). They manage the day-to-day needs of the office.
Graduate Students	Many DSPs employ graduate students to support the office's needs. Graduate students can access student information without breaking confidentiality, so what they can do is quite large. Some of the more common tasks for graduate students include helping manage student records, interpreting schedules, working with AT, overseeing certain accommodations (peer note-taking, exam proctoring), and increasing awareness of the DSO on campus.
Undergraduate Students	These students may or may not be using the services of the DSO. Due to confidentiality restrictions, these students cannot have access to any student files. They typically help the administrative staff with office projects and occasionally answer the phone. In some institutions, the DSO employs student workers to take notes for students with disabilities. This varies from institution to institution.

students rather than following best practices for an inclusive experience as an institution. For example, an influx of students who need interpreters might cause an institution to hire a full-time interpreter or an additional support staff member to coordinate the interpreters' schedules. If there is a sudden need for or reliance by students on AT or a spike in the number of alternative textbooks needed, an institution may hire an adaptive technologist or an alternative text specialist. With the increasing number of students struggling to master executive functioning skills in recent years, some institutions have provided a regular coaching service to SWDs through the hiring of learning specialists. The needs of the students vary from institution to institution, as does the response of the school.

While many schools have structured their DS response to focus only on the needs of current students, some institutions are proactively looking at the needs of all their students—beyond those with disabilities—and are considering the needs of future students. DSPs are aware of and have been touting the benefits of universal design for the last two decades, which we go into in more detail in Chapter 16. Universal design as it applies to higher education is "the design of college courses including the course curriculum, instruction, assessment and the environment, to be usable by all students, to the greatest extent possible, without the need for accommodations" (Behling and Hart 2008). The adoption of universal design by an IHE may influence the number of people in a DSO and their roles. If other offices are naturally building universally designed supports for students and faculty and creating more diverse methods of engaging with classes, then it is possible for a DSO to be smaller, as the needs of their students will be less.

Responsibilities Assigned to a Disability Services Office

When thinking of a DSO in higher education, most people—including prospective students, their families, and secondary educators—assume we are responsible for academic support of students. That is not necessarily wrong. Every DSO in higher education is there to ensure equal access to the collegiate experience. In a world of differences, this is one thing we have in common: the mandate to support students in their academic pursuits. Let us look back at that mandate one more time: "to provide access to the collegiate experience." The collegiate experience is much more than the classroom. It is living on campus (if available), eating in the dining halls, taking the shuttle between campuses, attending or playing in an athletic game, joining a club or watching a choir performance, accessing support from the library or career services, interning at a company, or registering for classes online. These are just a few of the collegiate experiences that can make up a student's journey. A DSO is responsible for making sure that students have full access to *all* of these experiences. Whoa.

In Chapter 7, we work through each of these categories (academic, housing, transportation, dining, social, etcetera) in more detail, including how to determine an accommodation and what accommodations might look like. For now, it is important to appreciate the magnitude of responsibility assigned to the DSO. As we noted earlier, the work of a DSP does not know any lanes. We must crisscross lanes, divisions, and offices depending on the student.

Centralized versus Decentralized Models of Disability Services

Each DSO must ensure that SWDs have equal access to the entire collegiate experience their institution offers. As we have noted, the ways in which the DSO supports students varies from institution to institution and sometimes even within institutions. This variation may continue in terms of who an office serves. Some DSOs serve all SWDs, while others focus efforts on specific types of disabilities.

Not all DSOs serve all SWDs. The decentralized model of DS (see Figure 3.1), in which students with mental health disabilities, for example, are served by the counseling office, athletes are served by the trainer, and residence life–related accommodations are served by the residence life office, is reminiscent of the first layers of support for SWDs—the idea of serving them where they needed to be served. Before the idea of a central office was realized and resources were dedicated to one person (or persons), the decentralized model was a way of supporting students without adding additional resources. Some campuses still follow this model. The centralized model of DS (see Figure 3.2) designates one office where students can go to register and receive accommodations no matter the nature of their disability. The centralized model is more common today as a central repository of resources and knowledge.

Split Based on Academic Level

Centralization and decentralization of DSOs can extend beyond type of disability to the academic level of a student. It is not uncommon for DSOs to

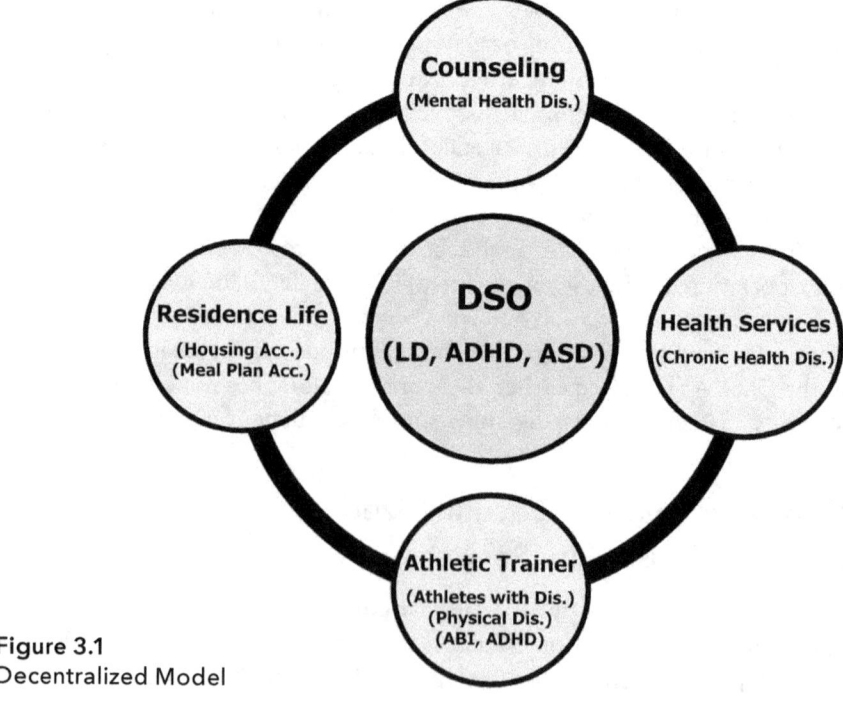

Figure 3.1
Decentralized Model

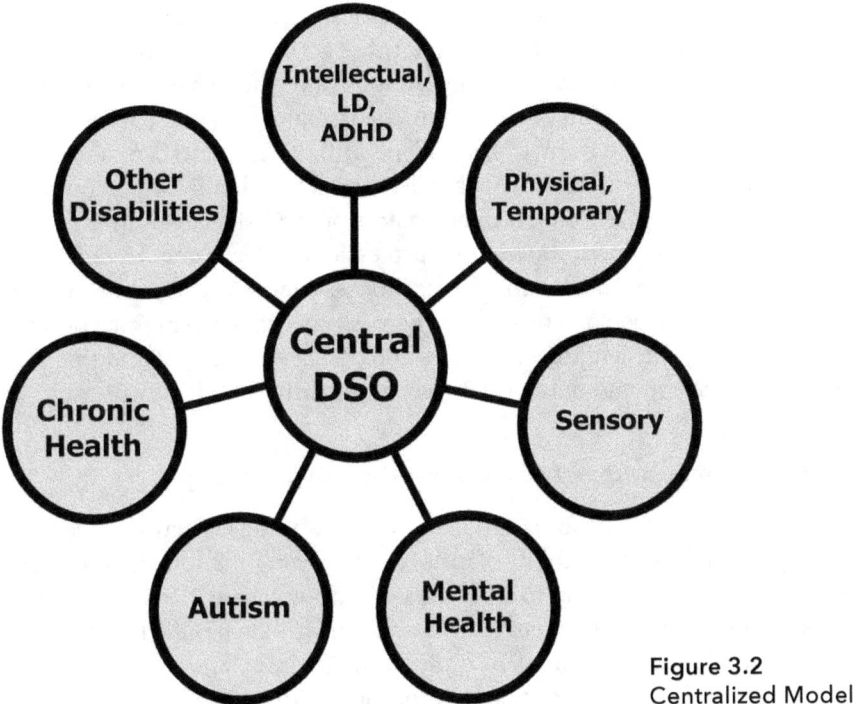

Figure 3.2
Centralized Model

split services between undergraduate and graduate students, especially for law and medical-related schools. Some institutions believe that the difference in course requirements between undergraduate and graduate programs requires a different knowledge basis for supporting students. Many times, the DSP supporting graduate students has some background in those fields (psychology, social work, rehabilitative counseling, sociology, education, etcetera) and is therefore more familiar with the experience their students are going through. Despite differences in curriculum, there is still a need for a common set of policies and procedures and clear communication across the offices, particularly if a student is considering enrolling in the graduate school and wants to transfer their services. We dive deeper into this topic in Chapter 11.

Split Based on School

Some IHEs have multiple schools within their larger university. A university may contain a business school, a liberal arts school, a medical school, an art school, a law school, a divinity school, an education school, etcetera. In some IHEs, these schools have separate majors, academic requirements, course offerings, and faculty but share university resources such as technology resources, admissions, libraries, transportation, and residence halls. The way in which

DSOs function varies here too. In some institutions, the DSO is centralized. Students seek services in one office, and those accommodations are enacted across the different schools. Other institutions value the idea of a DSO in each school. The thought is that DSPs know their school well and can tailor accommodations to meet the needs of students. This latter model can cause quite a bit of confusion for a student enrolled in one school but taking a course in another or a student who starts in one school but transfers to another. It also does not maximize the resources and professional development available to DSPs at the institution. If a university chooses to follow this method, then it should have one person ensure that there is consistency in how accommodations are determined, that processes and policies are steady, and that students can weave in and out of other schools within the IHE seamlessly.

Split Based on Campus Location or Modality Format

Some institutions have more than one campus. Campuses may be separated by just a few miles or hundreds of miles or may even function virtually. Online learning allows students to take courses from anywhere in the world where there is an Internet connection. How does an institution handle DS for a university with satellite campuses or online learning? The answer is that it depends. Generally things are centralized, though there is a point of contact on outlying campuses who, through communication and maintaining the same policies and procedures as the main DSO, can support SWDs. Often these professionals also have other roles, but they are at least available to students and aware of the processes set forth by the central DSO on how to accommodate SWDs.

International satellite campuses present a different challenge to supporting SWDs. If an institution owns an international campus and readily sends students to it, then it must accommodate SWDs under the ADA. The accommodation process should mirror the one on the main campus. However, it is highly unlikely that a satellite campus will have a full-time DS position. Instead, there may be a representative who wears many professional hats and can implement accommodations with guidance from the main office at the home campus. More complicated accommodations are arranged in advance of the student's arrival, which takes a lot of coordination between the home office and the international campus.

IHEs that offer online learning are still largely feeling out the best approach for supporting students online. Most do not require that the student physically come to the campus for an initial intake appointment. The process is more digital in nature; the student must submit documentation electronically and then meet with the DSP over the phone or through a synchronous chat room to determine the nature of their disability and the accommodations they qualify for. DSPs supporting students in the online environment are often tapped further to support faculty, especially around access and accommodation implementation in that modality.

The hierarchical and physical locations of a DSO vary from institution to institution. Often the location of the office, in both realms, is reflective of the university's approach to student services. If the office is situated in the academic affairs division, the institution may have a greater focus on academics and working with faculty to support SWDs. If it is based in the student affairs division, the approach to services is typically more holistic. Likewise, the physical location of the office offers insight into how DS are perceived and accessed on campus. If the office is secluded, the institution may be trying to reconcile the idea that SWDs desire a degree of anonymity. If the office is more front and center to students, the institution may be trying to normalize disability as another form of diversity. Each institution will approach the location of the DSO differently depending on its history, philosophy, and resources.

Fee-for-Service Programs

The ADA requires that IHEs ensure SWDs have full access to every aspect of the collegiate experience. This legal right comes at a cost to the institution, not the student. If a student meets admissions criteria for the institution and provides the appropriate documentation of their disability, then they have the right to individualized accommodations without cost.

Some IHEs, though, take the support model a step further and offer additional support—whether generalized to typical college needs (executive functioning and transitional support) or specific to a type of disability (summer programs for students with autism). These programs, in which students must pay additional money on top of tuition to work with a specialist or to join a group around a targeted set of needs, are called fee-for-service programs. There are many different types of programs. Table 3.2 outlines the five most common programs designed with SWDs in mind.

Fully integrated programs are the most common type of resource for SWDs in IHEs. These are the DSOs that work with students around individual needs and provide accommodations for courses or nonacademic needs. There are no specialized programs for SWDs; a DSO will refer them to the same campus resources available to any other student enrolled in the institution.

Integrated with additional support services are programs that might provide access to an academic coach on a weekly basis. The academic coach would help the student organize their work, study for exams, manage life skills (maintaining a good nutrition routine, exercise, and sleep hygiene), and refer them

TABLE 3.2 THE FIVE MOST COMMON TYPES OF SWD PROGRAMS	
Type of Program	Description
Fully Integrated	Fully integrated schools are IHEs that serve students through a DSO. All services are part of the cost of tuition. This is the most common type of program for any SWD.
Integrated with Additional Support	Students interested in this type of program enroll in typical college courses with their peers, may receive services from their DSO, and pay an additional fee for intensive academic and/or social coaching.
Specialized Programs	These programs are often designed for students with a specific disability. The students typically live together but separate from other college students. They usually take courses designed to meet their needs and have little interaction with the campus at large.
Hybrid Programs	These programs are often designed for students with a specific type of disability. Students take college courses (for credit or audit) with other students but may receive additional support in the areas of life skills, time management, social skills, or career skills.
Dual Enrollment Programs	These programs allow students still enrolled in high school to take college courses for credit. SWDs may receive services from either the university DSO or from their high school special education department. Many community colleges support students in this role.

to appropriate support as needed. These fee-for-service programs are popular among students who need a little extra support as they transition to college.

Specialized programs are just that: programs designed to support students with types of disabilities as they prepare for, transition into, or are fully enrolled in higher education. Several summer programs available for students, particularly those with autism, simulate a collegiate experience without the general student population on campus. Students might go to a college or university for a week or two during the summer.

Dual enrollment has been an option for high school students wishing to try out college for quite some time. In recent years, the concept of dual enrollment has extended to high school SWDs who have not yet graduated. Dual enrollment is an opportunity for these students to have the same college experience as their peers in an age-appropriate environment.

Fee-for-service programs are not necessarily run out of a DSO. Typically, these programs are developed through an alumni or parental donation or as a graduate student project that may be absorbed as a long-term program. They are usually run by professionals with experience in the disability that the program supports. DSPs are called on to be guest speakers, supply orientation activities, and to conduct intakes and provide accommodations to students enrolled in these programs.

In Summary

No two DSOs are alike. There is no federal or even state mandate that requires DSOs to look alike, be in the same place on campus, have the same number of employees with the same title doing the same things, or have the same resources and same name. The vast differences in DSOs from school to school or even campus to campus can be immensely confusing for an SWD, their family, and the guidance counselors and special educators advising in their transition to college.

But lack of required structure can also be an opportunity for a DSO to flourish. A DSO can morph across divisions, departments, and even campuses if needed. DS can and do essentially fit in anywhere on campus. The lack of a roadmap allows DSPs to be creative with funding, staff members, and resources when serving students. In recent years, this flexibility has become more apparent as DSOs relocate from within an office to a space of independence or within a diversity services office.

Reflective Exercise

Recently, the DSO at a small institution in the Northwest was organizationally relocated from the counseling services office to the division of student affairs. The director of the office wants to take advantage of this change to consider a new name and ask for a more central location on campus. What are some factors and steps they need to consider when asking for these changes? How might you propose these changes to your new boss? Finally, how would you roll out these changes to the student body?

Supplemental Job Aids

The following Supplemental Job Aids can be found at https://scholarshare.temple.edu/handle/20.500.12613/8373:

- Event Accessibility Checklist

4

The Day-to-Day Operations of a Disability Services Office

The goal of this chapter is to offer insight into the nuances of day-to-day DS management. The authors of this book have a significant history of navigating the intricacies of office management (even if just a one- or two-person office) across a wide range of IHEs. Throughout this chapter, we share lessons learned, with particular attention to the physical and virtual space of an office, budgets—where they come from, what they cover, how to advocate for more money—advocating for more staff and details around hiring, the importance of organization and management, and strategies for impactful communication. Each aspect of this chapter is designed to provide an example, not necessarily a roadmap, for other DSPs to draw on as they lead or advocate for resources at their institution.

▶ Guiding Questions

1. What factors should be considered in establishing a physical and virtual DSO space?
2. What are the nuances of a DSO budget? How can a DSP advocate for more support?
3. What are the best practices for managing a DS team?
4. How can data assist with advocating for more support?
5. What are the best ways to communicate to constituencies?

Physical Office Space

DS needs a dedicated office space. As discussed in Chapter 3, we can physically live in a lot of different locations across campus. Where we live impacts student traffic, potentially the stigma sometimes associated with disability, and the ease of building collaborative relationships with other student services offices. Where a DSO is housed matters. But so too does the physical space that it occupies.

Adequate space for a DSO is important and often overlooked. A DSO needs a space that allows for confidential conversations. Ideally, each DSP should have an office or at the very least access to a room with a closed door to meet students. The need for confidentiality extends to record keeping. In DSOs that rely on physical copies of documentation, accommodation letters or case notes should be kept in a locked cabinet, ideally in a locked room well within the DSO.

Space is at a premium on many college campuses, especially in urban areas where the costs of additional institutional buildings can be astronomically high. Thinking in terms of space logistics, at a minimum there needs to be one office or conference room and a surrounding open area for reception or exam proctoring. If the DS team is composed of more than one person who meets with students, each person should have access to a space to meet with students privately. Touchdown spaces may be an option in the absence of

Kirsten is frequently called to colleges or universities to assist with DSO evaluations—in-depth reviews of the services provided. The goal of these evaluations is for an outsider to determine what aspects of an office's work are going well and where additional support or specific recommendations for improvement can be made.

She was conducting an evaluation at a small college with a health profession focus. On arrival, she was led to a group of four cubicles and told that it was the DSO. The DSP poked her head up out of the cubicle and welcomed Kirsten to the cluster of cubes. When Kirsten spoke with the professional and some of her students, they all stressed the level of discomfort the space created. The DSP tried to find conference rooms or unused faculty offices nearby when conducting an intake, but when nothing was available, she was stuck meeting with students in the cube. She tried to offset the location with sound machines and a homemade shower curtain–type door to offer auditory and visual autonomy, but neither she nor her students ever felt truly comfortable talking openly about students' disabilities. The need for an office was one of the first recommendations Kirsten made to the college.

private offices. Touchdown spaces are shared offices or smaller conference rooms available to anyone working within the larger office space.

When considering best practices for setting up a DSO, it is important to review the critical functions of the office. Does the office proctor exams? Does it offer AT, and is a lab needed? Is there a place for students to gather to study or socialize? Does it offer space for professional development trainings or meetings with students and families (a conference room will often work)? With each of these functions come different needs for specific space.

Exam Accommodation Space

Exam accommodations are the most common type of accommodations granted in higher education. Exam accommodations may include extended time to complete an exam, use of AT, use of a reader or scribe, frequent breaks, and distraction-reduced testing. Within these accommodations, specific guidelines exist. Students who receive distraction-reduced testing, for example, could have access to a room that holds no more than three people at a time. Students who use AT may need a private space if their technology requires them to dictate out loud. Students who use a scribe need a space big enough for two people and private enough for the student to dictate to the scribe comfortably. These specific requirements quickly eat up space. At most institutions, space is prime real estate, and the possibility of having private testing rooms or a plethora of flexible space is not realistic. Many DSOs offer exam proctoring as a resource for faculty and students. Some are fortunate enough to have the space within the office.

While the provision of exam accommodations falls under the purview of faculty, many DSOs assist by coordinating alternative exam accommodations. Faculty often cite logistic challenges (i.e., not being able to secure a quiet space, teaching back-to-back classes) as reasons they ask the DSO to administer exam accommodations. These challenges are most notable for adjunct faculty, who may teach a couple of courses across multiple institutions.

Different institutions handle these requests differently. Some push back on their faculty, telling them to figure it out, ask department administrators to help find spaces, lean on their TAs to proctor exams in different locations (reserving classrooms nearby), begin the exam early for those who need more time, and, more recently, consider the possibility of online exams and remote proctoring. Others work to provide test proctoring through the DSO with DS staff.

Exam space or "testing centers," as some DSPs call them, are considered a luxury in the field. Because space is often at a premium, having access to a larger empty room is like finding a needle in a haystack. For those lucky enough to have it, we suggest designing the space to be multifunctional. It

Space at most institutions of higher education is at a premium. One institution recognized this and worked to make testing space flexible. They had two dedicated testing rooms, which also served as a conference room and an AT lab. In the conference room, they had one long conference table at which they would sit two students. The DSO's AT computer lab had six computer stations. Every workstation had an adjustable table and chair with sit/stand options for desks to accommodate multiple abilities and preferences. For proctoring purposes, each space was monitored by closed-circuit television, which was viewed from a central proctoring station. Each testing room had both a Mac and PC desktop and the ability to control browser access. Additional amenities included noise cancelling headphones, ear plugs, white noise machines, clocks that sweep (as opposed to ticking), large display/high contrast digital clocks, assistive and adaptive equipment and software, and adjustable lighting. Portable white boards were available for students who needed space to brainstorm and mind map.

The institution also was conscious about how it proctored exams. If two students needed to test at the same time, the DS staff made sure that the two students in the same room were not taking the same exam. Aside from obvious integrity reasons, this strategy eliminated comparisons that students may make, such as wondering why the other student already turned the page or finished first. The DSO worked to start exams at the same time to minimize disruptions for all students, as well as to make it easier on the proctor to sit all students at once.

should have movable and accessible furniture (desks and chairs that can change height), access to a multimedia station, natural light (if possible) with shades, sound machines, and a white board or some other board that can be used for projection and writing. Creating a flexible space allows DSPs to use the space for exam proctoring, staff meetings, student activities (hosting events, meetings, tutoring, study groups), or other uses as needed.

Testing centers require additional thought around functionality. Faculty can be hesitant to send students to a testing center for fear that students might cheat. To be fair, this does happen, but it can happen no matter the exam space. There are a variety of different ways that DSPs can address this concern, but the two most common methods are live and video proctoring. Offices that use a live proctor (often a paid student worker) ask that person to sit in the same room or a nearby room with high visual access of students taking the exam. The proctor administers the exam, holds a space for mobile devices and bags, connects with the student if there is a question (more on that in a moment), holds the student's exam if they need to use the restroom or take a break, and generally watches students take exams.

Other institutions use video proctoring. Some video systems involve installing a camera in the room with a direct connection to a monitor in the DSO or on a mobile device. Video proctoring can be cost efficient once the system is purchased and installed, as it does not require hiring someone to sit in the same room as students taking exams. If an office has different testing rooms, a video proctoring system may be a preferred, cost-effective strategy. Online proctoring is usually done by a third party—students leave their screen on, and someone hired by the faculty or the institution watches all the students.

Technology Space

Institutions with "healthier" budgets may also have a physical space for students to explore or use AT. AT spaces or AT labs, as they are commonly known, may live directly within a DSO or may be more centralized on campus but managed in partnership with the DSO. AT labs are typically spaces where students can learn about and try different types of AT with a DS provider teaching them. AT labs can range in size from a desk with a computer to large conference rooms filled with different types of assistive tech (low and high tech). We make more disability specific recommendations in Chapter 9.

While AT labs are helpful in demonstrating technology to students, they may soon be a way of the past. More and more computers and software systems are now embedded with accessibility resources. Apple, for example, has added text-to-speech and speech-to-text features directly into all its operating devices. Our laptops and mobile devices are wired to support a variety of potential accommodation needs; however, students may not be aware of these resources. So while an AT lab may be unnecessary, DSPs need to be aware of the accessibility features of student devices to teach students how to use them. The best way to do this is to have the student bring their device to a meeting and guide them as they "drive" the accessibility features. Think of a DS provider as a driver's ed teacher, guiding the student but ultimately letting the student discover and decide which way to turn.

Virtual Space

Another, less obvious space that is worthy of discussion is the virtual space a DSO occupies. Remember, it is our job to ensure that students have equal access to all our spaces. These include our websites, social media presence, learning management courses or spaces, any electronic forms we require, and any web conferencing tools we use. As IHEs grow, so too does their presence in and dependence on virtual space. DSOs are no different. Websites give us the chance to offer an overview of what we do and how easily we do it. High school students, families, and guidance counselors can review our websites to find out what documentation we require, what our due dates are, and how we function within the institution overall. This virtual space replaces trifolds and photocopied handouts and can be much more effective.

The challenge with websites, though, is design. It is very tempting to put *all* our information on the website. Unfortunately, most higher education websites are overwhelming and do not consider the user experience when adding information. This consideration is particularly important for DSOs, as students seeking DS support may struggle trying to find the forest for the trees. DS websites should be clear, have bulleted and succinct content, appropriately labeled images, and functional links. Annual DS website maintenance is a must; as content is added, outdated information should be removed. Ideally, a website update should be considered every summer.

Just as the content on a DS site is important, so too is where it is located on the university's main web page. Remember in Chapter 3 when we shared the many different names a DSO can have? For a prospective student, it is challenging enough to transition to college and seek out services without having to dig through pages and pages looking for a DSO. The institutional search feature should allow for words like "accessibility," "disability," and "accommodation" to all lead to the DS page. The DS page should be linked from all student services pages (dean of students office, counseling centers, health centers, athletics, residence life, orientation offices) as well as academic offices (advising, each academic department, the library).

Most institutions have two types of websites: outward facing, or what the public can see, and inward facing, or what students can access. Inward facing websites are sometimes called intranet or portals and are often secured behind a firewall. Enrolled students can gain access to content but must first log on to their university account. While outward facing websites are informative, providing information about a DSO, what it does, and how it supports SWDs, inward facing portals are where students might go to review their individual financial aid information, register for courses, and request accommodations.

As we move to a place of digital transactions, DSPs need to take into consideration the web forms we ask students, faculty, and providers to fill out. Each form must be accessible. What do we mean by that? A baseline for accessibility is that students who rely on screen readers or are unable to use a mouse are able to navigate through a form without assistance from someone else. We discuss this baseline in more detail in Chapter 16. In addition to being accessible, the forms need clear instructions for use. Should a student print the form out and then fill it out? Can they fill it out on the website and simply press submit? Where will it go when it disappears into the ether? When is it due?

More and more DSOs are turning to social media to bring awareness to the work they do and to promote student-run events and relevant resources across campus. Many DSOs ask their student staff to direct social media and help create effective messaging. Just like web forms, all social media postings should be accessible to a baseline of users. Setting a precedent of how to create accessible materials and messages will not only ensure that all students can view the DSO's content but also normalize the need to include accessibility considerations from the start.

If the DSO has a presence on the institution's LMS (Moodle, BlackBoard, Canvas, etc.), then that too needs to be not only accessible but also well organized. It is very easy to overcrowd an LMS site with content that we as providers deem critical but for students may be a pile of information difficult to wade through. When considering what goes on the DSO LMS site, follow the old acronym KISS (Keep it Simple, Silly). Add content thoughtfully. Update at least once a semester. Organize with well-labeled folders.

Budget Overview and Management

At the risk of sounding repetitive, budgets, budget amounts, budget allocations, and budget management also vary from institution to institution. When AHEAD asked its members in 2018 what their office budget was, the range was between $0 and $3,000,000 (Scott 2018). DSOs with larger budgets tend to be in larger schools, have more full-time staff members, and serve students across several campuses.

Some DSPs have full control over their budgets; others are given a certain amount to spend on specific things, and others are given no indication as to how budgets are determined. In this last case, DSPs must ask for resources as needed, usually with a lot of justification, from someone not closely familiar with their work. There is variability in what a budget might cover—staffing, accommodations, office resources, technology, etcetera. And finally, there is variability in how we are funded (from the institution directly, from fee-for-service work, or through gifts and grants). This section offers insight into general best practices and strategies for growing a DS budget.

Broadly speaking, budgets may be broken into two primary categories: compensation and noncompensation. Compensation covers the salaries of those who work in the DSO, including all or a combination of professional, hourly, part-time, consultant, and student worker staffs. Noncompensation, on the other hand, covers office supplies, accommodation resources, and other expenses as needed. In both situations, clear and detailed management of the budget is needed to both show expenditures and advocate for new resources.

Compensation

Some schools require the DSO to use its budget to pay the annual salaries of staff members. This requirement may also include the salaries of part-time or contracted employees, interpreters, and exam proctors. The budget may support undergraduate work-study students, graduate fellows or interns, and outside tutors and consultants, if the office employs them. The requirement to cover the salaries of staff will lead to hard decisions about what the office can and cannot afford. Any "luxury" services, like additional tutoring support, AT expertise, or disability-specific experts, may be cut when budgets are lean.

The rules of compensation vary depending on the type of employee. For full-time professionals, compensation is composed of the individual's annual salary plus a certain percentage (around 30 percent) of that salary to cover the individual's benefits (health and dental insurance, retirement plans, transportation support, and in some cases, tuition reduction). For example, if a staff member is hired in at a salary rate of $50,000, an additional $15,000 should be budgeted to cover the individual's benefit package.

It is also important to consider projected raises. In a strong fiscal environment, staff members should be considered for a raise year-to-year. Raises in higher education are not earth shattering. Typically, an institution will offer managers a pool of performance money to allocate among their staff. Raises tend to be 2–5 percent of an individual's annual salary (Sziron 2019). In our example of an employee beginning at salary of $50,000, this equates to an additional $1,000–$2,500 per year. A tip for those new to higher education employment—advocate for a higher salary when offered a position, as once someone is hired it is very hard to grow a salary significantly and quickly without a formal promotion.

When we consider our compensation budgetary needs, accommodations are not usually considered. However, a few accommodations require a DSO to hire additional staff, namely interpreters and notetakers. Interpreters are typically hired in pairs to negate the high cognitive concentration required to accurately interpret. DSOs may struggle to support students with approved note-taking accommodations. The easiest way to meet this need is to hire student workers to take notes for a course (we address variations within this system later in the book).

Another consideration are staff and faculty unions. Unionization primarily happens at state colleges and universities rather than at private institutions, since most state laws allow for such organizations. Unionized institutions use collective bargaining to negotiate terms of employment as well as wages. If the DSO is part of a unionized institution, the office's budget will likely not contain a compensation line. This portion of the university budget is managed by the institutional finance department. In terms of hiring new staff, a salary will be based on a number set by the union. Merit raises will be predetermined by the union cannot be decided by a specific supervisor.

While some DSOs have control over their compensation budget, others only have control over their noncompensation budget. In these instances, the central administration determines office staffing needs, budgets, raises, and whether additional team members can be added to the workforce. This model requires DSPs to have strong advocacy skills to make a case for additional support when needed. Either way, compensation management can consume a significant amount of time.

Noncompensation or Operational Budgets

Noncompensation budgets are funds that the institution allocates for the day-to-day running of the DSO, including the cost of accommodations. Day-to-day expenses range from office supplies (paper, ink cartridges, pens, notepads) and PR materials (brochures, fidgets, pens, etc.) to office equipment, database purchases, and mail accounts. Some institutions include a professional development budget line that may be used for books and journal subscriptions, memberships to professional organizations, or conference attendance and travel. This line is the most vulnerable when budgets need to be tightened.

The most common allocation of funds is for the accommodation needs of students, specifically, the purchase of AT, assistance proctoring exams, specific individual software or hardware purchases for a student, note-taking, and Communication Access Realtime Translation (CART) transcription or interpreting. Perhaps the most expensive accommodation an individual student may need is a sign language interpreter. Students who rely on ASL for communication will need an interpreter throughout their collegiate experience, including academic activities (classes, labs, workshops, internships, etc.) and nonacademic activities (student clubs, campus events, athletic events, etc.). For the academic side, there is quite a bit of planning a DSO can do in advance of the start of a semester. We need to figure out what classes the student will take, get as much information from professors as possible about those classes, and hire and coordinate the logistics of two interpreters to attend class and interpret for the student. In 2021, an average ASL interpreter makes about $28.00/ hour (Salary.com 2022). Let us think about this for a moment.

One student is taking four courses for a total of twelve class hours/week.

- Each class requires two ASL interpreters to be present.
- Therefore, there are twenty-four hours of academic time/week to be covered.
- If the average interpreter makes $28.00/hour, then the total charge/week is $672/week.

- Most semesters are fifteen weeks long: $10,080.
- Most students enroll for two semesters: $20,160.
- Most students take four years to graduate: $80,640.

$80,640 is the total cost to provide ASL interpreters for one student's academic experiences over four years. One student. Remember, this is just for academic experiences. We have not factored in any nonacademic events the student may need an interpreter for.

CART interpreting is an accommodation for students who require a live transcript of courses or nonacademic experiences. With the CART service, a third-party transcriber is called at the beginning of class. They listen in on the lecture and transcribe everything they hear in real time. The student's computer is set up to receive the transcription throughout the lecture. CART can be quite expensive—up to $100/hour (Collaborative for Communication Access Via Captioning, 2012). However, technology has advanced in such a way that minimizes our reliance on CART services. Many software and app options now allow a student to use their phone as a live recording device in a classroom.

Captioning is another costly accommodation. Historically, if a student required captions for equal access, it would cost the university upward of $3.00/minute of video content to be captioned. It would also require that a DSP organize and distribute the captioned content in a timely format. The impact of COVID-19 on captioning was very powerful. The different learning modalities meant heavy reliance on video as a course delivery method. To be compliant and support the diverse needs of learners, campuses explored autogenerated captions in presentation software and web conferencing tools. While autogenerated tools continue to improve their accuracy, we caution DSP and faculty against relying on them without checking the content they create. An inaccurate transcript denies equal access to the student dependent on it. We do believe, however, that as they improve, autogenerated captions will have the ability to reduce the overall noncompensation expenditures of a DS budget.

Supporting students with vision-based disabilities is another area of potential astronomical expense. Students who rely on braille or use text-to-speech software can absorb most of an annual DS noncompensation budget. Most braille readers utilize a device with a Refreshable Braille Display to read documents in electronic braille. Those who depend on text-to-speech software need academic and nonacademic content delivered electronically. Making a document electronic is fairly easy. Nevertheless, making it accessible is a challenge (as we discuss in Chapter 15). Making a brailled document for a science, technology, engineering, or math class (STEM courses) is a beast. The symbols, equations, charts, and graphs used in these classes take considerable time—three times the amount of time needed to braille a history text.

If a DSO is ensuring accessibility of course materials internally, it may need to increase its staff size, at least temporarily. Additional staff are hired to test documents, books, journals, and handouts and to fix them if they are inaccessible. This testing can cost a DSO about ten to twenty hours/week of staff time per student (depending on how many classes the student takes) per semester.

Outside of AT and ensuring academic access, some DSOs are charged with financing all accommodations on campus: academic, residential, university-wide computer labs and corresponding AT, and general programmatic access. DSOs may be called on to caption events like convocation, commencement, and open houses. Likewise, they may be held responsible to braille signs and install lifts, elevators, electronic door openers, and AT software to support third-party machines installed on campus (photocopying systems, ATMs, university dining cards). DSOs may be asked to fund the specific housing needs of their students: bed shakers, flashing alarm systems, accessible beds, and evacuation chairs. The potential drain on a DS budget can be massive depending on their jurisdiction for the campus and the student need.

The noncompensation line in a DS budget also covers the day-to-day expenses of running an office—things like the one-time purchase and annual subscription of a database, PR materials (pens, brochures, stress balls), general office supplies, events, and food costs for hosting and drawing students to events. These costs can be reduced by sharing with offices nearby and ordering in bulk. The technology needs of the office can also be minimized if the institution relies on the central IT division to cover the cost of new computers and work devices.

While it is difficult to predict the budgetary needs of a DSO, if a student needs an accommodation, an institution is legally required to financially cover it. This mandate does not come with a blank check, though. Institutions must accommodate students and faculty and staff with disabilities, but they can do so in a manner that does not cause an undue burden. DSOs can choose the equal but less expensive alternative; they can work with residence life to find alternatives to building new bathrooms and can reassign classrooms as opposed to building new ones. From a staffing perspective, there is no mandate on what the student to staff ratio must be. The lack of guidance often means that DSPs are working beyond a standard set of hours to support individual students as well as provide guidance for the university around access needs. DS staff burnout is a real concern.

Budget Management

Budgets across higher education are frequently determined on a year-to-year basis. As a reminder, the higher education fiscal year is July 1 through June 30. Typically, DSPs need to predict their budgetary needs for the following year by February of the current year. In the absence of a windfall of resources, most institutions expect DSOs to run year-to-year in a largely budget-neutral space. For example, if the DSO budgeted for $100,000 last year and spent $95,000 of that allocation, the institution will assume the office can run effectively with the same $100,000 budget the next year. If budgets are tight, there may be a university-wide decrease. If the university is prosperous, a DSO may receive a modest increase year to year.

Some institutions offset DS budgets with donations and grants. Donations may come directly from a student and their family or more formally through the university advancement office. The advancement office is charged with fundraising for the entire institution. Fundraising has the benefit of securing funds specific to a particular office. However, the timing of receipt of funds can vary. It is important to note that in many cases the DSO does not receive a sudden influx of money when donations occur. Rather, the donation or grant will offset the central administration's budget expenses, freeing up the funding required to run a DSO for another institutional cause. In most cases, the office gets a much smaller (10 to 20 percent) amount of the actual gift.

Some DSPs are active grant writers. They may write research grants or grants asking for specific types of technology or resources needed to fully support students. Grants are great because they can financially support a DSO above and beyond the standard budget. We have seen grant-funded positions become permanent positions at the conclusion of the grant.

Grants can be short-lived and not as financially prudent as one might expect. All institutions have something called an indirect rate that they take from the grant award. Indirect rates cover things like office maintenance (electricity, Wi-Fi, and water)—those critical yet invisible expenses. Indirect rates can vary depending on the institution receiving the grant and the granting agency, making it important to connect with the institution's office of research before applying for the grant.

If a DSO is struggling to get a new position funded, an assistive technologist for example, it may look to outside funding. The key to finding a permanent place for that position is keeping careful data on the impact with students, the reduction in time others in the office must spend on a task they handle, and the impact of the position on overall collaborative support of faculty. Think of grants as proof of concepts toward a long-term funded position.

DSOs frequently exceed their annual budget. No, we are not spending obscene amounts on pens and stress balls—it is very hard to predict our needs when a budget proposal is due. Budget projections are due prior to enrollment of the incoming class of students, so we are asked to predict our needs before we even meet the students. Some students may require expensive accommodations unknown at the time of the proposal. Legally, since we must accommodate, our institutions should adjust our budget to allow us to meet student needs. DSPs need to be prepared to justify why cutting other expenditures for the office is not the answer to supporting students with more significant disabilities. We may also be asked to consider the needs of these students in future budget proposals (finance administrators may be keenly aware of when particular students will graduate).

Disability Services Teams

Number of Employees

As noted previously, the number of employees, their roles, and their student caseload vary from institution to institution due to factors including institutional perception, values, and resources. As of the 2018 Biennial AHEAD Survey, almost half (48 percent) of DSOs are staffed by one to two full-time employees (Scott 2018). But what does that really mean? If a one-person office actively supports one hundred students, its ability to do anything other than intakes and check-in appointments is quite limited. Its ability to proactively educate faculty or think about larger university access policies is almost nonexistent. And, as we note later, it takes just one student with complex needs to consume a larger percentage of any individual's time.

A bit better for DSPs are one-person offices with access to an administrative assistant. Administrative assistants are often shared by multiple offices as a cost-saving method of providing some support without taxing a budget. Administrative assistants may help to manage the flow of traffic, send emails to students, and proctor exams. The dedication of a full-time administrative assistant is ideal for handling these needs though it often takes a report of increased student traffic and need to convince those who manage the budget of this necessity.

According to the AHEAD 2018 survey, 31 percent of campuses have three to six full-time employees. The way in which the work is split at these institutions varies from campus to campus. Some share the caseload equally between employees, others divide a caseload by type of disability, and others by student focus and/or institution focused work (education, policy development, committee membership, etc.).

DSOs with three or more full-time staff may have the luxury of having a specialist on their team. Universities with a more robust staff often create a job with at least half of a specialist role attached to it. For example, the DSO might have someone who provides expertise around AT or serves as an academic coach. Having a dual role adds a proficiency to a DSO, which benefits students. A dual role may need to be flexible, as the needs of students change over time.

Many DS models rely on graduate students for general administrative support. Graduate students may cover the front desk, welcoming students and getting them situated. Or they may manage a particular type of accommodation: AT, note-taking, or exam proctoring. Graduate students are wonderful short-term resources because they can access student data (undergraduate students are not permitted to for privacy reasons) and handle the day-to-day tasks of accommodation implementation with appropriate training. The challenge of relying on graduate students is that they are temporary, meaning DSPs will need to interview, hire, and train new support systems at least every two years.

Undergraduates might also be a resource for a DSO. Undergraduates can meet and greet new students, help them get situated, support AT needs, and serve as notetakers. The difficulty with hiring undergraduates is that they cannot access student data or easily proctor exams (some professors worry about conflict of interests and overall academic integrity). Just like graduates, undergraduate students are transient. Whether they move to another position in the institution or are balancing their own academic work, their inability to be fully present long-term does not create a reliable workforce.

Advocating for More Staff

The rate of students with identified disabilities will not decline anytime soon, making the need for additional DS team members inevitable. The key to advocating for more help is data. DSOs must keep track, semester by semester, of the number of students they serve, the types of services they provide, things they were unable to do because of caseload, and areas where students may be vulnerable because of lack of dedicated staffing time and resources. Showing increased registration, use of accommodations, and complexity trends, tied closely to the legal requirements of the ADA, should be at the beginning of any proposal for increased staffing.

Benchmarking the ratio of DSPs to students at peer institutions is another valuable exercise to prove need for more personnel. One of the first questions administrators will ask is, "Yes, but what is _____ school doing?" Seek a list of schools that the institution benchmarks against, and do a bit of digging as to how those schools serve SWDs. Collecting data about staff to student ratio at peer institutions or through comparable national data is helpful in a proposal for more assistance.

Another crucial tactic for increasing staffing is creativity. Historically, institutions have balked at requests to hire more support. Remember that a DSO is not just asking for a base salary—in most cases, benefited employees cost 30 percent more than the base salary. Could the office share a position with another office? Offices can share an administrative assistant, for example. Does the new position need to work twelve months, or could it be a shorter contract (nine to ten months)? Can this new position wear two hats within the office, answering two needs at once? Consider this tactic as the needs of the office change throughout the course of the year. August and September tend to be heavily filled with new student intake appointments and returning student check-in appointments. By October, a DSP's time adjusts to helping students prepare for and take midterm exams. Could the office hire a new employee who supports new students and has exam proctoring duty? If yes, the next step is to write a job description that effectively covers all the office's needs.

Create a proposal for increased staffing that answers as many issues as possible with as little asks of the institution as necessary. Once the position is approved, immediately begin tracking data again, because soon enough the DSO will be back at the budget table asking for more support. Bottom-line, coming to the table with no data and no creative funding solutions will almost immediately garner a "no."

Onboarding New Staff

Once the DSO has identified the right candidate, hired them, and worked out the specifics of start date, it is important to plan an effective onboarding process. Hiring someone and welcoming them onto the team is a significant undertaking. While it may be thrilling to grow the team, a DSP should expect about a three-to-six-month ramp-up time before a new hire can fully assume all their responsibilities. Of course, there are exceptions to this rule. If the DSO hires from within the university, the learning curve about the university is significantly less. The same may be said for someone with prior DS experience. Finally, both the nature of the job and the individual hired vary as to what is expected and how quickly they acclimate to their new position.

We recommend putting together a detailed onboarding process that covers the new hire's first month at the institution and within the office. The onboarding process should be a combination of reading and reflecting about the processes and policies within the office, as well as "get to know you" meetings with key stakeholders within and outside of the office. Each aspect of the job description should be reviewed in individual meetings so that the new hire has the chance to understand all the details of one responsibility before moving to the next. If the new hire will be meeting with students, we recommend they shadow those currently meeting with students before doing so on their own. Following the first set of student meetings, it is important to meet with the new hire to reflect on those meetings, add any information that may have been missed, and plan things moving forward. Regular check-ins with the new hire are a must to ensure that expectations are being met. University human resource offices offer a plethora of resources for onboarding, evaluating, and growing employees.

Various Departmental Meetings

Staff Meetings

While open door policies are good methods for immediate problem-solving, staff meetings should be held as dedicated time to discuss the day-to-day needs of an office. Staff meeting agendas may include a review of the numbers (student meetings, accommodations use, exams to be proctored, etc.), DS-sponsored events, upcoming university-wide events, plans for future semesters, budget needs, difficult cases, and other issues as they develop. Even if a DSO just has two staff members, it is important to set aside time to meet regularly.

Individual Meetings

Each staff member should have an uninterrupted hour with their supervisor at least once a month. An open door policy is smart for quick, need-to-know answers and resources but not for long-term planning. Scheduling hourly meetings allows for deeper conversations about the nature of the job, an issue that has arisen, or a particular student case. Advising staff to come to the meeting with a list of questions they have been gathering since the last meeting helps to make the most of the time together.

Specific Disability Services–Related Meetings

Some DSOs have meetings based around specific topics. These might include AT, housing, dining, transportation, exam accommodations, documentation review, or event planning, to name a few. The goal should be to set regular meetings where the duration of the meeting helps frame intake appointments and where review is focused on the topic at hand. Examples include meeting to learn about new ATs or planning how to support students through exam-based accommodations. Weekly documentation review meetings during busy intake months can help to establish a consistent framework for conducting intake appointments and the eligibility determination process. It is also helpful to have a meeting once a semester to discuss any campus events or trainings the DS staff may be asked to participate in (e.g., orientation, RA training, convocation, various workshops the office may be asked to give, and other events that occur on a regular basis across campus) and divvy up the work.

Advisory Board Meetings

Many DSOs find it helpful to have an advisory board. An advisory board is a group of individuals who do not work directly for the DSO but work with the DSO on a regular basis. Through annual or biannual meetings, this board should review any new policies the DSO is considering implementing, offer feedback, and help with proactive planning. Advisory boards may contain students—though some offices choose to separate out students and faculty/staff as a method of engaging in a deeper level of conversation. Advisory boards can share insights into what is happening in the individual worlds outside of the DSO but that might directly impact them in their role across the institution.

Committees Outside of the DSO

Because of the holistic work a DSO does, we are often called on to join committees and meetings beyond our day-to-day office work. Some committees meet just once or twice a year to plan an event or discuss a process change. Others meet as often as once a week to discuss student cases or offer support on behalf of SWDs. Membership in these outside committees offers the opportunity to both advocate for the needs of students and bring back key information about activities, trends, or happenings on campus that may impact students. If the DSO has more than one staff member, divide and conquer these meetings. If the office is a one-person office, it is important to lean on key stakeholders in other offices to be the voice of access in meetings the DSP cannot attend.

Record Keeping and Data Management

The amount of paperwork a DSO is responsible for gathering and creating is high. On the gathering side of things, we need students' documentation (which can be forty or more pages depending on the student), any intake forms a DSO might use, and any other forms we might require. On the information sharing side, we need to send out accommodation letters, confirmation of exam scheduling, and a mountain of emails referring students to one office or another across campus. The volume alone is enough to advocate for the use of an electronic database. The COVID-19 pandemic made it a necessity. As campuses closed, it became imperative that institutions have electronic databases for the continuity of business. It is important to understand what information we need to keep in the database and what information we need it to share back with us.

Having experienced a 200 percent increase in requests for alternative exam accommodations over a five-year period, the DSO at a small, private New England college sought to identify a more robust and flexible solution to an existing web form system—one that would improve workflow, simplify the user experience, and enhance customization of the accommodation request process for all users.

In its efforts to seek a more accessible solution for managing the logistics of exam accommodations, the DSO worked with students in a computer science capstone class to build an application that would automate this process. By the end of the semester, the computer science team had created and delivered an exam requesting system. This application integrated with the student information system, allowing for prepopulation of student profiles, courses, and accommodations. While initially the application was a success, ongoing maintenance by the college's IT team presented many challenges.

When IT determined it did not have the capacity to host an in-house solution, the DSO seized the opportunity to propose the purchase of an enterprise software solution. Outlining the steady growth of registered students and the need to manage student caseload more efficiently without adding staff, the DSO's proposal detailed the numerous benefits of a full-featured, market-available solution on office operations. With the support of IT, the proposal for an established DS database was approved.

Student Information and Records

Everything a student provides to the DSO, including documentation, signed forms, emails, and even phone messages, may be considered student data. Legally, these student records must be kept in accordance with the institution's record retention policy. Typically, records are retained for five to seven years (depending on specific state requirements) beginning from students' separation from the college—meaning their last date of attendance or graduation, whichever comes later. This record keeping is important, as students may transfer institutions or take leaves of absence without graduating. After the state-required set of time, a DSO may dispose of data through a secured system (shredding).

It is important for DSOs to keep track of the information students share for a variety of reasons. DSOs need to hold on to the diagnostic documentation and any corresponding supporting documentation (intake forms; Individualized Education Programs (IEPs); 504 plans; letters from doctors, high school teachers/guidance counselors, therapists). This record of disability may be referred to over the course of a student's time at an institution as validation of a disability. Students may request a copy of their documentation at any time, though many DSOs ask them to sign a record release before providing it. Students who plan to transfer to another school, apply to graduate school, or take a graduate entrance/professional licensing exam frequently contact the DSO seeking a copy of their documentation and a letter verifying their utilization of accommodations in college.

In addition to the information a student has shared, DSOs should keep all emails to and about the student on file, as well as all notes created by the DSP. This information serves as a record for information discussed, recommendations made, referrals suggested, and solutions to problems that may have occurred. If a DSO has more than one staff member, these notes serve to provide information about a student if they are referred to or are having their case covered by another team member.

If a student files a grievance, whether informal or formal, against the office or even the institution, the first thing the person hearing the grievance will want is a copy of all correspondence between the student and the DSO. If the situation rises to the level of a legal investigation, university lawyers will instruct DSPs not to erase, delete, or throw away any content related to the student's case. The simple fact of keeping very clear and detailed case notes, emails, and other forms of correspondence (including between the student, faculty, staff, and families) has often been the data point that clarifies grievance situations.

Data Analytics

Data, data, data—data is the key to advocating for more support and resources, accurately painting a detailed picture of what a DSO does, noticing and responding to trends, and making hard decisions about certain programs or specific resources. Unfortunately, there is no current mandate that DSOs need to follow with regards to data collecting or reporting. Most institutions are required to report the number of students with specific types of disabilities to federal agencies annually. While this is a starting point, it does not do justice to the work that we do; we need to dig deeper and paint a more robust picture. Many details in a DSO are valuable to capture throughout the year. Below we generalize data into two categories: student data and nonstudent data.

Student Data

Student data is an important tool to measure trends in students, which helps to predict the need for future services and accommodations. Student data might include general demographic information, type of disability, accommodation requests versus accommodation approvals, and use of accommodations. By looking at student academic achievement, a DSP can measure areas of impact—another reference point to use when advocating for more help.

Nonstudent Data

Nonstudent data are the data that an office might collect to accurately describe its functioning levels. This information can be helpful in outlining to supervisors and budget administrators about the day-to-day efforts put forth by the DSO. We provide more details as to what types of data a DSO might capture in Table 4.1.

The ability to quickly run a report sharing any of the information noted above (or even drilling down more specifically) can quite literally be the difference between getting an extra position, more financial resources, more space, more student workers, or not.

Databases

One of our most important recommendations to any DSO is to purchase a database. As the field has grown and evolved, so too have the options for a database designed distinctly for the field. While DSOs can rely on homegrown systems, issues will inevitably arise when those who created the database are no longer working at the institution or have moved to different projects. Excel is a wonderfully powerful tool, but it is not designed to house student files and personal information. Retrofitting DS databases into databases made for other offices is also not ideal.

It is important to invest in a quality DS database. A good database should be able to store scanned documents (think of diagnostic documentation), produce accommodation letters with the click of a button, and at the very least run reports. Some allow students to schedule appointments with their DSP, send emails back and forth, arrange for AT loans, and be associated with exam scheduling systems. The goal of a database should be to make the DSO more efficient.

When shopping for databases, it is important to involve the IT department. Ideally, the new database should connect with the university's system-wide database. If a student takes a leave of absence, the university-wide database can kick this information to the database, reducing hours of staff time spent tracking down accurate information. Another key aspect of the office database connecting to the institutional one is the ability to create accommodation letters customized to fit each student's classes and accommodation needs. This simple task can reduce the hours a DSO spends supporting students at the start of the semester drastically.

TABLE 4.1 DATA A DSO SHOULD TRACK

Category	Type of Data
Student Data	
Student Demographics	Number of students seeking support Number of students actually registered Number of graduates vs. undergraduates Number of nonmatriculated students Number of transfer students Breakdown of academic year Breakdown of academic major Commuter vs. residential status Number of international students Number of BIPOC, first generation, veterans, ELL, athletes, etc.
Types of Disability	Breakdown by type of disability (categories) Number of comorbidities Temporary vs. permanent Newly acquired/diagnosed
Types of Accommodation	Number of each type Number requested Number approved Number denied
Student Success	Average number of hours spent supporting students GPA analysis (by semester or annually) Academic standing (number of students registered with DSO) Retention numbers Graduation rates (including length of time to graduate)
Nonstudent Data	
Outreach Efforts	Number of faculty presentations Number of staff presentations Number of student presentations Number of student trainings offered Social media counts Newsletter clicks/openings
Public Relation Efforts	Number of PR materials ordered (year to year) Expenses of PR materials
Committee Work	Number of committees involved in Number of hours allocated to committee work
Budget Expenditures	Breakdown of compensation vs. noncompensation Amount spent on AT Professional development costs Office supplies Technology use
Staff	Number of staff (full-time, part-time, consultants, students) Number of overtime hours Salaries, merit, changes over time

A misconception, though, is that the database will make the DSO more efficient right out of the box. Setting up a database takes time. First, a DSP must work with IT to connect the database to the larger system. Once that has been done, a DSO must merge its list of students into the new system. Depending on the format of the student list, this may be done quickly or take some time. Each DSO will need to decide how to customize its database, from the look and feel of the system to the forms students need to fill out, the accommodation letter templates, the exam scheduling system, the report structures, and the ability for students to see certain information contained in the database. We recommend setting aside a considerable amount of time to set the database up—it can be a great summer project.

Communication Efforts

A DSO must maintain clear and concise communication with many different people in higher education. DSOs must communicate information about their services to currently enrolled students, prospective students, faculty, staff, and in some cases, parents and guardians. This is no easy task in a time of competing priorities and information overload. Figure 4.1 shares different methods of outreach that a DSP can use.

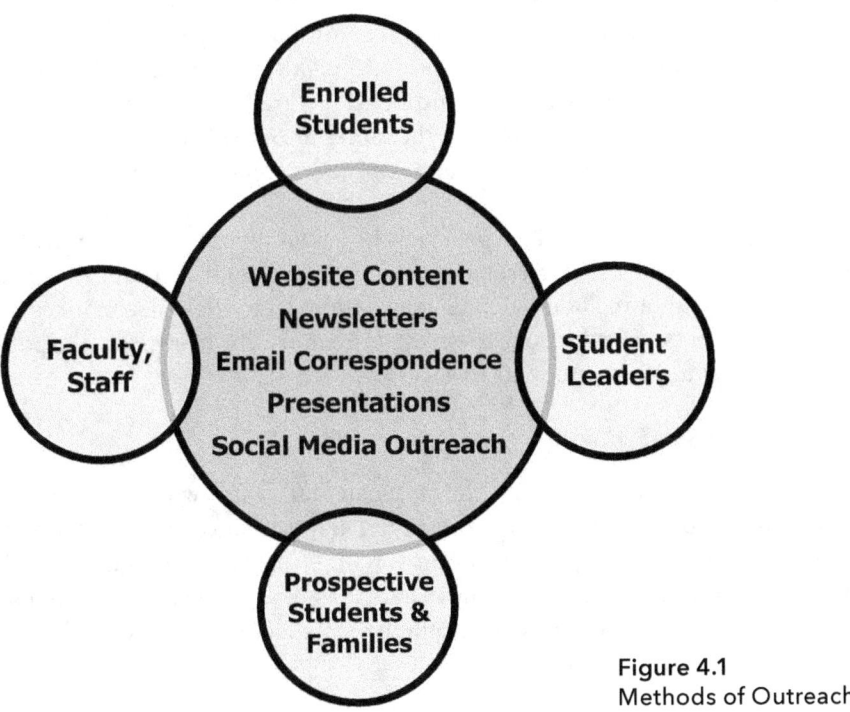

Figure 4.1
Methods of Outreach

Currently Enrolled Students

First and foremost, it is our responsibility to support currently enrolled students. The challenge that many DSOs face is how to do so effectively in a time when flyers and brochures are a thing of the past, students are inundated with emails, text messages are helpful but not always noticed, and overall attention spans continue to shorten with each generation.

A key to communication success is offering the same information in multiple formats, across multiple platforms, and at multiple opportunities. For example, an overview of a DSO should be on a website (connected to both the academic and student affairs sides of the house); on social media; on printed flyers and brochures available at admission offices, open houses, and within each department across campus; and given orally at orientation presentations, residence hall gatherings, and within classrooms. The more places information can be shared, the better.

A DSO officially begins all communication efforts with students the minute they express an interest in registering for accommodations. Detailed registration instructions should be available in a multitude of places. Instructions should include key dates (for housing accommodations, exam accommodations, requests for reduced course loads, etc.), if appropriate, and very clear information about what documentation is needed and how to submit it.

Once a student is registered with a DSO, the DSO will likely need to send reminders to the student to access their accommodation letters. Reminders may be needed for specific accommodations (alternative format of text, notetakers, interpreters, exam accommodations, and housing accommodations for upperclassman) throughout the semester. Some DSOs will use their database or scheduling systems to send reminders about upcoming appointments.

DSOs also send generalized overview information out to their students, whether through newsletters, social media posts, or emails. Specifically, this information might include welcome back letters from the office, notices of upcoming events, introductions to new staff members, or new processes, policies, and resources for students to access as needed.

Faculty and Staff

Information sent to faculty and staff typically falls into two categories: (1) individual student support, and (2) overall DS information. DSOs are often communicating, referring, and problem-solving with faculty and staff around an individual student through email, instant messenger, or live conversations. A summary of each conversation should be included in the student's file for reference at a later point in time.

More generalized communication about the DSO for faculty and staff may come in the form of newsletters, presentations at departmental meetings, faculty/staff space on the DS web page, and overview emails. Information may include updates to policies, procedures, and deadlines; introductions to new team members; and general reminders about what a DSO can and cannot do. This last point is important and worth reiterating. It is just as important to remind faculty and staff what DSOs do not do as what they do. This helps align expectations and share the responsibility of student support.

Faculty should include an accessibility or disability inclusion statement in their syllabi, signaling to students that they value individual learner differences and wish to make their course inclusive and accessible through barrier removal. As a point of reference, a DS statement might be as follows:

> I endeavor to provide a welcoming and inclusive learning environment. If you anticipate or experience disability-related barriers to your inclusion in this course, please let me know so that we can discuss options for meeting your needs. You are also welcome to contact [name of DSO and contact information] to begin this conversation. By working with [DSO], you can ensure appropriate accommodations for this and other classes.

In addition to simply including a statement in their syllabi, faculty should read the statement aloud on the first day of class and review it the week before the first exam or assessment. A DSO should have this statement on its faculty resource web page for easy copying and pasting.

Student Employees

Most IHEs rely on student employees to help them run efficiently. Student employees can be key figures in promoting the work of a DSO, as they interact with students more frequently and in spaces where students may feel more comfortable sharing their needs than faculty and staff. By educating student leaders, a DSO can empower them to respond to student needs with the most up-to-date, accurate information available.

While time consuming, it is important for the DSP to attend and present information at student leader trainings, including to residential advisors, teaching assistants, orientation leaders, admission guides, and tutors, as much as possible. These trainings should be short (ten to fifteen minutes) but impactful—not lecturing on the needs of SWDs but rather focusing on case studies and interactive discussions and leaving lasting handouts (stress balls, pens, brailled information cards, etc.).

Prospective Students and Families

Most DSOs are actively involved in admission events. Whether educating tour guides, holding sessions at accepted student days, serving on prospective parent panels, or acting as a resource for any prospective student and family, a DSO should make themselves available. Often, prospective students will visit a campus and meet with a DSO prior to deciding which IHE they want to attend. These meetings may help them to figure out if a particular college is able to support their accommodation needs ahead of time.

DSOs should have a presence at all orientation events, including those for specific groups (international students, transfer students, January-admit students, etc.). Be prepared for students to stare back with glazed looks from information overload. To combat this effect, consider sending an email to all new students two weeks later reminding them of the resources that the DSO provides.

In Summary

No two days are alike in a DSO in higher education. One day a DSP may be meeting with students for intake appointments and processing accommodations; another, they are advocating for a university-wide closed captioning policy by building a presentation for senior administrators. The work of this field is ever changing. Students are changing; their individual needs are growing in complexity. Our institutions are changing paths and focal points, and resources come and go. Despite these changes, the mission of any DSO should be the same: to provide equal access to those who do not otherwise have it. How we do that, who we do it with, and with what resources will vary from college to college and sometimes even within colleges.

▶ Reflective Exercise

Tiling University has seen exponential growth in the number of students registered with disabilities in the past two years. Currently, Tiling has one full-time equivalent staff member managing the bulk of accommodation-related work. Each year, the administration provides an additional graduate student to support the needs of the office. This year, the graduate students (two) are proctoring exams, helping to check students into the office, and meeting with students for initial intakes. The graduate students are hired to work ten hours a week. However, both report working additional hours unpaid and often leaving the office concerned that they did not have the time or expertise to meet student needs. Outline the steps, resources needed, and colleagues the DS provider might turn to in solving these problems.

Supplemental Job Aids

The following Supplemental Job Aids can be found at https://scholarshare.temple.edu/handle/20.500.12613/8373:

- *Examples of Job Descriptions*
- *Sampling of Interview and Evaluation Questions*
- *Onboarding Checklist*
- *DSO Overview Training*
- *Verifying Accommodations Process and Sample Letter*

Part III

The Interactive Process

5

The Transition from High School to Postsecondary

Do IEPs and 504s transfer to college? This perennial question asked of DSPs served as one catalyst for writing this book. The fact of the matter is that college is not grade 13, and educational and accommodation plans expire. While many school counselors and families do a fine job of helping students with the college search process, they often lack specialized knowledge and training to help SWDs plan for and navigate the postsecondary DS system. Confusion abounds about the legal, philosophical, and logistic differences between high school and higher education. While the transition can seem daunting, early and intentional preparation can ease the burden. This chapter offers a comprehensive overview of the transition planning process from the lens of various stakeholders. Focus will be given to illuminating the shift in rights, responsibilities, and culture post–high school.

▶ Guiding Questions

1. *How do different disability laws affect the provision of services in high school and college?*
2. *When should transition planning begin, and who should be involved?*
3. *How should various stakeholders help students prepare for the transition?*

Transition Planning Overview

Transitions are a rite of passage through the educational system often scaffolded by intentional practices that prepare students for increasing levels of independence. Integral to the transition process is preparing students to navigate bigger buildings, adapt to a larger student body, anticipate different routines, understand support systems, and balance increased freedom. For SWDs, special education teams and transition coordinators provide an added layer of support. Recognizing that transition planning is not an event but a process, these teams meet at least annually to develop a coordinated set of programs, services, and goals to enhance a successful shift. Families are included in this process. In K–12, the school-to-school handoff is an intentional effort to bring educational teams together to discuss each student's needs in the context of appropriate coursework, services, and supports. But what happens when the shift is from high school to college?

For SWDs, the transition can present unique challenges. Although IHEs have become increasingly accessible for SWDs, disabled students are enrolling at far lower rates than their peers. According to the National Longitudinal Study-2 (NLTS-2), 19 percent of SWDs attended four-year colleges and universities, compared to 40 percent of students without disabilities (Newman et al. 2011).

The good news is that improvements in postsecondary transition planning have helped close some of the gaps. To help students make a relatively seamless and successful transition to college, the student's planning team (e.g., educators, counselors, agencies, families) should be well informed about regulations, supports, services, and structures necessary to bridge the metamorphosis from childhood to adulthood.

Overview of Disability Laws and Accommodation Plans

Critical to helping students and families prepare for the transition is an in-depth understanding of disability legislation. The array of disability laws and the alphabet soup of acronyms can be confusing. However, one thing is clear: students' rights change as they enter college.

Individuals with Disabilities Education Act of 2004

Students from ages three through twenty-one may receive special education and related services under the nation's special education law, Individuals with Disabilities Education Act (IDEA), which mandates that public educational institutions are responsible for identifying disabilities, accommodating needs, and ensuring success (U.S. Department of Education n.d.a). IDEA is an entitlement law administered by the U.S. Department of Education that mandates a free and appropriate public education (FAPE) to SWDs. This means that families may not be charged for their student's education and related services and that educational services must be appropriate and provided in conformity with an IEP. It also ensures specialized instruction through an IEP to enhance educational outcomes. To be eligible for special education and related services under IDEA, students must be determined by a multidisciplinary team to meet the criteria of one or more of thirteen specific disability categories (U.S. Department of Education 2018b). Each of the thirteen conditions (shown in Figure 5.1) has its own eligibility criteria, but all require that a student's educational performance be adversely affected due to the disability.

Transition services are a coordinated set of activities developed and carried about by members of a multidisciplinary team. These services are federally required for all students who have an IEP. Transition planning must be in effect by the time the student turns sixteen and be updated annually thereafter. Consideration of transition services includes career counseling, college visits, accommodations, agency referrals, and community involvement.

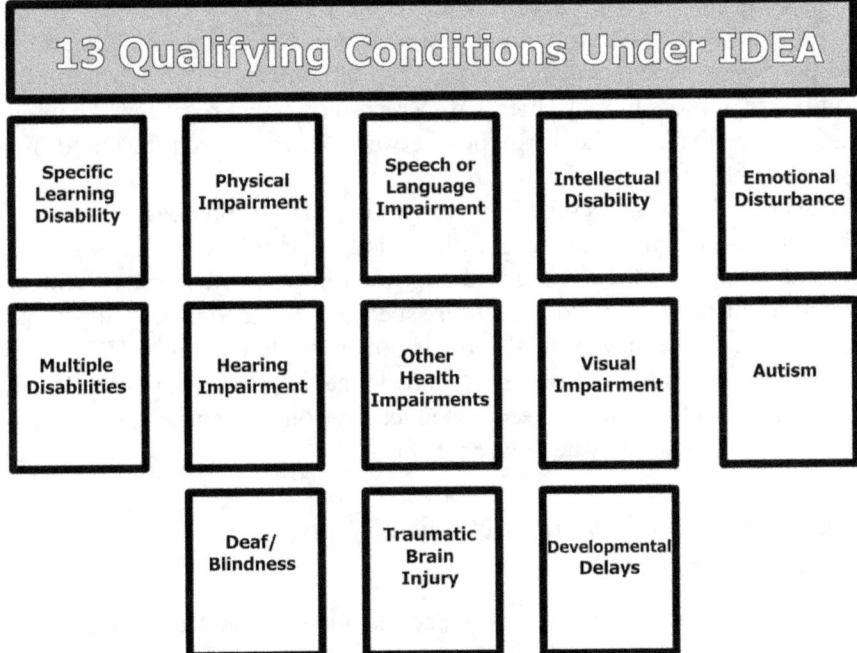

Figure 5.1 IDEA Qualifying Conditions

As part of the transition planning process, IDEA requires schools to provide a summary of students' academic achievements and functional performance. The summary of performance (SOP), typically completed the year before graduation, includes recommendations for meeting postsecondary goals. However, since the intent of the SOP is to provide guidance to professionals who may assist students in the future (e.g., DSPs or vocational rehabilitation counselors), timely preparation is recommended.

Since the SOP reflects students' abilities, needs, and aspirations, students should be actively involved in developing this document. While the SOP is very closely tied to levels of performance outlined in the IEP, it should be a separate document that condenses and organizes key information that should follow the student (Wright and Wright 2018).

Section 504 of the Rehabilitation Act of 1973

While Section 504 is a statute enforced by the OCR, the Department of Education also has a hand in upholding this statute. Subpart D applies to the K–12 environment, while Subpart E applies to postsecondary (U.S. Department of Education n.d.d). Like IDEA, Section 504 entitles students to FAPE regardless of the nature or severity of the disability (U.S. Department of Education n.d.b).

Section 504 and IDEA have different requirements for determining whether a student is disabled. An individual is considered to have a disability under Section 504 if they have a physical or mental impairment that substantially limits one or more life activities, have a record of, or are regarded as having such an impairment. The distinction between "having a record of" and "regarded as" is detailed in Chapter 6.

Section 504 is much broader in scope than IDEA and does not contain the same specific disability categories. Section 504 may be helpful to students who do not qualify for services under IDEA either because they do not meet the disability criteria or do not require specially designed instruction. Similarly, Section 504 may protect students no longer eligible under IDEA. For example, if a learning-disabled student no longer requires specially designed reading instruction but still needs extended time on tests and alternative text formats, a 504 plan may be most appropriate.

Americans with Disabilities Act Amendments Act of 2008 (ADAAA)

Eligibility under ADA is the same as Section 504—the student must have an impairment that substantially limits a major life activity. Unlike IDEA, ADA protections do not afford FAPE. However, in combination with Section 504,

ADA requires that every public and private institution, except those affiliated with religious organizations, make reasonable modifications to policies, practices, and procedures. Table 5.1 discusses these legal differences in more detail.

Private Schools

IDEA extends benefits to students who attend private schools, including religious schools, although the benefits differ from those in public schools. Essentially, students in private school settings waive their entitlement to FAPE.

Under IDEA, when the family of a privately placed student requests an evaluation to determine special education eligibility, the public school district where the private school is located is required to conduct an assessment (ASHA n.d.). Should the student be found eligible for special education services, the local public school agency is not required to provide students enrolled in a private school with the same services they would receive in a public setting. However, they are required to provide "equitable services." In fact,

TABLE 5.1 LEGAL DIFFERENCES BETWEEN HIGH SCHOOL AND COLLEGE

Legal Responsibilities	
High School	**Postsecondary**
IDEA FAPE and Section 504 Subpart D.	Section 504 Subpart E and ADA (if school is federally funded).
Students receive special education and related services to address needs based on an identified disability.	Formal special education services are not available.
Families must be informed of academic services, have access to student records, and can participate in the accommodations process.	Families do not have access to student records without written consent from the student via FERPA.
IDEA is about success.	ADA is about access.
Accommodations and services are designed to maximize a student's potential.	Accommodations are provided to level the playing field.
Districts are required to evaluate and identify students with disabilities.	Students must identify themselves and request accommodations.
IEPs provide specially designed instruction by trained teachers and support staff.	Unless a student chooses a college with a specialized program, services are generally the same for all students.
Progress toward IEP goals is monitored and communicated to families and the student.	Students are required to monitor their progress and communicate their needs to faculty.

through an IDEA stipulation referred to as "proportionate share funding," the local school district is only obligated to spend a portion of its federal aid moneys to fund the special education of private school students (National Archives 2022). The amount is usually insufficient to provide substantive services. Nevertheless, the local public school is obligated to develop a services plan, sometimes referred to as an Individual Services Plan (ISP), which outlines the services the school district will offer. While this plan may resemble an IEP, it is generally less comprehensive.

Section 504 prohibits disability discrimination and applies to all schools, both public and private, that receive federal funding. If the school receives federal funding, it is required to provide basic accommodations such as extended time on tests and AT. However, if the student's needs are more complex, a better-resourced public school may be recommended.

Informal Plans

Sometimes, high schools provide services and accommodations through informal means not memorialized in an official plan. An informal plan may be appropriate for students who do not have or are not suspected of having a disability but may be encountering challenges in school. Informal supports and accommodations include checklists for students who need help breaking down assignments, after-school tutoring, and access to an adjustment counselor.

Another way students may receive informal accommodations is via well-intentioned teachers or guidance counselors who allow accommodations such as extended time or flexible assignment deadlines to support students with an undocumented disability. Test anxiety, which alone is not a disability, is the most often cited reason for offering extended time or a distraction-reduced location for taking exams.

Sometimes, students who are no longer eligible for an IEP are provided a monitoring plan through which some accommodations are continued. In other cases, students who have undergone psychoeducational testing but do not meet disability criteria under IDEA may be provided with informal accommodations. Often, this situation occurs when a particular domain of functioning (like processing speed) or subtest score (like reading fluency) falls below average. While below average or relatively lower domain and subtest scores in and of themselves do not necessarily constitute a disability, well-meaning professionals may feel that weaknesses warrant informal accommodation.

A challenge for students who have been informally accommodated in high school is that they will not meet the eligibility requirements for establishing disability at the postsecondary level without appropriate disability documentation. While potentially helpful in establishing a history of accommodation, these informal plans hold little weight at the postsecondary level in the absence of a substantially limiting disability, as we discuss in Chapter 6.

Key Differences between IEPs and 504 Plans in High School

Through high school, Section 504 and IDEA have many similarities. Both protect the rights of SWDs, provide free and appropriate public education, outline accommodations based on individual needs, and list accommodations in a written plan. Although similar in their goals and outcomes, they differ in scope and detail. Table 5.2 highlights the key differences between a 504 plan and an IEP (U.S. Department of Education 2020b).

Transitioning from an IEP to a 504 Plan

One objective of special education is to help students become more independent. As students progress through school, the goal is that they become less reliant on supports and services.

TABLE 5.2 DIFFERENCES BETWEEN AN IEP AND A 504 PLAN

	IEP	504
Laws and Authority	IDEA Department of Education	Section 504 of the Rehabilitation Act of 1973 OCR
Eligibility Requirements	Must have one of thirteen recognized disabilities under IDEA Significantly impacted educational performance; not making effective progress; requires specialized instruction or related services	Must have a disability that substantially limits one or more major life activities Does not need specialized instruction to make effective progress, only accommodations and related services
Plan Contents	Formal written document outlining how FAPE will be provided to ensure educational progress	Does not have to be a written document; outlines how FAPE will ensure the same access to the learning environment as nondisabled peers
Created by	IEP team with strict legal requirements about participants	A team of people familiar with the student who understand evaluation data and service options
Evaluations	Comprehensive evaluations required by multidisciplinary team; conducted triennially	Evaluation draws on information from a variety of sources; periodic evaluations required
Monitoring	IEP team must review the IEP at least once per year	Rules vary by state; 504 plans generally reviewed annually

Transitioning from an IEP to a 504 plan may be a good option for students who demonstrate they can perform well in the general education environment with accommodations. For example, a 504 plan is likely appropriate for a student who no longer requires specialized reading instruction but needs books in alternative formats.

Transition to Postsecondary Education: Legal Obligations

A common misconception about IEPs and 504 plans is that they transfer to college. This is simply untrue. There are no postsecondary regulations entitling students to the same level of support they received in high school.

Students are no longer covered under IDEA when they leave high school, either from graduating or aging out of the system. Because IDEA no longer applies once students leave high school, the educational rights of students change. One of the most significant changes involves the goal of federal regulations. Under IDEA, the goal of educational services is to ensure students are successful and making effective progress. By contrast, the goal of ADA and Section 504 shifts from success to access. IHEs are required to afford students equal access as a way of leveling the playing field. They have no obligation to ensure students make academic progress or have successful outcomes.

Once a student matriculates to college, even if they are not yet an adult, parents and guardians no longer have access to student records (e.g., financial aid, student accounts, academic progress, disability files) without the student's written consent. In college, student records are protected under the Family Education Rights and Privacy Act (FERPA), "a federal law that protects the privacy of student education records" (U.S. Department of Education 2021a). When a student turns eighteen or enters a postsecondary institution at any age, rights under FERPA transfer from the caregiver to the student. Families should not expect college faculty or staff to talk with them about their student's progress or attendance. Even if students waive FERPA rights, college professionals may choose not to discuss student progress without the student's direct involvement. At the postsecondary level, students are expected to self-advocate while families are relegated to mentors or guides on the side. Postsecondary institutions have significantly different responsibilities from those of K–12 school districts. Consider the unique relationship between students and colleges in pre- and postadmission practices.

Before Admission

IHEs are not allowed to make preadmission inquiries about a prospective student's disability. While there is no legal obligation to disclose a disability to a prospective school, students may voluntarily choose to do so. Not surprisingly, we field many questions from students and families about whether disclosure is a good idea and how it might impact a student's chances of admission. Ultimately, it is a personal choice.

As a rule, disclosure of a disability in a student's applications or interviews may help explain anomalies or discrepancies in their academic profile. For example, if a student had a difficult transition to high school resulting in a less than stellar first-year GPA but demonstrated a steady upward trend in their grades, disclosure might signal the ability to pivot after a challenging start. Another reason to disclose might be to explain why a student has not met a specific academic college requirement (e.g., two years of a foreign language). While colleges are not required to waive or lower their entrance criteria, verification that the high school waived the foreign language requirement because of the student's disability might help to elucidate why a particular requirement was not met.

Preadmission disclosure might also be considered if a student's academic achievement is not reflected in their standardized test scores. Many students report that disability negatively impacts their ability to perform on high-stakes testing. It might be helpful for admission counselors to understand not only how the disability impacts performance but also the strategies the student utilizes to mitigate its impact and effectively manage learning. Some students feel so strongly that their disability has shaped their identity that they choose to write about it in their college essay or supplemental questions.

At the postsecondary level, a qualified student is one who meets the academic and technical standards required for admission or participation in the institution's educational program or activity (U.S. Department of Education n.d.c). In other words, SWDs must meet the same admission and programmatic requirements as their nondisabled peers. While colleges can inquire as to whether a prospective student can meet the academic and technical standards required for admission, they need to ensure that inquiries are not designed to inadvertently reveal a student's disability.

Following Admission

IHEs are required to have an office that coordinates accommodations for SWDs. Unlike K–12, IHEs have no legal obligation to identify SWDs. They are not required to conduct evaluations to determine whether a student has a disability and requires services.

Students wishing to be considered for disability-related accommodations must self-identify to the DSO. While disclosure is strictly voluntary, the institution is under no legal obligation to provide any adjustments without the student initiating and engaging in an eligibility determination process. IHEs must provide reasonable adjustments to ensure equal opportunity—in essence, to level the playing field. In providing an academic adjustment, IHEs do not have to eliminate or lower essential requirements or make modifications that would result in a fundamental alteration of the programs or activities being offered or impose an undue burden on the institution. IHEs have a right to establish reasonable procedures for requesting academic adjustments, and students have a responsibility to know and follow these procedures.

Students may request accommodations at any point in their postsecondary career but are encouraged to do so as early as possible to ensure timely accommodation provision. For example, a Deaf or hard-of-hearing student who requires an assistive listening device or sign language interpreter should identify to the DSO before enrollment. This will allow the DSO reasonable notice to coordinate accommodations and deliver them in a timely manner, ideally by the first day of classes.

Other Key Differences between High School and College

While there are many legal differences between high school and college, there are philosophical, logistic, and programmatic ones as well. It is important to note that, fundamentally, the goal of the K–12 system in supporting SWDs is to help each student reach their full potential and be successful. In college, however, the foundational goal is not to discriminate. Table 5.3 details some of these key differences, especially in relation to the need for self-advocacy and expectations within a course.

Planning for the Transition from High School to College

Our collective experience working with SWDs affirms two critical factors in determining postsecondary success or failure: adequate transition planning and self-determination. As previously noted, a successful transition from secondary to postsecondary education is not a static activity. Intentional and ongoing planning allows students to develop the skill sets essential to independence in adulthood.

Expectations are central to a student's postsecondary success. Students perform better when they are provided with appropriate challenges matched by appropriate support. Conversely, "low expectations are often cited as significant barriers to academic and career achievement for students with disabilities" (U.S. Department of Education 2020b).

TABLE 5.3 DIFFERENCES BETWEEN HIGH SCHOOL AND COLLEGE FOR SWDs

Public High School	College
\multicolumn{2}{c}{Self-Advocacy}	
Schools have an obligation to identify disabled students.	Students must self-disclose a disability.
Schools assist in connecting students with community support agencies.	Students are responsible for making or maintaining connections with community support agencies.
High school professionals will often approach students if they believe assistance is needed.	College faculty and staff expect students to seek help when needed.
Schools are responsible for ensuring accommodation needs are communicated to relevant professionals.	Students are responsible for notifying faculty and staff of accommodation needs.
\multicolumn{2}{c}{Assessments, Grading, Instruction}	
Students follow a school-directed schedule within the school day, moving from one class to another.	Students are responsible for registering for classes and coordinating their schedules.
Twenty-five to thirty hours per week of classroom instruction.	Twelve to sixteen hours per week of classroom instruction with an expectation of two to three hours of work outside of class for each hour spent in class.
Emphasis on in-class learning; independent reading and studying is limited.	Emphasis on independent learning with substantial reading assignments and out-of-class research/study.
Classes are dictated by state graduation requirements and district policies.	Classes are based on graduation requirements, which often include general education courses and major requirements.
A school year is typically thirty-six to forty weeks long.	A typical semester-based institution is fifteen to seventeen weeks per semester including final exams.
Many opportunities for grading/assignments.	Fewer opportunities for assessments; each assignment can carry significant weight.
Learning is primarily about remembering and understanding information.	Deeper learning is expected, including application, analysis, syntheses, evaluation, and creation.
Teachers might provide students with materials missed when absent.	Faculty expect students to check with peers about missed material when absent.
Teachers are often available to meet before/after class or school.	Faculty hold scheduled office hours that may be only a few hours each week.
Teachers will often review assignment and test dates.	Faculty expect students to follow the course syllabus without prompting.

High expectations can be fostered in a couple of ways. First, students should be placed in courses where the level will challenge them. Decisions made in early high school related to course level and requirements will have a significant impact on their preparation and eligibility for college admission. Second, IEP goals and support services should focus on enhancing independent skill development. Too often, we hear about supports that undermine students' potential for independent learning and class engagement. These supports may include substantial curricular and pacing adjustments, class notes and study guides, and assessment modifications. Unfortunately, while lowering standards and expectations may ensure student success, they may inadvertently undermine educational opportunities and impede skill development.

Despite the protections afforded under the ADA and Section 504, students bear the ultimate responsibility for their success at the postsecondary level. Students' success in college hinges on their ability to manage themselves and their situations. Self-determination is a comprehensive concept that incorporates a wide array of attitudes, skills, and knowledge that leads people to set goals, execute decisions, and plan for the future. These include decision making, problem-solving, goal setting, planning, self-management, self-advocacy, and self-awareness, to list a few (Bremer, Kachgal, and Schoeller 2003).

Like transition planning, the development of self-determination is not a static process. It happens over time with practice, feedback, and failure. Cultivating self-determination is most effectively accomplished through real-world experiences, which inherently involve taking risks, making mistakes, and reflecting on outcomes. Learning self-determination skills while adjusting to college independence is a formidable task, so students should begin building these skills no later than high school. While self-determination is an essential skill set for all students, it is particularly crucial for those with disabilities. Oftentimes, well-intentioned people attempt to shield disabled students from challenges by making decisions on their behalf, removing obstacles, or speaking for them.

Transition Guidance for Student Support Team Members

While IDEA requires transition planning to begin when the student turns sixteen, the process can start sooner if determined necessary by the school team. At the center of this process is the student; the process is facilitated by strong partnerships between team members including the family, school professionals, and outside agencies. As these constituents reach out to us for guidance in preparing students for the transition, we impart some words of

TABLE 5.4 TRANSITION PLANNING TEAM

Role	Transition Guidance
Family	• Take a less active role in students' day-to-day planning/organization. • Guide students in making decisions; do not make decisions on their behalf. • Encourage students to take an active role in IEP/504 process and meetings, leading these discussions by senior year. • Help students compile a file of disability documentation (e.g., IEP/504, medical records, psychoeducational testing).
School Professionals	• Help students understand and articulate how their disability impacts them, strategies that have been effective/ineffective in mitigating barriers. • Scaffold development of self-regulated learning skills. • Understand and communicate how laws, accommodations, and services differ in college. • Conduct comprehensive evaluations per established timelines; encourage students not to waive their right to testing.
Community Agencies (e.g., Vocational Rehabilitation, Agencies for Deaf/Blind)	• Attend high school transition planning meetings. • Evaluate AT, auxiliary aids, independent living, mobility, and orientation needs.
Students	• Lead an IEP/504 meeting. • Practice and enhance self-determination and executive skills. • Research college disability accommodations and services by contacting DSOs. • Understand the impact of disability and strategies/accommodations that have/have not worked.

wisdom to share with each. Table 5.4 shares how each member of the team can guide the student through the process.

The Higher Education Opportunity Act of 2008

The Higher Education Opportunity Act (HEOA) of 2008 assists underrepresented students (e.g., low income, first generation, and disabled) transitioning to postsecondary education with financial aid programs and support services with the goal of improving retention, graduation rates, and financial and economic literacy. Under HEOA, two programs that specifically target support and financial assistance to SWDs are the TRIO Student Support Services (SSS) program and the Comprehensive Transition and Postsecondary (CTP) programs for students with intellectual disabilities.

While HEOA does not mandate IHEs offer programs for students with intellectual disabilities, many do. As of May 2021, 308 postsecondary programs enrolled over 6,500 students. As colleges have opened their doors to students with intellectual disabilities, these individuals experience significantly better employment, social engagement, and community living outcomes (Think College National Coordinating Center 2021).

In Summary

As more and more high school SWDs prepare to matriculate to postsecondary institutions, being well-informed and prepared to support students' transitions is paramount. At the heart of this preparation is being knowledgeable about federal antidiscrimination statutes that afford students equal access to all a higher education institution has to offer. One key distinction between laws that govern K–12 and college relates to the matter of entitlement versus access. In K–12, accommodations and services are in place to maximize a student's potential and ensure success. At the postsecondary level, accommodations are provided to ensure access. Stark differences in the identification, accommodation, and oversight of SWDs punctuate the IHE setting. Understanding these differences will enable a successful transition. Central to the success of launching students into adulthood is their development of self-determination skills. Proficiency with self-advocacy begins with students understanding their disability and knowing how it impacts them across multiple contexts. Assisting students with postsecondary goals is a shared responsibility facilitated by early and comprehensive planning. The college search process is daunting enough; for SWDs, there are added complexities. Students should evaluate the depth the breadth of campus supports and services within the context of their needs. Meeting with the college DSO will illuminate available options and the processes for accessing them.

▶ Reflective Exercise

Jordan is a high school junior considering college options within a thirty-mile radius of his home so that he can commute. He plans to study business. Jordan has cerebral palsy, which limits his gross and fine motor skills. Jordan has his license and plans to drive to campus, but mobility limitations impact how far he can walk. Jordan types with one or two fingers. Dysarthria complicates speech intelligibility to some degree. Jordan's reading speed and decoding accuracy is below average.

Jordan's IEP lists academic support services one period per day, five days per week. Accommodations include extended time on exams; scribe, reader, and oral exams; and teacher-provided notes. Some of his workload is modified (e.g., reduced number of math problems, oral papers vs. written). Jordan has not had an AT evaluation or participated in an IEP meeting.

How would you advise Jordan to prepare for his college transition? As he weighs college options, what are some key questions he should be asking the DSO?

Supplemental Job Aids

The following Supplemental Job Aids can be found at https://scholarshare.temple.edu/handle/20.500.12613/8373:

- Questions to Ask the Disability Office

6

Establishing Disability in Higher Education

In becoming DSPs, we take on the responsibility of verifying a student's disability, evaluating the impacts of their disability or disabilities as they pertain to daily life in postsecondary education environments, and working with students to develop and implement plans of accommodation for the purpose of providing equal access to the full range of opportunities at our institutions. By and large, the professionals in our field are not qualified evaluators, nor are we medical or mental health care providers who can appropriately diagnose a disability. We are, however, charged with evaluating the evidence a student presents by way of self-report, documentation from evaluations, and records of academic and accommodation history. In this evaluation, we must make the determination for the institution as to whether the impacts a student is presenting rise to the level of disability and qualify them for reasonable accommodations. In this chapter, we explore the legal definition of disability, interpret the guidance of AHEAD for determining eligibility of services, discuss established practices for verifying an individual's disability and the level to which it impacts academic and nonacademic activities, and navigate the nuances of the interactive process from a student's initial disclosure to determining and granting reasonable accommodations.

▶ Guiding Questions

1. *How does the accommodation process in higher education differ from the process in a K–12 setting?*

2. What constitutes "good" supporting documentation?
3. How do DSPs engage with students in the interactive process?
4. How does the DSP determine the eligibility of a student for reasonable accommodations?

Disability, Defined

The ADA, which provides us with the legal definition of the term "disability," is fundamentally a civil rights law. The purpose of the ADA, at its core, is to protect individuals with disabilities against discrimination. The specific language of the law outlines a number of arenas where this protection is afforded, and specific language from the ADA definition are discussed in this chapter as they pertain to determining disability. The legal definition of disability, as defined by the ADA (section 12102), is as follows:

Disability
The term "disability" means, with respect to an individual—a physical or mental impairment that substantially limits one or more major life activities of such individual; a record of such an impairment; or being regarded as having such an impairment (as described in paragraph (3)).

Major Life Activities
In general
For purposes of paragraph (1), major life activities include, but are not limited to, caring for oneself, performing manual tasks, seeing, hearing, eating, sleeping, walking, standing, lifting, bending, speaking, breathing, learning, reading, concentrating, thinking, communicating, and working.

Major Bodily Functions
For purposes of paragraph (1), a major life activity also includes the operation of a major bodily function, including but not limited to, functions of the immune system, normal cell growth, digestive, bowel, bladder, neurological, brain, respiratory, circulatory, endocrine, and reproductive functions.

Regarded as Having Such an Impairment
For purposes of paragraph (1)(C):
An individual meets the requirement of "being regarded as having such an impairment" if the individual establishes that he or she has been subjected to an action prohibited under this chapter because

of an actual or perceived physical or mental impairment whether or not the impairment limits or is perceived to limit a major life activity.

Paragraph (1)(C) shall not apply to impairments that are transitory and minor. A transitory impairment is an impairment with an actual or expected duration of 6 months or less. (U.S. Department of Justice Civil Rights Division 2010c)

The legal definition of disability does not include a list of conditions or impairments that qualify; rather, it provides a broad set of guidelines by which the impact(s) of an individual's impairment(s) can be assessed. This is an important starting point, as it represents a major difference for students transitioning from secondary to postsecondary education—under IDEA, a list of qualifying conditions is provided. In this way, "covered under ADA" becomes more dynamic, which establishes our job as more interpretive than diagnostic.

Paragraph (1)(A) is what DSPs cite as the legal definition of disability: "physical or mental impairment," "substantially limits," "major life activities." ADAAA regulations refer to a disability under (1)(A) as "actual disability," suggesting a demonstrable impact. The spirit of Paragraph (1)(A) is to establish the least-restrictive definition of the term "disability" by allowing for the provision of services based on functional limitations and not diagnoses. The idea of broad coverage is further enforced by Paragraph (4)(A):

(4) Rules of construction regarding the definition of disability
The definition of "disability" in paragraph (1) shall be construed in accordance with the following:
(A) The definition of disability in this chapter shall be construed in favor of broad coverage of individuals under this chapter, to the maximum extent permitted by the terms of this chapter. (U.S. Department of Justice Civil Rights Division 2010c)

Because of this definition, theoretically, more students qualify for services in college than in high school. Paragraph (1)(B), indicating an individual with a record of such an impact, refers to an individual who has a history of having a disability under this definition paragraph (1)(A) but is not currently substantially limited in their daily life activities. A person could have a "record of" a disability because they were falsely diagnosed, a condition is in remission, daily life activities that would be impacted are not applicable in a particular setting, etcetera.

Paragraph (1)(C), dealing with "regarded as," offers protection for individuals thought to have a disability. This section also covers individuals who have "transitory" impairments—impairments lasting six months or less, which are not classified as "actual" disabilities. While students with transitory impairments, such as broken fingers, may not meet the legal definition of having a disability, and we may not be obligated to offer services under the ADA, DSOs can (and in many instances, do) extend services. It is important to note, however, that this choice relies on institutional discretion. Some institutions encourage faculty to accommodate through other channels, such as the dean of students office or health and wellness center. In either case, an institution must recognize when it is appropriate to afford ADA coverage, which we explore later in this chapter. In some cases, temporary accommodations are not provided.

It is important to reiterate that the ADA is, by nature, an antidiscrimination law. Paragraphs (1)(B) and (1)(C) refer to the fact that it is against the law to discriminate against someone who used to have a disability, has a temporarily impairing condition, or is thought to have a disability regardless of whether the disability is impacting the individual.

Here are a few examples that illustrate these points. The first example relates to the experience of a student who had a seizure in class. The student may have returned to campus with medical clearance and be declared seizure-free. Prohibiting this student from handling chemicals in a lab environment would constitute discrimination of a person who has a record of having a disability. A second example of having a record of a disability could involve a student who previously had a cancer diagnosis being denied an internship opportunity out of concern that they may experience a recurrence and need to miss time to receive treatments. Under Paragraph(1)(C), an example of discrimination would be a student who presents with some social difficulties not being placed in a project group; they might experience discrimination as a person regarded as having a disability.

In order to qualify for services, including but not limited to access, accommodations, and auxiliary aids, the daily life activities of a student must be impacted. The ADA provides a list of major life activities, which are broad in scope. The ADAAA of 2008 saw the addition of "major bodily functions," which further broadens the types of impacts that warrant coverage under the ADA, translating into even more students qualifying for services in college. For instance, a student who has a food allergy or asthma but is otherwise qualified to participate could be eligible for accommodations under the ADAAA.

The daily life activities listed under Paragraph (2)(A) provide guidance in determining the scope of impact of a student's disability. As student service providers, we should consider how the list compares to the student experience on our campuses to make further sense of the tasks that will be impacted. Understanding how particular activities overlay with our unique physical campuses, virtual environments, academic and cocurricular opportunities and standards, and every aspect of campus life provides that construct. For instance, performing manual tasks can mean very different things for students taking an online course in tax accounting versus pursuing a culinary degree; reading varies between literature majors and analytical chemistry majors. With the magnitude of what is encompassed under the need to provide equal access, our interpretation of each student and each activity will range from broad to granular. Ultimately, the activity and the way in which it is impacted by a specific student's disability profile dictates services, not the diagnostic criteria met.

Determining Disability

According to Kincaid (2019), there are two ways to establish that a student has a disability: condition analysis and "predictable assessments." We have established that there is no finite list of conditions that qualify as disabilities, which means that any physical or mental condition that impacts a major life activity could meet the eligibility threshold. There are, however, a list of conditions set forth in the 2016 ADAAA regulations that, "given their inherent nature, these types of impairments will, as a factual matter, virtually always be found to impose a substantial limitation on a major life activity" (U.S. Department of Justice Civil Rights Division 2016a). This guidance dictates the term "predictable assessment" in that "the necessary individualized assessment should be particularly simple and straightforward" (U.S. Department of Justice Civil Rights Division 2016a). Kincaid goes on to state that "this list is subject to rebuttable presumption of disability status," referring to the conditions as presumptive disabilities. The list of predictable assessments and their primary impacts, as outlined in the 2016 regulations, is as follows:

- Deafness substantially limits hearing.
- Blindness substantially limits seeing.
- Intellectual disability substantially limits brain functioning.
- Partially or completely missing limbs or mobility impairments requiring the use of a wheelchair substantially limits musculoskeletal function.
- Autism substantially limits brain function.
- Cancer substantially limits normal cell growth.
- Cerebral palsy substantially limits brain function.
- Diabetes substantially limits endocrine function.
- Epilepsy, muscular dystrophy, and multiple sclerosis each substantially limits neurological function.
- Human Immunodeficiency Virus (HIV) substantially limits immune function.

- Major depressive disorder, bipolar disorder, post-traumatic stress disorder, traumatic brain injury, obsessive compulsive disorder, and schizophrenia each substantially limits brain function.

For conditions outside those outlined above, we must analyze the student's condition as it applies to the definition of disability. To do so, we analyze the information presented and/or gathered to the standard of "substantially limits." In this way, a student who has a diagnosis of ADHD or a learning disability is not inherently "disabled," but if they are determined to be substantially limited in one or more major life functions, they qualify for ADA protection and may qualify for reasonable accommodations. The standard we evaluate "substantially limited" against is the functioning of "most people in the general population" (U.S. Department of Justice Civil Rights Division 2010c). This means that we should not compare functions within a specific population, such as chemistry majors, graduate students, college athletes, etcetera. Given this information, the need for an interactive process and protections against overscrutinizing becomes apparent.

Part of the evaluation of impact to daily life activities is the relevance of mitigating measures. Mitigating measures are factors that reduce the impact of a physical or mental impairment. Examples include medication, hearing aids, AT, medical equipment, daily living aids, etcetera. While mitigating measures are, in essence, designed to reduce the impact of an impairment, in some circumstances negating the limitation, they are not factored into the determination of whether an individual has a disability. A graduate student who uses hearing aids can still be considered to have a disability and be eligible for services even though they may not be presently impacted because their current classes are taught in a small seminar style.

The one exception to the rule of mitigating measures deals with "ordinary eyeglasses or contact lenses" that are "intended to fully correct visual acuity or to eliminate refractive error" (U.S. Department of Justice Civil Rights Division 2010c). The extent of the ameliorative effect that glasses or contact lenses have on a student's vision must be taken into account when determining whether the student has a disability to warrant services. For instance, a student who wears reading glasses might not be eligible for alternative format materials because proper reading glasses would correct their vision back to 20/20. However, a student who has low vision may have correctable vision to some extent but not necessarily or sustainably within a nonimpaired range.

Documentation

There are lasting impressions in the field that documentation is the be-all and end-all, yet according to a guidance document published by AHEAD in April of 2012 after the ADAAA went into effect, "no legislation or regulations require that documentation be requested or obtained." Part of the history and intention of the ADAAA was to overturn a narrowing effect on the protection afforded to individuals with disabilities at the mercy of case law that set the burden of "docs" higher and higher in the decade and a half after the inception of the ADA. Obtaining documentation from a full-blown neuropsychological evaluation every three years, which was the old standard, was costly to school districts and families. This process allowed IHEs to hold recency standards for documentation, which usually meant documentation needed to be updated every three years (or sooner, depending upon the condition). In many instances, this meant provision of service was easier for those who could afford testing, which was never the intended purpose of ADA protections. In some cases, relevant documentation is much more effective than recent documentation.

AHEAD's 2012 guidance on documentation provides updated guidelines for how to incorporate verifying information related to a disability into our decision-making processes. The guidance document presents a list of acceptable sources for forms and documentation, which are listed below as they appear in the guidance document.

Primary Documentation: Student's Self-Report

The student is a vital source of information regarding how he or she may be "limited by impairment." A student's narrative of his or her experience of disability, barriers, and effective and ineffective accommodations is an important tool which, when structured by interview or questionnaire and interpreted, may be sufficient for establishing disability and a need for accommodation.

Secondary Documentation: Observation and Interaction

The impressions and conclusions formed by higher education disability professionals during interviews and conversations with students or in evaluating the effectiveness of previously implemented or provisional accommodations are important forms of documentation. Experienced disability professionals should feel comfortable using their observations of students' language, performance, and strategies as an appropriate tool in validating student narrative and self-report.

Tertiary Documentation: Information from External or Third Parties

> Documentation from external sources may include educational or medical records, reports and assessments created by health care providers, school psychologists, teachers, or the educational system. This information is inclusive of documents that reflect education and accommodation history, such as Individual Education Program (IEP), Summary Of Performance (SOP), and teacher observations. External documentation will vary in its relevance and value depending on the original context, credentials of the evaluator, the level of detail provided, and the comprehensiveness of the narrative. However, all forms of documentation are meaningful and should be mined for pertinent information. (AHEAD 2019)

Primary information comes directly from the source; thus, the student self-report is monumental in the verification of functional limitations. According to AHEAD guidance, a student's self-report may be sufficient evidence to establish need for an accommodation. An example based on a presumptive disability could concern a student with a vision-based disability. The student may readily demonstrate a functional limitation, in which case a self-report may suffice.

Secondary sources are pieces of information gathered by the DS provider, as a second party, about the primary source—the student making the self-report. This piece of guidance empowers DSPs to collect and use information about their interactions with the student. Factors such as body language can support or contradict a student narrative.

As DSPs, we also may need to gather additional information on a number of factors from campus partners. This information could include evidence from faculty and staff regarding a student's performance and behavior. Such information may be provided if a student is referred to our office through a number of different channels, such as a faculty member providing information about a classroom interaction or performance concern, the student disclosing to their tutor, or referral through a Concern, Assessment, Response, Evaluation (CARE) team. We may need to collect additional information relevant to specific accommodation requests. Examples could include information from academic records, tutoring appointments, standardized testing records, card swipe information from residence life or dining services, etcetera. FERPA affords privacy to a student's education record information. However, information can be shared to a school official who has a "legitimate educational interest" (U.S. Department of Education 2018a). As such, DSPs should feel empowered to gather information relevant to the decision-making process.

Tertiary sources are what we would traditionally refer to as "docs" but can be more encompassing if necessary. These are reports from third parties that include diagnostic evaluations and educational records. The pivotal statement in the AHEAD guidance is that "all forms of documentation are meaningful and should be mined for pertinent information" (AHEAD 2019). The pre–Amendments Act thinking was that documentation—for example, a neuropsychological evaluation for a learning disability—needed to be (1) thorough and (2) recent (within the last three years). Some DSPs did not even want to see a student's IEP. But the IEP can be a valuable document and at least establishes that a student has a record of having a disability. In many cases, the IEP provides enough diagnostic information to verify a disability, though in some cases, additional docs may be necessary. Other examples of tertiary sources include direct information from your campus' counseling center, where a student met with a qualified clinician, or speaking with a student's care provider or case manager. We would even consider information reported by family members or advocates and/or current faculty or staff under these criteria, as they represent third parties who can help paint the picture of a student's demonstrated impairments.

The ultimate goal is not to overly scrutinize or put barriers, perceived or otherwise, between the student and accommodation services for the impacted activity. Given the information provided by a student's self-report, with some combination of valid, relevant, supporting third-party report, we should be able to make an informed decision on whether it is more probable than not that the student is experiencing substantial limitations in one of more daily life activities.

Primary Documentation: Student Self-Report

The initial meeting and the vehicle by which the interactive process of requesting and granting accommodations is put into motion is typically referred to as the intake interview. There are necessary skills and several desired outcomes for conducting a successful intake, and in this section, we discuss them in detail.

Essentially, the intake is a meeting held between the student and the service provider to discuss the student's formal disclosure of a disability and request for accommodations. It is also the process by which the DS provider gathers the student's self-report. Either during or after the intake, the DS provider evaluates the student's profile for the purpose of determining eligibility and granting accommodations. We explore this evaluation in detail later in this chapter.

It is in the spirit of the ADA that no undue burden be placed on the provision of equal access. In this way, it is our philosophy to provide as succinct a process for granting accommodations as possible. The intake represents the last step to establishing an accommodation plan, meaning documentation will have already been collected and reviewed, and accommodation requests will have already been submitted. Ideally, the student will walk out of their intake understanding (1) their rights and responsibilities, (2) the role and responsibility of the DSO, (3) what their accommodation plan entails, (4) the protocol for establishing and using each accommodation, (5) how to disclose their relationship with DS to faculty and staff, (6) grievance procedures, and (7) how to renew, update, and/or request additional accommodations.

Pre-intake Information

While the process of determining a student's disability begins with self-identification, the DS provider often establishes a formal process that assists the student in making a formal disclosure. This process can vary from institution to institution, but often includes a way for a student to disclose information pertaining to a diagnosis, accommodation history (if applicable), and accommodations they intend to request. Collecting information pertaining to a student's diagnostic and/or accommodation history is critical and is the point at which tertiary documentation is often requested. Though not always feasible, in an ideal situation the DS provider will have the opportunity to review secondary documentation prior to meeting for an intake appointment as well. At this stage, documentation review should be used for the purpose of gathering information and verifying that information exists to substantiate a student's self-report. The information provided can inform the intake conversation but should not be used to predetermine eligibility or accommodations, as this would not be representative of an interactive process. Secondary documentation is covered in more detail in the following section.

The Intake Interview

The intake interview itself is central to the interactive process between a student and their college or university. It is where the DSP has direct communication with a student who has disclosed and requested accommodations for the purposes of (1) verifying the information that the student has disclosed, (2) determining whether the student's self-report "rises to the level of disability," and (3) determining whether the student meets eligibility for requested accommodations. This interview is where we cultivate our primary source of documentation from our student. "Cultivate" is a carefully chosen word to the extent that as DSPs, we have an obligation to be interactive in the student's self-reporting, not just receive requests. The more thorough and transparent our interview process, the more complete and informed our decision-making process.

The intake interview is a conversation guided by questions about the student, their disclosed disability, their academic and accommodations history, and their requested accommodations. As a general rule, we recommend asking first about the interviewee as a person, next as a student, and third as a student with a disability. This progression can serve to build a rapport that will be the basis of the student–service provider relationship moving forward. The ultimate objective of the intake interview is to address accommodation requests and either grant accommodations and provide an implementation plan or deny the requests and provide clear reasoning. More information regarding the intake interview is discussed below.

The typical flow of an intake session should adhere to three fundamental principles. The intake interview should provide (1) an individualized assessment of the student's eligibility under the ADAAA, (2) an interactive process between the student and service provider, and (3) a process consistent with the standards by which your institution evaluates *all* accommodation requests. The typical flow of an intake interview can include, but is not limited to, the following exercises:

- Welcome and introductions
- Provision of student self-report
- Fact-finding to clarify student self-report
    - Review of diagnostic and/or accommodation history
    - Review of student's reported functional limitations
    - Exploration of the "substantially limits" standard
- Determination of student disability status
- Interactive process for reviewing accommodation requests, including determination of eligibility for each accommodation requested
- Review of other applicable accommodations and/or auxiliary aids and services
- Determination of whether additional information (i.e., documentation) is needed, clear communication of what is required from the student
- Communication of whether each request is granted or denied
    - Clear communication of reason for denial
    - Provision and review of information pertaining to grievance/appeal procedures when a requested accommodation is denied
- Review of accommodation details and associated protocol
- Creation of an accommodation and implementation plan
- Discussion of additional campus resources

There may be steps added to these general guidelines; it is important to note that each institution may set its own standards, and each service provider has their own style of approaching intake interviews. It is recommended for new professionals to shadow several service providers in determining what style works best for them. This is why training programs in DS and/or higher education administration typically require a practicum or other field placement experience.

Secondary Documentation: Observation and Interaction

During the intake and throughout the DSP's relationship with the student, observations of the student's behavior and presentation—factors such as affect, appearance, demeanor, body language, and use of language—can significantly inform the interactive and accommodation process. It is important to note that while the presence of observed behaviors consistent with a disclosed condition and self-report may support the decision-making process, the absence of those behaviors does not rule out the determination of eligibility. There are also a number of ways in which behavior should not impact academic or administrative decision making.

Making observations falls into the category of "more art than science." While we may look for characteristic or consistent behaviors, remember that every person we meet is an individual, no two disability experiences are the same, and everything we do is case by case. Does the student's presentation appear consistent with what a reasonable person would consider to be in line with what the student is reporting? Essentially, does the student seem to be a reliable source of the information they are providing?

One common theme in the field is that there is no direct path into DS in higher education. Specifically, service providers may not have formal training in behavioral observation. While this is not a requisite skill for the profession per se, the ability to make appropriate and informed observations based on a student's presentation is an undeniably necessary skill to include in the DSP's repertoire.

Pre-intake Communication

The nature and manner in which a student and/or their family/advocates communicate with the DSP can offer insight into how to prepare for the intake. In some cases, the DSP takes this information directly; in other cases, another administrator is responsible for fielding communication. If there are specific behavioral cues worth collecting—which are in many cases collected informally—appropriate guidelines for the administrator can be helpful. Sharing this information can range from a simple debrief to notes attached to the appointment to the generation of a formal case note. Keep in mind, any information collected and maintained by the institution is subject to FERPA, so any information collected should remain objective. Essentially, we collect all information available and keep it in mind as we engage in the interactive process.

The key is to be mindful of the information collected and not make assumptions or judgments. As service providers, we want to use information in a way that positively impacts the interactive process. For instance, information gathered during pre-intake communication can inform the way we prepare to discuss advocacy and the rights, roles, and responsibilities associated with the use of accommodations.

Intake Observations

In many ways, we are the institutional gatekeepers of the accommodations—and affiliated resources—our institutions can offer. There are a number of ways to view and interpret this charge, and it may change depending on institutional culture, as well as a host of other variables. However, one of the guiding philosophies of being a DSP is to respond to and, with a good faith effort, investigate every request made by any student. We should engage in this process with a mind for establishing eligibility without overly scrutinizing. There is a reason why a student is disclosing and seeking services. It has been our experience that the vast majority of students requesting services have a legitimate claim. Through a review of the information presented—some combination of self-report, observations of the interactive process, and a documented diagnostic and/or accommodation history—we can make an informed judgment about whether a student's disclosed impacts "rise to the level of disability."

An overwhelming number of disabilities are not visible or apparent. In the case of apparent disabilities, observations pertaining to the direct demonstration of functional limitations may be possible or in some way inform the process of making a predictable assessment. For nonapparent disabilities, while we are not prohibited from reviewing documentation, a combination of a self-report and observation may be enough to establish eligibility. Other types of observations could include, but are not limited to, student behaviors (disability related or other), demeanor, language (disability related or other), nonverbal communication, and appearance.

Observations from Secondary Sources

Sometimes when students disclose and request or are referred to seek accommodations in response to a negative experience on campus, observations from interactions with community members may help inform our judgments as service providers. Like a number of factors listed above, these types of observations should not constitute a determination of disability or eligibility for services. However, gathering as much observational data as possible may better serve the interactive process in the long run.

Tertiary Documentation: Evaluator's Reports and Diagnostic Documentation

Providing evidence that supports a student's eligibility for reasonable accommodations is a core responsibility of the student in the interactive process. Documentation from a third-party provider falls under the category of tertiary documentation. Typically, this type of documentation comes in the form of either a diagnostic record or a record of accommodation history. In this section, we discuss examples of these two types of tertiary documentation.

Diagnostic Records

Collecting documentation from qualified professionals is an institution in the field of higher education administration, and rightfully so. This is especially true when it comes to students requesting adjustments based on "physical or mental conditions" that "substantially limit one or more major life activity." Such documentation is often the most direct path to providing verification to both clauses of the previous statement. Good documentation provides a clear diagnostic statement from a qualified professional and an assessment of functional limitations. Great documentation provides empirical evidence collected by formal evaluation and recommendations for accommodations, though this information is not always required to determine disability or provide accommodations.

Tertiary documentation can fall under a number of categories. Common types of documentation that students submit include, but are not limited to, neuropsychological evaluations, psychological evaluations, psychoeducational assessments, medical evaluations, and letters of diagnosis. In any event, documentation should be official, on letterhead, and provided by qualified professionals.

For cognitive-based disabilities, the neuropsychological report is often considered a marquee piece of documentation because of the depth of knowledge it provides related to brain functioning and the breadth of diagnoses it can identify. The assessment itself consists of a battery approach, including clinical interview and skills-based tests. "The evaluation measures such areas as attention, problem solving, memory, language, I.Q., visual-spatial skills, academic skills, and social-emotional functioning" (Golden and Tomb 2016).

All of the domains assessed have the potential to directly relate to "major life activities" associated with postsecondary education, such as learning, reading, concentrating, thinking, communicating, and interacting with others. A typical "neuropsych" includes historical information (e.g., developmental, educational, and medical), clinical interviews, test results (often including methodology and analyses), clinical impressions, a diagnostic statement (if applicable), and individualized recommendations (Schaefer, Thakur, Meager 2022). The recommendations section may include academic (and other) accommodation suggestions, instructional modifications, intervention strategies and support services, and additional resources for the student and family. When determining disability, a clear diagnostic statement with supporting, empirical evidence can be invaluable. A neuropsychological assessment can be used to diagnose conditions such as ADHD, dyslexia, autism spectrum disorder, nonverbal learning disability, alcohol or drug-related damage, brain injury or concussion, mood and personality disorders, and other neurological conditions (Neurodevelop.com). A comprehensive evaluation can expedite the progression of the interactive process to the stage of evaluating individual accommodation requests.

Although typically less comprehensive than neuropsychological testing, psychological assessments may evaluate similar domains of functioning—cognitive, social-emotional, behavioral, and executive—and include similar elements—clinical interview, record reviews, test results summaries, and recommendations for treatment planning and adjustments or accommodations to maximize the individual's potential.

A psychoeducational evaluation is an assessment completed by a licensed psychologist, school psychologist, or special education professional (Bellefeuille 2020). Its goal is to identify patterns of strength and weakness in an individual's cognitive and academic functioning to formulate diagnostic impressions and recommend supports and interventions. The assessment may also include elements such as parent/caregiver and teacher questionnaires and rating scales to provide information about an individual's social, emotional, and behavioral functioning from a variety of perspectives and in various settings. As stated in the AHEAD documentation guidelines, "all forms of documentation are meaningful and should be mined for pertinent information."

Because of the complexity of the data, some training may be necessary for DS providers to learn how to properly interpret results. These types of documentation generally include summary and recommendation sections that provide diagnostic impressions and justification for recommended accommodations, which are typically written so that the "reasonable person" can interpret them with little difficulty. In thorough evaluations, explanations of individual tests are provided, and these can give insight into the nature of the exercise and what can be gleaned from the data. Some basic familiarity with standardized test statistics (e.g., standard scores and T-scores) can be helpful in understanding the data, but as in other areas, we do not need to be experts in specific disabilities or psychometrics to make informed decisions based on the information included.

Neuropsychological, psychological, and psychoeducational assessments are utilized heavily in a K–12 setting to determine eligibility for IEP and 504 accommodation plans. In many cases, SWDs transition to postsecondary education with recent assessments completed to satisfy that process. While intended to provide the essential information to determine eligibility for a K–12 accommodation plan, these assessments are often recent and relevant enough for eligibility determination in a postsecondary setting—two birds, one stone. For this reason, we often encourage prospective families to continue testing on the secondary level when possible or appropriate.

Other documentation can include medical evaluations, letters of diagnosis, and statements of disability. Because the categories of disabilities are so broad, the types of documentation we receive from medical providers can vary greatly. Documentation should be provided in an official format that allows the interpreter to verify it was completed by a qualified professional.

Some of the documentation that falls into this category is relatively simple to interpret. Doctors' letters, for instance, may be specifically written to inform the DSO of a student's diagnosis. Sometimes the letter only includes a diagnostic statement; other times, the letter may include information such as how the doctor is working with the student to manage symptoms or even recommended accommodations. It should be incumbent on the DSO to provide guidelines for what type of information should be included in submitted documentation. Anecdotally, there seem to be mixed responses from the field as to whether a letter might be sufficient. We purport that it might be and that all information received from a qualified professional should be reviewed as part of student accommodation requests.

Other medical documentation might include records and results from medical examinations. These can include anything from medical test records to hospitalization records, discharge paperwork, medical history records, etcetera. Some documentation may be very specific and technical, such as allergy titration results or an audiogram. Sometimes the evaluation report includes information that assists with interpreting the results, but sometimes it does not. In these cases, it may be necessary to research how to interpret the records or to communicate with the student's care provider. In these cases, it will be necessary to obtain the consent of the student, and their care provider may require the same.

Qualified Evaluators

Academic institutions and test agencies describe qualified professionals in similar ways. According to the Law School Admission Council (LSAC), which publishes the Law School Admissions Test (LSAT), a qualified professional is "a person who is licensed or otherwise properly credentialed and possesses expertise in the disability for which modifications or accommodations are sought" (Law School Admission Council 2022). Other institutions and organizations add different factors, such as the qualified evaluator having experience working with an adult population. In the evaluation of whether the student's diagnosis and self-report "rise to the level of disability," we must consider the source of the student's diagnostic records. As DSPs, we have some flexibility to use our judgment in validating the source of documentation with regard to each accommodation request. For instance, a request for a housing accommodation based on an allergy could easily be supported by diagnostic records from an allergy specialist, but a primary care physician may also be able to provide substantiating evidence. A mental health clinician might not be qualified to make this assessment.

Records of Accommodation History

Often, the most immediate documentation students are familiar with and able to provide is a record of past accommodations. This record can come in several forms including an IEP, a Section 504 accommodation plan, documentation of accommodations on high stakes tests, records of accommodation from previous institutions, and so on. Bona fide accommodation records should follow similar guidelines to medical documentation, being completed by a qualified professional and presented in a formal way (standard report template, letterhead, etc.). While they, in essence, document granted interventions, they are representative of an evaluation. Sometimes, accommodation records make direct reference to data from formal evaluations like neuropsych assessments; other times, they may not. In any event, a previous accommodation plan is a record that qualified professionals made an evaluation against the standards of whether a student qualified as having a disability. If there is an IEP or 504 plan, it might represent a more detailed analysis than what is necessary at the postsecondary level (AHEAD 2019).

Section 504 of the Rehabilitation Act of 1973 establishes that SWDs who qualify are entitled to a plan that includes reasonable accommodations. A 504 plan will typically include specific accommodation supports (paired with the area of educational need), services for the child, names of who will provide each service, and the name of the person responsible for ensuring the plan is implemented (Understood for All 2019).

Many students seeking accommodations at the college or university level have, at one time, had either an IEP or Section 504 plan. Some students seeking accommodations have had both, either at different times or simultaneously. Given the information above, it is clear that both plans are representative of a thorough and qualified evaluation and can stand as qualifying tertiary documentation for our purpose of establishing eligibility.

Family/Advocate Participation

A wide range of types of family involvement can be present at the intake interview and beyond. Often, family members who have been the advocate for their student have a number of concerns the DSP needs to be aware of. For one, they may be intimately aware of the diagnostic and accommodation history of their student—often more so than their student. They may have a better understanding of the successes and failures the student has experienced than the student themself. The other thing to consider is the level of involvement they have had up until this point. Not only have families learned the ins and outs of accommodations in a K–12 setting, but they have often had to fight for services for their student. One of the difficulties we can face in an intake is that sometimes, students and families are provided with little information about the transition to higher education.

There are essentially three methods for managing the involvement of family members at the intake. DSPs can support full participation with the student's permission; support partial participation, which can be done with or without the student's permission; or deny access to family participation. Any given program may need to be flexible enough to offer a combination of these methods based on the way in which a particular student case may present. It is recommended to have a preferred protocol.

Gathering information, including diagnostic and/or accommodation history, from family members or other advocates (provided doing so falls under your preferred protocol) should be part of the fact-finding phase of the intake interview. In any of the above scenarios, the student should be the primary participant in the interactive process with the DSP, and an individualized assessment should never take place without the student present.

Making Documentation-Based Decisions

Documentation can vary greatly, as can the nature of a student's requested accommodations. When making decisions based on documentation, there are a few key factors to take into consideration. According to AHEAD, four main guidelines are applicable to making documentation-based decisions. The guidelines tell us that documentation-based decision making should include individual review, commonsense standards, a nonburdensome process, and current and relevant information.

The individual review guideline states that "institutions should consider the student's disability, history, experience, request, *and* the unique characteristics of the course, program, or requirement in order to determine whether or not a specific accommodation is reasonable" (AHEAD 2019). The key is to consider all relevant information against each accommodation request the student makes using a commonsense approach. According to the AHEAD guidance, "the question is 'Would an informed and reasonable person conclude from the available evidence that a disability is likely and the requested accommodation is warranted?'" (AHEAD 2019). This commonsense standard can often dictate how DSPs review documentation. For instance, enough information might be provided by a diagnostic statement (considering the standards for presumptive disabilities) or the recommended accommodations of a qualified evaluator.

The concept of a nonburdensome process stems from the ADA and the ADAAA. This guideline suggests that "postsecondary institutions cannot create documentation processes that are burdensome or have the effect of discouraging students from seeking protections and accommodations to which they are entitled" (AHEAD 2019).

As covered earlier in this chapter, the idea that relevant documentation outweighs recent documentation in our reviews is supported in the guidance from AHEAD. The AHEAD guidance states that "disabilities are typically stable lifelong conditions. Therefore, historic information, supplemented by interview or self-report, is often sufficient to describe how the condition impacts the student at the current time and in the current circumstances" (AHEAD 2019).

These guidelines provide DS as a field with an updated paradigm, in line with the ADAAA, for approaching fair and consistent determinations of a student's eligibility for services and whether accommodation requests meet the standard of being reasonable. While this holds true, as highlighted in this chapter, students often submit documentation that is fairly technical and may not be readily interpreted without some background knowledge. It may be incumbent on the DSP to research a nontypical diagnostic report for the purpose of making an appropriate evaluation. Numerous resources and professional development opportunities in this area are available.

Insufficient Documentation

There are times when the documentation a student provides may not give sufficient evidence to establish eligibility for disability-related accommodations. Insufficient documentation can be a bit of a gray area, so it is important to review a few scenarios.

One type of scenario is when the student is not able to provide any documentation. An example could be a student in the process of seeking a diagnosis or in the early stages of the evaluation process who does not yet have documentation. As covered in this chapter, a DSP can rely on their judgment (recall that a student's self-report might provide enough information). There are not many clear guidelines in these cases, but we strongly encourage DSPs to take a holistic view of the situation.

Conversely, there may be instances when we need to question the information presented in the documentation. Though less common in our experience, there may be times when a student submits documentation that is not representative of a formal evaluation. Of these examples, it is not uncommon for a letter from a clinician to include language such as "the student reports" a specific symptom or need for an accommodation. The absence of a clinical impression or evidence of an evaluation may be cause to request additional documentation.

In any of the above scenarios, and in the spirit of minimizing undue burden to the student, it may be appropriate for the DSP to request contact with the student's care provider. For the student in the process of seeking an evaluation, a clinician may be able to provide enough initial clinical impressions to substantiate a request. You may also find that a primary care provider completed an initial assessment and referred the student for more complete testing. When documentation is unclear or incomplete, or if you are uncertain as to whether it supports a particular request, speaking to the clinician may provide clarity. As mentioned earlier, the process includes obtaining the student's consent, and your intention to speak with a care provider should be communicated clearly as part of the interactive process. In any of these cases, as a DSP, it is critical to clearly outline what is expected and the type of additional information you need to make an informed judgment.

In Summary

The determination of a student's disability status as it applies to accommodation requests in a postsecondary education setting lies with the DSP. It is the student's responsibility to self-identify, provide supporting materials, and engage in the interactive process with the institution's designated service provider. Supporting materials from third-party providers should include a diagnostic and/or accommodation record provided by a qualified evaluator and should be relevant to the student's requests. The process for determining disability and evaluating a student's requests for reasonable accommodations must include an individualized assessment that takes place during an interactive process and follows a process consistent with the institution's standards for evaluating such requests. While many types of documentation can be provided by diagnostic and accommodation records, as well as observations and self-reports, ultimately, it is a commonsense standard, along with the good faith efforts and informed judgments of the DSP, that are central to the process of determining disability.

▶ Reflective Exercise

Bai is a transfer student from a large institution across the country from yours. They are coming to your university for your engineering program after initially going to art school. They have submitted their IEP from high school and their approved accommodation letters from art school. They are asking for the same accommodations at your institution. They have not submitted any other information as of yet and are insistent that they see you as soon as possible, as they have an exam at the end of the week. What do you need prior to meeting with them, and what might your approach be once you connect with them?

▶ Supplemental Job Aids

The following Supplemental Job Aids can be found at https://scholarshare.temple.edu/handle/20.500.12613/8373:

- *Documentation Review Form*
- *Student Intake Form*

7

Determining Reasonable Accommodations

If there is one central function of the DSP in higher education, it is to evaluate students' accommodation requests. As we saw with defining disability, there is no exhaustive list we can provide of all possible accommodations offered in an IHE setting. In fact, doing so would be a disservice to students and institutions. There are, however, common accommodations and themes that must be explored. Students have the right to request an accommodation to all aspects of the college experience. Subsequently, there are several considerations for what constitutes a reasonable accommodation as it pertains to a student's unique eligibility. In this chapter, we explore the process for evaluating individual requests, what constitutes a reasonable request, when a request may be unreasonable and how to respond, as well as the types of accommodations offered at the postsecondary level. In many ways, accommodating student requests can be more art than science, but approaching this process with an understanding of well-defined standards is one of the most important competencies of being a successful DSP.

▶ Guiding Questions

1. What is the difference between access and accommodation?
2. Do accommodations provide an unfair advantage?
3. What are the roles of our campus partners in the process of determining reasonable accommodations?

Disability-Related Accommodations in Higher Education

There are a few mantras in the field of DS. One of the most beloved is that "it depends," especially when we talk about how to evaluate a student's request and provide appropriate and reasonable accommodations. The law and the professional standards held by the field of DS dictate an interactive and iterative process for evaluating requests and providing accommodations. There is not, nor should there be, a "cookie cutter" or "one size fits all" approach to granting accommodations. Not all students with ADHD have the same needs, so not all students with ADHD receive the same accommodations. If two students happen to have the same accommodation plan, they may need accommodations for different reasons and use them in different ways. As we explored in the previous chapter, it is the role of the DSP to help drive this process, and it is the responsibility of the DSP to determine the methods to provide adjustments or accommodations students need to receive independent, meaningful, and equitable access to all our institutions provide. Accommodations are how we provide that access.

There is a bit of a paradox when it comes to accommodations, but the process through which accommodations are granted is based on practicality, efficiency, and the importance of a consistent approach. There is no set list—and no finite list—of accommodations; we do not take a cookie-cutter approach, but there are standard accommodations. Some accommodations are standardized across the field of DS and education in general. For instance, extended time and "time and a half" for testing tends to be universal. It is an accommodation we see in elementary, middle, and secondary school, postsecondary and postbaccalaureate education, as well as high-stakes testing such as college entrance exams, graduate school entrance exams, and professional licensing exams. But just because a standard accommodation often fits a student's accommodation need does not mean it is entirely a cookie-cutter accommodation. In this way, accommodations are our tools—we can use them in multiple applications or multiple jobs, if you will. They can also be viewed as the building blocks we use to create customized accommodation plans with each student. Having some standardization is critical. It allows us to accommodate students in a consistent way.

Defining "Accommodation"

Accommodations versus modifications—there are a lot of semantics to be aware of when considering accommodations, and the nuances are critical. Accommodations are essentially adjustments, alterations, modifications, adaptations, or changes to our curriculum, living and learning environments, college or university policies and procedures, and so on. Essentially, accommodations are the changes we make to adjust for significant impacts students experience to the major life activities associated with being an SWD.

However, there is an important distinction to make in the way we use the terms "accommodation" and "modification." The term "accommodation" is used to signify adjustments that provide access to the same opportunities all students have. In the act of accommodating, we preserve the integrity of our academic and community standards. Accommodations adjust the way a student participates in a course, for instance, but they do not adjust the learning objectives, academic standards, or the fundamental nature of the course. The term "modification" is used to signify changes in course standards, pedagogy, curriculum requirements, or the fundamental nature of the course. In a college or university setting, we must provide reasonable accommodations in the name of access, but we are under no obligation to reduce our academic or community standards.

College is different from high school, and the ADA is different from the IDEA. The educational laws and regulations that pertain to a K–12 education setting ensure success. Success can be achieved through reasonable accommodations but may also require curricular and instructional modifications. Anecdotally, students are often surprised that many, if not all, of their high school accommodations transfer to a higher education environment seamlessly. The modifications, however, do not in most cases. Accommodations in high school can include curriculum modifications, such as a reduction in required coursework and assessments. For a five-page paper, students with modifications may be required to write three. On a math exam with thirty questions, a student with modifications may be required to complete fifteen. These modifications, in many cases, work in conjunction with accommodations like extended time to complete assignments or extended test time. In a higher education setting, the applicable laws and regulations are designed to ensure access by way of nondiscrimination. The amount of work and integrity of assessments are generally not modified in the ways they are in a K–12 setting.

Instructional modifications mean that the way a student is taught can be fundamentally different, in part or in whole, from the typical academic program. Examples relate to both content instruction and classroom behavior management. In most traditional college or university settings, those types of modifications are not considered reasonable.

Accommodations in a higher education setting are designed to level the playing field without being advantageous. This point is important to consider for two reasons. The first is that the accommodations process allows us to preserve integrity and not provide undue benefits. The second relates more to the perception of the impact of a disability and the need for reasonable accommodation. In the case of preserving integrity, modifications like those mentioned above (reduced academic standards, specialized instruction, provision of personal services, etc.) would, in essence and by design, lower the threshold for attaining a desired outcome, such as a conferred degree. But let us flip that script. We would be doing a disservice to SWDs by fundamentally modifying their educational program. A modified program may mean that a student receives less content mastery, professional competency, and opportunity to engage in experiential learning. The focus should be on providing the same opportunity to achieve those things.

With regard to the concept of perception, adherence to providing accommodation and not advantage supports our equity and inclusion initiatives. Clear messaging that accommodations do not provide unfair advantages combats the stigma related to seeking support. Students report on a regular basis that they have hesitated to seek accommodations to avoid this perception. When faculty understand the concept of a level playing field, they may be better partners for providing reasonable accommodations. When students understand this concept, they may be more willing to use accommodations.

Having established the difference between accommodation and modification, further nuances need to be addressed. *Some* modifications might be appropriate. The main distinguisher is whether a modification fundamentally alters the activity. We explore the terms "reasonable" and "fundamental" as they pertain to accommodations later in this chapter.

Consider the sports metaphor. Accessibility puts the player in the stadium and accommodations level the playing field. However, players might play in different positions and have different roles in the game. Not everyone on the field needs to stand in the same spot to participate in the game. Take public speaking, for example. For a student with anxiety, a reasonable accommodation may be to allow the student to present to a smaller group—same assignment, same expectations, accommodated environment. But what about a student who does not have the ability speak? In some cases, an alternative assignment might be necessary. The student is, however, expected to participate in a way that demonstrates their mastery of the content even if the parameters of the assignment are changed. Would a paper be appropriate? Or creating a prerecorded video using synthesized speech? How about creating a PowerPoint presentation or poster? The idea is to engage in the interactive process with the student and faculty and determine what reasonable alternative might approximate the learning objectives: different assignment, comparable expectations, modified assessment. Keep in mind, there are technical standards and discipline-specific competencies that cannot be modified.

Limitations?

While there are conventions, remember that there is no finite list of accommodations. We cannot deny an accommodation because it is our policy to do so or because we do not "have that one" already. An individualized assessment must take place for every request. We use the intake to explore the impact of a student's disability as it pertains to the requested accommodations. Impacts differ by student, and sometimes the factors being accommodated are complex.

In fact, students can request accommodations to any campus policy, process, or procedure. While academic accommodations account for most of the accommodations we grant, housing, dining, and transportation represent other significant categories. IHEs have operations beyond living and learning opportunities. A Deaf student may require an interpreter on a campus tour. A student with autism may request a social interpreter to be present in a conduct hearing or Title IX investigation. A student may need to request an extended deadline to submit a petition to be released from a housing contract.

DSPs must engage in the interactive process with good faith efforts. While there is standardized language for conventional accommodations, the process is more developmental than transactional. There will be requests for which there are no prescribed processes. Some of these requests may be complicated; some may be difficult to assess, unconventional to grant, and require considerable resources. This is where consistency is critical. We must assess every request in the spirit of the interactive process, without preformed opinions and, least of all, predetermined outcomes. We are biased in some ways, of course, by the fact that at the end of the day, we represent the institution, but our professional code of ethics dictates that we represent the best interest of the student equally.

IHEs must provide DSPs with commensurate authority to make evaluations and determine when a reasonable accommodation is warranted. We need access to content experts and campus partners who set the policies and procedures. We need to be able to question without being scrutinized. In some situations, this is easier said than done, but community education on the importance of the interactive process can make great strides. We grow one ally at a time.

Defining "Reasonable"

The term "reasonable" is used in the language of ADA laws and regulations to qualify the term "accommodation." "Reasonable" is a fluid concept. What is reasonable for one may not be reasonable for another. It bears repeating that the key here is that we conduct our assessments in a consistent way.

While it is written from a Title I (employment accommodations) perspective, the Equal Employment Opportunity Commission (EEOC) provides the following definition of "reasonable":

> A modification or adjustment is "reasonable" if it "seems reasonable on its face, i.e., ordinarily or in the run of cases"; (8) this means it is "reasonable" if it appears to be "feasible" or "plausible." (9) An accommodation also must be effective in meeting the needs of the individual. (10) (JAN n.d.a)

Another way to define "reasonable" is by defining what is unreasonable. As previously established, an accommodation is considered unreasonable if it fundamentally alters an academic or community standard. In this way, an unreasonable accommodation is one that provides not an equal opportunity but a reduced experience. So, a reasonable accommodation, in part, is one that provides equal access. An accommodation that does not mitigate the effect of a student's disability would be considered unreasonable. For instance, postponing an exam date may provide equal access to a student who experiences migraines, but would be unreasonable for a student who has dyslexia.

Some accommodations, like the provision of personal aids and services, are not required by the ADA. In a residential setting, providing building access to a Personal Care Assistant (PCA) would be a reasonable accommodation; providing the PCA would not. Providing captioning, interpreting, or real-time transcription—providing access to our curriculum—would be reasonable accommodations; providing hearing aids would not.

Reasonable accommodations are for the qualified individual, and they affect the qualified individual. Accommodations that negatively impact other members of the community might be deemed unreasonable. Any accommodation that poses a significant disruption or is a direct threat to the health and safety of others would not be reasonable. This might be evident at the time of the request. For instance, during the COVID-19 pandemic, some students requested accommodations to mask requirement policies. These requests could be related to respiratory conditions or sensory integration differences. If the requested accommodation is deemed as a direct threat to the health and safety of other members in the community, there may not be an obligation to accommodate. A granted accommodation might become unreasonable after the fact if it becomes disruptive. Take, for instance, a granted Emotional Support Animal (ESA) accommodation. If the student is allowed to have a dog, and the dog does not allow residence life staff or campus police into the room, this would constitute a disruption to campus operations and would become unreasonable. Some accommodations might positively impact members of the community—captioning can be beneficial for all learners—and that is an added bonus.

Ultimately, "reasonable" is another paradox. It is where the art of our interpretation comes up against the science of our evaluation. With a good, consistent process, an understanding of when to step back and assume the "reasonable person" perspective, and an understanding of what constitutes an unreasonable accommodation, we can make informed assessments to determine whether a request is reasonable.

Regarding Standards

Many of the "fundamental components" or "essential elements" we have explored so far relate to curriculum and grading standards. There are finer points to make, though. Academic leadership determines the curriculum—what an education at your institution entails and what a degree from your institution stands for. Typically, this education involves a core curriculum or set general education requirements and major-specific requirements.

The core curriculum comprises classes all students must successfully complete to meet the standards of earning their degree. A well-rounded education is often part of what is considered at a liberal arts institution, including writing classes, quantitative reasoning or analysis classes, humanities, world languages, social sciences, natural sciences, and so on. The core may differ from major to major. For instance, natural science or some business majors may require a higher level of quantitative analysis; international relations may require more world language courses; psychology, sociology, marketing, and political science might require statistics.

Major-specific requirements are determined by content experts in a field of study. There is a fundamental difference between completing some courses of interest and obtaining the formal education for success in a chosen field. Individual programs may have standards that further define the field beyond the major-specific curriculum. For instance, a theater production major may require students to master both analog and digital production equipment; film production may adhere to film industry standards; psychology may follow APA standards; and chemistry may follow the standards of the American Chemical Society.

The question is whether there is any flexibility in these requirements, and what competencies are fundamentally nonnegotiable. Students can request an accommodation to any policy, process, or procedure, so a request against a standard will not necessarily be automatically disqualified. A request to alter the standards could be viewed as a modification, but it is our job as DSPs to drive the interactive process toward determining whether the requested accommodation fundamentally alters the standard.

Sometimes, students have disabilities that significantly impact their ability to complete a particular course. A student with a language-based learning disability may experience barriers to completing a world language requirement; a student with a specific learning disability in math may experience barriers to completing a math requirement. These are probably two of the most commonly requested course waivers. How fundamental are these requirements to the curriculum? Are the waiver requests reasonable? Are there reasonable alternatives? Does the student qualify?

Ultimately, in these cases (as with all accommodation requests), an individual assessment must take place of both the student's eligibility and the nature of the standard. Some assessments are self-evident. Precalculus or calculus is not negotiable for a physics major; statistics is not negotiable for a psychology major. Study abroad programs may require an immersion-level language course. Some assessments may not be as evident. A student may question the math requirement in a history major, or a world language requirement in a graphic design major.

The evaluation of a student's eligibility may need to include some additional information beyond their diagnostic and accommodation history. Some students received previous course waivers, either in a K–12 setting or at a previous institution. That information can be useful to consider in an assessment. However, a previous accommodation of this kind will not necessarily be evidence enough to grant the accommodation.

Evaluating what is fundamental regarding the standards themselves is a prime example of how the interactive process should work. A thorough assessment should include, at minimum, both content experts and accommodations experts. Evaluations can include DSPs, course instructors, course coordinators, department chairs, deans, and provost-level leadership. Some guiding questions include the following:

Individual courses:

- What is the purpose of the course?
- What does the course intend to teach?
- What is the content?
- What are the learning objectives and outcomes of the course?
- How are the course outcomes assessed?
- What underlying cognitive processes are required to master the content?
- How does the course relate to program and major requirements?
- Is the course a prerequisite for other courses?
- Are the resulting core competencies prerequisites of future courses?
- How much person-to-person interaction takes place?

- To what extent is attendance and participation required to master the content?
- Are there physical requirements?
- Are there experiential learning components?

Major programs:

- What are the overall goals of the major?
- What are the core competencies of a successful degree candidate?
- Is the program accredited by an outside authority?
- Are there licensing requirements or other professional credentialing?

Broad curriculum:

- What content must a successful degree candidate master?
- What qualifications and core competencies must a successful degree candidate obtain?
- Are there licensing requirement or other professional credentialing?

A common saying in the field is that "courts give deference to content experts" to determine the standards. For this to hold true, the institution must show that a determination was reached through a reasoned and informed process. In the case of a legal complaint, the institution bears the burden of proving the extent to which the decision is an academic one related to the necessary achievement of the successful degree candidate. Courts do not, however, give deference to academic determinations if the decision is more about adjustments needed to complete program requirements. Consistency in making these determinations is of equal importance to the determinations themselves.

One guiding question for the DSP to ask in evaluations is whether there are alternative ways a student can achieve mastery of the content. Can it be done in a way that does not compromise the integrity of learning and achievement or negatively impact a student's peers? Again, we are not striving to ensure success; we are striving to provide a fair pathway. Institutions must hold an understanding of the difference between equality and equity when making assessments. Is our goal to ensure that our successful students achieve the same mastery or a comparable mastery? Diversity of learning should be a guiding principle of our institutions.

There are two possible outcomes to the assessment of a course, program, or curriculum-level accommodation request. Either the request is deemed reasonable, and appropriate accommodations, or reasonable alternatives, are determined, or the request is deemed unreasonable. These outcomes are discussed in further detail below as they pertain to commonly requested accommodations.

Technical and Professional Standards

Additional standards apply to educational programs that involve professional preparation and career-specific licensing. Technical standards announce the requirements for accessing the program of learning. In other words, the technical standards of a program indicate what is fundamental for successful participation in said program and ultimately in the profession.

> Technical Standards are those physical, personal skills and attributes academic departments with professional/graduate programs expect students to acquire and display; they are, by their nature not academic or met solely through the acquisition of academic knowledge, however some technical standards may be related to academic knowledge. (University of Scranton 2021)

Technical standards are for preprofessional programs that directly prepare students for careers and vocations with like requirements. For example, an EMT/paramedic training program may post that a standard for admission to the program is the ability to lift and carry a certain amount of weight. This standard is either self-evident or dictated by the field as a necessity. Technical standards identify functions required for participation that must be met without accommodation.

Some technical standards pertain to core competencies and essential job functions. Take, for example, a culinary education program. This program may have standards related to lifting a certain amount of weight (i.e., pots, pans, bags of flour). Some of these standards may be able to be accommodated, such as by having an assistant place ingredients near a student's station. Some may not, such as moving a skillet on and off the flame. Other standards may include the ability to discern color. In some cases, this ability could be necessary for a chef. An evaluation could explore whether the presorting of ingredients can be done by an assistant. Other standards may be more self-evident as fundamental. These standards could include smelling, tasting, and feeling. It is an absolute requirement for chefs to constantly be tasting. The inability to do so alters in a fundamental way the ability of the student to complete the task.

There are also technical standards dictated by the nature of the field. A good example pertains to technical standards associated with law school programs. The Socratic method is foundational to the process of teaching law and preparing students to practice.

> Socrates (470–399 BC) was a Greek philosopher who sought to get to the foundations of his students' and colleagues' views by asking continual questions until a contradiction was exposed, thus proving the fallacy of the initial assumption. (University of Chicago 2019)

This method involves cold-calling on students and is infamous for tearing students down to build them back up. It can, at times, be intense for students. A common request from students who have mental health diagnoses such as social anxiety is to not be cold-called in class. The Socratic method, though, is fundamental to the way the learning takes place. Moreover, it directly relates to the practice of law in the field. Communication in a court room, a negotiation, a conference room, and so on, will invariably involve cold-calling and continual questioning.

Other technical standards relate to safety. Safety is of paramount importance. No accommodation can compromise the health and safety of the community, especially when professionals in the medical field are working with patients. Seeing and fine motor ability, in addition to other functions, are essential for surgery. Hearing may be essential for evaluating the safety of a patient when taking a report. Vision-related requests for accessible textbooks may be considered reasonable, but vision-related requests for reading an X-ray may not. Individual evaluations must be made to determine the nature of the request, the student's eligibility, and when the standards apply.

When technical standards are involved, evaluations still must take place. Not all requests involving technical standards are automatically determined to be fundamental alterations. Through the interactive process, we must investigate the major life activities impacted by the student's disability and evaluate them against the factors related to each request.

Community Impact

An accommodation cannot significantly impact college operations, community standards, or other members of the community in negative ways. The major factors to consider are health and safety and significant disruption.

Health and safety are of paramount importance. Not many accommodations pose a direct threat to the health and safety of others, but when one does, it should immediately be deemed unreasonable. This is nonnegotiable. Again, this does not mean that a student is not identified as having a disability or that they are not eligible for reasonable accommodations. An individual assessment must be made regarding the impact of the accommodation.

Some examples are clear. There should be a process in place for addressing and removing a granted animal accommodation if the animal bites another student. We have seen examples where students have requested to smoke cigarettes on campus property to alleviate acute anxiety. The ADA makes clear that it "does not preclude the prohibition, or the impositions on, smoking in places of public accommodation" (U.S. Department of Justice Civil Rights Division 2010c).

The ADA references a case relating to the health of an infectious individual and the impact the individual may have on the community. In the case *School Board of Nassau County, Florida v. Arline*, a test was established to determine if there is a significant health and safety risk (Powell, White, and Robinson 1987):

> A public accommodation is required to make an individualized assessment, based on reasonable judgment that relies on current medical evidence or on the best available objective evidence, to determine: The nature, duration, and severity of the risk; the probability that the potential injury will actually occur; and whether reasonable modifications of policies, practices, or procedures will mitigate the risk. (U.S. Department of Justice Civil Rights Division 2010c)

Significant disruption caused by an accommodation must also be considered in determining whether said accommodation is reasonable. An accommodation that significantly disrupts learning or other campus operations will not be implemented. It bears repeating that an individual assessment must be made. The test outlined above may serve as a guide in making an assessment during an intake and initial evaluation of a request. For example, it may be disruptive for a student to have a reader for exams in the classroom. The disruption may be easily mitigated by other accommodations, such as taking tests in a separate location.

Timing of Accommodation Requests

The timeline of accommodation requests can affect implementation and efficacy. There are two general rules we follow: there can be very few firm deadlines associated with accommodations requests, and accommodations cannot be granted retroactively.

In college, everything is cyclical. While some colleges deviate from this schedule, the vast majority run on a fall semester, spring semester academic year. The semester is finite, and end dates cannot be extended by accommodation. Grades are due when grades are due (more on this later). Key dates throughout the academic calendar pertain to the current semester, and some pertain to future semesters. There are admissions deadlines, financial aid deadlines, housing placement deadlines, registration deadlines, and so on. Every course will have its own pace with respective deadlines.

The timing of an accommodation request might be critical. For typical, in-semester academic accommodation requests, students can request accommodations at any time. Take, for instance, a student who wishes to request exam accommodations. Obviously, the preferable timeline is to make requests prior to, or early in, the start of a new semester. We want students to hit the ground running and be able to take full advantage of their accommodation plan. We have found time and time again that doing so results in the highest opportunity for success. Students can, however, request accommodations after their first exam, around midterm time, or closer to finals. While it is not recommended, it is still possible. We cannot set a cutoff date for requesting accommodations, but it must be made clear that accommodations are not applied retroactively.

There are many reasons why a student may request accommodations later into the semester that help explain why we do not set deadlines. A common reason is that students simply want to attempt to start college with a clean slate and not use their accommodations. A student owns the responsibility of self-identifying, and they cannot be denied accommodations—or be penalized or discriminated against—because of when they are comfortable doing so. Students may wait to request accommodations until after they experience impacts in their classes. They have the right to do so. Recall from Chapter 2 that disability can be transient. A student may become disabled at any time. They may simply not know the process. Our responsibility is to always actively engage students in the interactive process with good faith efforts.

There are deadlines for nonacademic requests as well. For instance, housing placement takes place when housing placement takes place. For full consideration, it is in the student's best interest to request a housing accommodation prior to room assignments being made. We do not automatically deny a housing accommodation request because that deadline has passed. Again, a student can become disabled at any time. It is critical to be clear that our ability to furnish accommodations beyond these types of deadlines will be diminished. Beds can fill up, and at many campuses, single rooms, spaces in on-campus apartments, and spaces in the residence hall closest to the dining center or academic buildings may become nonexistent past a certain point. Our role is to engage in the interactive process, determine a student's eligibility, and advocate for reasonable accommodations we may grant. Based on the timeline, it may be difficult or even impossible to implement the accommodation.

In other cases, students may request accommodations to the deadlines themselves. Students may need to take leaves of absence due to extenuating, disability-related reasons, or they may need to request to be released from housing based on similar impacts. Depending on the nature of the request, release from a housing contract might be considered reasonable after the deadline to back out of the contract. However, there are often other considerations. In this type of case, a student may request a refund for housing costs for the semester, but they remain financially responsible for their time spent in residence. There are other operational deadlines as well. For instance, students may have a fixed amount of time to respond to a conduct violation. We would conduct an individual assessment to determine if the request is reasonable. If the student is the sole participant in the violation, a reasonable accommodation may be warranted. A student may need additional time to process the information contained in the violation, to write their personal statement, and to obtain proper advocacy. There may be requests that involve other community members or in which the nature of the timeline is such that it is fundamental to the operation. A student might not, for instance, be able to request an extension to the timeline involved in a Title IX investigation.

The timeline of other accommodation requests can be complicated by the community impact. Some requests might be deemed reasonable; others may not. Potential community impacts do not factor into the decision of whether a student meets the threshold of qualifying as a SWD or determining said student's eligibility for reasonable accommodations. They do, however, weigh in on how the accommodation is implemented, if (1) the request is reasonable and warranted and (2) it can be granted in a way that does not significantly affect the community. For instance, a student may request to have an ESA with them in their residence hall after students have moved into their rooms. We cannot deny this request simply because we have a policy to adhere to a deadline. This accommodation might, however, raise the issue of conflicting accommodation needs purely because of the timing of the request.

Conflicting Accommodations

There are some cases when accommodations or access needs conflict with other accommodations. The most prominent examples of this relate to assistance animal accommodations. A student may be granted the accommodation of an ESA under the Fair Housing Act. One of the appropriate steps of implementing this accommodation is to notify pertinent community members, including roommates and suitemates. The purpose of the notification is twofold. First, notice should be made that there will be an animal living in the space. The second reason, from a DS perspective, is more important: to allow students who may share the space an opportunity to request their own accommodation. This process is set for identifying and preempting a scenario where there may be conflicting accommodation needs. The conflict would come when a student identifies, for instance, having an allergy to the animal.

In these cases, there needs to be a review of the impact of said conflict. There are a lot of factors to consider in these cases. Provided that a proper evaluation has taken place to determine the eligibility of the first student to have an animal, a second evaluation must take place of the student who reports a conflicting disability and, subsequently, the conflicting accommodation request. Ideally, this evaluation takes place after the initial notification and before the students move into the space. The desired result is to be able to provide a space that meets the accommodation need of both students.

There are a few ways to look at this specific type of request. First, removing the presence of a conflicting disability, the granted ESA accommodation cannot be contingent on the approval of other students. Second, in the case of an allergy, while the student has a physical condition, it would not significantly impact the major life activities related to living on campus in the absence of the animal. In this way, without the first student's accommodation, and in this circumstance, the condition might not be considered disabling. There would need to be an evaluation of the entire relationship to determine a way to grant both accommodations.

Undue Burden

Granting some accommodations may result in an undue burden to the institution. The concept of undue burden can apply to factors such as institutional finances or instructional burden. A requested accommodation that poses an undue burden is unreasonable.

Title III of the ADA defines undue financial burden in the following way:

> Undue burden means significant difficulty or expense. In determining whether an action would result in an undue burden, factors to be considered include:
> 1. The nature and cost of the action needed under this part;
> 2. The overall financial resources of the site or sites involved in the action; the number of persons employed at the site; the effect on expenses and resources; legitimate safety requirements that are necessary for safe operation, including crime prevention measures; or the impact otherwise of the action upon the operation of the site;

3. The geographic separateness, and the administrative or fiscal relationship of the site or sites in question to any parent corporation or entity;
4. If applicable, the overall financial resources of any parent corporation or entity; the overall size of the parent corporation or entity with respect to the number of its employees; the number, type, and location of its facilities; and
5. If applicable, the type of operation or operations of any parent corporation or entity, including the composition, structure, and functions of the workforce of the parent corporation or entity. (U.S. Department of Justice Civil Rights Division n.d.b)

Based on relevant case law, the standard for determining undue financial burden is variable across institutions and often significantly higher than many DSPs realize. There is no specific dollar amount we can lean on. Rather, the determination of undue burden needs to be based on an assessment of the accommodation requested by DSPs and critical stakeholders on campus, up to and including the president or chancellor of the institution.

In the case of an accommodation that is denied on the basis of undue financial burden, alternative accommodations must be provided. For example, funding a transportation program, an evaluation of the specific needs of the student must take place. For instance, is the student requesting transportation to class due to a mobility-related disability? If the cost associated with accommodating in this way is undue, there may be other options to evaluate, such as relocation to a residence hall closer to academic facilities or relocation of classes so that they are in close proximity to one another.

Sometimes, academic accommodation requests have implications for the methods of instruction and content delivery that are considered an undue burden. After evaluating pedagogy for what is fundamental (e.g., the Socratic method in law school) and evaluating the request for whether it represents a personal service (e.g., assigning a classroom aide), we turn to burden. There is no way around the fact that some accommodations add additional work for the faculty member. However, an accommodation that poses a significant impact on a faculty member's workload, rising to the level of hardship, may be considered an undue burden.

One common reason faculty claim hardship relates to an accommodation for postponing an exam. Once the exam is distributed to the class, there may be concerns for preserving the academic integrity of the assessment. In these cases, one possible solution is to create a different exam for the student requesting the accommodation. Depending on the entirety of the evaluation, creating a second exam may be an undue burden. Take, for instance, a comprehensive final exam for organic chemistry. Exam questions include complex problem sets, supporting lab data, tabular data and graphics, and rendered models of chemical compounds. In this case, it would be fair to ask the faculty member to quantify the time and effort associated with this task and use our reasonable standard to assess the level of burden. If the burden is deemed to be undue, alternate accommodations must be considered but may be difficult to ensure. For some classes, such as precalculus, it might be possible for new problem sets to be generated by an algorithm. This might be a reasonable request.

Unreasonable Accommodations and the Evaluation

To define unreasonable is, in a way, tantamount to identifying one of the ways we choose to deny accommodation requests. It may seem counterintuitive, but the first step to defining whether accommodations are reasonable is to rule out the factors that would render them unreasonable. A process of elimination takes place. To review, a request may be deemed unreasonable if it does the following:

- Poses a fundamental alteration to the curriculum
  - Compromises the academic integrity of a course, program, or major
  - Reduces the quality and quantity of learning
  - Reduces the ability to meet technical standards or achieve core competencies
- Poses a direct threat to the health and safety of the campus or campus community
- Requires the provision of personal aids and services
- Represents an undue burden

By applying our "reasonable person" standard and ruling out the factors that make a request unreasonable, we are well on our way to granting the accommodation and supporting our student!

Determining Accommodations

Approvals

When a reasonable accommodation request is approved, the student should receive written confirmation of the approval along with procedures for how the accommodation will be implemented and who to contact for further information. Typically, approved academic accommodations are communicated via written letter of accommodation or faculty notification letter. However, some academic accommodations (e.g., course substitutions) and others (e.g., housing, dining) are memorialized in writing via email or other formal notification method.

Alternative Accommodation Approvals

There are times when, after careful consideration of the options, a particular accommodation is determined not to be the most appropriate given the requirements of the program, nuances of the setting, availability of accommodation, or alternative suitable options. DSPs have the authority to suggest alternative reasonable accommodations as long as alternatives are relevant to the student's disability and barriers. A common example of an alternative accommodation approval is when a student requests a notetaker, but the DSP deems that recorded lectures will provide equal access. Such might be the case if, through the interactive process, the DSP learns that the goal of the accommodation is to supplement notes, not provide a complete copy of them. In this example, the student is capable of independently taking their own notes, but they can become easily distracted and miss portions of the lecture. When denying this student's request for a notetaker, we would highlight research outlining the benefits that active note-taking has on engagement and memory. We might then introduce different technologies for recording lectures and suggest a note-taking workshop. Remember, the goal is to provide accommodations that mitigate barriers while allowing the student to be as independent as possible. If a student finds the alternative accommodations unacceptable, they may request reconsideration or initiate the grievance process.

Provisional Accommodations

Sometimes, given the whole of the available information, a reasonable accommodation analysis cannot be achieved. This is often the case when external documentation is not readily available or does not fully support some or all of the requested accommodations. In such instances, it is advisable to offer the student a provisional accommodation with the expectation that the additional requested information be provided within a reasonable period. Be explicit in communicating expectations about missing elements of the process and elements that need clarity or elaboration. Also, be sure to communicate how long the provisional accommodation is in place and potential determinations once the additional information is received (e.g., accommodation may be approved, adjusted, extended, or denied). Determination of provisional accommodation does not obligate the institution to provide the accommodation on a long-term basis. Instead, it shows a flexible and good faith effort to consider the student's access needs while affording the student more time to engage in the interactive process.

Denials

When denying an accommodation, it is important to show that the institution has engaged in a good faith effort by complying with all steps in the interactive process. This objective can be achieved by adhering to reasonable or established timeframes in considering and responding to student requests. Compliance is further demonstrated through attempts to engage expert college officials in balancing the right of the college to determine basic requirements with the right of the student to participate. We must be prepared to defend our determination by detailing in writing our rationale for denying the request and remain responsive to conflicts regarding the denied accommodation, including offering guidance on how to initiate a grievance process.

Grievance Procedures

Students have the right to appeal the denial of a requested accommodation or seek resolution of a discrimination complaint. Any denial of an accommodation or complaint about violations of antidiscrimination policies should be accompanied by information detailing the right to seek review of such concerns. It is well established that, at a minimum, institutions should publish grievance procedures on any web page dedicated to accessibility, including where and how complaints may be filed. More on grievance procedures is discussed in Chapter 13.

Implementing Accommodations

Within the classroom, the responsibility for implementing academic accommodations lies with instructors. Exceptions occur where DSPs or other campus partners provide proctoring, document conversion, or interpreting services. In those cases, the relevant provider will take responsibility for implementing the accommodation.

The faculty accommodation letter is a confidential document that serves as official notification to instructors that a student has been approved for academic accommodations. The main components of an accommodation letter may include:

- Student's name and ID
- Course/professor name

- Exam/classroom accommodations
- Confidentiality statement
- Fundamental alteration statement
- DSO contact information

Letters should not include:

- Student's disability
- Nonacademic accommodations (e.g., housing accommodation)

In the interest of inclusive pedagogy, consider adding verbiage that alerts faculty that inclusive course design should be their goal so that unintended barriers and the need for accommodations are eliminated or minimized. Faculty should be advised to contact the DSO as soon as concerns about the provision of accommodations arise—but to be aware that they may not deny a student's accommodation request. DSPs may consider adding to the accommodation letter some version of the following statement from Georgia Tech:

> The College is committed to providing inclusive learning environments. Equal access can often be achieved through course design. However, barriers to learning or assessment may still exist for a student with a disability in your course. Where access cannot be achieved through design, reasonable accommodations are required under Section 504 and the ADA. The following accommodations may be requested by this student to facilitate access. Please reach out to our office if the methods listed do not eliminate barriers or are in conflict with essential course requirements. We are here to be a resource to you and look forward to working with you to ensure that you course is accessible for all students. (Georgia Tech n.d.)

As a best practice, the letter should be accompanied by a communication instructing the student on how to notify faculty of an accommodation, how to report concerns about accommodation implementation, rights and responsibilities, general office information, and timelines for specific accommodation requests.

Many institutions require the student to notify faculty of intent to use an accommodation and discuss how the accommodation will be implemented (Figure 7.1). Students should be aware that they are under no obligation to discuss their disability—only the course-related barriers that result from the disability. Further, students should know they are not obligated to discuss any accommodations they are not requesting. However, they are required

DELIVER YOUR LETTER OF ACCOMMODATION (LOA) TO YOUR INSTRUCTOR
- Send a brief introduction email and attach your LOA; or
- Print your LOA and deliver it in person
- Do this as early in the semester as possible

MEET WITH YOUR INSTRUCTOR
- Schedule an appointment to determine when you will meet
- Accommodations are not in effect until you deliver your LOA <u>and</u> discuss which accommodation you'd like to use in that class

DISCUSS YOUR ACCOMMODATIONS
- Review each accommodation you plan to use for that class
- Share a little bit about why you need that accommodation
- You do not need to disclose your disability
- Ask how the accommodation will be applied

QUESTIONS OR CONCERNS: CONTACT OAR
- If you have concerns about your accommodations
- If your accommodations are not working or if you need new ones
- If you want to check in; we are here to help!
- ☏ 888-555-1212   ✉ dsp@college.edu   📅 schedule appointment

Figure 7.1 Letter of Accommodation Process

to discuss accommodations they will be using and to make requests in a timely manner so that requests can be appropriately facilitated. Reasonable notice timelines should be clearly communicated, as should notice that accommodations are not retroactively applied. Finally, students should be instructed to contact the DSO immediately if they have concerns about the provision of accommodations or encounter new barriers. It may be helpful to summarize these steps in both written and graphic form.

Several options should be offered to students for communicating accommodation needs to professors, including the following:

- Meeting individually (and privately) after class or during office hours (virtually, by phone, or in person).

- Emailing the instructor a brief introduction and correspondence about accommodation needs. This initial outreach may serve as an icebreaker for students who are anxious or hesitant.
- Sending a verification email from their student accommodations portal. The portal allows students to specify which accommodations they plan to use in each individual course.

As a best practice in supporting student agency, we do not recommend emailing faculty accommodation letters on students' behalf. However, there may be instances where discussion with faculty in advance of an official accommodation letter is advisable. Such may be the case when prepping faculty for students with sensory disabilities. To support inclusive efforts from day one in class for a student with hearing loss, we might offer instructional tips for working with Deaf/hard-of-hearing students (e.g., face class when speaking, repeat questions/comments, provide captioned videos) or acquaint instructors with technology aids (e.g., demonstrating how an FM system works). This advanced notice does not necessarily mean identifying a particular student—of course we cannot do that without the student's expressed consent. Instead, we can offer some general suggestions for working with student populations.

Just as students may need some guidance on how to engage faculty about accommodation disclosure and requests, faculty can also benefit from reminders and best practices for talking with students about accommodations, as detailed in Chapter 11. For now, though, it is important to remind faculty that the request for accommodations is, for some students, a very difficult task and should be treated with utmost sensitivity and confidentiality. For this reason, faculty should take care to arrange a private space to meet with the student. It is not uncommon for students to complain about being inadvertently outed by an instructor. Faculty should never disclose disability-related information to others without the student's expressed consent—not a department chair, not a co-instructor, and not a teaching assistant—unless there is a legitimate need for that person to know under FERPA.

Ensuring appropriate implementation of the listed accommodations is a joint effort between the student, the instructor, and the DSO. Each requested accommodation should be facilitated by the instructor (or, in some cases, the DSO) unless reasonableness concerns emerge. When faculty raise concerns, as part of the interactive process, it is our responsibility—not the student's—to engage the professor in discussion. Our role is to ensure that all partners meet their obligations by understanding their rights and responsibilities. As we review accommodation eligibility with students, we should take care to ensure they are duly informed of their obligations to remain actively engaged in the interactive process and bear the primary responsibility of meeting established standards and timelines. A summary of standard responsibilities follows.

Students have the right to the following:

- Equal access to courses, programs, services, facilities, and activities offered through the institution
- Protection from discrimination
- An equal opportunity to learn
- Not self-identify if accommodations are not being requested
- Confidentiality of all disability information; choice regarding to whom information about their disabilities will be disclosed
- Reasonable and appropriate accommodations from each faculty/staff who has received notification from the DSO
- Challenge a decision or submit a complaint through the institution's or an external channel's grievance procedures

Student responsibilities include the following:

- Demonstrating how their disabilities limit them within the context of institutional barriers
- Requesting faculty notification letters from the DSO per established scheduled (e.g., usually each semester)
- Advocating for their needs
- Notifying the disability office of their desire for continued accommodation
- Providing reasonable notice to implement accommodations (e.g., abiding by established timeframe for requesting exam accommodations)
- Discussing the implementation of accommodations with each of their instructors and contacting the disability office as soon as possible with concerns or questions
- Meeting and maintaining the institution's academic, behavioral, and technical standards, as any other student
- Following published procedures for filing an appeal

The DSO has the right to the following:

- Request appropriate documentation to support a request for reasonable accommodations
- Select the most appropriate or equally effective accommodation through discussion with the student and others as necessary

- Refuse an accommodation that imposes a fundamental alteration of a program or activity, poses a direct threat to the health or safety of others, or poses an undue financial or administrative burden

DSP responsibilities include the following:

- Determining reasonable and appropriate accommodations through an interactive process
- Communicating approved accommodations to instructors and other relevant providers
- Serving as a resource to assist in facilitating campus access
- Denying any request for accommodations, academic adjustments, auxiliary aids, and services determined unreasonable or not requested in a timely manner
- Advocating on behalf of students to ensure access

Instructor/staff responsibilities include the following:

- Ensuring approved accommodations are implemented in a timely manner on receiving official accommodation notification
- Contacting the DSO to discuss concerns or questions related to the implementation of accommodations as soon as possible
- Treating accommodation information as confidential and protecting the privacy of students who receive accommodations
- Providing materials in accessible formats
- Referring students to the DSO if they suspect or a student reports a disability

Instructor/staff have the right to the following:

- Receive official verification of a student's eligibility for any requested accommodations
- Maintain academic/program standards
- Determine course/program requirements
- Determine an accommodation is unreasonable through consultation with the DS provider

Continued Interaction

An essential but often forgotten part of the interactive process is monitoring the effectiveness of accommodations. As we have established, students bear the responsibility of alerting the DSO of concerns about the implementation or effectiveness of accommodations. At most schools, students are required to request academic accommodation letters each semester or, for housing or dining accommodations, annually. And while students are obligated to alert us to their accommodation needs (e.g., requesting CART services or a classroom assistant for a new course, ensuring their classrooms are accessible), we are often one step ahead of students in coordinating supports and services proactively.

Implementing accommodations is hardly ever a one-and-done situation. Even for students who have a fairly basic accommodation plan with only extended time on exams, we have a duty to ensure that students are informed about their obligations to maintain access to their accommodations. At least annually, students should be informed about their rights and responsibilities as a student registered with the DSO as well as our responsibility to ensure the timely provision of accommodations and serve as a resource and advocate for any disability-related needs.

As a final note about the interactive process, Table 7.1 shows tips for ensuring a good faith effort to consider students' needs.

In Summary

The determination of reasonable accommodations is not made solely by (1) establishing disability and (2) receiving accommodation requests. Whereas the initial disclosure and disability establishing processes are the first phase of the interactive process, reviewing requests and determining reasonable accommodations are the second. These are separate determinations but can typically be accomplished during the same intake interview. The process begins with an evaluation of impacts to major life activities. We use the "most people in the general population" standard to gauge the significance of the impacts SWDs experience. We also use the reasonable/unreasonable standards (or guidelines) to determine eligibility for each individual accommodation. Ultimately, the interactive process is a shared process. There are rights and responsibilities for each party, and it is important for the DSP to understand and uphold them. If done right and with "good faith efforts," the interactive process ensures a fair review of students' accommodation requests, preserves the integrity of our programs and offerings, and can be the driving force for equal access and opportunity on our campuses.

▶ Reflective Exercise

Maddy is a junior at Labrie University. She is studying at Labrie's satellite campus, which is in a different state than her home and the institution. Maddy has an eating disorder and has experienced a relapse at midterm time. She

TABLE 7.1 TIPS FOR ENGAGING IN THE INTERACTIVE PROCESS

Do	Do not
Approach the process with a success mindset—finding a way for the student to have the same level of access as their nondisabled peers. Be helpful and sincere in your words and actions.	Approach the process with an adversarial mindset (e.g., that the student is trying to game the system or obtain an unfair advantage).
Work through the process by considering all reasonable alternatives.	Adopt a "take it or leave it" approach.
Determine the final manner in which the accommodation will be provided.	Put faculty or an untrained college administrator in the position of having to make a reasonable accommodation determination.
Serve as an intermediary between students and faculty. Engage other relevant people in conversations (e.g., faculty, facilities, campus police, dining staff).	Require students to negotiate accommodation needs with instructors. That is an unfair power dynamic.
Give individualized consideration to each request no matter how unreasonable it seems.	Fail to act on or delay a request for accommodation.
Conduct a course-by-course analysis of the reasonable accommodation standard.	Make a blanket determination that an accommodation is unreasonable without consulting with the instructor.
Document, document, document all steps of the interactive process and especially the rationale for denying accommodation requests.	Skimp on notes, especially during the intake meeting and any time a student makes a request or you deny a request.
Give primary consideration to students' preferred method of effective communication accommodations (Title II).	Insist that a particular auxiliary aid will afford access or that the student's preferred method is expensive or difficult to coordinate.
Be flexible and creative in identifying new or alternative accommodations.	Make assumptions about limitations based on stereotypes of disability or ignore students' preferred method of accommodation.

needs to return home to attend a Partial Hospitalization Program (PHP) for treatment. Maddy is taking four courses this semester. Two of the courses can be completed remotely. However, the other two classes have in-person components. Her art history class has mandatory museum visits and walking tours of the city, and she is taking a biology class with an in-person lab and a planned trip to a local marine fishery. Maddy is requesting an accommodation to remain in her courses and complete the semester remotely. What information is needed to determine if her request is reasonable? How would you approach the process of determining what is fundamental for her art history and biology classes? Who should be involved in the decision-making process? What alternatives can you think of to investigate/propose for the in-person components of those classes? If granted, what other accommodations might be necessary?

Supplemental Job Aids

The following Supplemental Job Aids can be found at https://scholarshare.temple.edu/handle/20.500.12613/8373:

- *Sample Accommodation Letter (Accommodations Grouped by Category)*
- *Sample Accommodation Letter (Accommodations with Descriptions)*

8

Accommodations

Accommodations are necessary adjustments to eliminate barriers where design is either ineffective or inefficient. They are determined after examining the nexus between the disability-related barrier and the environment. It is through this framework that we explore various accommodations, academic and cocurricular. Some accommodations are fairly straightforward to implement while others require a little more effort and collaboration. While the list of accommodations is inexhaustive and grows with every passing year (some institutions offer hundreds), we decided to consolidate accommodations into broad categories—academic, housing, dining, transportation, contingency, experiential learning, and temporary—for easier consumption.

> ### Guiding Questions
> 1. Which factors help distinguish ESAs from service animals?
> 2. How can dietary restrictions be accommodated?
> 3. Who is responsible for determining accommodations in experiential learning settings?

Understanding that accommodations are essentially changes to the way things are typically done, it is helpful to categorize their purpose into several areas:

- Modifications to policies and practices
- Removal of architectural barriers
- Adaptations or modifications that allow equal access to and enjoyment of the benefits and privileges of an institution's programs, services, and activities
- Provision of auxiliary aids and services
- Adjustments to the educational environment that allow equal access to meeting academic requirements

As we explore the various accommodation categories, it is important to remain cognizant of an accommodation's purpose in reducing or eliminating barriers. It is through this barrier-removal lens that we strive to improve meaningful access to our campuses.

Academic Accommodations

Academic accommodations are designed to eliminate disability-related barriers in the classroom and curriculum that impact access to learning. While the following list is not exhaustive, we have categorized some of the most common accommodation categories.

Alternative Testing Arrangements

Accommodations in this category are appropriate when a student's disability affects their performance on assessments. These accommodations are appropriate for, but not limited to, students with cognitive disabilities (e.g., dyslexia, ADHD, TBI) and mental health conditions (e.g., depression, OCD) that impact processing speed, arousal level, recall, or distractibility; students who require certain environmental adjustments (e.g., lighting, sound reduction) or medical considerations (e.g., access to food for diabetic students); and students whose impairments may impact motor functioning, mobility, or sensory organs. Table 8.1 highlights different assessment-based barriers a student may face and examples of different accommodations to address these barriers.

Classroom Accommodations

Accommodations in this category are appropriate when the student has barriers to learning or navigating classroom spaces, requiring adaptations to the way information is presented, the way the student responds, or the way the student accesses information. Table 8.2 identifies options for mitigating various classroom barriers.

TABLE 8.1   ALTERNATIVE TESTING ARRANGEMENTS

Barrier Related To	Examples
The characteristics of the setting	Distraction-reduced location Headphones/earplugs (noise cancellation) Private/semiprivate room Access to food/beverage Breaks/bathroom breaks
The way in which the student is expected to respond to exam questions	Scribe Dictation software Alternative to scantron Breaks Use of computer Extended time (1.5x, 2x)
The way in which the student accesses the room	Adaptive furniture (e.g., adjustable tables, chairs, standing desks, adjustable lighting)
The way in which the student accesses or processes content	Access to computer Exam enlargement AT (e.g., text-to-speech software) Technical aid (calculator, spell-check, dictionary) Memory aid Reader Extended time

Communication Accommodations

Accommodations in this category are related to the understanding of spoken communication for deaf and hard-of-hearing individuals. Institutions are obligated to provide effective communication to afford deaf and hard-of-hearing individuals the ability to share and receive information in a manner equitable to those without hearing loss. Title II institutions are required to give primary consideration to the service or device requested by the deaf student unless it can be determined that another equally effective means of communication is available. Title III institutions are only encouraged to consider the specific service or device requested (University of Texas at Austin 2019). We review this information in Chapter 9 in a bit more detail. Options for addressing communication barriers are outlined in Table 8.3.

Modifications

There are times when accommodations are insufficient to level the playing field. In such circumstances, it may be reasonable to modify a policy or procedure. A reduced course load is an example of such an accommodation. For students whose disabilities may impact their ability to maintain full-time sta-

TABLE 8.2 CLASSROOM ACCOMMODATIONS

Barrier Related To	Examples
Information access	Alternative formats (e.g., braille, content magnification, digital files, captioning) Permission to record lectures Access to notes (e.g., notetaker, note-taking technology) Advanced copies of lecture slides Use of personal laptop/tablet (e.g., to take notes, use AT, type assignments) Auxiliary aids/services (e.g., assistive listening device, interpreter)
Navigation, mobility	Adaptive furniture (e.g., adjustable height, seating to fit stature) Classroom relocation Classroom/lab assistant
Environmental stimuli	Preferential seating Movement breaks Air conditioning Headphones/hats/sunglasses
Timing	Extensions on assignments Breaks Flexibility with class arrival
Attendance	Flexible attendance agreement Alternate test dates
Participation	No cold-calling Alternative ways to participate (e.g., attending office hours, responding to course blogs) Alternatives to class presentations (e.g., videotaped presentation, private presentation to faculty)

TABLE 8.3 COMMUNICATION ACCOMMODATIONS

Barrier	Examples
Hearing acuity	Assistive listening systems/devices
Hearing acuity, facilitates communication between deaf and hearing individuals through visual interpretation	ASL Interpreter Transliteration Tactile interpretation (e.g., used by those who are deaf-blind)
Hearing acuity, provides textual representation of audio content in video format including dialogue, sound effects, and speaker identification	Closed captioning/descriptive captioning Speech to text (e.g., CART, C-Print, TypeWell)

tus, this accommodation allows them to take fewer credits (usually eleven or less) while remaining entitled to the benefits of being a full-time student (e.g., on-campus housing, financial aid). Table 8.4 suggests other examples of policy modifications.

TABLE 8.4   MODIFICATIONS

Barrier	Examples
Scheduling challenges due to a service, medical, or mental health-related need. Students who may qualify include: Students with mobility impairments or who work with personal assistants Students who have a strict medical regimen Students with sensory impairments impacting navigation or who require alternative formats or communication access providers	Priority registration
Even with accommodation, the student's disability precludes them from accessing the course or demonstrating their knowledge. Students who may qualify include: Students with language-based learning disabilities or who are deaf/hard of hearing	Course substitution/ waiver (e.g., world language)
Attending class in person presents an access barrier (not a preference). Must consider whether remote access poses a fundamental alteration determined by academic officials. Students who may qualify include: Students who are pursuing some form of disability-related treatment	Remote attendance

Housing Accommodations

Accommodation requests are not only relegated to the academic side of our institutions. We must make living opportunities accessible to all students as well. For some students, an integral part of their educational experience is learning how to live in a community and share space with others. To this end, we strive to ensure that disabled students have opportunities to fully participate in and equally benefit from communal living. Housing accommodations are intended to address functional limitations at no additional cost to eligible students. For example, students who have difficulty navigating stairs may need to live on a lower floor. Deaf students may require visual and tactile emergency alerts such as strobe lights and bed shaker. A proven way to evaluate requests is to structure them according to factors. Factors will vary greatly by campus based on existing facilities. Table 8.5 pairs factors with associated accommodations.

Emotional Support Animals

ESA accommodations are residential accommodations, whereas service animals are an access necessity.

TABLE 8.5 HOUSING ACCOMMODATIONS

Barrier Related To	Examples
Cohabitation: living space	Fewer roommates Single room Double room (as opposed to triple+) Triple room (as opposed to quadruple+) More roommates Placement in suite Placement in apartment
Cohabitation: bathroom space	Private bathroom (in suite) Access to private bathroom Semiprivate bathroom (shared with as few students as possible)
Location	Within building: Near bathroom Near kitchen Near elevator Lower floor (e.g., for evacuation) Higher floor (e.g., less street noise) Building itself: Near campus buildings (e.g., classes) Near transportation Near parking
Amenities	Wheelchair access Lighting (e.g., adjustable, natural light) Environmental control (e.g., air-conditioning) Adaptive furniture Accessible bathroom, kitchen, and laundry facilities
Caring for oneself	Emotional Support Animal (ESA) Personal Care Attendant (PCA)

By the ADA, "service animals are defined as dogs that are individually trained to do work or perform tasks for people with disabilities" (U.S. Department of Justice Civil Rights Division 2020a). Examples of such work or tasks include guiding people who are blind, alerting people who are Deaf, pulling a wheelchair, alerting, and protecting a person who is having a seizure, reminding a person with mental illness to take prescribed medications, calming a person with Post Traumatic Stress Disorder (PTSD) during an anxiety attack, or performing other duties. Service animals are working animals, not pets. The work or task a dog has been trained to provide must be directly related to the person's disability. Dogs whose sole function is to provide comfort or emotional support do not qualify as service animals under the ADA.

This definition does not affect or limit the broader definition of "assistance animal" under the Fair Housing Act or the broader definition of "service animal" under the Air Carrier Access Act. Some state and local laws also define service animal more broadly than the ADA does. Information about such laws can be obtained from the relevant state attorney general's office (U.S. Department of Justice Civil Rights Division 2020). Table 8.6 outlines the differences between emotional support and service animals.

Evaluating an ESA request should follow the same essential process as evaluating other accommodations: investigate a student's self-report and review documentation. All the same processes for determining a student's disability status and evaluating whether the accommodation is reasonable and appropriate should apply. Specific intake questions can be included to tailor the evaluation for an ESA request. Here are some examples:

- What benefit does the ESA provide?
- What are the effects of not having access to the animal?
- What conversations have you had with your clinician pertaining to an ESA accommodation?
- Do you have an existing, proven relationship with the animal?

TABLE 8.6 THE DIFFERENCES BETWEEN EMOTIONAL SUPPORT AND SERVICE ANIMALS

Factor	Emotional Support Animal (ESA)	Service Animal
Applicable law	Fair Housing Act (FHA)	ADA
Function	Comfort, companionship	Disability-related work
Animal	Any (except prohibited species*)	Dog (or in some cases a mini horse)
Location	Student's individual residential unit (e.g., individual dorm room)	Anywhere student is permitted, with few exceptions (e.g., chemistry lab)
Process	Intake and DS registration	"Two questions." Registration not required
Documentation	Required	Not required
Training	Not common	Required*

*Important notes
- Some states, cities, and towns prohibit ownership of certain species (some require a permit).
- Consider a legal review or local ordinances (breed and species restrictions, licensing laws, vaccination requirements, leash laws, and so on).
- In some states, service animals in training are permitted (e.g., Massachusetts).
- If there is concern for illegitimate requests—individuals can purchase credentials online—consider researching sources and fact-checking provided documentation.
- Removal of an ESA due to disruption does not automatically remove the accommodation—e.g., "student can have an animal, but not *that* animal."
- Student must retain control of the animal at all times.
- A sample ESA contract is included in the supplement for this chapter.

- How do you provide care for the animal?
- What other strategies or coping mechanisms do you have for managing your symptoms?

There are also some animal-specific questions to ask:

- What kind of animal do you have?
- How long have you had the animal?
- Is the animal housebroken or otherwise capable of living on campus?
- What needs does the animal have?

Dining Accommodations

Dining accommodation requests can stem from physical or mental conditions or bodily functions. Students may present with a medically restrictive diet, significant and/or multiple food allergies, an eating disorder, obsessive-compulsive disorder, autism, compromised digestion, and so on. Dietary preferences, such as a vegetarian, vegan, keto, or paleo diet, avoiding gluten or dairy, or religious dietary requirements, do not qualify unless medically necessary. Table 8.7 highlights different dining barriers that students may identify and examples of accommodations to address those barriers.

Transportation and Parking Accommodations

Transportation is considered a personal service unless transportation services (e.g., fixed route buses, on-demand shuttles) are made available to the general student population. When available to all, accessible transportation options equivalent to the service offered to other students must be provided. The most ideal scenario is that all applicable vehicles are accessible, meaning they are equipped with lifts, ramps, securement devices, signage, communication devices, and allow for a service animal. Where standard transportation op-

TABLE 8.7 DINING ACCOMMODATIONS	
Barrier Related To	**Examples**
Food access	Meal plan reduction or exemption Dedicated food prep areas Custom-order meals Point-of-service allergen labels/ingredient list Procurement of special dietary products Allergen-free or allergen-conscious zones (e.g., pantries)
Dining hall access	Accessible menus Accessible seating

tions are not achievable or feasible, alternative yet safe and timely accessible options should be made available. Examples include paratransit vans, reservation-based shuttles, and golf carts.

Disabled parking spaces are not considered an accommodation for students who have a state-issued placard. However, placards alone do not authorize student access to permit-parking facilities. Class-year restrictions and space availability may require exceptions. Most parking accommodation requests stem from issues related to parking space limitations, parking lot location, or class-year restrictions. Table 8.8 highlights different transportation and parking barriers that students may identify and provides examples of corresponding accommodations.

Contingency Accommodations

Places of public accommodation naturally have emergency protocols in place. With all other accommodations, these protocols must be made accessible for all students. This category of accommodation rises to a higher priority than many others because it has implications for the health and safety of campus community members. Protocols include emergency notification, management of adverse weather, evacuation procedures, and other contingencies, such as the response by campuses to the distancing, isolation, and quarantine requirements of the COVID-19 pandemic. Table 8.9 identifies different contingency accommodations a DSP may use for emergency situations.

Experiential Learning Accommodations

Internships, Practicums, Clinicals

Accommodations for practicum and internship opportunities may include, in part, involvement from a DSO. This area requires careful evaluation, a clear understanding of roles and responsibilities, advocacy and education for students, and partnerships with academic departments, career services operations, and external sites.

TABLE 8.8 PARKING AND TRANSPORTATION ACCOMMODATIONS	
Barrier Related To	**Examples**
Mobility and ambulation Exposure to adverse elements Getting to off-campus providers	Permission to have a car on campus Modified parking lot assignment Permission to park in a nonstudent lot Paratransit Shuttle service Scooter/golf cart loan

TABLE 8.9	CONTINGENCY ACCOMMODATIONS
Barrier Related To	Examples
Emergency notification systems	Auditory AND visual fire/emergency alarms Bed shaker alarms Emergency text notification system Prior notice for preplanned fire (and other) drills Orientation training to campus emergency notifications
Evacuation procedures	Evacuation list provided to emergency response personnel and first responders Placement on a lower floor Favorable placement on an evacuation route Orientation training for evacuation procedures
Weather	Snow removal plans, especially for curb cuts and ramps Remote attendance and participation Residential placement in proximity to key locations Classroom relocation Access to air-conditioning Transportation and/or parking
Crisis contingency	Accessible evacuation protocol Remote attendance and participation Meal delivery Orientation training for contingency protocol ESA point of contact if the student is removed from campus

- Training should be provided to emergency response personnel and first responders.
- Campuses should have access to emergency evacuation equipment/evacuation chairs placed in each building and in first responder vehicles.
- Every DSO should have a thoroughly vetted contingency plan (partners can include emergency response personnel and first responders, crisis management team, environmental safety team, general counsel, facilities, residence life, and so on).

The first evaluation is whether the internship or practicum is a curricular requirement. Students may choose to accept internships for extracurricular job experience and resume building. These experiences are akin to having an outside job, and while they support what the student is learning, they are not required of the institution in any way. However, many academic programs establish internships and practicum experiences as curricular requirements. Since these experiences are tied to an academic program, the institution has some responsibility in ensuring that accommodation needs are met.

The analysis of which entity is responsible for providing access can be tricky. There is some gray area. Scenarios can be dynamic and depend on both what the institution and the employer can offer and what processes are in place. Some employers handle the entire accommodation process, and the DSO can take a back seat. Some employers defer to the institution to determine disability, collect and store documentation, and consult on possible accommodations. The employer is then responsible for implementation. We have experienced some cases where the employer accepts an accommodation letter as verification of eligibility. In these cases, the employer either takes the institution's recommendations or engages in communication to determine what is reasonable. In either situation, the interactive process often mirrors Title I, which examines accommodations needed to perform essential job functions.

One possible solution is for the academic unit to make an inquiry on the student's behalf. Ideally, this inquiry should be done during the recruitment phase for appropriate sites. Questions about site accessibility, accommodation process and procedures, and types of accommodations that can typically be provided should be part of the recruitments and contracting phases of approving sites. Guiding questions might include the following:

- Is the proposed accommodation available?
- Will the proposed accommodation result in a failure to meet essential job functions or program requirements?
- Will the proposed accommodation jeopardize the safety of others?
- Will the proposed accommodation fundamentally alter the program or pose an undue hardship?

Ultimately, the institution (DSO and academic unit) and the employment site share responsibility. Each site's level of responsibility should be factored into the interactive process. When internships or practicum opportunities are offered and required for students, the opportunities must be accessible.

Accessibility Abroad

Whether spending a semester or two abroad or opting for an intensive but short-term excursion overseas, SWDs have many opportunities to explore the world. Because the ADA and Section 504 are U.S. laws, they generally do not apply to extraterritorial boundaries. That said, IHEs have an affirmative duty to comply with U.S. federal laws by proactively ensuring equal opportunity to participate and programmatic access during the abroad application and acceptance process. Fortunately, many countries have ratified the UN Convention on the Rights of Persons with Disabilities or have laws like the ADA entitling students to some accommodations.

While all U.S.-based international exchange organizations are required to make their programs inclusive of those with disabilities, some locations may be better suited to meeting accessibility needs than others. Not all host countries will offer the same resources students are accustomed to in the United States. Cultural norms around accessibility may vary depending on the type of disability a student has. Of course, students should select locations that are aligned with their personal and academic interests, budget, travel opportunities, and sense of adventure, but they should also consider factors that match their disability-related needs.

Early preparation is the key to ensuring that the experience abroad is as seamless as possible. Students should find out as much as they can about the host culture by reading, attending predeparture orientation meetings, and consulting online resources such as Mobility International USA (MIUSA). MIUSA is an outstanding resource for information on how students with a wide array of disabilities can prepare for and make the most of their time abroad (MIUSA 2014). It offers suggestions for identifying accessible programs, negotiating accommodations, navigating health conditions, finding accessible restaurants, and locating mental health professionals. Talking with other disabled students who have traveled overseas is another great resource to help students consider how their needs can be met in an unfamiliar environment. Students with medical or mental health needs should consult with their provider about the type of care they may need abroad and how to maintain their treatment regimen. They should discuss the impact of cultural adjustment and acclimation to different therapeutic options on their overall health and well-being.

Temporary Accommodations

Students with temporary, nonchronic disabilities—those that are transitory, minor, and have an actual or expected duration of six months or less—are typically not afforded protections under the ADA. In some cases, however, a temporary impairment expected to last less than six months can be sufficiently severe to be considered a disability under the law. For this reason, every accommodation request must be given individualized consideration. Most campuses provide temporary courtesy accommodations for short-term disabilities such as injuries to limbs, mild to moderate concussions, impairments following surgery, or medical treatments. Students with common minor illnesses such as seasonal allergies, viral infections, mono, or the flu are not eligible for temporary accommodations. Instead, students with these conditions may be advised to work directly with faculty regarding attendance or assignment flexibility or may be referred to health services or another office in student affairs to provide absence verification and other types of support.

DSOs may assist students by engaging in an interactive process to understand the nature of the impairment and its expected duration. Medical documentation is often required to substantiate needs and timelines. When temporary accommodations are approved by the DSO, faculty and relevant staff are provided with a letter or email outlining the approved accommodations and noting that they are time limited. Faculty should neither expect nor ask for doctor's notes to substantiate accommodations such as excused absences. Some DSOs have the capacity to coordinate alternate exam accommodations, scribes/notetakers, and transportation assistance. As is true for students with ongoing disabilities, the DSO, in most cases, is not required to provide assistance with homework, personal needs, or transportation to off-campus medical appointments.

Students with temporary impairments may benefit from assistance with applying for state-issued temporary disabled parking placards, hiring personal attendants or scribes, identifying accessible campus routes, or locating providers that rent or sell medical equipment. Table 8.10 highlights different experiential learning barriers that students may identify and various accommodations a DSP may utilize.

In Summary

Reasonable accommodations are alterations to the status quo. They serve to bridge between the limitations posed by a disability and the barriers that exist in the environment. The range of possible accommodations is essentially limitless and can include changes to policies, practices, services, environments, as well as the provision of assistive aids. In this chapter, we distill accommodations into broad categories—academic, housing, dining, transportation, contingency, experiential learning, and temporary—and examine them from a barrier removal perspective.

TABLE 8.10 EXPERIENTIAL LEARNING ACCOMMODATIONS

Barrier Related To	Examples
Writing, dexterity	Voice recognition software Peer notes Use of computer for notes or exams Permission to record lectures Scribe for exams
Reading print materials	Electronic format of books Text-to-speech software
Focus/concentration	Extensions on assignments Extended time for exams Peer notes
Campus mobility, physical stability, and comfort	Transportation services Residence hall relocation Accessible bathroom Medical parking Adaptive furniture
Attendance (e.g., medical appointments, feeling unwell)	Excused absences Remote participation

Reflective Exercise

Dominique, a second-year student at a state institution, is hard of hearing. It is the second week of the spring semester, and she schedules an appointment with you to discuss challenges hearing her engineering professor. The professor has a strong, unfamiliar accent that is proving difficult for Dominique to interpret. Up until this point, she has been accommodated with an assistive listening device, preferential seating, and captioned videos. During the conversation, Dominique shares that she is planning to study abroad next spring. How would you address the new barrier Dominque has encountered to ensure effective communication? What kinds of challenges might emerge in providing appropriate accommodation(s)? How would you mitigate those challenges? In what ways can you help Dominique prepare for future accommodation needs?

Supplemental Job Aids

The following Supplemental Job Aids can be found at https://scholarshare.temple.edu/handle/20.500.12613/8373:

- Attendance Accommodation Agreement
- Assistance Animal Request Intake Form
- Emotional Support Animal Agreement

9

Assistive Technology and Auxiliary Aids

Rapid advances in smart technology for the consumer market have made assistive applications commonplace. Listening to an email, enabling captions on a video, downloading a transcript from a video conference call, using your voice to change the thermostat or adjust the lights in your house—these are all adaptive tasks that have high value for people with disabilities that have entered the mainstream with appeal to much broader audiences. There is an obvious difference between technology as an access need and technology as a convenience (or, in some cases, a novelty), but there is an important connection between the two. It is undeniable that mainstream use of assistive applications has driven both awareness of access needs and advancement of specialized technology to meet needs of people with disabilities. This shift has transformed the field of AT in higher education. The ways we approach granting tech-related accommodations have changed. The concept of an AT lab is obsolete in most cases. As higher education paradigms shift, however, the need for understanding AT applications is more important than ever—as is the ability to delineate access needs from mainstream applications. In this chapter, we explore the guidelines that define AT and auxiliary aids and how they shape our practices and obligations.

▶ **Guiding Questions**

1. What impact has consumer "smart" technology had on the AT industry?

2. How can a DS provider who is not a "tech guru" provide AT/auxiliary aid–related accommodations?
3. What are the costs associated with AT and auxiliary aids?
4. What are our obligations related to personal medical devices and daily living aids?

What Is Assistive Technology and What Are Auxiliary Aids?

When we think of assistive devices, a few examples immediately come to mind. Numerous everyday items have been adapted to reduce barriers and increase ease of use. A lot of items we rely on, day in and day out, were developed using universal design principles for the purpose of reducing barriers for individuals with disabilities and our aging population. Amenities such as wheelchair ramps have a dedicated access purpose, but they also benefit those who use crutches or push a stroller. Closed captions are a necessity for a Deaf student, but they are beneficial to language learners. How would people of all abilities watch the news in an airport terminal without them?

Smartphone technology has driven rapid change in the area of assistive applications and mainstreamed their use. Voice-to-text applications used to be specialized technologies used predominantly by individuals with limited dexterity or a learning disability. Now, it is easy to dictate a text message or email because we have the capability in our pocket. It is getting easier and easier to interact with the web, access and manipulate content, engage in multimedia and social media, and control our environments with consumer technology. These applications have revolutionized access for individuals with disabilities, lowered the threshold of availability of previously specialized functions, and helped to mainstream the concept of accessibility.

AT is an umbrella term that covers the myriad of devices—high tech and low tech, software and hardware, digital and analog, purpose built and multifunction, native and peripheral—designed and used to remove or reduce barriers. Our working definition of AT devices comes from the Technology Related Assistance to Individuals with Disabilities Act of 1988, or the Tech Act. The Tech Act defines AT devices as:

> Any item, piece of equipment, or product system, whether acquired commercially off the shelf, modified, or customized, that is used to increase, maintain, or improve functional capabilities of a child with a disability. Exception—The term does not include a medical device that is surgically implanted, or the replacement of such device. (ECTA 2012)

In many ways, AT has become a field unto itself within the K–12 special education setting and within DSOs in higher education. When we apply the definition of disability, we can link AT devices to major life activities such as reading, writing, walking, speaking, standing, and so on. Different activities may require different devices, and there are often multiple solutions for each activity, allowing for factors such as flexibility, robustness, affordability, convenience, and preference. In an education setting, we can narrow the scope to where major life functions intersect with activities associated with living and learning at our institutions. For instance, technology can be applied in an exam setting and for note-taking, or we may provide adaptive equipment to make accessible the opportunity to join a club, participate in a sport, or live in a residence hall. While it is not necessary for all DS providers to be experts in AT, familiarity with key functions can be considered a core competency.

AT is not the only way to use devices to support functional limitations. Auxiliary aids and services will often employ assistive and adaptive devices to provide access to SWDs. In addition to technology as an aid or service, auxiliary aids can include non-tech-based services, access services, and ancillary materials. The ADA defines auxiliary aids and services in the following way:

> (1) Qualified interpreters on-site or through video remote interpreting (VRI) services; notetakers; real-time computer-aided transcription services; written materials; exchange of written notes; telephone handset amplifiers; assistive listening devices; assistive listening systems; telephones compatible with hearing aids; closed caption decoders; open and closed captioning, including real-time captioning; voice, text, and video-based telecommunications products and systems, including text telephones (TTYs), videophones, and captioned telephones, or equally effective telecommunications devices; videotext displays; accessible electronic and information technology; or other effective methods of making aurally delivered information available to individuals who are deaf or hard of hearing;
>
> (2) Qualified readers; taped texts; audio recordings; Brailled materials and displays; screen reader software; magnification software; optical readers; secondary auditory programs (SAP); large print materials; accessible electronic and information technology; or other effective methods of making visually delivered materials available to individuals who are blind or have low vision;
>
> (3) Acquisition or modification of equipment or devices; and
>
> (4) Other similar services and actions. (U.S. Department of Justice Civil Rights Division 2010c)

By the definition above, the role of the DS provider in acquiring AT constitutes an auxiliary aid in and of itself. The definition also outlines our institutions' obligations to provide AT and auxiliary aids as reasonable accommodations.

The role of the DSP is evolving as quickly as the technology. Knowledge of the historical and legal foundations of AT and auxiliary aids provides useful perspective. Awareness and understanding of the categories of AT and auxiliary aids, their functionality, how they can be applied toward reasonable accommodations, the scope of our obligation, and the ability to provide and implement AT and auxiliary aids have become core competencies of the DSP. Even the least tech savvy of us can become effective AT and auxiliary aids providers.

A Brief History of AT and Auxiliary Aids

There are three eras associated with the development of AT: the Foundation Period (prior to 1900), the Establishment Period (1900–1972), and the Empowerment Period (1973 to present) (Gatchalian 2019). These three periods are defined by transformative acts or occurrences in the disability world (Table 9.1). For instance, the Foundation Period is separated from the Establishment Period by a change in social thinking and advocacy in additional to early acts and laws for individuals with disabilities beginning in the early twentieth century. The Establishment Period is separated from the Empowerment Period by the passage of the Rehabilitation Act of 1973.

We currently operate in what is known as the Empowerment Period. It is unclear if or when another major transformation will take place that

TABLE 9.1 THREE ERAS OF ASSISTIVE TECHNOLOGY		
Three Eras of Assistive Technology		
The Foundation Period (prior to 1900)	The Establishment Period (1900–1972)	The Empowerment Period (1972–present)
Key Events		
Pre-nineteenth century, needs of individuals addressed (correction of functional limitations) Foundation of Gallaudet University (1817) Invention of Braille (1834)	Early twentieth century, passage of foundational laws and foundation of disability advocacy associations Formation of Council for Exceptional Children and the Speech Language Hearing Associations Founding of Easter Seals	Disability as a civil right, protections of equal opportunity AT and auxiliary aids as a means to access The Rehabilitation Act of 1973 The Tech Act of 1988 The Americans with Disabilities Act of 1990

defines a new era—or whether it has already happened. Time and hindsight will tell. It is likely that advances in smart technology and the norming of assistive features, in addition to the advent of virtual and augmented reality, will be that threshold. While our focus and application of AT still revolves around empowering students, there are larger objectives to strive for. Empowering students to use technology to access the world around them still constitutes retrofitting and, ultimately, a reactive approach. As more entities and institutions adopt the accessibility standards proposed by the World Wide Web Consortium (W3C), awareness of universal accessibility continues to spread. The ideal would be a world proactively designed to provide accessible technology to all. Maybe one day, the AT specialist will become obsolete, but there is a lot of work to do in the meantime.

Laws That Guide the Use of AT in Education

The Rehabilitation Act of 1973 had a major transformative effect on the field of DS and provided a strong foundation for the provision of AT and auxiliary aids. Some of the laws that came after the Rehabilitation Act further defined our usage of technology to support SWDs. Perhaps the most prominent of those was the Technology Related Assistance to Individuals with Disabilities Act of 1988 and its amendment in 2004.

The Tech Act gave us our first working definition of AT (included above). This is the definition we use today, though narrowed—by device, category, application, and so on. The purposes of the Tech Act are included below:

> To provide financial assistance to States for capacity-building, advocacy activities and designated to assist each State to maintain and strengthen a permanent consumer-responsive comprehensive statewide program, that is designed to:
> - Increase the availability of, funding for, access to, and provision of AT devices and services;
> - Increase the active involvement of individuals with disabilities and their family members, guardians, advocates or authorized representatives in decisions related to the provision of AT devices and services;
> - Increase and promote coordination among and between State agencies, local public agencies and private entities (e.g., managed care providers) that are or could be involved in carrying out activities under this Act;
> - Increase the probability that individuals with disabilities of all ages will, to the extent appropriate, be able to secure and maintain possession of assistive technology devices as these individuals

make the transition between services offered by human services agencies or between settings of daily living;
- Increase the capacity of public agencies and private entities to provide and pay for AT devices and services on a statewide basis for individuals with disabilities of all ages.
- To identify Federal policies which facilitate payment for AT devices and services, to identify those Federal policies that impede such payment, and to eliminate inappropriate barriers to such payment. (Education and the Workforce, and Howard McKeon. Bill, GovInfo §. H.R.4278 [2004])

The ADA provides IHEs, as public and private entities, with the most relevant mandates regarding AT and auxiliary aids. The mandate for auxiliary aids and services included in the ADA states that places of public accommodation "shall take those steps that may be necessary to ensure that no individual with a disability is excluded, denied services, segregated or otherwise treated differently than other individuals because of the absence of auxiliary aids and services" (U.S. Department of Justice Civil Rights Division 2010c). The provision of AT falls under this mandate.

Assistive Technology: Categories and Examples

AT and auxiliary aids and services are well defined and well categorized. We are working in a time of a wealth of tech-based solutions and alternatives. We have a plethora of examples from the field concerning the successes and failures of AT and auxiliary aids related to the provision of access and accommodation.

Historically, assistive devices were developed for apparent disabilities. Examples include hearing cones, large print, tactile options, and mobility aids. The field of AT experienced a significant boom in the twentieth century, and now, in the twenty-first century, it continues to experience rapid advances and refinement. AT can now be organized into thirteen categories.

Aids for Daily Living

These devices and/or services fall under a category defined by the ADA as personal devices and services. From the ADA:

> Section 36.306 Personal devices and services. This part does not require a public accommodation to provide its customers, clients, or par-

ticipants with personal devices, such as wheelchairs; individually prescribed devices, such as prescription eyeglasses or hearing aids; or services of a personal nature including assistance in eating, toileting, or dressing. (U.S. Department of Justice Civil Rights Division 2010b)

In addition to some of the devices listed above, other examples include prostheses and adaptive daily devices (eating or hygiene tools, school supplies such as adaptive writing implements, devices that assist with typing, and so on).

One example of a personal service commonly requested in higher education is the provision of a Personal Care Assistant (PCA). A PCA may assist with the functions listed above or with providing medical care. This service may be required for different reasons. A student may need a PCA at the beginning and end of the day (for hygiene and dressing). In this case, providing access to a residence hall may be necessary for the PCA. In other cases, a student may require 24/7 support, which would require an evaluation of supporting accommodations that include access to classrooms, residence hall, dining center, and other appropriate facilities for the PCA. The student is responsible for the provision of the service.

Blind and Low Vision

Technology and services in this category depend on the nature of the student's disability. The major distinction in the technology is the difference between blindness and low vision. Essentially, technology will depend on the level of usable vision the student has. Technology geared toward low vision addresses factors such as magnification (Figure 9.1), color contrast, and field of vision. Technology geared toward blindness relies on alternatives to visual content such as text, video content, and graphics. As with every category, the specific approach is student dependent. For instance, a student with low vision may prefer to use computer-generated speech and/or magnification, and a student who is blind may prefer braille to a screen reader.

Many materials are already available in braille formats through institutions such as the National Library Service (NLS) at the Library of Congress. Other materials need to be converted. Some DSOs convert materials into braille in-house; some outsource it to organizations such as the National Braille Press. Others take a hybrid approach, formatting documents so that they can be read using a Refreshable Braille Display (Figure 9.2). Production of braille can be costly and time consuming. As much advance notice as possible is necessary to be able to provide content to the student in a timely manner. Ideally (and for true accessibility), all materials are provided to the student prior to the beginning of a semester. Some DSOs create a production schedule to be able to provide sections of the content prior to their use throughout the semester.

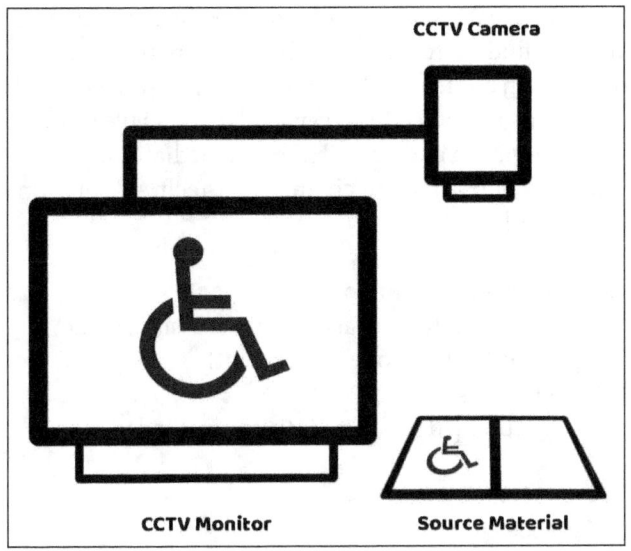

Figure 9.1 Personal Magnification Device (CCTV)

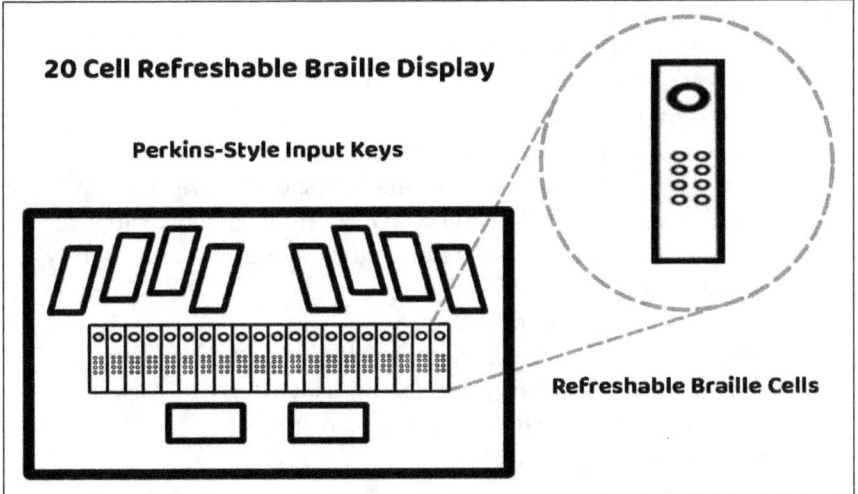

Figure 9.2 Refreshable Braille Display

Screen reader technology is one of the standards by which blind individuals access content. A screen reader has two major functions: to read text and to announce navigational structure of a document, web page, or other template. A sighted individual may look at a website and be able to visually determine how to navigate the page. They may go through operations such as scanning from heading to heading, assessing pictures and their relation to content, skipping over ads, and so on. A screen reader will announce the heading structure of a page, number of images, links, and so on. The screen reader allows the user to tab through each item as opposed to reading the full page, left to right, top to bottom, to find useful content. The next function is to read the text, which includes written content and alternative text associated with visual content. Content must be presented in screen reader accessible formats. This may require careful evaluation and considerable remediation.

Below are some examples of both low-tech and high-tech AT solutions for students with blindness or low vision:

- Examples of Low-Tech Vision Technology
  - Wayfinding: Large print/high contrast directional signs; ADA compliant signage (braille and proper placement)
  - Braille; braille label makers
  - Tactile indicators (e.g., "bump dots," raised stickers applied to computer keys)
  - Raised line paper
  - Canes (personal device)
  - Large print, high contrast reading materials
  - Magnifying glasses
  - Writing and signature templates
  - Markers/highlighters (for contrast)
  - Low scent markers
- Examples of High-Tech Vision Technology
  - Screen reader (includes text reading and spoken navigate—JAWS is the industry standard and NVDA is an open-source application. Both are used by blind individuals, along with accessibility testing tools).
  - Text reading devices or software.
  - Personal Magnification Devices (screen magnification software, handheld devices, and closed-circuit televisions or CCTVs).
  - "Talking" devices (calculator, dictionary).
  - Refreshable Braille Display.
  - Braille typing devices.

In addition to AT, an auxiliary aid and service is often required for students who are blind or have low vision. Alternative formats of course content, for instance, must be provided in conjunction with the chosen AT. Alternative format materials, which we typically refer to as "alt texts," provide a way for students with vision or other print-related disabilities to access material. Materials may include course content—such as textbooks, notes, associated readings, and web content—and any marketing and communications content. Alternative formats may include large print, high contrast, audio formats, braille, tactile graphics, and screen-reader accessible documents.

Communication

Communication is essential in a higher education setting. Centering on the student, communication either comes from or is directed toward them. This category refers to assistive and adaptive software or hardware as well as auxiliary aids and services that provide alternative ways to communicate with SWDs.

This category addresses major life activities such as speaking, listening, seeing, and hearing. While there are numerous examples of the ways in which our institutions communicate with students—course participation, emergency notifications, and so on—this category focuses primarily on technology associated with verbal and written communication.

Augmentative and Alternative Communication (AAC) are included as assistive technologies for communication. AAC as an auxiliary aid and service includes the type of technology and services provided by speech and language pathologists in a special education setting. In most cases, students who have utilized these services in elementary and secondary education settings will come to college with an established plan in place. Speech and language services are categorized as a personal service and not subject to provision by the IHE.

There are both high-tech and low-tech examples of AAC. Low-tech examples include simple solutions such as communication boards that allow students to point to icons that represent ideas or emotions they wish to convey or small blackboards/whiteboards that allow the student to communicate in writing. Other low-tech options include specialized interpreters. High-tech examples include computerized speech generators, of which there are sophisticated options for both desktop/laptop computers and mobile devices. A number of specialized devices are geared toward teaching speech and written communication, but these are far less common in a postsecondary setting.

Computers

Computers and mobile devices reign supreme these days in terms of AT for providing both access and accommodation. So many assistive functions that used to only exist in specialized devices and software are now baked-in features. Functions such as screen readers, text-to-speech, speech-to-text, display settings (high contrast, icon and cursor size), magnification, optical character recognition (converting images of text to readable text), and auto-generated captions are readily available. These features are regularly used by nondisabled users as well. Other accessibility features include sticky keys (allowing for one touch operation of complicated functions such as ctrl+alt+del), mono audio (eliminating information loss through independent left ear/right ear audio mixes), customizable keyboard shortcuts, on-screen keyboard (accessed with a point device or joystick control), speed controls (cursor speed, blink rates, double-click speed), and so on.

Computers are heavily utilized to access the web and other computer-based content. Students with sensory disabilities rely on computers to access captioned video content or in conjunction with a screen reader and keyboard-only navigation to access documents or web content. Accessibility of electronic content is covered in detail in Chapter 16.

While the student's computer is considered a personal device, there are settings in which the IHE may provide computers, such as computer labs, design and studio classes, science labs, libraries, laptop loaner programs, printing stations, and kiosks. If the institution provides computers, they must be accessible to all students. This might include providing accessibility software, such as a student's preferred screen reader or magnification software.

Deaf and Hard of Hearing

As with vision-related disabilities, there are categories of hearing loss with unique technology needs. Some hard-of-hearing technology presupposes a level of usable hearing. Deaf individuals or those who are hard of hearing may use personal devices such as hearing aids or cochlear implants. These devices can be used to amplify ambient and acoustic sound or to interface with other technology.

A major subcategory of this technology is assistive listening devices (Figure 9.3) that amplify the sound for either an individual or the entire audience. Something as simple as a microphone and PA system in a classroom may meet the needs of some students.

The basic premise for a personal amplification device is that the person speaking wears a transmitter (usually a lavalier, or lapel-style microphone), and the person listening wears a receiver. The message, which can include a feed from the microphone or a direct feed from other audio sources in the classroom, is broadcasted directly to the receiver device, which is then relayed to a listening device worn by the student. The listening device is typically either headphones or hearing aids. Most modern hearing aids are equipped with telecoils (T-Coils) that receive the broadcasted signal directly from the relay device. The signal can be broadcasted in multiple ways, such as FM signal, infrared (IR), or Wi-Fi; modern relay devices typically transmit via Bluetooth. The ADA requires that all new classrooms be wired for assistive listening devices with what is called a "loop." An individual inside the loop is able to receive the transmission, and those outside of the loop (i.e., not in the classroom) are not. This allows for students to receive the audio from the class they are in and not the neighboring one.

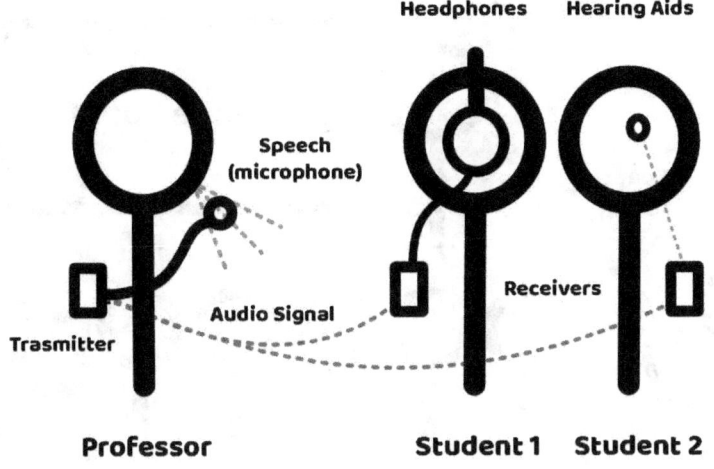

Figure 9.3 Assistive Listening System

Another major subcategory provides text alternatives to sound and spoken words. Most people are familiar with closed or open captions. Closed captions exist as a supplement and can be turned on or off; open captions are always on. Recorded content will need to have captioning tracks added, which should include spoken word and descriptions of additional audio. This can either be done by a captioner or by a number of options that autogenerate captions. These options are getting better as voice recognition technology progresses, but accuracy is a major consideration and content must be reviewed and remediated if necessary. Captions can also be created "on the fly," and the same options are available: created by a trained professional (Figure 9.4) or autogenerated. For DS providers, this choice typically means deciding between cost and accuracy. Trained professionals can be placed in the learning environment or can operate remotely, receiving an audio feed and transcribing the content live. As with hearing devices, the captioned content can be openly displayed or displayed to the student individually, usually on a mobile device or laptop. For captioned video content, both a caption track and a written transcript should be provided (Utah State University 2020). Provision of transcripts and captioning is an auxiliary service.

Examples of captioning/transcription (or speech-to-text services) are included below.

Verbatim: Nearly every word that is spoken is transcribed into text, including false starts or misspeaks and speaker repetition. Communication Access Realtime Translation (CART) is the system used to provide verbatim transcription services.

168 / The Interactive Process

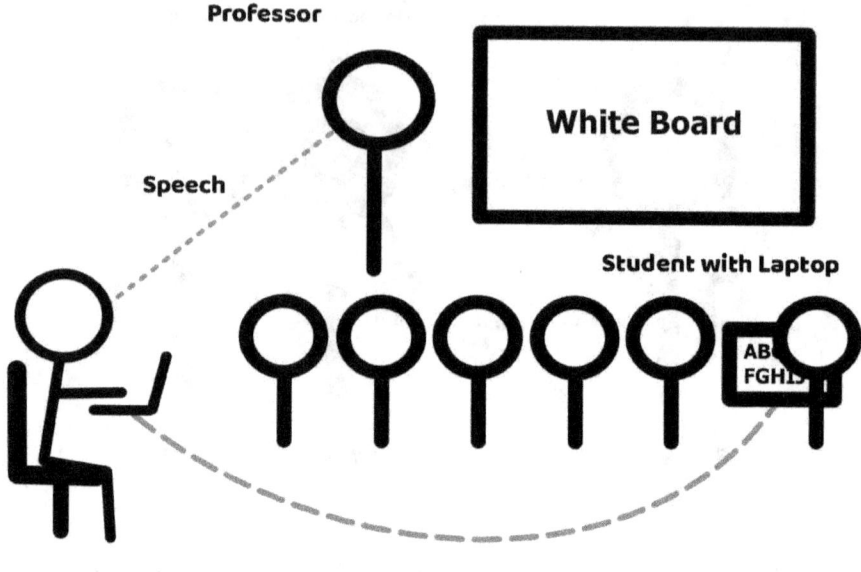

Figure 9.4 Real Time Captioning/Transcription

Meaning-for-Meaning: This type of system conveys the intended meaning in fewer words and formatted more visually, such as eliminating false starts, misspeaks, or repetition. C-Print and TypeWell are two systems that provide meaning-for-meaning transcription. (University of Texas at Austin 2021)

The other major category of auxiliary service is interpreting, typically ASL interpreting. Interpreting is a necessary auxiliary service that provides access to individuals whose primary mode of communication is ASL. It may need to be arranged as a service for individuals and for events. Individuals receiving ASL interpreting include students, campus community members, and anyone who may need to access our place of public accommodation.

For students, arranging interpreting will need to happen, first and foremost, for all classes and educational opportunities such as campus programming and events. These events can include student clubs and organizations, floor meetings in residence halls, guest speakers and conferences, performances such as plays or concerts, and so on. DSOs work with either independent contractors or interpreting agencies. When contracting interpreters for classes, the best approach is to create a contract on a semester-long basis. Fees for interpreting vary but include the interpreter's pay, an agency fee (if applicable), and travel/parking fees. It is an industry standard to schedule two interpreters for any engagement over an hour.

For our place of public accommodation, interpreting needs to be scheduled for campus visits and marquee events. Marquee events include events such as convocation, commencement, awards nights, induction ceremonies, etcetera. A general rule to follow is that for campus visits, the visitor should request interpreting as an accommodation in advance of the event, and for marquee events, interpreting should be arranged as part of the event.

Deafblind

Deaf-blindness refers to the condition of having concomitant hearing and vision losses. As with individual hearing or vision losses, there are spectrums of the nature of the condition. It is a common misconception that all Deafblind individuals have a complete loss of both senses, when in actuality, a considerable number of individuals have a combination of hearing loss and low vision. A combination of AT and auxiliary aids meeting the need of each individual disability should be considered.

A specific Deafblind auxiliary service is tactile interpreting (Figure 9.5). This type of service may be employed when an individual is not able to receive sign language interpreting through visual means. A tactile interpreter communicates through touch, such as finger spelling and other signs performed on an individual's hand.

Education

Educational AT are solutions geared toward learning, cognition, and development (Minnesota Guide to Assistive Technology n.d.). For the AT professional, or the DSP providing AT and auxiliary aids, educational AT are some

Figure 9.5
Tactile Interpreting

of the more common applications in our repertoire. A majority of the direct student contact we have as DSPs relates to academic support. Educational AT function to meet individual access and accommodation needs of SWDs, but they also support general college-level learning strategies.

Below are some examples of educational AT:

- Memory aids (words banks, vocabulary lists, formula sheets)
- Text-to-speech
- Speech-to-text
- Reminder systems
- Note-taking systems
- Mobile devices with assistive and accessibility features
- Audiobooks
- Recording applications
- Calendars
- Picture dictionaries

Environmental Applications

Environmental AT are devices used to adapt physical places of public accommodation. We are obligated to make our places of public accommodation accessible. Like all other categories and applications on this list, environmental AT provide necessary access to individuals with disabilities and benefit the community at large.

Below are some examples of environmental AT:

- Wheelchair ramps
- Wheelchair lifts
- Automatic door openers
- Wayfinding signage
- High visibility stair markings; tactile stair indicators (textured tape usually used on first and last step of staircase)
- Handrails and grab bars
- Dimmable lighting; light filters
- Buttons for environmental control
- Auditory indicators (such as for elevators)

Orthotics and Prosthetics

This category includes personal medical devices that are not provided to students by colleges or universities. Orthotics are devices employed to strengthen weakened muscles and connective tissue and/or realign or stabilize bones and joints. These include braces, specialized clothing and footwear, and footwear inserts. Prosthetics are devices or implants used to augment or replace missing or impaired digits or limbs.

Recreation, Sports, and Leisure

Beyond academics, our institutions offer activities, as part of orientation events or campus-life programming, that include physical games, contests, team-building exercises, games, puzzles, sports, and so on. One way to make such programming accessible is to provide activities that allow for multiple ways to participate, choice of activity, or alternatives. Another strategy is to employ AT and adaptive equipment. Some examples of devices in this category are listed below:

- Switch-enabled devices
- Sensory-adapted devices, such as talking devices
- Adaptive sports equipment
- Sensory games and toys (such as braille-embossed game boards and pieces)
- Accessible sports recreation locations; accessible facilities at these locations

Safety and Security

Safety and security are of utmost importance. Emergency notifications and alarms must be accessible. Fire alarms should include a visual indication, such as a strobe, in addition to the auditory tone. For emergency alarms in a residence hall where a Deaf student may sleep, a bed shaker alarm may be required. An auxiliary aid or service would be the creation, practicing, and enactment, if necessary, of an evacuation plan with a student and campus partners. These partners may include residence life, facilities, campus police or security, and any others who may assist in navigating and exiting spaces or who need to be aware of where students may be located during emergency scenarios.

Other safety and security technology is listed below:

- Adaptive door controls and locks
- Bathroom safety (grab bars and call buttons)
- Clearly marked exits and wayfinding
- Multisensory and accessible campus alert messaging systems

Seating and Positioning

Seating and positioning may be combined with mobility and transportation, but the separation here indicates the difference between campus-provided amenities (included in this category) and personal devices (included in the next category). The campus provides furniture for student use. Once something is provided, it must be accessible, or as we say in the field, "the ADA attaches." Classroom furniture (desks, chairs, lab and studio benches) and residence hall furniture are primary examples. Students may require desks or tables in the classroom, for instance, that are wheelchair accessible or stature/size appropriate. In residence halls, students are typically provided with a bed, desk, chair, and storage amenities. Many campuses have adjustable furniture in these locations, such as desks that raise and lower; some do not. One option for accessible furniture would be to provide a high-tech solution, such as an electric, adjustable desk. There are low-tech solutions as well, such as providing a higher or lower desk or even using blocks to raise a desk from the floor to the necessary height. In some cases, there are low-cost or no-cost solutions our facilities partners can provide. In other cases, assistive or adaptive devices may need to be purchased by the DSO.

Mobility and Transportation

This category includes personal devices (provided by the student), such as wheelchairs, canes, and crutches, in addition to environmental adaptations (provided by the campus) that allow the user to access our spaces, such as ramps, elevators, and chair lifts.

For campuses that provide transportation, accessible vehicles are a must. Owning and maintaining a fleet that consists entirely of accessible vehicles is ideal. If we think of "the ADA attaches" (as established above), when we provide transportation, at least one vehicle must be accessible to individuals with mobility-related disabilities. These types of vehicles can include features such as ground-level entry, wheelchair lifts, seating, storage capacity, and accessible seating.

Assistive Technology in Higher Education

AT is now a cornerstone in the provision of DS. It is a means of providing access and accommodations to SWDs, and it has grown to mean more than individual devices or a collective of devices. AT is a subset of what we do as DSPs and is often its own functional unit in DSOs.

For some DSOs, AT is coordinated by individual service providers and is part of the case management process. Other offices have dedicated AT specialists. Some offices have dedicated auxiliary aid specialists to oversee coordination of aids and services such as interpreting, captioning, and providing alternative format course materials. It is becoming more common for offices to have or create roles for specialists who focus on a combination of the two.

Like other DS roles, formal training in AT and auxiliary aids is not common. Many of the professionals who specialize in these areas come from other DS roles or have a background working in another educational or higher education setting, and there tends to be a lot of on-the-job training. There are, however, more opportunities for professional training in these fields, particularly in AT, than in DS provision overall. There are numerous degree and certificate programs on the postsecondary or postbaccalaureate level. In addition, many local and national organizations offer ongoing professional development related to AT, often offering free resources such as webinars and resources.

The field of DS has developed some conventions when it comes to AT and auxiliary aids. For instance, audio recording smart pens are a common way to support note-taking accommodations, and text-to-speech software is commonly used in conjunction with exam proctoring (these two examples are likely the most common high-tech AT applications used in the field today). DSOs differ, to some degree, in the types of accommodations, but these are a fairly common approach.

Ultimately, if we think back to the concept of major life activities and the way we define disability, we can quickly identify the functions associated with being a college student. Abilities such as reading, writing, typing, walking to class, sitting in a chair, hearing, seeing, listening, communicating, and participating are all part of the deal. When a student has a physical or mental condition that affects these abilities, chances are that a tech-based solution can assist in providing access. In this way, an AT evaluation can be woven into an intake appointment organically.

There are essentially two things you need to make work: you need to know the AT pieces that fit the functions, and you must have the pieces at your disposal. Knowing the pieces comes with time, a little research, communicating with colleagues, and listening to students. This chapter covers the most prevalent examples. Having the appropriate pieces of technology can take time, research, and know-how, but it takes resources too. It is important to know that there are options. Very few assistive applications are so proprietary that there are no alternatives. DSPs are a passionate bunch, and they are nothing if not curious, creative, and resourceful. It is hard to find a contemporary DS conference that does not include a presentation on low-cost/no-cost AT alternatives.

We already know that DSOs are often resource limited. Some fortunate offices have fully outfitted, state-of-the-art AT programs run by AT specialists and staff members dedicated to coordinating auxiliary aids and services. There are full-time staff positions in the field dedicated to coordinating captioning and interpreting, and they may have sufficient funding at their disposal. This takes dollars, institutional commitment, and sometimes grant funding and donor sponsorship. In many cases, resource allocation is driven by student population and disability demographics. Some schools have a higher population of Deaf students than others, for instance. On the other end of the resource spectrum, there are offices with one staff member with a one-pager on popular mobile apps and a dusty box of audio recorders. The majority of our colleagues sit somewhere in the middle. The important thing is how you make your resources work for students.

Table 9.2 lists some general rules for the DSP. These are presented in no particular order and are further defined throughout the remainder of this chapter. It is as simple and as difficult as that. Mastering this list takes time, and if it is approached with a student-centered mind, it will never be complete.

Determining if a Student Needs AT

Students' AT needs are initially evaluated during the intake interview. Many times, a student will request AT and auxiliary aids prior to the intake, and it is the responsibility of the DS provider to respond to these requests. DSPs should use good judgment when reviewing student requests, using the "reasonable" standard. Does the request align with what the student reports and documents regarding their disability, functional need, and other accommodation requests? A particular technology solution may be granted to address multiple needs. For instance, a student may request a recording solution based on hearing, speech, and language processing or a physical need that affects writing. In determining whether a technology solution is reasonable, functions must match.

Students will not always request AT. As DS providers, we build our repertoire and tailor our intake to include a variety of AT functions. For instance, it is good practice to include questions related to academic exercises such as reading, note-taking, taking exams, and writing papers. Technology solutions such as text-to-speech, speech-to-text, and smart pens or other audio notetakers may be broadly applicable. These can be provided through dedicated AT applications or built-in accessibility features on laptops or mobile devices. One approach is to introduce and provide a brief demo of the technology during the intake to discuss its application and gauge student interest. If necessary, the next step could be to provide resources, such as how-to guides for technology a student already uses, or to schedule a follow-up appointment with the student's service provider or an AT specialist.

Factors to consider when making the decision to grant AT and supporting accommodation include student history (previous accommodations and

TABLE 9.2 AT GUIDELINES TO FOLLOW	
Goals	Objectives
Research the field	• Be knowledgeable about options in the thirteen categories of AT • Have a sense of how different options work, what functions they address, and accepted practices in the field • Source and collect training resources for students
Stay current; stay competitive	• Watch the field for trends • Understand the technology students are using • Be mindful of AT that students expect (understand the trends, communicate with colleagues, and listen to students)
Conduct a cost analysis and know your alternatives	• Consider the cost of single licenses vs. institutional licenses for software • Explore low-cost/no-cost alternatives • Familiarize yourself with assistive and adaptive features built into consumer devices such as smart phones • Consider single function/multifunction solutions as they pertain to your needs and resources
Identify multifunction implements and applications	• Some software solutions are single function (e.g., dedicated text-to-speech application); others are multifunction (e.g., text-to-speech platform with note-taking, word prediction, mind-mapping, and other features built in) • Identify AT solutions that can be used in multiple settings (e.g., a portable CCTV can be used in class to view the board as well as in an exam setting to view exam materials)
Know the necessary resources	• Be aware of readily available adaptive solutions (such as mobile accessibility applications and operating system features) and how they mitigate functional limitations • Identify your state's AT project funded under the Tech Act • Find out if your institution has contracted vendors for ASL or captioning (sometimes other offices engage these services); research options in your area • Understand the cost, lead time, and production time offered by your vendors (ASL, captioning, braille, etc.)
Take stock of what you have	• Inventory the tech owned by the DSO (common solutions include text-to-speech, speech-to-text, and recording devices) • Identify "consumables" such as batteries, ink, and paper for smart pens, extra charging cables, and so on • Determine whether other departments have technology that can be used as AT or for accessibility initiatives (e.g., does media services have software that can create captions? Do the library or print shop have equipment that can unbind or rebind a book or access to scanning equipment?) • Understand what classroom technology is used on campus; understand the capability
Know how and why it works	• Learn your tech (at least in principle) • Be able to perform simple tasks such as installing software and providing hardware; be knowledge about setup, configuration, and basic troubleshooting

(continued)

TABLE 9.2   AT GUIDELINES TO FOLLOW (*continued*)

Goals	Objectives
Cultivate partners	• Identify other departments that can leverage AT solutions (e.g., text-to-speech can be used by international students and writing tutors); there are often significant volume discounts for software licenses • Identify where other departments can help defray costs • IT can assist with installation, configuration, and troubleshooting of AT devices

interventions), level of functional need, resource availability, and the "stakes." Remember, there are often multiple solutions for providing AT, such as dedicated platforms or low-cost/no-cost alternatives. Students may also have their own specialized AT or have AT applications at their disposal, whether they know it or not. In these cases, the DS provider's role may be to grant supporting accommodations, such as allowance for AT in the classroom and on exams. Also remember that the stakes will vary from accommodation to access-level needs. Accommodation-level needs have more wiggle room for discussing alternatives. Access-level auxiliary aids and services may require a considerably higher level of coordination and resources, so in some cases, deeper evaluation may be needed.

Auxiliary services such as live captioning and ASL interpreting are among the highest in level of cost and coordination but, coincidentally, may require a lower level of evaluation. Think back to Chapter 6 on documentation and the intake process. Some diagnoses adhere to the "predictable assessment" standard. For instance, Deafness may not require as high a level of documentation to establish. Once established as a disability, which may be accomplished by demonstration alone, the interactive process shifts to evaluating the right solution. Asking students about the impact of their disability, as well as their other abilities, helps determine the appropriate level of AT and auxiliary aids. For sensory-based disabilities and accommodation requests, it is important to know the student's preferred mode of communication and the level at which they can communicate this way. For instance, is the student requesting interpreting fluent in ASL? If so, when and where will they require interpreting? Is the student requesting braille fluent in braille? If so, do they read contracted or uncontracted braille? If a student is requesting alternative format materials, what factors must be considered, and what formats are required? Does the student just need readable text, or do graphics need to be described? Is a PDF or Word document preferable? Why? What software does the student use to access materials? Is text size, color contrast, pagination, heading and navigation structure, or number of columns necessary to consider? And, as always, what resources and capabilities does the DSO have at its disposal, what technology may need to be acquired, what services may need to be arranged, and what additional training might the DSP or your student need?

Implementing Assistive Technology and Auxiliary Aids and Services

Once an eligibility determination is made, the appropriate AT or auxiliary aid is selected, and supporting accommodations are granted, there needs to be an implementation plan. Typically, a student will make the initial disclosure to faculty regarding their status with the DSO and the types and nature of accommodations they are permitted to use. In some cases, advanced notice and additional preparation are required, and having outreach come directly from the DSO is appropriate. This process can be done by having the student make an initial disclosure, coauthoring outreach with the student, or obtaining the student's consent to outreach on their behalf. Outreach begins with notification of a granted accommodation. For instance, a faculty member should have advanced notice that an ASL interpreter will be attending their class. The classroom itself may need to be evaluated for size and arrangement of space. A student should notify their professor if they need to record, and if necessary, the DSP should be available to navigate the accommodation. If an assistive listening system will be used, we need to make sure that faculty have access to the right equipment and training.

Another important implementation measure is sourcing the technology or auxiliary aid or service. This step, too, may require lead time. It is important to recall the adage that we do not build the ramp when the wheelchair user shows up. Anticipating needs is important, but as discussed, covering all bases in advance is not always possible. Planning may include having preferred vendors lined up, having technology on hand, knowing how technology works, understanding classroom technology on campus, having infrastructure and workflows for sourcing, creating alternative format materials, and so on. Sometimes, however, we need to find solutions and learn how to implement them on the fly. Know the vendors and be familiar with common features of mobile and desktop technology. Create or tap into a network of colleagues in the field; there is a wealth of knowledge out there.

In some cases, it will be necessary for the DSO to provide technology, which may, in turn, require training. Remember, there is a difference between personal devices and AT the school can provide. In most cases, a student's laptop and mobile device will be their own responsibility. Some IHEs provide students with laptops. These need to be accessible, which may require the school to purchase and provide AT, such as screen reader software. There are strategic decisions a DSO can make regarding provision of technology.

For instance, in some cases, it is more cost effective to purchase a Refreshable Braille Display for use with digital files of texts than to have all course content physically printed in braille. If this is the first time the student is using a Refreshable Braille Display device, training may be necessary and must be provided by the institution. Typically, vendors of these types of devices offer training, which may or may not be included in the cost of entry.

Many pieces of AT require consumables. Audio recording smart pens use ink and require the use of special paper. Various devices require specialized charging cables. And do not forget the batteries! It is important to include consumables in your implementation plan with your student, including what you will provide and what the student will provide.

From an operational standpoint, tracking AT loans and collecting signed loaner agreements from students are standard practices. AT can be expensive, and many devices can be reused. Consult with campus officials to determine if and how students can be billed if a piece of AT is lost, stolen, or damaged.

Current and Emerging Trends in Assistive Technology

The most important and disruptive change to the field of AT has been the advent of smart technology. More and more students have assistive and adaptive features at their fingertips, and many students are already using these tools. These applications are getting better and better and are becoming more mainstream with every new generation of iPhone or Android device. Native accessibility tools and third-party applications are rapidly taking the place of specialized devices. This is not exactly new technology, but it is here to stay, and every DSP should be familiar with how this type of technology can meet the access needs of students.

Some emerging technology applications have clear connections to the field of AT, and others have the potential to be high impact but may take creative leveraging. Rapid prototyping and 3D printing have been used extensively in the creation of medical devices, implants, and prosthetics. Devices such as adaptive tools, buttons, joysticks, tool and utensil grips, book holders, and so on are being printed and becoming more mainstream every day. Emerging technology is not without challenges, though. Some technology, such as virtual or augmented reality, may be the next disruptive technological force to be reckoned with by higher education. The ability to interact with a real-time environment or explore virtual recreations of real environments and imagined worlds holds undeniable teaching power. How does a student with low vision participate? Hand tracking technology is rapidly advancing and is often required to navigate virtual reality applications. How does the person without the ability to grip a control or move with precision use this technology? As DSPs, we are not yet equipped to answer these questions, but we can educate our communities and urge caution with implementation. We can be part of the process for brainstorming alternatives. If workarounds and alternatives do not exist, the technology should not be used until it can be made accessible.

We recognize that many campuses do not have identified processes for conducting accessibility audits at the time of technology procurement. We also recognize that DSOs may not have the authority to deny the adoption of a piece of technology. If the technology is something a faculty or academic department is using in an exploratory way, the DSO might not even know about it. Make inroads with campus partners. Make accessibility and the appropriate use of technology to enhance education your new mantra. Evaluating technology for accessibility is covered in detail in Chapter 16.

In Summary

Today, AT is a field unto itself. AT is not just about its collective devices and software applications but the way we evaluate and meet the needs of diverse learners. The more we learn about AT and the more the technology progresses, the more it becomes apparent that AT has broader applications. It will become easier to accommodate students moving forward, and accessibility awareness and compliance efforts are advancing. DS is nowhere near putting itself out of work when it comes to AT. In fact, quite the opposite. As campuses incorporate more tech-enhanced learning, AT usage will likely advance. This development provides an opportunity for DSOs to form stronger partnerships with other offices on campus. More partnerships and more awareness can translate into more resource sharing and, ultimately, better tools for SWDs. The more we can leverage and share these tools, the more we can advocate for campus-wide accessibility. AT is more important now than ever before, and DS has a unique footing. We may not be tech experts, and we may not have all the best tools or be replete with resources, but we know accessibility. Even if we do not know all the ways to make accessibility happen, we know the spirit behind it and how to advocate for students. Technology—in particular, Assistive Technology—is the way forward.

▶ Reflective Exercise

Professor Clayton teaches Contemporary Moral Issues, a highly discussion-based course for which weekly debate sessions are part of the curriculum. Professor Clayton moderates the debates, and students are expected to bring topics for discussion. Students are made aware at the beginning of the semester that there will be a section of questions on the midterm and final exams pertaining to the content of these discussions. Lauren, a philosophy major in the college's honors program, is eligible for audio recording and note-taking accommodations. Her preferred method of note-taking is to use an audio recording smart pen. Given the sensitive nature of the content, Professor Clayton is concerned that Lauren's use of audio recording will alter the integrity of the discussions and sanctity of the learning environment. Specifically, he is concerned that students will be hesitant to participate if they know they are being recorded. What are your IHE's policies related to audio recording? What are the applicable laws in your area regarding consent to record audio? How might you enter the interactive process with Professor Clayton to evaluate (1) the impact of Lauren's use of AT and (2) possible alternatives?

Supplemental Job Aids

The following Supplemental Job Aids can be found at https://scholarshare.temple.edu/handle/20.500.12613/8373:

- Assistive Technology Evaluation Form
- Equipment Agreement Option 1
- Equipment Agreement Option 2
- Alternative Course Material Request Form
- Faculty Resource: Working with Disability-Related Interpreters

10

Case Management

Just about every job description for a DSP includes some mention of "case management," followed by a series of responsibilities further contextualizing what that entails. While case management duties within a DSO are operationalized differently from campus to campus, the core objectives remain relatively the same: remove barriers; provide timely and effective interventions to ensure full and equal access; and build bridges between students and resources. These goals cannot be accomplished by working in silos. As such, case management is predicated on effective collaboration and communication—a sense of shared responsibility to align students with resources and support. An equally important element of case management—for which many of us have limited time—is record keeping. For an office charged with upholding legal mandates, documenting interactions with students is essential and ongoing; plus, it keeps our general counsel's office happy in the event of a complaint. This chapter outlines the role of case management throughout the life cycle of a student.

▶ Guiding Questions

1. What are some important qualities of case managers?
2. What are the core components of the case management process?
3. What are some best practices for conducting an intake interview?
4. What are some effective ways to establish rapport with students?
5. How should DSPs respond to sensitive student disclosures?

Introduction

Case management is a generic term with no singularly recognized definition. According to the Case Management Society of America (CMSA), case management is "a collaborative process of assessment, planning, facilitation, care coordination, evaluation, and advocacy for options and services to meet an individual's ... needs" (CMSA 2021). While this definition is intended for those who work in health care professions, it seamlessly translates to what case management means to DSPs.

Since case management has been variously described and operationalized in our discipline, we can turn to AHEAD's Professional Standards (AHEAD 2021a) outlined in Table 10.1 for a point of reference outlining the work we do directly with and on behalf of students:

> Direct Service: Providing services directly to students or acting on behalf of students with members of the campus community. (AHEAD 2021a)

Rather than a single, time-limited encounter, case management is more of a process that encompasses a range of steps. Distilled into smaller components, case management's four primary stages are explored in greater detail.

Intake

Case management begins on the first substantive interaction with a student. Typically, this interaction occurs after matriculation at the point of an intake assessment, but in more complex cases can occur sooner. During an intake meeting, the DSP gathers information from the student, establishes trust, and determines how the student can be supported.

Needs Assessment

The needs assessment stage builds on information collected during the intake and delves into greater depth about a student's strengths, interests, goals, needs, and barriers. Needs assessment is not a static step but rather an ongoing process of engagement as a student's circumstances change over time.

Service Coordination

Service planning requires collaboration with on- and off-campus partners to enhance service delivery. This stage involves identifying and connecting a student with appropriate resources to facilitate their needs and goals.

TABLE 10.1 AHEAD'S PROFESSIONAL STANDARDS FOR DIRECT SERVICE

AHEAD's Professional Standards for Direct Service		
Maintains confidential student records	Communicates information regarding program activities and services to student	Distributes program brochure or handbook to campus department
Serves as an advocate for students with faculty or administrators	Consults with faculty regarding the instructional needs of students	Processes complaints/ grievances from students
Determines program eligibility for services based upon documentation of a disability	Consults with institutional administrators regarding the needs of students	Provides personal/ individual counseling to students relating to disability issues
Determines program eligibility for services based upon documentation of a disability	Consults with other campus departments regarding the needs of students	Coordinates assistants for students
Responds to inquiries from prospective students or their parents	Communicates information regarding program services to the campus community	Provides academic advisement to students relating to disability issues
Consults with students about appropriate individualized accommodations based upon documentation	Arranges auxiliary aids for students	Provides counseling/ advisement to enhance student development
Provides information to students regarding their legal rights and responsibilities	Arranges individualized accommodations for students	Assists students in self-monitoring the effectiveness of accommodations

Source: AHEAD 2021a

Monitoring

During the monitoring stage, DSPs evaluate the effectiveness of accommodations and interventions, identify service gaps, and strategize new referrals or supports to provide comprehensive and holistic student support.

Before we dive deeper into each of these stages, let us explore the various case management roles on campus.

Case Manager Roles

Centered on providing holistic student support, case managers coordinate efforts toward bettering the experiences of students. Integral to our role is gathering data, assessing needs, and deploying individualized interventions. We "broker resources and referrals while empowering the individual to advocate for themselves and their desired outcomes. Case managers maintain an ongoing connection with students to provide guidance, evaluate changes . . . ensure efficacy of interventions, and monitor the need for adjusted or additional resources" (NABITA 2020). If there is one word underpinning the work we do, it is collaboration. In our role, we work with students, families, health care providers, community agencies, and colleagues in an ever-broadening array of settings.

Many of our student service–oriented colleagues also serve as case managers. While the scope of case management responsibilities may vary across settings, our practices remain relatively similar: engage students in a collaborative process of identifying, assessing, coordinating, and monitoring supportive resources. As such, it is important to distinguish between those of us operating in a clinical versus nonclinical capacity. A summary of the scope and privacy differences is referenced in Table 10.2.

Our colleagues in college counseling and health centers are considered clinical case managers. The institution hires them to operate in a clinical capacity by providing treatment to students with chronic or shorter-term medical and mental health needs. Like us, they conduct intake interviews, evaluate needs, triage, facilitate services, and monitor students' well-being.

With the rising tide of students in distress and our efforts to retain them, we are seeing a proliferation of nonclinical case manager roles within the higher education space.

Nonclinical case managers are housed within their own student support and case management office or in the offices of dean of students, residence life, student conduct, or Title IX. They work adjacent to behavioral intervention teams with the primary function of supporting students who are facing crises, experiencing stress, and encountering barriers that impede success.

Like DSPs, academic advisors, academic support staff, and residence life liaisons provide case management services with a shared goal of providing support, not therapy.

TABLE 10.2 CLINICAL VS. NONCLINICAL PRIVACY REGULATIONS	
Clinical	Nonclinical
Hold a clinical license	May be licensed but does not operate under it
Provide *treatment* or care for medical or mental health needs	Provide *support*, resources, and nonclinical counseling
Governed by state confidentiality laws/ HIPAA	Governed by FERPA
Notes kept in a privileged database	Notes part of a student's educational record
Source: Adapted from Schiemann 2019	

Qualities of Case Manager

The work of a DSP is not easy. Centering our work is our obligation to level the playing field, advocate for best practices, and enable a high-quality academic experience for SWDs, and case management is essential to facilitating the interactive process. Often, we are called on to be nimble and efficient problem solvers in a high-need, high-demand, no-two-days-are-the-same environment. As case managers, we facilitate the interactive process and serve as the vital link between students and institutional partners. Foundational to our role in providing a welcoming, supportive, and inclusive environment are core interpersonal qualities that underlie our work: empathy, advocacy skills, cultural competence, communications skills, agility, and patience.

Recognize, Respond, and Refer: Student Disclosures

At the outset of the intake process and as part of establishing rapport, it is good practice to communicate the intent to treat all personal information with the strictest confidentiality. Further, out of respect for privacy, we should consider advising students that we will err on the side of confidentiality whenever possible and not release information without their expressed consent. At the same time, it is crucial that we let students know up front the boundaries of confidentiality—for compelling and legitimate educational reasons, we may be required to release information without consent. While federal, state, and/or ethical mandates and guidelines differ, such instances may include (1) imminent danger to self/others; (2) disclosure of an incident of sexual harassment, sexual assault, dating violence, or stalking; or (3) when ordered to release information as part of a court order. What happens when we observe, suspect, or when students disclose information that we are required to share, as in cases of threats involving harm to self/others or unmitigated disorderly, unresponsive, or incoherent behavior? Every institution should have a protocol for recognizing and responding to students in distress, and we should be familiar with and have handy contact and referral information.

Due to the personal nature of the conversations we have with students in concert with the rising mental health epidemic, it is not uncommon to encounter students who disclose suicidality or self-harm. While this disclosure can be very distressing, it is incumbent on us to communicate our concern and take immediate action. One of the first steps following disclosure is to offer reassurance of the DSO's willingness to help. Appropriate responses might be, "You are not alone in this. I'm here to help you," or "You may not believe it now, but the way you are feeling will change." The next step is to determine whether the student is in danger of acting on suicidal feelings. DSPs may consider asking the student in a direct but sensitive manner whether they have a specific plan and intend to act on it.

When imminent danger is known or suspected, such as in the case of a student with active suicidal ideation and intent, campus protocol may indicate calling campus police for on-campus situations or 911 or the local police department for off-campus situations. In cases where it is unclear, it may be appropriate to call behavioral health services, the dean of students' office, or case management. Be familiar with campus protocols and resources, as each campus should have a guide setting forth specific procedures for various levels of student distress.

Another type of sensitive disclosure is that of gender-based harassment or interpersonal violence (IPV). During the intake process, we may find ourselves in the position of suspecting or knowing that a student has been impacted by IPV (i.e., sexual assault, intimate partner violence, sexual exploitation, stalking, or harassment). This information may come by way of direct disclosure from the student or through documentation. Statistically, we know that most victims of sexual violence and stalking (of all gender identities) report that it first occurred prior to the age of twenty-five (Smith et al. 2018) and that 90 percent of sexual assault victims on college campuses choose not to report their experience to anyone.

Unless we are serving in a capacity as a chaplain, counselor, or medical provider, we are considered nonconfidential and mandatory reporters of sexual misconduct. It is important to let the student know that disclosures of IPV need to be reported to the institution—should they not desire to file a report, it might be best to keep the details vague. If it appears a student is about to disclose sexual misconduct, a potential response is the following:

> I apologize for interrupting, but I want to let you know that I am not a confidential resource on campus, which means that I will need to share anything you tell me about an experience of sexual misconduct with our Title IX Coordinator. This is just our college policy, which aims to ensure you receive the resources and support you may need. I can let you know who the confidential resources on campus are or connect you with them. I want you to be able to make a choice about who you feel comfortable sharing with.

If the student chooses to disclose, they should be met with a supportive, nonjudgmental response. One of the most important things is to listen attentively and show compassion and concern. Responses such as, "I am so sorry you experienced that," "No one deserves to be treated that way," or "How can I support you" help the students know that they are not alone and that help is available. Avoid blaming the student or asking questions that could imply fault, such as "Were you drinking?" Acknowledge the disclosure and affirm that sharing their account takes courage: "Thank you for sharing that with me. I am here to support you." Avoid offering any advice on what the student should do but encourage the student to report the incident or seek medical or mental health attention. It is important to help the student regain power lost in the incident. If the student would like assistance, connect them with the appropriate campus office where they can speak confidentially or seek resources. If appropriate, assist them in setting up a counseling appointment or walk them over to health services. Remember, mandated reporters must follow up by submitting a crime-related report or contacting the Title IX office. Timelines and reporting details may vary by institution.

Behavioral Intervention Teams

In recent years, behavioral intervention teams have either broadened their mission or morphed into different entities tasked with not only assessing threats but also offering more generalized and coordinated support to students in need. With names such as Students of Concern Team (SOC), CARE Team, Campus Assessment Team (CAT), these multidisciplinary teams have as a mission to proactively share information and formulate plans to assist students struggling with challenges presented by physical or mental health, personal loss, academics, finances, or relationships.

Many DSOs have representation on the behavioral intervention team. As consultants, we identify disability-related behaviors that may impede student success or act as a referral source for students who present with concerning behaviors. Be sure to consult the campus framework for guiding students in distress to behavioral intervention teams and other support resources.

The Four Components of Case Management

Current trends in DS student data suggest that the profiles of entering college students are becoming increasingly complex. The reality is that many students are presenting with multiple and comorbid conditions that require a higher level of case management. If prospective students have done their due diligence, they have reached out in advance of enrollment to inquire about access to supports and services that will facilitate their success. As such, it is not uncommon for case management to begin before the official intake appointment and even before depositing. Some of us work closely with our admissions and student engagement offices to coordinate accommodations such as interpreters, transportation assistance, or alternative text formats during welcome events and other precollege events such as orientation.

Earlier in this chapter, we identified four phases of the case management process—intake, needs assessment, service coordination, and monitoring. We now take a deeper look into each of these components.

Intake

The technical and operational components of intake are detailed in Chapter 6, but given that intake is the entry point to the case management process, it is important to cover intake in this chapter. The success of case management is dependent on the relationship between the DSP and the student. Intake is not only a meeting to comply with the interactive process requirements of the ADA and to generate information but also a place to establish a rapport.

Intake Interview

As detailed in Chapter 6, intake meetings are semistructured interviews that serve as an opportunity for students to clarify their needs and familiarize themselves with the DS staff, services, procedures, and facilities. While this meeting is often structured via guiding questions, students should expect an interactive and open dialogue through which their needs will be explored. During intake, the DSP listens intently to the student's narrative and makes observations about their conversational style (e.g., eye contact, speech characteristics, response latency, thought processes), movements and gestures, and memory. It is important to note that not all DSOs have the time and resources to go into the level of detail discussed below. The intent of this information is to outline the ideal so that DSPs can scale to their needs but still obtain the essential information.

Recognizing that students may be seeking accommodations independently for the first time or requesting them at a time of considerable distress, we need to remain mindful that the process can feel overwhelming. Some students may not be fluent in discussing their needs and barriers or may feel uncomfortable communicating personal information. They may have many questions or not know what to ask. It is essential to provide a welcoming and safe space where students are invited to be authentic and share their lived experiences. One way to facilitate a productive meeting is to provide interview questions in advance and encourage students to solicit information from others as appropriate to plan talking points for the discussion.

The role of DSP as case manager is multilayered and cross-functional. It starts at the first point of contact with the student but really takes shape and springs into action post-intake and throughout the student's experience. Effective relationships between DSPs and students require trust. We are asking students to disclose very personal and often stigmatizing information. The vulnerability of this moment should not be overlooked, and these first few interactions are critical in setting the tone for a safe and respectful dynamic.

A key to building rapport is breaking the ice and putting the student at ease about the process. Engaging in the accommodation process can be very intimidating, and many students may be coming from situations where they or their support systems had to fight for additional resources throughout their schooling. Their guards and defenses may already be activated at the initial point of contact. That, combined with the dramatic differences between high school special education services and college accommodations, can cause additional friction because the institution can be interpreted as not being accommodating or sensitive to the needs of the student. These factors, if not handled with care, can set the process off on the wrong foot and make it challenging to right the course.

To assuage any worries about the meeting and clarify expectations, it is good practice to begin by framing the meeting's objectives and agenda. Consider a variation of the following:

> Thank you for completing the disclosure form and submitting documentation. I understand that you are interested in discussing academic and housing accommodations. I look forward to assisting you through this process. In the next hour, I would like to understand your needs better, so I will be asking questions about your disability and how it has impacted you in various settings. Together, we will explore your needs and goals and figure out which accommodations, supports, and services will best support you.

Another way to break the ice and send the message that this relationship can be about more than just academic accommodations is to make sure students know that the DSO is a private space. It is important to differentiate between private and confidential. Most of us are not confidential and fall under the mandated reporter obligations. By letting students know, they are informed about what can and cannot remain private, which creates trust. Always let students know of the confidential spaces on campus (usually mental health counseling services) and break down the mandated reporting process. Even though it is not technically confidential, the privacy offered by the DSO can be a relief to students who are trying to build autonomy and develop their identities.

DSPs should always lead with openness and authentic interest about where the student is coming from and their expectations, strengths, challenges, and concerns. The student and DSP form a type of alliance to ensure appropriate coordination of services (Lukersmith, Millington, and Salvador-Carulla

2016). There will be time to educate students and their support systems about how the ADA differs from the IDEA, but the focus should remain on what we *can* do to assist the student in accessing the programs and services of the institution instead of what supports and services are not available in college.

Reframing the conversation from IEP and 504 accommodations or suggested accommodations from a neuropsychological evaluation to a focus on barriers to access in college is an effective strategy for building rapport with students. Highlighting the rich array of resources available—such as tutoring, academic advising, mental health counseling, financial aid resources, campus employment opportunities, mentoring, clubs and organizations, recreational activities, health and wellness supports, and the myriad of other opportunities that exist on college campuses—encourages the student to seek the built-in collegiate support they need. Listing and encouraging students to seek out these resources can be destigmatizing because it emphasizes that these are common challenges for all students regardless of disability status. An added benefit to noting these resources is that doing so helps to define reasonable accommodation in terms of barrier reduction.

The meeting is also an opportunity for the DSP to assess the need for additional services and supports beyond the student's requests. Depending on the completeness of a student's request and whether the DSP makes individual (vs. committee) determinations of eligibility, accommodations may be approved during the intake meeting.

Establishing the Role of Parents and Families

At admissions events and through preentry phone calls, emails, and meetings, we often field concerns from parents and families long before their student decides to enroll. We understand the active role that many families play in the K–12 setting and the trepidation that accompanies their student's impending independence. Some families have had to battle to get their student's needs met and anticipate a continued adversarial experience; others are accustomed to being overinvolved, influencing every facet of their student's development. Regardless of whether family involvement has been appropriate or not, families may be fraught with legitimate concerns about their student's potential for a successful college experience and how we will meet their needs. This concern is especially common for students who have not developed a sense of personal autonomy or who are easily overwhelmed with transitions. The role families play in the success of their students should not be underestimated. Peripheral support can be helpful as students navigate complex and intimidating institutional structures. For these reasons, it may be appropriate to allow some level of family engagement in the process per the student's wishes, most notably as students are transitioning to college.

Most of us are guided by a model of student empowerment. We understand that while disabled students have limitations and face barriers that others do not, self-determination should be the goal for every college student. As such, we educate and guide students about their responsibility to initiate contact and engage with our office. It is important to make it clear that the process for requesting accommodations requires active participation by the student. While many of us feel comfortable allowing a family member to accompany the student to the intake meeting, we only do so at the student's directive. To gauge a student's comfort level with parent participation, we might address the student by saying the following:

> I see that you have someone with you today. It is up to you as to whether you would like for them to join us. If you'd like, we can talk first and have your family member join us at the end of our meeting, or they are welcome to sit in with us from the beginning. It's your choice.

With overbearing families, take the opportunity to establish boundaries sensitively but firmly at the start of the meeting. One way to navigate this tricky conversation is through the lens of skill building. Consider setting the tone by communicating that one of the learning objectives of involvement with the DSO is to help students develop self-advocacy skills. To facilitate participation, assess how well students understand their disability, are aware of their strengths and challenges, identify barriers, and articulate their need for accommodations. Follow up by acknowledging that the student's insights and input are welcome and valued.

Needs Assessment

The information gathered during the intake process begins to organize and take shape to advise the next component of case management—needs assessment. During this stage, the case manager assesses all the information at their disposal and develops an understanding of the student's needs and goals and potential pathways for addressing them. Keeping in mind that case management is an ongoing, iterative process, needs may require reassessment at any point in the student's life cycle. We have established that case management is a collaborative process of which the student's sense of agency and effort are critical components.

Advocacy

Advocacy and self-agency are essential skills for success, and students come to college at varying levels of proficiency in these areas. As case managers, DSPs are well positioned to introduce these concepts to the students on their caseload. Assisting students in building self-advocacy skills can be a great bridge from the initial intake/accommodation determination portion of the relationship to a longer-term connection with the student as they advance in their academic career.

Helping students build this skillset moves the connection beyond the transactional to a dynamic that really focuses on the individualized needs of the student. While many large IHEs do not have the service model or resources to sustain this level of service, there are most likely people or departments at these institutions responsible for providing these types of supports. Referrals are an essential component of quality case management, and more information on that topic is found later in this chapter.

Strong self-advocacy skills are boosted by a student's understanding of their disability and of what works best for them in terms of taking in information and demonstrating knowledge. Case managers have a variety of tools at their fingertips to help students gain a better understanding of who they are as learners. Learning style inventories, interest assessments, informational interviewing strategies, and time management resources are all excellent ways to start this conversation and help the student realize that they need to take responsibility for their academic and social experience.

An understanding of how relevant access laws and legislation interact with students' needs (and how they do not) is another powerful tool for building self-advocacy skills. This understanding can be very helpful with students who are reluctant to access the supports to which they are entitled because they do not want special treatment or are sick of being labeled. Educating students about how these supports are rooted in important and groundbreaking legislation and have benefits extending beyond college may help them reach their goals.

Normalizing the fact that having a disability can be very challenging and frustrating and that the case management relationship is a great place to work out those emotions can clear the space for a student to take ownership of their situation. The combination of knowing the impact of a disability, understanding legal rights, normalizing struggle, and finding a sense of community is a confidence-boosting package. Case managers can facilitate the evolution to empowered self-advocacy by helping students develop these skills and knowledge areas throughout their college experience. This is not a quick process, but it is essential in helping SWDs acclimate to the college environment and beyond.

Identify Key Challenges, Needs, and Interests

Undoubtedly, some of our meetings with students can seem very transactional. Students may come to us with an unremarkable history, a routine accommodation request (e.g., extended time on exams), and a low need for future engagement with our office. For other students, our encounters are more relational. Given the intimate nature of our conversations and our access to sometimes deeply personal information gathered through families, colleagues, and health care providers, we are in a unique position to connect with students, cultivate a sense of belonging, introduce resources, and facilitate personal development.

As DSPs, we are trained to identify disability-related environmental, programmatic, and attitudinal barriers that limit access and to determine remedies—through reframing and awareness conversations, inclusive design, or accommodations—so students can enjoy full and equal participation in all that our campuses offer. Our analysis takes into account academic, housing, dietary, AT, and personal needs: self-advocacy, executive functioning, communication, and socialization. In our role as case managers, our scope is broadened to a more holistic lens through the consideration of non-disability-related barriers that prevent students from fully participating. For some students, societal inequalities or personal circumstances pose impediments to basic needs being met. When assessing needs, consider barriers and marginalization through a broader perspective. Do students need assistance with health care, food, transportation, technology, books, housing, or finances?

We also consider needs from a strengths-based perspective. What talents, goals, and interests do students have that they would like to cultivate? How can we direct them to opportunities where they can develop their interests and showcase their capabilities? As we strive to connect students with services and resources to enhance their wellness and optimize their success, it is important that we remain aware of programs and activities to help them find a sense of belonging, feel connected, and shine in areas where they have potential.

Service Coordination

As we have established, the role of a case manager not only involves direct services but also coordination and referral. Because we cannot be all things to all students—though that sometimes feels like the expectation—being able to connect students with appropriate resources is vital to our role.

For first-time college students transitioning from high school, independent management of academic and social environments may be a very new concept. Students may be very accustomed to the prescribed routines of the school day and to their time outside of school being micromanaged by extracurricular activities and family supports. A large part of the case management process, especially at the beginning of a student's college experience, is assessing a student's environmental and attitudinal barriers to performance and participation in campus life. Do students know how their responsibilities have changed from high school? Do they realize that the gaps in their class schedule are not all free time and that professors are expecting them to use that time to cover topics not explicitly discussed in class? Can they figure out how to access the many clubs, organizations, and other special interest activities? Are they prepared to manage their health-related conditions? Thorough case managers go beyond academic barriers to access and look at the big picture of the student experience.

Knowing when and where to refer a student can sometimes be difficult. Sometimes, students are unable to identify underlying challenges. As we are assessing needs, it is vital we pay attention to both explicit and implicit concerns. For example, a student may come to us with an academic concern, but as we peel back the layers, we may learn that their challenge stems from a personal matter.

Making an effective referral involves more than simply telling a student about a particular resource. We never want students to feel that they are being bounced around. First, we need to provide more specific information about a resource, such as how the referral can be beneficial or even a specific contact person. It is always helpful if we can facilitate a referral by alerting the person to whom we are referring the student. We can notify the party ourselves or, even better, have the student call or email the person with a brief description of their need and by whom they were referred. For more urgent matters, we may consider walking over to a resource with the student. Second, it is helpful to brainstorm a list of questions or needs to cover with the referral. Have the student jot down notes about how they can get the most out of their visit. Finally, be sure to ask the student whether they have any questions or concerns about accessing the resource. Students often feel uneasy about seeking support. It is our job to make them feel comfortable and assured that the resource or person we are referring them to will be helpful and friendly. Keep in mind that campuses vary in the breadth of resources offered and offices' names and functions.

Monitoring Caseloads Throughout the Student Life Cycle

Benchmarks for Outreach—Rarely does a DSP's relationship with a student end after intake. There is immense value in maintaining contact and lending support to students throughout their collegiate careers. The key is to identify periodic times to check in with students and to be available when students need support at random moments.

DSOs are not typically staffed to provide regular meetings to everyone on their caseload. And we certainly cannot count on students to consistently reach out to us in a timely manner. To avoid being bombarded by students in a state of turmoil and to establish some sense of order to caseload management, we need to identify regular benchmarks for outreach throughout the year. Some ideas of how to set up an outreach calendar are

- Outreach to incoming students who have attended intake appointments two weeks prior to the start of the semester to reestablish the connection and share pertinent information
- Outreach to students two weeks after receiving accommodation memo/letter to see if there are any questions or concerns
- Midterm exam check-in leading up to exams or outreach to students who receive a D or below as a midterm grade
- Two weeks before course registration
- Before the housing selection deadline
- Final exam grades and planning for the next semester
- Outreach to students who received poor GPAs the semester prior

Maintaining Connections with Elusive Students—Some students cannot possibly receive enough time or attention from us while others are a bit more difficult to engage. Unfortunately, it is often the students who are less connected who need the most support, so we need to use our rapport building and service provision skills to demonstrate our value to those who can benefit the most from holistic and comprehensive case management (Lukersmith, Millington, and Salvador-Carulla 2016). In these situations, it is essential to deliver tangible results right away. Go the extra mile and make the call to the student organizations office with the student to find out when the club meets or walk them over to the tutoring center so they can schedule an appointment.

Tracking Outreach Efforts—Documenting outreach is important for case management systems. It provides a paper trail if any part of the interactive process is called into question or if you need to report quantitative data to illustrate the value of the DSO.

Engaging Stakeholders to Increase Equity—We are in a unique position in that we obtain a lot of information from students; they tend to disclose things to us whether relevant to our work or not because we are a safe, private space where a certain sense of comfort tends to develop. Just as it is important to help students develop self-advocacy skills and their ability to independently ask for what they need, we need to model these skills by taking the input they provide and using our voices to advocate for making our campuses more accessible and usable for all. Everything from event planning to construction, curriculum requirements, and policies can have a significant impact on accessibility and equity.

Making Connections—We have already mentioned the importance of helping SWDs make connections and feel a sense of belonging to our campuses in the context of self-advocacy. This is such an important component of the student experience, and disability case management is well positioned to help students feel welcome and included. A few tips and tricks can help to send the message that students are welcome as they are and to encourage them to bring their whole selves to campus. Highlight all the different types of clubs and organizations on campus and watch students light up when they hear about the anime club or the theater group. This is a powerful tool to help students realize they have a community on campus.

The shift of ownership of the process catches a lot of students off guard. Many students arrive at college completely unaware that some of the services they received in high school were unique to them and not part of the school experience for all their peers. Sometimes, accommodations and supports were just implemented and did not need to be initiated by the student at all. And if things were not put into place, often parents or other supports addressed gaps in service provision with the school. The higher education process is much more hands off and relies on the student and professor to be aware of the accommodation and how to implement it and to reach out to DS as needed for assistance. It often feels like students and their support systems think there is a master database where all student information is stored and that we can just transfer everything over and implement the supports.

Record Keeping—Quality case management depends on the DSP's caseload management. While case management refers to individuals, caseload management involves the entire caseload (Roessler, Rubin, and Rumrill 2018). Providers must be skilled in managing multiple cases at one time, transitioning between cases, making sure there is a system in place that facilitates the progress of all cases, and always checking back into the client's goals and the purpose of the relationship (Roessler, Rubin, and Rumrill 2018). The varying demands of the work combined with often very large caseloads of students with a variety of complexities and needs make caseload management critical to effective service delivery.

Follow-up, Monitoring, and Evaluating Needs—The intensity and frequency of case management can be difficult to gauge. In general, the frequency of case management should be based on student needs. The level of need can be found along a continuum from least to most complex, least to most intense, while the timeliness of our response varies from proactive to acute. How and when to follow up with students is likely a function of staffing levels, philosophy, and available campus resources, but the following are good indicators of when to conduct outreach:

- Academic standing
- College withdrawal
- Leave of absence

- Behavioral intervention team
- Appeals

The follow-up and monitoring of case management needs to be systemic. The system will vary depending on the needs of the student, but it is wise to set a benchmark of a minimum of one point of contact per month. This can range from an email to a five-minute check-in call or a fifty-minute meeting, but having regular contact puts the DS provider in a position to be prepared to assist the student with whatever may come up, expected or unexpected. A weekly drop-in hour or outreach hour can be a great way to build in time for brief touchpoints. It also allows for time for externally requested outreach from counselors, professors, behavioral intervention teams, etcetera (Roessler, Rubin, and Rumrill 2018). Low grade reports/midterm/final grade reports and academic probation lists are all great prompts for student outreach.

In Summary

At its core, case management in our field encompasses the coordination of services to provide holistic, individualized support to optimize student success and well-being. While one of our fundamental objectives is to remove disability-related barriers for students, we recognize that access and inclusion are a shared responsibility. As such, collaboration with campus resources underpins the work we do. Case management is not unique to the role of the DSP; many other student services providers assume case management responsibilities. We differentiate clinical from nonclinical case managers in terms of scope of service and privacy expectations. Quality case managers are empathetic problem solvers who feel comfortable being a conduit between students and other service providers. Often, they need to be nimble and calm in addressing contentious or highly distressing situations where students' needs are not being met or understood or when student safety is in question.

This chapter provides a detailed review of four key components of case management—intake, needs assessment, service coordination, and monitoring. These components are cyclical and can be revisited at any point in the student life cycle. We offer thoughtful suggestions for conducting a comprehensive intake interview, analyzing a variety of needs, and connecting students with appropriate resources. While some of our encounters with students can seem transactional—one or two meetings with students during their enrollment—many are relational. Sometimes students reach out to us, such as when they need a new accommodation or assistance considering career or study abroad needs. Other times, we reach out to students as part of our ongoing monitoring efforts, such as when they have deficient midterm assessments or final grades or are referred to the behavioral intervention team (Wilson 2016).

DSPs often need to play detective to get the whole picture of a student's needs in the higher education environment. Do they really require a notetaker as a reasonable accommodation, or is that just something that was provided in high school and is a preference? If the latter, empower the student to develop academic skills that are lacking and connect them with university resources in that area. It is a fragile dance between setting a hard line about what is and is not a reasonable accommodation for each student's individual situation and being open to hearing where the student is coming from and what they think they are entitled to. Remember that when you have met one student with a disability, you have met *one* student with their own individual story.

▶ Reflective Exercise

You are meeting with a transfer student who has disclosed a learning disability and is seeking academic accommodations for which you have supporting documentation. In advance of your meeting, you receive a call from the student's father, who discloses that the student transferred from their first institution because they did not make any friends and felt isolated. The father asks for a follow-up call to see how the meeting went and review next steps. During the intake process, the student discloses a mental health diagnosis and reports difficulty obtaining treatment due to insurance and financial issues. They do not share much about their experience at their prior institution other than to say that their peers were interested in sports and partying and that they have other interests. Use this information to describe how you will approach the case management process. How will you document each step? How often do you anticipate needing to meet with this student? What factors about this case influence you decision? What considerations should you take when determining how involved to be with service coordination versus how much independence to expect from the student?

▶ Supplemental Job Aids

The following Supplemental Job Aids can be found at https://scholarshare.temple.edu/handle/20.500.12613/8373:

- *Differentiating between Intake, Service Coordination, and Case Records and Reports*
- *Intake Interview Questions*
- *Case Management Communication Tools*
- *Campus Resources*

11

Roles and Responsibilities of Faculty

Faculty play a pivotal role in ensuring access for SWDs. The process is one of mutual communication by the student, DSP, and the course instructor. Faculty become partners with the DSO in the application of accommodations provided in their course. The DSO provides support to students and assists faculty in understanding their roles as well as providing a "how to" for delivery of accommodations. As content experts, faculty have the right to evaluate how accommodations apply to their course. This chapter explores the responsibilities faculty have to their course or program, the process of accommodation, the determination, sometimes in partnership with faculty, of reasonable accommodations, and the delivery of accommodation in the classroom. Beyond accommodation discussion and implementation is the need to collaborate with faculty on short and long-standing initiatives. Ultimately, this chapter highlights the need for a close partnership between faculty and DSPs.

▶ Guiding Questions

1. How does a DSO actively involve faculty in the accommodation implementation process?
2. How does a DSO navigate faculty who are either overly supportive or not supportive enough?
3. What are strategies for increasing faculty engagement?

4. What are strategies for working with departments to identify fundamental requirements if unclear?
5. How does a DSO facilitate the importance of confidentiality for students?

Most faculty want to make their courses accessible to SWDs. They might not understand what is expected of them or that the law requires their compliance, but DSPs should assume the desire to accommodate is there. The challenge for many DSPs is to figure out how to educate faculty about their role in the accommodation process. Let us start with the first step in the accommodation process: receiving the accommodation letter.

Receiving an Accommodation Letter

Of all the possible roles on campus, faculty have the most frequent interactions with students, making them wonderful conduits for sharing information. Ideally, every course within the IHE should have a DS syllabus statement. Putting the disability statement on the syllabus not only shares faculty desire to be inclusive with students but also offers students another informational point as to the existence of the DSO. If a student asks for an accommodation directly from a faculty member without an accommodation letter or shares with the faculty that they are experiencing disability-related impacts, then the faculty should refer the student to the DSO rather than granting the accommodation. The syllabus statement provides context for these conversations.

Students formally engage faculty when they deliver a current and official accommodation letter. The accommodation letter should clearly state what the accommodation is, how it should be implemented (if the "how" is not included in the letter, it should be available on the DSO website for reference), the semester it is for, and how to connect with the DSOs if needed. This connection may be needed for clarification purposes, to brainstorm ways to implement the accommodation, or to discuss potential concerns around the fundamental requirements of the course. These are wonderful opportunities to build collaborative relationships.

It is important that faculty understand and value the confidentiality of the student when discussing their accommodations. Faculty should pull the student aside privately, if the student wishes to engage with them, or respect the student's desire to simply hand over the letter without conversation. Regardless, faculty do not need to know the nature of the student's disability. Likewise, when faculty are setting up an accommodation like extra time for exams, they can make a general announcement to the class that those who get accommodations should follow the procedure they have determined, but they should not name students individually.

Faculty often ask for a list of SWDs in their course, and sometimes even a list of what the disabilities are. Neither are appropriate, and both break the confidentiality of the students. Students have the right to choose which courses they may need accommodations for and in some cases may choose not to use their accommodations for a particular class. As a reminder, students legally own the right to disclose their disability, therefore faculty do not have the right to know what the disability is. Faculty breaking confidentiality is one reason a DSP may need to reach out to faculty or the department chair as a form of education. The good news is that once corrected, it rarely occurs again.

Informally Accommodating Students

Can faculty be too accommodating? Indeed they can. There are occasions where faculty go rogue and decide to handle accommodation requests on their own, without referring students to the DSO or in the absence of an official accommodation notification letter. With these seemingly good intentions to be accommodating, faculty in fact might put themselves and the institution in jeopardy.

Faculty risk personal jeopardy by being subject to discrimination complaints if they establish themselves as gatekeepers for determining eligibility. As an example, if faculty agree accommodate x but not y, they may be subject to complaint for failure to fully accommodate a student. Additionally, if an instructor agrees to accommodate a student for one disability—let us say migraines—but requires another student with a different disability—anxiety, for example—to get accommodations from the DSO, they may be subject to a discrimination complaint.

Faculty who provide unofficial accommodations may be inadvertently setting precedence, in which case a student may expect (and be entitled to) accommodations in other courses. There are potential grounds for a discrim-

---

A DSP saw how a professor's attempt at kindness inadvertently harmed the student when a student with a visual disability required all content to be electronic. The DSP met with and taught the professor about what they could do and assured that the DSO could provide alternative format of texts when the professor could not. Well after the student had finished this course, the DSP ran into the professor, who confessed that he had not altered his lecture materials because it was too time consuming. Instead, he met with the student during his office hours, asked her what she had learned in his course, and passed her through. The DSP later learned that the student had had to take the subsequent course twice in order to fully grasp the material.

ination complaint if a different professor denies the accommodation request and in doing so comes across as unreasonable—or worse—in the eyes of the student.

Finally, providing an unofficial accommodation may put the student in jeopardy. Without official record of accommodations, the student may have a difficult time establishing a need for accommodation in the future. For example, postgraduate programs or testing agencies may look for verification of accommodation from the student's undergraduate institution.

Accommodations are not always appropriate for courses. Faculty are content experts. They are responsible for establishing the goals of their course and designing corresponding learning objectives for students to master those goals. Ideally, these goals and objectives should be highly visible to students in the course catalog and on the syllabus. If an accommodation fundamentally alters a course learning objective, then an interactive process between the faculty and DSP needs to occur. The goal of the interactive process is to determine whether the accommodation truly does impact the fundamental requirements of the course as written in the syllabus and conveyed to the student. If the accommodation is found to conflict, the faculty and DSP begin looking into options for the student.

Students should also be part of the interactive process. Once it is determined that an accommodation may alter the fundamentals of a course, the student should be notified that an interactive process has begun. Offering

An example of this interactive process occurred when a DSP navigated a request made by a nursing student. The student asked for physical assistance when transferring patients over certain poundage. The DSP looked closely at the syllabus and course catalog and found a weight requirement that all nursing students needed to be able to lift to complete the course. Because this was a fundamental requirement of the course, the accommodation request of assistance with transferring patients was denied. However, the DSP did engage with the faculty and the student to brainstorm alternative accommodations for the student. Ultimately, the student circled back with their physician for a medical plan that could get the student to the point of lifting the required poundage. The plan for the student to work on their health first to reach the required goal would take time. The conversation at this point went back to the faculty and ultimately the department chair to allow a leave of absence and adjustment to the course sequence. In this case, the written expectation for essential requirements was clearly stated in the syllabus and course catalog. The knowledge the faculty had about who to go to with concerns allowed the student to be an active participant in the process, and ultimately, a solution was agreed on.

students full transparency as the DSP navigates appropriate accommodations gives students the opportunity to be part of the brainstorming process, provide more details about their accommodation needs, and choose whether the course is something they wish to pursue. Depending on the nature of the course and/or the professional field it is designed to prepare students for, students who cannot be accommodated may choose a different class or even major.

Once the fundamentals of a course are determined, appropriate accommodations are granted, and the student has handed the accommodation letter to their faculty, the DSP can often step out of the conversation and trust that the student will be accommodated. That is, of course, unless the accommodations are complex in nature.

Complicated Accommodations Faculty Might Navigate

A few accommodations can be more difficult to navigate and require a strong partnership between faculty and the DSO—specifically, note-taking support, alternative formats of materials, assessment-related accommodations, and remote access learning. As always, each institution handles these accommodations differently, but we want to share some common themes and words of advice for DSOs working through how to support both faculty and students with these accommodations.

Note-Taking Assistance

As discussed in Chapter 8, students who qualify for note-taking assistance do so for a variety of reasons, which are important to distinguish. DSOs must determine if the request for a notetaker is due to an access issue, meaning the student is physically or cognitively unable to take notes due to their disability, or is due to a preference, usually easing the concern a new student might have about taking a college-level class. Many DSOs will notice a pattern of declining requests for note-taking assistance between the fall and spring semesters. This trend tends to be due to a common thought among first-year students that college classes will be more difficult than high school classes. This concern is just, and as a result, many IHEs are creating college-level note-taking workshops for students. Often the skills gained in these workshops can satisfy the concerns of students without the need for a formal accommodation.

While workshops and auxiliary programs are impactful, there will still be students who need note-taking assistance because of an access issue. Note-taking assistance can come in many forms. Some institutions rely solely on peers within the class. Others use a combination of accommodation strategies including peers, access to the professor's notes or PowerPoints ahead of time, and/or use of AT. The DSO should determine which type of note-taking assistance is appropriate to meet the access needs of each student rather than only offering one type.

Regardless of the type of note-taking assistance, this accommodation requires coordination with the faculty member beyond the delivery of letters. Let us look at the peer-assisted version of note-taking for a moment. Peer assisted note-taking can include asking volunteers to share a copy of their notes with the student with the disability. In these instances, the DSO can direct the faculty member on how to ask for a volunteer at the beginning of the semester. The DSO should include a description of what the volunteer notetaker is being asked to do. In some cases, the volunteer simply connects with the SWD, and they work out a system for note sharing. If the system breaks, the SWD should connect with their DSP for advice on next steps (usually asking for another volunteer). In other situations, a DSO might get a copy of the class roster from the professor and send an email (without naming the individual SWD) to the entire class asking for a volunteer. In these situations, the DSO usually serves as the logistic manager of the note-taking accommodation by seeking a volunteer, receiving the notes, and passing them on to the student (through email, LMS, or accommodation database).

From a faculty's perspective, whether the notetaker is paid is of little importance. Some faculty raise concerns about having a course captured in notes (or even in audio notes) with regards to the confidentiality of other students and their intellectual property rights. Faculty can be reassured that students who qualify for a note-taking accommodation are required not to share their notes with others in the class. This conversation should occur between the DSP and the SWD when the note-taking accommodation is approved.

Recorded Lecture Agreements

The recorded lecture accommodation includes use of an audio recording device to allow eligible students equal opportunity to receive and process information presented in class lecture by supporting their note-taking needs. Methods of making an audio recording include computer software, smart pens, cellular phones, or other devices that record audio. Sometimes faculty object to their lectures being recorded, citing concerns for breach of copyright or right to privacy. A professor's concerns about infringement or privacy do not override a student's right to accommodation. Specifically, Section 504 states that

> A recipient may not impose upon handicapped students other rules, such as the prohibition of tape recorders in classrooms or of dog guides

in campus buildings that have the effect of limiting the participation of handicapped students in the recipient's education program or activity. To allow a student with a disability the use of an effective aid and, at the same time, protect the instructor, the institution may require the student to sign an agreement so as not to infringe on a potential copyright or to limit freedom of speech. (U.S. Department of Education 2020b)

Our responsibility as DSPs is to assure concerned faculty that we respect their concerns by offering a formal agreement between the instructor and student that details the specific, limited use of recordings and arranges for their disposal when the purpose of the recording is fulfilled.

Occasionally, instructors object to the use of recording devices in classes that involve a great deal of self-disclosure, fearing students will be inhibited from freely sharing. If open discussions are not an appropriate time for any student to be taking notes, it would be appropriate to ask the SWD to not record during these periods.

Alternative Format of Course Materials

Alternative format of course materials can cover just about anything related to the course, including textbooks, PowerPoints, documents, access to the course LMS, and the in-class course itself. When we reference alternative format of materials as an accommodation, we should quickly follow with the caveat that what "alternative format" means depends on the individual student. Some students may need all course materials in a digital format, while others may need them in an auditory format and others in brailled format. The key to working with faculty around this accommodation is to connect with faculty as soon as a DSP is made aware that a student with these needs has enrolled in their class. Ideally, students who need alternative format of course materials may be given the accommodation to register for classes early, even if just a week or so, to give the DSP and faculty a bit more lead time to prepare the course.

Once a student has been identified as needing alternative format of materials for a course, we recommend setting up a meeting with the lead professor. Request a copy of their syllabus, ask what additional texts and/or resources they plan to use, and review their course style and what and when they release materials to students. Legally, any institution that receives any form of financial aid from the government must post text choices in advance of the course selection process (Ingeno 2013). If a faculty is wavering between texts, this little reminder—combined with a nudge about how much easier it will be to plan their course if texts are selected in advance—usually helps move the process along.

One of the most helpful ways to educate a faculty member on the needs of their student is to demonstrate how a student accesses information with the course material at hand. If, for example, a student is dependent on a screen reader, use a text-to-speech application to show the faculty how a student will access the LMS. Access demonstrations are rarely smooth, leading to lots of "ah ha" moments from the faculty. Once faculty realize that their students cannot access the assigned material, a DSP can engage them in fixing the problem.

The degree to which faculty need to be involved depends on the nature of the accommodation. The easiest requirement of alternative course materials is to make all course content digital. That includes finding digital copies of the textbook. While we recommend that faculty make the digital textbook available to any student as a universal design strategy, this task is the ultimate responsibility of the DSP. We should be the ones searching for the digital text at the publishers or at one of the many digital textbook clearinghouses. Faculty, though, can be held responsible for students getting digital copies of all course materials (handouts, slides, syllabi, and assessments). Faculty can either do this for the whole class on their LMS or arrange with the student to email it directly. A DSP's role here is to facilitate this planning process.

While DSPs can adjust course content to fit the access needs of the student, they are not content experts. Many of the course materials used in higher education have images, charts, and graphs associated with them. Each image needs an alternative text tag, or an alt-text tag. These are short (one to two sentence) descriptions explaining the image and its importance to the text in which it is nestled. In situations where images, charts, and graphs are used, we recommend leaning on the faculty to help create accurate descriptions. The easiest way to do this is to ask faculty to send a document with alt-tags corresponding to the images in the document/text they have assigned. In some cases, creating a worksheet helps facilitate the process. If a faculty member pushes back because this process takes a lot of time, remind them that by creating alt-tags, they are also supporting the needs of English language learners who may struggle to understand the importance of an image, chart, or graph. Explain that once this work is done, they will not have to do it again for quite some time and suggest that they lean on someone in their office, a TA, or a graduate student to help. If necessary, remind them that the law requires us to provide this accommodation.

Interpreting or CART Reporting

Students who require ASL interpreting and/or CART reporting should be given the accommodation of an early registration. As noted in Chapter 7, these accommodations take a bit of time to set up and arrange, and in most cases, the IHE will need to work with an outside vendor to provide this accommodation. DSPs should provide a brief overview of how the accommodation works to the student and what their role is in facilitating it. In some instances, it might involve wearing a microphone so that the CART reporter can capture all the content. When an ASL interpreter joins a classroom, a DSP should discuss how faculty should and should not interact with the interpreter. Setting expectations around communication and what the outside vendor will do in the classroom will help to ease any concern the faculty may have.

For some faculty, sharing course content with someone outside of the institution can feel vulnerable and might lead to questioning their intellectual property rights. DSOs should respond to these concerns by acknowledging them and sharing that any students using accommodation services, including outside vendors, are not permitted to share the course content in any manner not related to participation in the course (Alley 2012). It might help to allow faculty to see the content, if it is being recorded, as a method of reassurance.

Supporting students who use interpreting or CART reporting takes time and money. DSPs should plan to connect with faculty as early as possible to inform them of the process, ask for any materials the interpreter or reporter may benefit from having, and set expectations about their role in class with the vendors. DSPs should also review the processes of requesting these services and the policies for what happens if the student does not show up to class. It may be helpful to meet with the student and faculty at the same time; however, this is not a requirement and may be a burden to the student, so check with the student first.

Exam Accommodations

Exam accommodation confusion is by far the most common issue that DS providers navigate with faculty. Exam accommodations, after all, are a legal requirement for the students who have them, but the law does not state who needs to implement them. Exam accommodations are the most common accommodation a DSO provides. As a reminder, exam accommodations include extended time, testing in a distraction-reduced environment, use of AT, use of a reader or scribe, frequent breaks, and other nuanced accommodations specific to the student. In most institutions, DSOs do not have access to a state-of-the-art testing facility. Many of us have access to one or two rooms we can use to proctor exams with more complex accommodations—but by no means all exam accommodations, especially those with just extended time. DS providers are very reliant on faculty to manage their own exam accommodations.

Exam accommodations are one of the few accommodations that may require faculty participation outside of the class, meaning an additional time commitment. When a faculty member receives an accommodation letter, especially if it only vaguely describes an exam accommodation, they will inevitably call a DSO. DSPs can help to reduce confusion with clear descriptions of the accommodation in the accommodation letter and corresponding detailed instructions on their website, in a follow-up email, or in the disability database.

The ultimate role of faculty when proctoring exams for students with accommodations is to provide those accommodations in a seamless fashion. Ideally, this means finding a space where a student can begin and end their exam in the same space without disruptions. Space and time are the two issues that faculty note cause the biggest disruptions to their day-to-day work. Space on a college campus is at a premium no matter how big the institution is. It can be difficult to provide extra time in the classroom where the class occurs, since another class is likely to need the room right before or after. Faculty offices are often in a different location than classrooms, requiring them to be in two places at once to proctor an exam. An extra classroom, office, or conference room space is hard to come by, especially within proximity to the classroom.

DS providers should acknowledge this difficulty and offer assistance in the form of ideas for where to find space without assuming the responsibility of solving the problem. Remember that most DSOs are already understaffed as is. By empowering faculty to solve this problem with some suggestions, DSPs can create allies among the faculty and redirect attention to other areas that need our assistance. Some institutions advise academic departments to reserve neighboring classrooms or conference rooms near the course classroom at the start of the semester on the exam date and at the exam time. Other institutions determine which faculty offices may be free at that time and ask to borrow one ahead of time. Others find central spaces on campus (the library, student center, and even residence halls) that they can reserve ahead of time. A DSP can work with a faculty and their department administrator to brainstorm different spaces and encourage them to think ahead, but we should not be the ones reserving the space.

The other sticking point for faculty is time. Extended time, which is the accommodation we most frequently ask faculty to handle, requires them to find the time to proctor exams. The average extended time is time and a half, or 50 percent more time. If the exam is an hour, the faculty and student will need to spend an hour and a half together to ensure the student is accommodated. Faculty frequently complain that they do not have the time to proctor these exams. In truth, they may not. But that does not mean doing so should be the responsibility of the DSP. Remember, it is the university's responsibility to seamlessly support SWDs, not just the responsibility of the sole DSP on campus.

DSPs can be supportive by helping faculty brainstorm solutions based on what they have seen work in the past. Examples include the following:

- Starting exams early or staying late if the classroom is available
- Asking a graduate assistant or teaching assistant to proctor exams with extended time in a location that does not require students to move
- Asking a colleague or administrative assistant to help proctor exams
- Combining sections of a course with another professor and sharing proctoring responsibilities
- Utilizing remote proctoring if the exam is offered online to everyone

DSPs should be empathic but firm in their conversations with faculty about time commitments. Understanding constraints and helping come up with solutions will forge a better relationship in the future than assuming responsibility for students with accommodations. We recommend reaching out to faculty early in the semester, individually or through department or all-faculty meetings, to remind them of their responsibility and help them prepare for the semester before space and time become a problem.

For students who receive more complex exam accommodations (AT, scribes and/or readers, distraction-reduced space), it may be easier for a DSO to proctor. These exams require the DSO to set up equipment, identify a scribe or reader, and train them on what and what not to do. If a faculty member is unable to find a distraction-reduced space, the DSO might offer to proctor those exams if they have the space and bandwidth to do so.

Exams taken with the DSO require advanced coordination with faculty. Ideally, faculty send the DSO the exam (by email or physical drop-off) at least one business day prior to the start of the exam. Faculty should be available via cell phone, text, or email during the time the SWD is planning to take the exam to answer questions or serve as a resource if needed. A DSO should have an exam process for faculty to follow and should advertise that process frequently throughout the semester (at overview meetings but also in a separate email to faculty when a student is approved to take their exams with the DSO). DSPs should feel comfortable being firm with faculty who send exams late or fail to respond that if faculty do not follow the outlined process, they will be responsible for proctoring the exam. The more DSOs and faculty support each other through the exam accommodation process, the better the long-term relationship and outcomes will be.

Remote Access Accommodations

Prior to the global COVID-19 pandemic, DSPs may have responded to requests to take classes remotely just a few times a year. Students navigating in-patient treatment, whose provider felt it may be harmful for them to physically be on campus due to a chronic health disability, or who were recovering from a significant accident may have been candidates for this accommodation. Remote access accommodations permit students to take classes but not be physically on campus. In some cases, remote access means video conferencing a student into a class in real time. In others, it involves sending the student the class materials and a copy of the class notes and asking them to complete assignments on their own. There is great variability in how remote access works depending on the class and the faculty teaching it.

DSPs should determine if a student qualifies for remote access accommodations. However, just because a student qualifies does not mean that each class can be turned into a remote format. DSOs must meet with each of the student's intended faculty to determine if being physically in the class is a fundamental requirement for the class. In most cases, it is not a fundamental requirement to be physically present, but faculty might prefer students to be there. A preference for an in-person experience is something an accommodation can override. Therefore, it is critical for faculty to identify course goals and learning objectives and to state them on their syllabi.

If a learning objective is to engage in meaningful practice of physical movement in a class (consider an occupational therapy class in which students work in pairs to understand therapeutic placements, for example), then it could be argued that remote access is a fundamental alteration to the class. However, if a history professor is running a seminar-style class and feels that the other students would be negatively impacted by a student's absence—and a learning objective is to engage in meaningful debate with peers—then a student could be remote, but it would need to be in a way that allows them to both listen and contribute to the class in real time. If a biology class has both a lecture and lab section, a DSP would need to work with the faculty around both sections. Perhaps students do not need to be physically present or present in real time in the lecture, but they need to be present in the lab, as there is no way to learn about chemical reactions or how lab equipment works remotely. Each class requires an in-depth look at course goals and learning objectives to determine whether the approved remote access accommodation is a fundamental alteration of the curriculum or not. If not, the DSP should serve as the conduit between the faculty and IT, a notetaker, or an outside proctor (if the student needs to take exams remotely), organizing the student's remote access experience. These conversations should begin as early as possible.

Accommodations Requiring Agreements with Faculty

Some accommodations require individualized agreements between the student, the instructor, and the DSO about implementation. Federal law requires that institutions consider flexibility with attendance and assignment deadlines as a reasonable accommodation for qualified students. As such, institutions may not have a blanket policy of prohibiting extensions on assignments. Doing so obviates individualized assessment and effectively ends the interactive process.

When a student has a chronic condition with random or cyclical acute episodes, or one that requires ongoing specialized treatment, modifications to attendance policies may be appropriate. The accommodation does not apply to absences unrelated to the disability (e.g., common illnesses, car trouble, childcare). Modifications may include additional absences beyond what is stated in the syllabus and the ability to submit late or make up missed assignments and assessments without grade penalty or additional work. As DSPs, our role is to first determine the reasonableness of the accommodation overall and to then consult with faculty as to how much flexibility, if any, can be extended to the student without compromising essential components of the course or fundamentally altering the curriculum.

Class attendance is generally one of the most important learning components in a course, and due dates are established to assess learning progression. For many classes, there is some room for flexibility. However, the extent to which flexibility can be afforded to students requires an individualized assessment by the instructor to determine if the accommodation would pose a fundamental alteration to course objectives. Adapted from the OCR decision regarding Cabrillo Community College, Case No. 09-96-2150 (U.S. Department of Education 1996), the following questions provide a framework for determining if and how many disability-related absences are reasonable:

- What is the format of the course (e.g., in person, hybrid, online, remote)?
- Does the fundamental nature of the course rely on student participation as an essential method for learning?
- Do student contributions in class constitute a significant component of the learning process?
- According to the course description and syllabus, what are the classroom practices and policies regarding attendance?
- What does the course description and syllabus say?
- Is the attendance policy consistently applied?
- How is the final grade calculated?
- To what degree does a student's absence constitute a significant loss to the education experience in the class?

After an analysis of these factors, a reasoned judgment can be made as to whether a modification to the attendance requirement is acceptable. It is important to consider any differential treatment an instructor has given others (e.g., student athletes) in allowing exceptions to their policy.

Attendance accommodations should be established in advance, not retroactively. Therefore, the conditions of an attendance modification need to be established before a student misses classes or assignments. Instructors are only required to provide accommodations about which they been notified through a letter of accommodation, with the recommendation that the student discuss each requested accommodation with them. Syllabi with detailed attendance, lateness, or participation policies are an indication that requests for flexibility may require a mutually agreed on plan. To facilitate development of such a plan, we suggest soliciting information from instructors about course parameters involving maximum absences, communication expectations, timeframes for submission/completion of late work and assessments, and participation point alternatives. This deliberative process should be well documented to demonstrate a good faith effort to consider alternatives and the reasons for the final decision.

An attendance flexibility agreement, generally, covers three broad areas:

- Disability-related absences: The maximum number of absences permitted as an accommodation beyond what is stated in the course policy and the timeframe and communication method for notifying an instructor of a disability-related absence. Vague terms such as "flexible" and "to be determined" should be avoided.
- Assignments/assessments: The communication plan and maximum timeframe for a student to submit late work or to make up a missed exam, quiz, or lab.
- Participation points: Alternatives to make up for missed class participation.

While the work required of DSPs to negotiate with each professor and course is time intensive at the forefront, averting misinterpretations about how the accommodation was implemented at the end of the semester is worth the initial investment.

Strategies for Working with Resistant Faculty

Some faculty are resistant to providing accommodations. Others provide too much flexibility in their desire to support students. DSPs are consistently educating faculty about their role and responsibilities, encouraging them to be more flexible in some cases and less flexible in those with long-term consequences. At times, faculty education can seem like an uphill climb. We encourage DSPs to celebrate successful conversations, embrace allies, and tackle one resister at a time.

Faculty, more than DSPs, are on the front line of student support. They have the most contact with a student, allowing them to observe behaviors, watch academic progress, and connect with the student privately before or after class. Faculty also frequently receive doctor's notes from students, calls from parents, cryptic student emails, or requests for extensions. They tend to worry about a student after class but can be altogether dismissive.

DSPs can support faculty in providing structured assistance to their students. All too often, faculty are unaware of where to send a student who is struggling for support. Making faculty aware of the resources on campus (the DSO, the tutoring center, the counseling center, advisors, or the dean of students, for example) is an excellent method of getting the student the trained support they need. It also unburdens the faculty member.

There is power in teaching faculty to use the word "no." If a student asks for extended time on an exam the morning of the exam when the policy clearly states it is not permitted or is not feasible, giving in to the student does not teach the student and makes the faculty's life more complicated. Some faculty are afraid to say "no" for fear of not being supportive or breaking the law. A DSP can quench that fear with an overview of faculty roles and responsibilities, by sharing the consequences of being too nice, and by empowering faculty to support students appropriately.

Those who resist accommodating students are counter to overly supportive faculty members. As we discussed previously, DSOs are the first stop for students who feel they have been denied their accommodation or been discriminated against. Each of us has navigated or will have experiences where faculty have not provided exam accommodations or alternative format of course materials when the student was clearly entitled to them and followed the process for receiving those accommodations. In most cases, it is a matter of educating faculty about their role and responsibility. DSPs should meet with the student, hear their complaint, and ask them to write their account of the situation. DSPs should then meet with the faculty member to gather more specific information and, if appropriate, have a learning moment to review their roles and responsibilities as faculty. If remediation is warranted, the DSP should work with the faculty member to determine a fair response and circle back to the student. If the student still feels that the situation is unwarranted, then the DSO should encourage them to meet with the ADA official on campus or advise them on the IHE's grievance options.

We use these examples as case studies when we connect with faculty at the beginning of the semester. Many faculty actively seek guidance on what they can and cannot do or should do to support students. Using case studies is instrumental in situating real experiences to potential ones that faculty may face. We recommend leaving quite a bit of time for questions and answers at departmental presentations so that the DSP can help faculty think through their unique situations.

In Summary

Faculty understanding their role in the process is at the core of delivering seamless accommodation to students and allowing for the full educational experience within the class. As discussed, the DSO plays a critical role in communicating expectations and facilitating relationships to further understand those expectations. Developing a structure of reaching out to faculty and even departments can create opportunities to collaborate more directly. Never underestimate the power of unexpected conversations in unexpected places. Look for opportunities to join faculty during training experiences, explore ways to highlight those who understand the process, and facilitate exemplary practices of adhering to the accommodation exercise. Faculty often learn best from their peers—what better way than to champion those who embrace their responsibilities with the accommodation process?

▸ Reflective Exercise

Professor Johnson calls the DSO enraged. They just received an email from a student requesting to use his extended time exam accommodation on tomorrow's final exam. Professor Johnson does not understand why this student did not come forward before now and even goes so far as to suggest that the student is trying to ask for more time as a method of cheating on the exam. They exclaim that there is no way for them to accommodate the student's request, as they are leaving campus directly after the exam for a family engagement. How can you begin to deescalate this situation immediately? What long-term strategies might be helpful to avoid situations like this in the future?

▸ Supplemental Job Aids

The following Supplemental Job Aids can be found at https://scholarshare.temple.edu/handle/20.500.12613/8373:

- *Roles and Responsibilities of Faculty*
- *Managing Student Attendance/Absences: Attendance Guidance for Faculty*

Part IV

Compliance

12

How Legal Cases Influence Our Work

While very few of us have been to law school, all of us need to be legal scholars in our corners of the institution. Some institutions have in house general counsels while others contract out their legal services; no matter how IHEs handle legal support, it is rare that they engage with disability law specialists. Many law specialists employed by IHEs are generalists or focused on employment law as opposed to higher education or civil rights law. The onus is on DSPs to fill in knowledge gaps and keep their finger on the pulse of trends in disability litigation. Luckily, there is a treasure trove of case law that teaches us what to do and, more importantly, what not to do. The resolution agreements of the past guide us and are a powerful tool not only to make sure we keep our institutions in compliance but for motivation and incentive to think about inclusion and universal design.

▶ Guiding Questions

1. *What is the difference between the OCR complaint process and the DOJ complaint process?*
2. *What are the steps involved in responding to OCR and DOJ complaints?*
3. *What are some positive results of participating in the complaint process?*
4. *What are some proactive steps IHEs can take to prevent complaints?*

Complaints: The Good, The Bad, and The Progress

Many of the authors of this text have been on the other side of a letter from the OCR or DOJ, and we survived to tell the tale. While it is certainly an intimidating situation and creates an enormous amount of time-sensitive work, we can honestly say that as a result, we are better professionals, and our institutions have made great strides toward accessibility. Before we walk into the weeds of this chapter, we want to share the positives that can come out of participating in the process. Table 12.1 highlights the results of an OCR or DOJ experience.

The U.S. Department of Education Office for Civil Rights and the Department of Justice Civil Rights Division: A Brief Overview

When doing this work, one often hears the acronym OCR. The acronym stands for the Office for Civil Rights—what many DSPs think of as our governing agency. Likewise, the DOJ Civil Rights Division has a role in protecting students' rights in higher education. A memorandum of understanding (MOU) signed in 2014 "reinstated the intentions that the OCR and DOJ work together to enforce civil rights laws in higher education." The two agencies recognized the overlap and agreed to work together on issues such as "Title IX, enforcement, public outreach, and technical assistance" (Lhamon and Samuels 2014).

OCR is a governmental agency responsible for investigating allegations of discrimination in agencies that receive federal financial assistance. OCR investigates claims in state education agencies, elementary and secondary schools, IHEs, and municipalities such as libraries and even museums. If an

TABLE 12.1   POSITIVE RESULTS OF AN OCR OR DOJ EXPERIENCE

Positive Result	Example
Highlights the need for accessibility to be part of everyone's job.	A website accessibility complaint resulted in the creation of a web accessibility policy and the assignment of technology services staff to maintain accessible public-facing websites.
Accelerates action on initiatives not otherwise prioritized by the institution.	An OCR complaint by a student with a visual impairment resulted in a long overdue budget increase for the creation of accessible course materials.

institution agrees to take federal aid, that agency must not discriminate against an individual based on race, color, national origin, sex, disability, or age. Specifically, OCR oversees two laws dealing with educational access: Section 504 of the Rehabilitation Act of 1973 and the ADAAA (2008) Title II.

Any individual who believes they have been discriminated against based on disability has the right to contact the agency for assistance with their concern. OCR also takes complaints from people or institutions on behalf of individuals, which they investigate and work to resolve. If OCR decides to investigate the complaint, it will engage in a neutral fact-finding process to determine if a violation occurred. This process can be comprehensive and involve DSPs or just the IHE's legal team. The agreements made between OCR and the educational institution often result in a more accessible physical and online environment for individuals with disabilities.

The DOJ will prosecute individuals and organizations who may have violated the civil rights of individuals with a disability. Examples of discrimination that the DOJ Civil Rights Division investigates regarding disability can include harassment, denied admissions, segregation in an educational setting, denial of requested accommodations, and failure to provide granted accommodation. The department also works with the public, so members of the public understand the laws protecting them, and coordinates with other federal agencies to enforce civil rights laws (U.S. Department of Justice Civil Rights Division n.d.a).

Case settlements present in many different forms depending on the type of complaint and jurisdiction. The two federal level complaint types we see in higher education are through the Department of Education's Office for Civil Rights (DOE-OCR) and the DOJ Civil Rights Division. The DOE-OCR is the federal agency responsible for enforcing Section 504 of the Rehabilitation Act and Title II of the ADA (U.S. Department of Education 2022). The Civil Rights Division of the DOJ enforces Title III of the ADA (U.S. Department of Justice Civil Rights Division 2013). In addition to federal laws, states have their own discrimination laws and regulations that may be used in disability litigation. People may choose to file a lawsuit in federal or state court in lieu of or in addition to making civil rights complaints via OCR or DOJ. Table 12.2 outlines the differences in legality between the DOJ and OCR.

An Overview of State Laws

Some state laws expand protections under the ADA or offer the same protections, and others narrow the scope of protections for disabled people. Dissecting state laws related to disability discrimination is beyond the scope of this book, but the following example illustrates the importance of being aware of individual state and municipal laws and regulations:

TABLE 12.2   THE DIFFERENCES BETWEEN OCR AND DOJ

OCR		DOJ
Rehab Act Section 504	**ADA Title II**	**ADA Title III and Civil Rights Legislation**
Prohibits any program receiving federal financial assistance from discriminating against an individual because of disability. Covers any IHE that receives direct or indirect federal financial assistance.	Prohibits all state and local governmental entities, including public IHEs, from discriminating against people with disabilities.	Prohibits private IHEs from discriminating against people with disabilities. Title III of the ADA covers private IHEs.

The ADA identifies service animals as "trained" and does not cover animals that are in training. Massachusetts expands protections to those training animals as well. However, Hawaii's state laws do not include service animals in training. Therefore, service animals in training in Massachusetts would be afforded more protections than the ADA and those in Hawaii would not. (Graymore 2021)

The ADA rule of thumb is that if state or local law provides fewer protections, the ADA brings it up to speed. However, if the state or local law goes further than the ADA, that standard needs to be met (Mid-Atlantic ADA Center 2012). "A specific provision that is of greater benefit to people with disabilities will override one that is less generous" (Mid-Atlantic ADA Center 2012). DS providers must keep apprised of specific state and local regulations in addition to federal civil rights laws and federal court judgments. Doing so is especially important if a state expands protections because lack of compliance may add complications if a case is filed in state court. Regional ADA centers are a great source of information on state-specific disability rights laws and regulations.

The OCR Complaint Process

The OCR complaint process follows a very specific formula. The complaint is made, relevant parties are notified, information is requested, and a determination is made. The goal of complaints is resolution, so the focus is on information gathering, communication facilitation, and solutions. While complaints do not always go in this direction, the process is solution focused and gives many opportunities to avoid escalation.

OCR is a neutral body assigned to process complaints and facilitate resolutions within any state. A complaint is filed (typically within 180 days of the offending occurrence), and if OCR has the jurisdiction to process the complaint, it either initiates a Facilitated Resolution Between the Parties (FRBP) or launches an investigation.

An FRBP is the quicker of the two options, as depicted in Figures 12.1a and 12.1b. If both parties are agreeable to an FRBP and OCR supports moving forward with the process, discussions between the two sides are facilitated

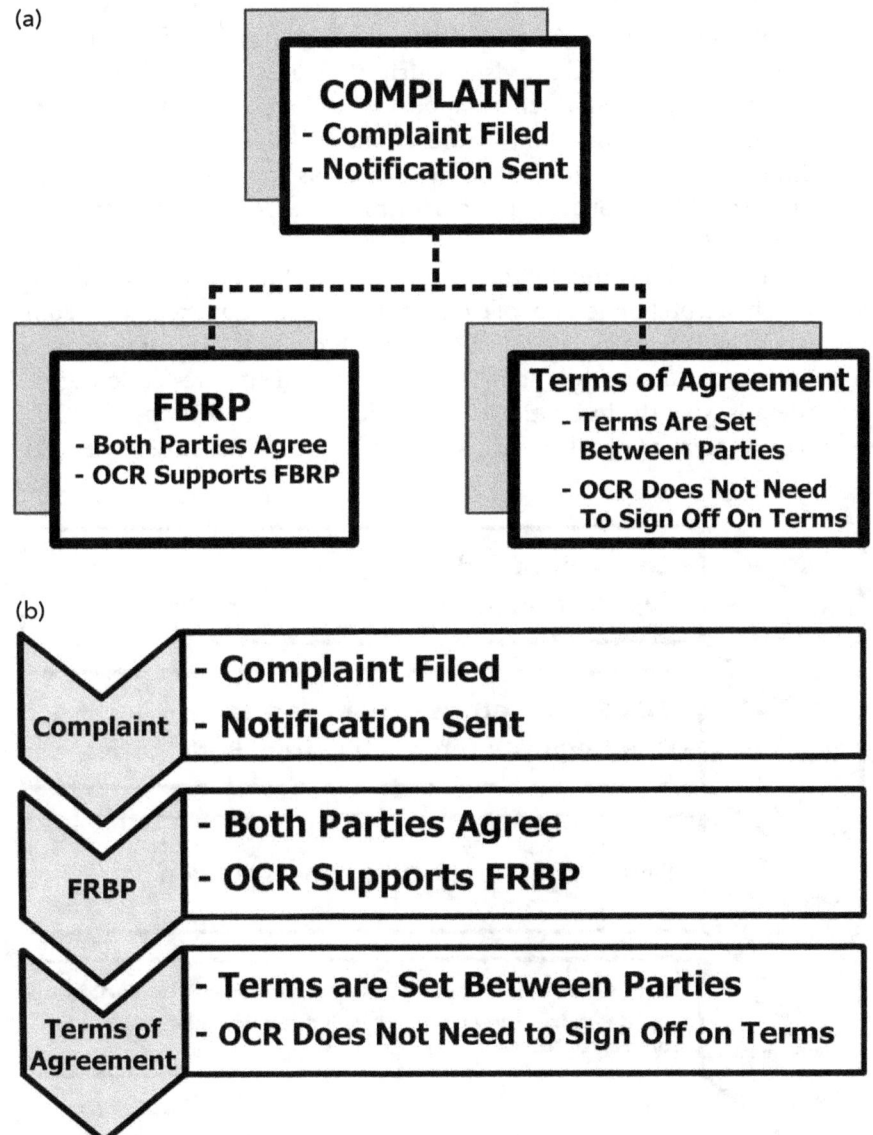

Figures 12.1a and b OCR Resolution–Terms of Agreement

by OCR, and terms of an agreement are set. OCR does not sign off on or enforce the terms of the agreement. If the terms of the agreement are not met, however, another complaint can be filed for failure to comply with the agreement (U.S. Department of Education 2020a).

If neither side wants to engage in an FRBP, or if OCR deems the specifics of the complaint cannot be addressed through a resolution agreement, an investigation is launched. As shown in Figure 12.2, OCR issues letters to both sides notifying them of the opening of the investigation and requesting information relevant to the case. Information may come in the form of documentation, interviews, and site visits. During the investigation, OCR tries to determine whether the evidence supports the charge that the institution violated the law. It is important to understand that the legal standard OCR is looking for is a "preponderance of evidence," as opposed to evidence beyond a reasonable doubt as required of criminal cases (U.S. Department of Education 2020b).

Letters of findings are sent to both parties detailing the results of the investigation. If a preponderance of evidence is found to support that the complainant's rights were violated, OCR will reach out to the institution to see if it agrees to engage in a voluntary resolution agreement. A resolution agreement details what the institution needs to do to comply with the law. OCR tracks the agreement to ensure terms are met and corrections are implement-

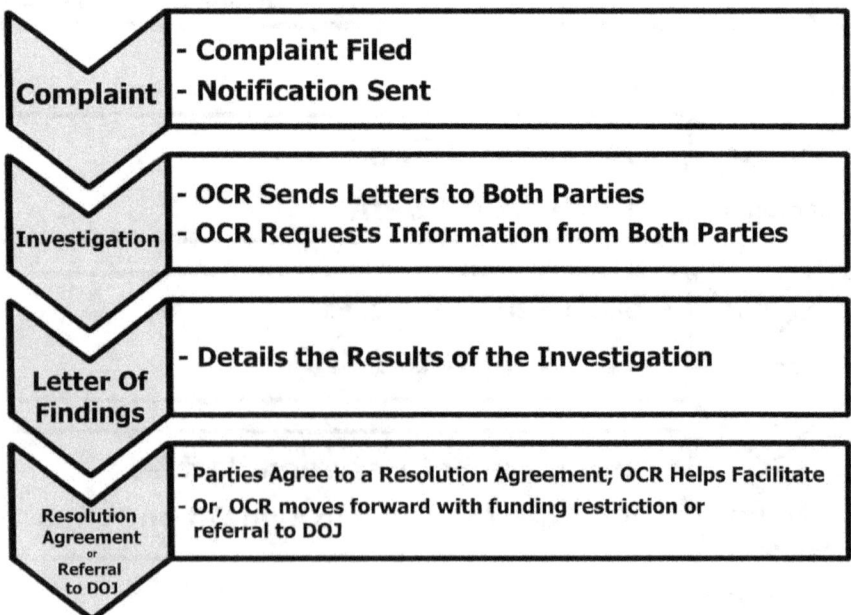

Figure 12.2 OCR Resolution–Letter of Findings

ed. If an institution does not agree to engage in a voluntary resolution agreement, OCR may restrict federal financial assistance or engage with the DOJ on any next steps (U.S. Department of Education 2020a).

A common example of a complaint filed with OCR relates to inaccessible web content on IHE websites. A real-world example of an OCR resolution agreement is the 2017 complaint against Brown University citing the inaccessibility of its public-facing website. A complaint was filed, an investigation was initiated, and the ISE decided to engage in a resolution agreement prior to the completion of the investigation. This decision resulted in a signed resolution agreement in which Brown agreed to fix the identified accessibility issues of its website as detailed in the Remedies and Reporting section of the OCR agreement.

Department of Justice

A DOJ process follows a path similar to an OCR process in that there is a complaint, a response, and either an investigation or a voluntary agreement. However, the jurisdiction is different, and the resolutions can include monetary damages. The Civil Rights Division of the DOJ enforces Title III of the ADA (places of public accommodation including private IHEs) in addition to other civil rights laws such as the Civil Rights Act of 1968 and the Fair Housing Act. The DOJ can choose to bring a lawsuit on behalf of the complainant and is therefore not considered a neutral party in those cases. DOJ resolutions come either in the form of a consent decree or a resolution agreement as shown in Figures 12.3 and 12.4. A consent decree is enforceable by the court (in the form of a court order), while a resolution agreement is resolved outside of court via a signed agreement or MOU. Any violation of the agreement or MOU may result in the government filing a lawsuit to enforce the terms (U.S. Department of Justice 2018).

An example of a DOJ resolution agreement is the case between the United States of America and Lesley University whereby the private IHE was found to have violated Title III of the ADA

> by failing to make necessary reasonable modifications in policies, practices, and procedures to permit students with celiac disease and/or food allergies (collectively "food allergies") to fully and equally enjoy the privileges, advantages, and accommodations of its food service and meal plan system. (U.S. Department of Justice 2012)

In this case, the ISE entered into a voluntary agreement with the DOJ to remedy the identified violations that led to noncompliance with Title III of the ADA. The terms of the agreement included the following:

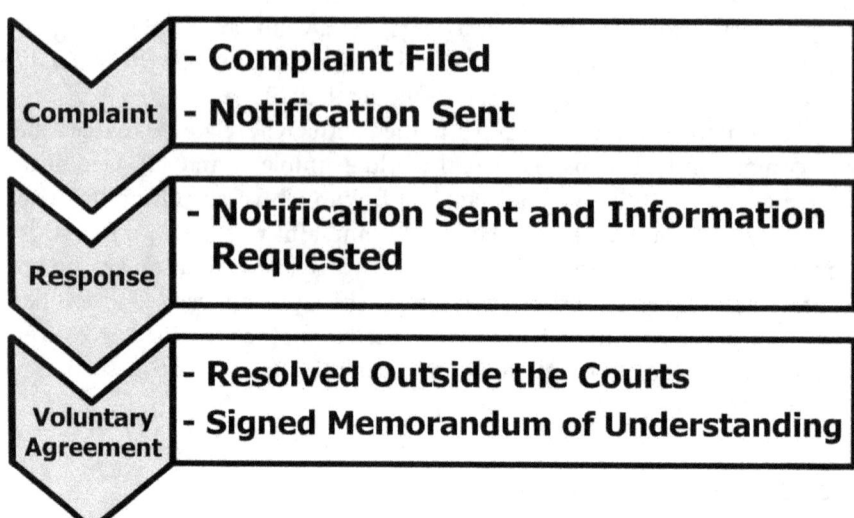

Figure 12.3 DOJ Resolution—Voluntary Agreement

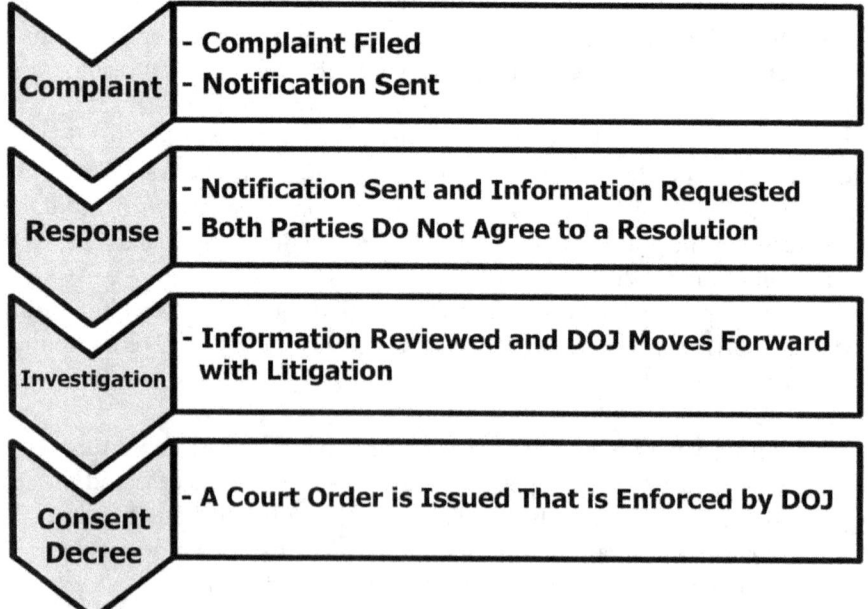

Figure 12.4 DOJ Resolution—Consent Decree

- Availability of ready-made allergen-free meals
- Development of individualized allergen-free meal plans
- Options for preordering allergen-free meals
- Space allocated for storage and preparation of allergen-free foods
- Allowance for the request of allergen-free food
- Contracts with vendors allowing students to purchase allergen-free food via prepaid meal card
- Posting of information regarding food allergies and foods that contain certain allergens
- Allergy-related training for food services and ISE staff
- $50,000 in damages to students involved in the complaint

How to Navigate a Legal Complaint

As we stated before, anyone who feels they have been discriminated against based on race, color, national origin, sex, and/or disability may file a complaint with OCR. OCR also accepts filings on behalf of individuals who have experienced discrimination. The DOJ follows similar processes for receiving and investigating complaints. For many DSPs, the idea of either governmental agency investigating their campus can produce anxious feelings. Some offices may even be fearful of their role in the matter and worry about the repercussions it might cause. This is not usually the case, and many complaints filed with both agencies happen far beyond the purview of the DSO.

OCR is not a punitive body looking to hurt institutions. When a claim is filed, OCR investigates and often fosters a feeling of cooperation. That said, the process does take time, attention, and sometimes money to settle. OCR can also initiate its investigation without a complaint to determine whether a school's practices comply with federal laws (U.S. Department of Education Office 2022a).

OCR sees its role as an educating body, answering questions in the hopes that an institution can resolve concerns and make a welcoming environment for all; it also provides written guidance for institutions to help with compliance. OCR relies on Dear Colleague Letters to relay critical information to institutions. An example of a Dear Colleague Letter is the "Joint 'Dear Colleague' Letter: Electronic Book Readers" sent in June of 2010. This letter explained why "electronic book readers are not accessible to students with low vision, blindness, and learning disabilities." OCR entered into settlement agreements with ISEs that used such devices in the classroom not to purchase, require, or recommend the use of the Kindle DX or any other dedicated electronic book reader until the devices are fully accessible to individuals who are blind or have low vision or until the ISEs provides reasonable accommodations or modifications so that SWDs can acquire the same information, engage in the same interactions, and enjoy the same services as sighted students with substantially equivalent ease of use (Perez and Ali 2010).

The letter went on to "ask that you take steps to ensure that your college or university refrains from requiring the use of any electronic book reader, or other similar technology, in a teaching or classroom environment as long as the device remains inaccessible to individuals who are blind or have low vision." The letter stated that "technology is the hallmark of the future, and technological competency is essential to preparing all students for future success" (Perez and Ali 2010). OCR ended the letter by asking to work with institutions to ensure that American technological advances benefit all. The agency also provided information for institutions, such as a toll-free technology line to answer questions and a separate line to help with technical assistance. The Dear Colleague Letters serve as a form of guidance without the difficulty a complaint may bring.

So, what happens if OCR or the DOJ opens an investigation? An OCR complaint can use institutional resources and a professional's time. It is crucial to have a team familiar with the agencies manage information gathering and to distribute work among the members of the assembled group. To understand who should be involved in a complaint, it might be helpful to understand what a complaint looks like. As we discussed earlier, OCR must investigate any complaints that meet essential criteria. A written explanation of the allegations is provided to the IHE describing a matter under OCR jurisdiction then identifying the individuals and understanding the allegation of the discrimination. It is only after OCR investigates the complaint that a case number is generated and given. The complaint provided to the institution lists out the allegations under investigation, and the institution receives notification that a case has been opened for OCR to investigate. This complaint is often obtained by the ISE legal team, which initiates an internal investigation. It is typically during this phase of the inquiry that the DSO is brought in as a team member.

The investigation scope will differ depending on the concern. The institution may need to direct certain individuals to collect information and documentation. Each district has its authorities share the appropriate time frame for a response to the data request. It is essential to mention that the institution is the responsible party, even if a specific office such as DS is mentioned, the individuals in the office will not be the target.

Stress can be impactful when staff is tasked with responding to OCR requests for information while managing day-to-day jobs. Information must be provided even if doing so adds stress to the team, as not complying with requested information can result in a deferral of federal funds and ultimately become a referral to the DOJ, which, as mentioned before, has the ability to collect damages in addition to the cost of the agreement to mitigate the concerns stated in the case.

The time frame from receipt of the complaint by the ISE to resolution varies and is unique to the case and institution. An early complaint resolution may be offered to the ISE during the complaint process. OCR decides if an early complaint resolution is appropriate in the initial evaluation of the case. Suppose the institution and complaint filer agree to the early complaint resolution. In that case, the investigation may be suspended for up to thirty days while OCR begins its role as impartial moderator. This resolution is done in hopes that a mutually acceptable agreement can be reached. If the ISE agrees to the early complaint resolution, it is important to know that OCR is not responsible for monitoring compliance by either party.

At the conclusion of the investigation, OCR will focus on whether a preponderance of evidence supports that an institution failed to comply with the law and discriminated against the individual who brought the complaint. When the conclusion is reached, OCR issues a letter of findings to explain the basis for the decision. At this time, both the institution and the individual who filed the complaint are notified. If the ISE is found responsible for a violation of the law, a statement is issued, and a resolution is drafted. At this time, the institution is encouraged to enter into a voluntary resolution agreement to bring the institution into compliance. The resolution agreement enables OCR to monitor the institution's implementation of steps outlined in the agreement and the statute and regulations named in the case. This information is made public and is often how we as professionals learn and grow.

It is important for the assigned team to work on the casework with their institution's attorneys throughout. This collaboration ensures the evaluation of the allegation was thorough, coordinates the institution's response, and oversees negotiation with OCR if there is participation in the resolution discussion. If the institution enters a resolution agreement, attorneys can help with the administration's work, allowing for relief from the process and monitoring period (which can take several years).

Those of us in this field, along with both agencies, want to protect students from discrimination. Our primary purpose is to focus on a student's learning experience without barriers that can sometimes become an unequal practice. With this mutual focus, the institution and OCR may collaborate and achieve the common goal of an educational experience equally accessible to all. With that outcome in mind, hearing of an OCR complaint may initiate a different response than anxiety—a feeling of mutual interest in making the ISE more equitable for the learners it serves.

Putting a Big Case into Perspective: How the University of Nebraska at Kearney Changed Our Practices

A civil rights lawsuit against the University of Nebraska by the DOJ claimed that the IHE violated Title III of the Civil Rights Act of 1968 as amended by the Fair Housing Amendments Act of 1988 by denying two disabled students the accommodation of having their ESAs live with them in ISE owned housing. The result was the following:

- $140,000 in damages to two former students denied reasonable accommodation
- Change in housing policy to allow ESAs for people with disabilities in campus-owned housing

A large public IHE found this case pivotal in enhancing policies around animals in residence halls. The case was resolved at the same time the ISE began to receive requests for assistance animals in residence halls. The DS and residence life staff met to develop wording for the handbook for living on campus as well as language for the residence life website. The DSO was listed as the location to request and submit documentation for the decision of whether an animal is an appropriate accommodation. When the process was finalized, the ISE needed to determine how to refer to animals designated as accommodation in the residence halls. It was decided to use the terminology from the resolution itself, and the adoption of the term "assistance animals" was agreed on. This choice was important because many institutions and colleges were using the term "emotional support animal," when the animals we were evaluating for accommodation were not all accommodating emotional needs—they were doing other tasks for the student living in the hall. For one of the author's offices, this was the slow shift in the thinking around animals as accommodation in the dwellings.

The DS and residence life staff agreed that a committee would be needed to evaluate requests. The committee was formed with a team from both offices. It met frequently and had discussions around the accommodation's appropriateness and the many situations that having an animal on campus would bring up. One area that needed to be addressed was that appropriate behaviors and vaccination status for the animal are required. It became clear that the area responsible for conduct violations was also required at the table. Once everyone was brought together, a comprehensive educational process was developed to allow for the complete understanding by students of the expectations—as well as the consequences of the expectation—of a healthy environment for an animal to live in the residence halls. We discussed a process for fire drills and emergency evacuations as one of many anticipated areas of concern identified by this collaborative group.

As DSPs know, processes are ever evolving. The DSO and residence life continue to meet regularly to discuss how the process is working and whether anything needs to be reevaluated. Training needed to be developed for professional staff and student staff. It was discovered that campus police needed to be brought into the conversations to understand complaints that might come to them. Staffing responsibilities needed to be addressed in both the DSO and residence life. In the DSO, one individual assumed responsibility for this accommodation, which then spurred a discussion around that individual's job description and possible changes within the office. We might not have anticipated this process while reading a resolution for a case, but it became a need for us.

Overall, the University of Nebraska case became the flashpoint in our work around this growing accommodation. The fact that it was a DOJ case, allowing for damages to be discussed, caught the eye of many DSPs, creating synergy around the common goal of making the process for assistance animals as transparent as possible. This case is an excellent example of how OCR and DOJ resolutions can spur change in our institutions without us even receiving a complaint. It is also a great example of how the two governmental agencies can shape blanket change and provide essential guidance for our work as DSPs.

In Summary

The fork in the road for DSPs presents two choices: react to complaints or be proactive to reduce the likelihood of complaints. If we think about these choices from a cost/benefit perspective, it is far less costly in both time and money to invest in accessible solutions from the outset. However, the reality of many of our situations is that it can be hard to make a case for prioritizing our work without the pressure of potential litigation. The upside to being involved in a complaint is the subsequent actions that take place to push our institutions toward becoming more accessible and inclusive spaces. By staying two steps ahead of the courts, we position ourselves to plant seeds of accessibility and take action quickly when the time comes.

Maintaining a proactive position is no easy task. There is constant change and jurisdictional differences, and all of it exists in a gray area. The line between the roles of DOJ and OCR is very blurry; it can be very difficult to differentiate between the two. We are not lawyers, so the goal of this chapter is to provide a broad overview of how court decisions influence our work and how we can apply court rulings to our practices. Readers of this text are encouraged to consult with their institution's legal counsel given the dynamic nature of the legal landscape.

Reflective Exercise

A DSO at a unionized, medium-size public institution has begun to see an increase in student requests for accessible course materials. Many of the requests revolve around inaccessible PDFs, photos of documents needed to fulfill assignments, and inaccessible platforms for supplemental instruction. The requests come from students who use screen readers primarily. You identify that minimum accessibility standards need to be adopted. What steps need to be considered? Who will be your audience and your partners? Is there a formal process for adopting changes to faculty workflow? If so, do you need to consider the faculty union as a partner, and how will you develop the support? Should you consider legal cases as part of your plan to promote the production of more accessible course materials? If so, what cases would be relevant to include?

Supplemental Job Aids

The following Supplemental Job Aids can be found at https://scholarshare.temple.edu/handle/20.500.12613/8373:

- Helpful Resources

13

Distinguishing between Policies, Processes, and Procedures

Not all processes and procedures are policies, but every policy needs a process and procedure. This chapter defines and differentiates between policy, process, and procedure and provides specific examples of each. Particular attention is paid to how the three functions are interconnected and how each plays an important role in maintaining compliance and equity in service provision.

▶ Guiding Questions

1. What key characteristics require something to be a policy versus a process or procedure?
2. How do policies, processes, and procedures relate to one another?
3. Why is it important to consistently apply policies?
4. What are the important policies, processes, and procedures for a DSO?

IHEs are responsible for regulating a wide variety of areas including but not limited to equity, learning outcomes, quality control, funding, and assessment (Viennet and Pont 2017). The terms "policy," "process" and "procedure" can be inconsistently used and applied, further complicating the already complex management of these broad parameters. For example, some schools have policies for everything, resulting in policy overload that dilutes the message

(ACICS 2021). Others are reined in by institutional requirements (also known as a policy for policies) that, if too restrictive, can result in policy gaps, leading to inconsistency and confusion (Viennet and Pont 2017). This lack of standardization can feel a little chaotic and make it challenging to know who owns what. A happy medium between the two is a policy playbook for potential scenarios that provides general guidelines around the rules and regulations of the game (the game being compliance). Within the playbook are the actual plays (the processes) and the instructions on how to execute those plays (the procedures).

One way to maintain clarity is to streamline policy governance. Let the institution own the policies whenever possible and use DSO processes and procedures as channels for engaging with the policies. For example, instead of writing a separate housing accommodation policy, create a procedure connected to the institutional housing policy that instructs students on how to request housing accommodations via the reasonable accommodation process.

Being discerning about how policies are used does not negate their importance. Case precedent shows us time and time again that clear and consistent policies are an essential component to institutional risk mitigation and management. Chapter 12 dives into more detailed explanations of the impact of policy (or lack thereof) on resolution agreements and legal decisions, but it is important to note that the legal sticking points tend to be ease of access to the interactive process and consistent application. The courts have shown time and time again that a critical component of accessibility compliance is not having an overly burdensome process for accessing and receiving accommodations, hence the importance of clear processes and procedures.

According to the Accreditation Council for Independent Colleges and Schools, smart policy design is clearly justified and provides solutions to the problem a policy is seeking to address (ACICS 2021). A rule without a policy to back it up is difficult to enforce when challenged (see the second example below), while a policy without an accompanying process and procedure can be hard to apply. The goal of this chapter is to encourage judicious use of policies where appropriate and DSOs not taking on more than is reasonable or legally prudent. Doing so not only prevents policy fatigue but also supports operational efficiencies that result in a more accessible experience (Viennet and Pont 2017). Be mindful that IHEs may have their own definitions and guidelines; readers of this text are strongly encouraged to consult with their institution's compliance and/or general counsel staff as needed.

It can be overwhelming to think about how many areas DSPs need to manage. The AHEAD Program, Standards, and Performance Indicators name three areas for equity and accessibility considerations: higher education ex-

A University of Massachusetts Boston (UMB) student filed a complaint with OCR claiming their rights were being violated because a professor refused to grant an extension as a reasonable accommodation. The complaint was initially handled through the UMB internal grievance procedure, and the student filed an OCR complaint for failure to provide academic adjustment, retaliation, and failure to equitably investigate internal grievance. UMB had clear procedures for students who qualify for assignment extensions, but OCR took issue with some of the components of the procedure (failure to provide academic adjustment); because the IHE had an established internal grievance process, the latter two complaints were dismissed.

A nonresidential student began bringing his dog to campus during the day. The student would bring the dog to class, the library, the campus center, and other indoor areas of campus. The student was stopped from bringing the dog into the cafeteria because of board of health regulations but continued to disregard requests from faculty and staff to remove the animal. The DSO began getting calls from all different areas of campus—the department that manages the campus center, the student's faculty members, and other staff who would observe the student walking through campus buildings with the dog. Everyone regarded the student as having a disability and wanted the DSO to intervene and either restrict the dog from campus or provide an accommodation for the student to bring the dog into campus facilities. After a lot of teachable moments about the ADAAA regarding people as having disabilities and highlighting a lack of IHE policy about allowing animals inside campus facilities, DS providers were able to work with campus building managers to develop a policy for animals in campus facilities with provisions for service animals and people with accommodations.

periences, campus environments, and academic policies (AHEAD 2021c). These are broad categories that encompass the entire student experience from enrollment management (the application process, tours, open houses) to onboarding (orientation programs, placement exams, precollege programs) to the student experience (commuting, housing, curriculum, extracurriculars). Further complicating the situation is the fact that students can request accommodations at any point during the student experience. Therefore, DSPs must be equipped to engage in the interactive process at any time.

Distinguishing between Policy, Process, and Procedure: What Does It All Mean?

Policies are high-level statements of the rules and expectations guiding an institution, while processes and procedures implement the structure for fulfilling the directives of policies (Viennet and Pont 2017). Processes are the overview of how to interact with policy, and procedures are the step-by-step instructions on what exactly needs to be completed to obtain the deliverable. In other words, policies are the destination, processes are the map, and procedures are the step-by-step directions on what exactly needs to be done to arrive at the final target.

Instead of authoring every policy, student-facing DSOs can (and should) look to the established institutional rules and requirements, provide input on how to incorporate paths to accessibility into the actual policy/rule/regulation, and develop processes and procedures for requesting accommodations. Since the ADA is a federal law that prohibits discrimination against people with disabilities and requires provision of accommodations for those who qualify, there need to be established mechanisms for disabled students to request and receive accommodations or auxiliary aids that reduce or remove barriers to access (U.S. Department of Justice 2010a). This does not mean that there needs to be a policy for every single potential accommodation request. The bottom line is that if something cannot be backed up by an established rule, regulation, or law and cannot be consistently enforced (or enforced at all), it may not need to (and probably should not) be a policy. This is where processes and procedures come into play.

A process is a mandatory sequence of actions that results in specific deliverables. Process language describes the overview of what it looks like to engage with the policy and possible end results. For example, an IHE or a specific course may have an attendance policy that requires students to be present for a certain percentage of the semester to pass the class. SWDs may need to request an accommodation to this policy. DS does not need to write an attendance policy for disabled students; rather it needs to establish a process for interacting with the existing attendance policy by requesting an accommodation. For example, students seeking exceptions to the attendance policy need to engage in the academic accommodations process at the institution, which may look something like Figure 13.1.

As DSPs conduct individualized assessments as part of the interactive process, it is a good idea to engage with the authors of the original policy. Collaborating to create guidelines about how accommodations will work and setting parameters about receiving and providing accommodations is much more effective than creating an entirely new policy. This is an important step

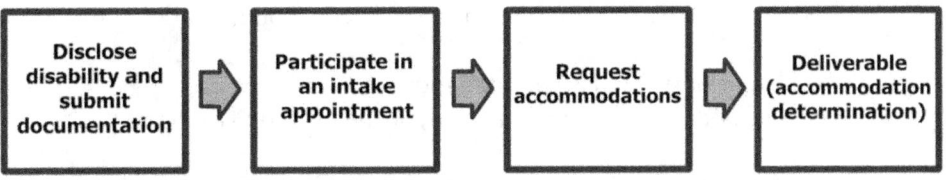

Figure 13.1 Academic Accommodations Process

in preventing accommodation processes from having unintended negative impacts on other areas and is discussed in more detail later in this chapter.

The procedure takes the process and breaks it down into step-by-step instructions. The process for accessing reasonable accommodations should have follow-up procedures specific to the area of need. For example, the academic accommodation process may have many procedures associated with it, such as an exam accommodation procedure or an alternative text request procedure. Using our example of a request for an accommodation to the attendance policy, the procedure for engaging with the academic accommodation process may look like the following:

- Student completes disability disclosure form.
- Student submits documentation that supports the request.
- Student schedules an intake appointment.
- Student attends intake appointment and shares information about how the disability functionally impacts the ability to meet the attendance requirement.
- DSP reviews the information provided by the student, the documentation, and the fundamental goals/objectives of the attendance

A 2018 class action complaint resulted in Stanford University entering into a resolution agreement with OCR. Current and former students alleged that IHE leave of absence polices violated the rights of students with mental health disabilities. The resolution agreement had serious implications for IHE policies, processes, and procedures. Stanford was required to rewrite the involuntary leave of absence policy, include a voluntary leave of absence provision, and review and update communication procedures with students. The agreement mandated that Stanford post a resource for students on how to interact with the process for mental health leaves of absence. It required the provision of specific accommodations such as course load requirements, changes after the add/drop deadline, recording of classes, and assignment extensions (Anderson 2019).

requirement to determine whether requested accommodations are reasonable.
- Student is notified of accommodation decision.
- Accommodations are implemented, or the decision is appealed.

The accommodation policy and request process will remain relatively static throughout institutional areas because they are connected to established access laws that cover all services and programs of IHEs. The procedures will differ depending on the type of accommodation that needs implementation (i.e., test taking, interpreters, physical access, parking/transportation, housing, etc.).

Common Disability Services Policies, Processes, and Procedures and a Framework for Management

This section provides a framework for policy development to assist DSPs in distinguishing between when to create processes and procedures for an existing policy and when to author a new policy. Let us review the three Ps:

- The *policy* is the statement of the rules and expectations guiding the institution.
- The *process* is the overview of how to interact with the policy—the high-level view from start to finish.
- The *procedure* is the specific steps to take to achieve the output intended by the process—exactly what to do, when to do it, and with whom to engage to get to the endpoint identified by the process.

An example of the three Ps is as follows:

- *Policy*: No unauthorized audio recording of lectures in compliance with institutional intellectual property standards and state privacy laws and regulations.
- *Process*: Student must obtain permission to audio record lectures.
- *Procedure*:
  - Student requests permission to audio record lectures via the institution's accommodation process.
  - Student brings audio recording notification and agreement to faculty for signature.
  - Student returns signed notification and agreement to DS.

- Signed notification and agreement are stored in the student's DS record.

Common policies that live in DSOs may include reasonable accommodation policies and grievance or nondiscrimination policies. We are the gatekeepers of reasonable accommodation requests and provision, and these policies override almost any institutional requirement. The reasonable accommodation policy is the umbrella policy under which we keep the processes and procedures used for requesting access to the plethora of campus programs and services. Examples of processes and procedures that live under an accommodation policy are those for housing accommodations, assistance animals, dining accommodations, and interpreter requests.

The DS policies, processes, and procedures provide guidance on how SWDs can fully participate in the programs and services of the institution. Institutional academic policies around attendance, registration, course requirements, and course load minimums may interfere with equal access for disabled students. For example, full-time student status often requires a minimum number of credits and can impact student financial aid eligibility and ability to live in on-campus housing. DS providers are often called on to authorize reduced course load accommodations for students unable to access the academic program as prescribed, and the reasonable accommodation process is implemented to determine the most reasonable course of action. Nonacademic processes such as the discipline and sanctioning process, residential and meal plan requirements, and even some components of Title IX proceedings may present access barriers to SWDs. For example, a student on the autism spectrum may need to request a social interpreter for a conduct hearing, or a person with PTSD may receive an accommodation to have advanced access to the agenda of a Title IX proceeding.

Keeping tabs on every area that has the potential to present access issues is daunting. Using a clearly defined structure for determining when something is a policy, process, or procedure in addition to defining the parameters of each component is important for consistency and ease of management. This text defines policy as the umbrella under which processes and procedures exist to guide interaction with the policy. We see this as a best practice but are aware that IHEs vary in their thoughts about how policies, procedures, and processes should be developed and implemented. We encourage using this chapter as one method for simplifying the policy management process.

We present the following framework to look at DS policy, procedure, and process management. These are not exhaustive lists of all the areas that may require provision of services for disabled students, and IHEs may categorize things in different ways, but this framework can be a basic guide on how to think about classifying policies, processes, and procedures. Of course, it is important to think beyond compliance; compliance is the floor, and universal design methodologies (see Chapter 16) should be the paradigm in higher education. However, the reality is that until universal design becomes the standard—and the medical model of disability is replaced by the social model (see Chapter 2)—we need to be acutely aware of the compliance issues faced by our universities.

A Management Framework

Experiences, environments, and academic policies (AHEAD 2021c) encompass every touchpoint during a student's time at an IHE. DSOs do not have ownership over most of these areas, yet we are responsible for providing reasonable accommodations for students to fully participate in the college experience. This responsibility may result in the temptation to create a laundry list of our own policies for providing reasonable accommodations, much to the chagrin of IHE legal counsels and compliance staff. Doing so inevitably results in "policies" that are not actually policies giving conflicting information to the consumers of the services. An audit of IHE rules and regulations will most likely result in the realization that many DS policies can be converted into processes and/or procedures because they are either not backed up by legal requirements or institutional rules or because an institutional policy already exists. The moral of the story is to resist the temptation to write policies for every possible situation; instead, write processes and procedures to correspond with existing IHE policies whenever possible.

Conducting a comprehensive review of the institutional regulations relevant to the work of the DSO is the first step to identifying what works, what needs revision, and what is missing. This process is not static; new situations, updates to case law, and compliance-related changes occur throughout the life cycle of a policy. IHEs should establish a review schedule (annually, every three years, etc.) to make sure the original intentions of regulations still hold up. An example of the review process is illustrated in Figure 13.2.

The following two questions should guide the review:

- Is there a legal obligation or institutional rule/requirement this policy seeks to enforce?
- Does the IHE have an established policy that can be used to develop processes and procedures that facilitate the interactive process?

We have already agreed to leave the heavy lifting of policy development to the high-level administrators at our IHEs whenever possible. Once we know what we are working with at our IHEs in terms of current policies and reg-

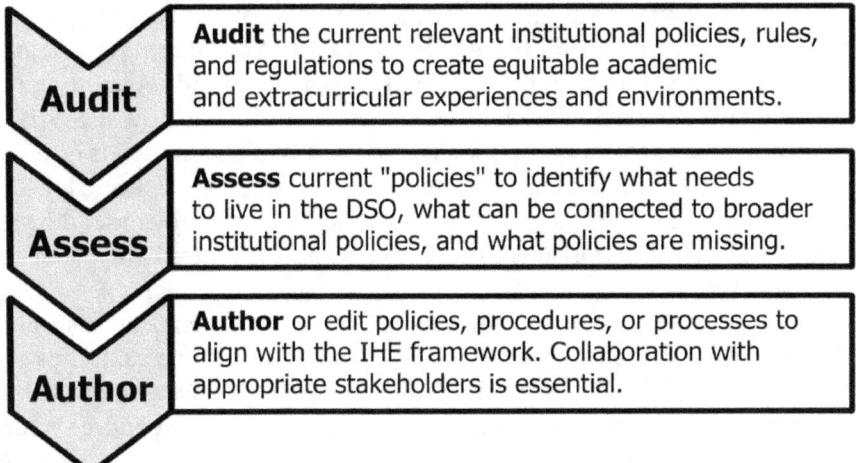

Figure 13.2 Comprehensive Review of Institutional Regulation

ulations, we can begin the process of editing: the development phase. In this phase, DSPs can utilize the reasonable accommodation policy to showcase our knowledge of how laws and regulations governing the rights of people with disabilities interact with the laws, regulations, institutional rules, practices, and standards upheld by IHEs (Pasquini 2016). The interactive process for requesting accommodations is the path DS providers must take toward larger institutional compliance.

Engaging with Appropriate Campus Stakeholders to Author Policies

We cannot emphasize enough how important it is to check on IHE-specific policy writing guidelines for before creating or adopting another institution's template. Even if the IHE does not provide specific information about what should be in a policy, there may be a mandatory policy approval process. Less is more with policy language, and using a consistent formula can help keep focus on the situation the policy is intended to enforce. The goal is to establish boundaries for areas that come under DSO jurisdiction. Most of the issues we deal with have gray areas and can become quite complex, so it is tempting to go off on tangents to make sure every single possible scenario is covered. However, it is more effective to keep policies broad and general and let processes and procedures do the legwork for the particulars.

If IHEs do not provide guidance for policy management or if there are few policies to use as guidelines for determining reasonable accommodations, resist the temptation to author a policy in a DS vacuum. Seize the opportunity to connect with relevant stakeholders and work in partnership to develop inclusive policies rooted in the universal design framework. According to the Accrediting Council for Independent Colleges and Schools (ACICS 2021), "stakeholder engagement for policy writing and implementation is critical because higher education is multi-directional." In other words, even though we often operate in silos, our actions have a ripple effect throughout the institution. We need to work together to promote a truly accessible experience for students.

Policy should be used not only for inclusion in what already exists but also as a means of transformation for what could be (Strangio 2021). It is an opportunity to help our colleagues build accessibility considerations from the ground up. Chapters 16 and 17 of this text go into detail about the value of applying universal design principles throughout the institution and of engaging with the IHE community. However, since accessibility issues are so pervasive, we would be remiss not to highlight the opportunity for collaboration in policy development and management.

DSPs do not need, want, and probably do not have the authority to create a policy on how to request every single type of possible accommodation. However, a lack of internal policies or regulations can cause headaches when it comes to enforcing the mandates set forth by the ADAAA and other access legislation. For example, a lack of IHE-wide attendance policy results in course-by-course determinations. This lack of consistency opens the door for potential subjectivity with providing accommodations, such as two professors teaching sections of the same course but implementing different policies because they have different ideas of what is fundamental.

Policies not only provide protection against noncompliance but also send a loud message about institutional culture. If there is an opportunity to push IHEs to adopt more inclusive and equitable policies, take it! Does the IHE have a campus-wide accessibility policy or statement? If not an overarching policy, do they have accessibility-related policies in specific areas like web accessibility, accessible electronic and information technology, course materials, or accessible procurement? If not, this work can serve as an opening for collaboration as shown in Figure 13.3.

A Note on Appeals and Grievances

A policy without accompanying clear, efficient processes and procedures can hinder participation in the interactive process required by the ADAAA. In this way, policies mitigate institutional risk but do not eliminate the need for systems that address questions or disagreements about how policies are

When one institution's DSO explored ways to improve the accessibility of course materials, it started with the procurement process. Initially, DSPs thought they should author an accessible procurement policy. When they drilled down a little further, they realized that a procurement policy already existed through the purchasing office. The DSO and the purchasing department met to discuss the proposed addition of accessibility criteria to the existing purchasing procedure. Universal design principles and case law (Pennsylvania State University 2015) helped provide the rationale for implementing a system to catch inaccessible products before purchase orders are signed. The DSO then partnered with the faculty senate and budget managers to develop a system to establish minimum accessibility criteria and require all purchase orders to include a completed accessibility checklist from the vendor. This change did not happen overnight and did not catch every single purchase made at the IHE, but it established a solid foundation to expand on and provided more justification for the development of an IHE-wide accessibility policy.

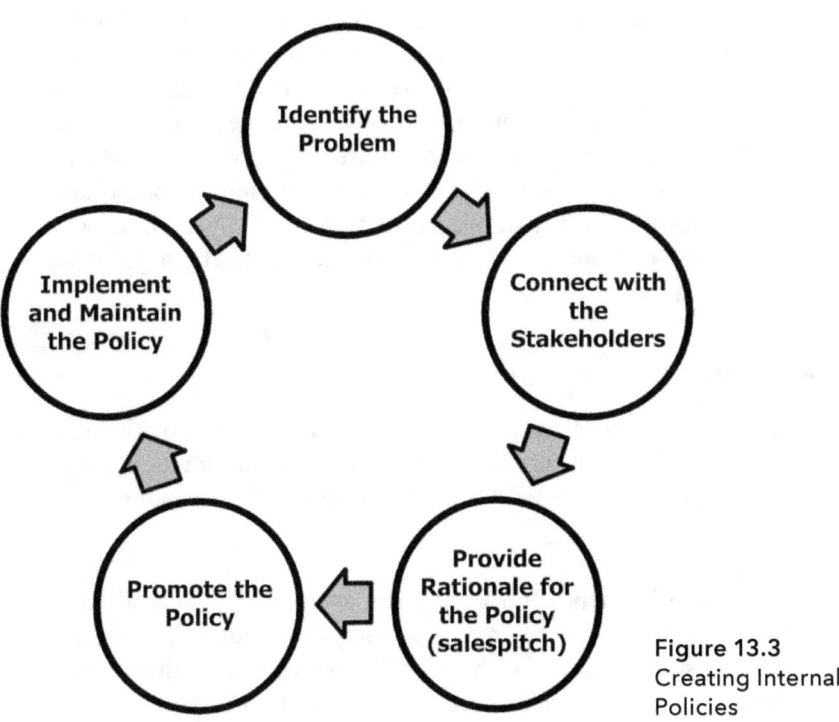

Figure 13.3 Creating Internal Policies

applied. DSOs must have an official procedure for appealing and filing a grievance if students disagree with a decision or feel their rights are being violated.

The interactive process is a fancy way of describing a conversation. Students request accommodations; DSPs discuss the request with the student and other stakeholders (faculty, program heads, housing, etc.) and make decisions about reasonable accommodations. In cases where decisions result in a different accommodation than the one requested or a denial of accommodations, it is essential to have a mechanism for appeal and grievance to facilitate additional opportunities for the interactive process.

There are typically three tiers of communication about an accommodation decision: appeal, informal resolution attempt, and formal grievance complaint.

Appeals

Appeals are a formal review of a decision that requires additional consideration of new information.

- Procedure: The student appeals the decision and submits additional documentation supporting their request. The appeals committee reviews the additional documentation, meets with stakeholders where appropriate, and issues a decision either upholding the original decision or issuing a reasonable accommodation based on new information. If the student disagrees with the decision of the appeal, the student may initiate the informal grievance procedure.
- Example: A student is denied a housing accommodation because they provided insufficient documentation. They appeal the process and submit additional documentation that qualifies them for an accommodation.

Informal Resolution Attempt

An informal resolution attempt is a complaint about a decision that requires informally coordinating with key players to determine whether the policy, process, and procedure were followed correctly to affirm or adjust the decision.

- Procedure: The student discusses the issue with the individual directly responsible for accommodation implementation (faculty member, housing staff, etc.). If this discussion does not result in a satisfactory resolution or if direct communication with the person responsible for implementing the accommodation is not appropri-

ate under the circumstances, the student contacts the DSO to discuss the situation.
- Example: A student alleges a faculty member did not provide them with extended time on the midterm. The DS provider calls the faculty member for clarification, and it is determined that the student has not used the accommodation all semester and did not plan to use the accommodation for the midterm. The student confirms this information. The faculty member, DS provider, and student meet to clarify roles in the accommodation process to avoid future confusion.

If the result of the informal resolution is not satisfactory to the student, the student is advised on how to file a formal grievance.

Formal Grievance

A formal grievance is a complaint filed via the IHE's nondiscrimination policy complaint process where a formal investigation is conducted to determine grounds for upholding or overturning an accommodation decision. Formal grievances are best managed via a committee structure to ensure a comprehensive and impartial response to the student concern. Committee members can include representatives from DS, counseling services, housing and residence life, academic affairs, student health services, dean of students office, and any other relevant components of the institution. Many IHEs may already have an ADA compliance committee that can serve as the appeals board.

- Procedure: The student files a written complaint within ten days of the end of the semester that the alleged infraction occurred. The complaint must include the grievant's contact information, a detailed description of the problem and any attempts to resolve the issue, and a statement detailing the requested solution. The student sends the written complaint to the ADA compliance committee for review. The ADA compliance committee convenes to review the complaint, investigate, and issue a finding.
- Example: A student files a formal complaint alleging that a school club is discriminating against them because they have a disability by holding events in an inaccessible location. An investigation conducted by the ADA compliance committee determines that the student was being discriminated against because they were offered a separate but equal option of attending the events virtually instead of the club moving the meetings to an accessible location.

In Summary

This chapter attempts to present a policy strategy that walks the line between too much and not enough to help maintain compliance and limit risk while providing the institution with clear, consistent, and fair parameters that promote accessibility and equity. DSPs can create and maintain processes and procedures that allow people with disabilities to engage in the interactive process and request accommodations when institutional policies create barriers to access. We live in a litigious society, and people can be quick to use legal arguments to push back on rules. We need to have sound arguments rooted in reasonable policies that are consistently applied when approving or denying accommodation requests.

There are multiple factors to consider before embarking on a policy development initiative:

- Understanding how policies, processes, and procedures are managed on an institutional level
- Identifying policies that need to be authored and maintained in the DSO versus institutional policies that need a channel to the interactive process required by the ADAAA
- Ensuring policies are backed by an institutional rule or legal mandate
- Establishing processes and procedures for each policy
- Engaging with campus stakeholders to create policies, processes, and procedures that promote access to the IHE's programs and services

The landscape of higher education is dynamic, and the needs of students and scope of access laws and regulations continue push the boundaries of DSOs. There is no area of the college experience untouched by potential barriers to access. IHEs are continuously adding rules and requirements to their academic and extracurricular programs and services, often without thinking about access implications. Using clear and consistent applications of policy, process, and procedure—where policy is the umbrella term referring to laws or institutional rules, process is the roadmap of how to interact with the policy, and procedure is the step-by-step guide to get to the end result—will help DS providers be prepared to act efficiently and accurately when it comes to advising the institution on compliance in accommodation provision and assisting students with accommodation requests.

▶ Reflective Exercise

A student asks their professor for more time on an exam. They explain that they were diagnosed with ADHD in middle school but that those classes were easy, so they never needed any additional support. They are finding college-level work very challenging. When asked for authorization from DS, the student responds that they do not have time to request accommodations because they are balancing school, work, and family responsibilities and have a very long commute. The professor feels bad and grants the student's request without official notification from DS. The professor tells the student that they will need to provide the required authorization for all future exams. When the next exam approaches, the student once again requests the accommodation without providing supporting authorization from DS. The professor declines to provide the student the accommodation, and the student files a grievance. Discuss how the professor's actions compromised the accommodation process and how available policies could have maintained the integrity of the exam and connected the student with available supports. How could the professor grant the student's request without creating a case for a grievance filing?

Supplemental Job Aids

The following Supplemental Job Aids can be found at https://scholarshare.temple.edu/handle/20.500.12613/8373:

- *Tips from an ADA Compliance Office and Key Terms and Definitions*
- *When to Write a Policy*
- *Policy Topics and Associated Processes and Procedures*
- *Example of a Reasonable Accommodation Policy*

Part V

Inclusion by Design

14

Access to the Built Environment

While there have been great strides in recent years to improve the physical accessibility of our campuses, much work remains to achieve the desired result—elimination of all barriers. SWDs must be able to access all aspects of an institution's campus, including getting to campus, getting around campus, and navigating campus buildings and facilities. While DSPs have expertise in evaluating barriers and working to remove them, they alone do not bear the burden of responsibility to achieve access. Access to the built environment should be addressed via a comprehensive plan with representation from campus partners including facilities, equity and inclusion, compliance, campus planning, DS, and students. Many campuses have an advisory group inclusive of some or all of these members to address a wide range of accessibility efforts. As with all facets of accessibility and inclusion, physical access is a shared institutional responsibility and should be treated as such.

▶ Guiding Questions

1. Which accessibility standards apply to the built environment?
2. How does a DSP address and prioritize physical accessibility on campus?
3. What systems are in place to report and respond to access barriers?

Within the context of a college campus, the phrase "physical accessibility" typically conjures thoughts of ramps, door paddles, and accessible bathrooms. Often overlooked are equally important features such as accessible seating, protruding objects, and wayfinding. Compliance problems may not be uncovered until a complaint is made.

As DSPs, one of our many roles is to ensure students have equal access to the built environment. The built environment consists of a campus's buildings, grounds, and infrastructure. Think about academic buildings, residence halls, libraries, administrative offices, sports facilities, dining halls, etcetera. It encompasses open spaces on campus, including athletic fields, parking lots, amphitheaters, courtyards, transit points, lawns, and any other common student space. Essentially, the built environment is any space on campus—indoors and outside.

As DSPs, ensuring access in a myriad of spaces can feel overwhelming. We are often tasked with triaging complaints about broken elevators, inoperable door paddles, obstructed pathways, unsuitable furniture, and insufficient accessible parking. We are called on to relocate classes and events from inaccessible spaces to accessible ones, reimagine spaces, research furniture, and plan alternate routes of travel during construction projects or inclement weather. Thankfully, we are not required recite architectural standards, measure tolerances, or gauge door forces. Those responsibilities likely fall under facilities or buildings and grounds departments. However, it is incumbent on us to be aware of the broad areas in which access should be built in. The goal of this chapter is to give DSPs guidance on where to focus their attention and who to partner with to share the responsibility of access.

Legal Standards

Four federal laws govern physical campus accessibility. Along with state and local regulations, they establish a basis for access, design, and construction standards. While Table 14.1 provides a summary of each statute, DSPs should consider exploring each in greater detail on their campus. Given the breadth of the ADA, Table 14.2 outlines nuances between Title II and Tile III.

According to the ADA Checklist for Existing Facilities, when selecting which accessible elements to address first, elements that provide the greatest access should be prioritized (New England ADA Center 2017).

- Priority 1—Accessible approach and entrance
- Priority 2—Access to goods and services
- Priority 3—Access to restrooms
- Priority 4—Access to other necessary measures (e.g., amenities such as water fountains)

TABLE 14.1   A SUMMARY OF EACH LEGAL STATUTE

Law	Summary	Application	Implication
Architectural Barriers Act (ABA) of 1968	Mandates that people with disabilities have "ready access to and use of" federal buildings and facilities built or altered after the bill's signing.	Any building designed, built, or operated with federal dollars.	Since most institutions receive federal dollars, they are obligated to comply with the ABA.
Rehabilitation Act of 1973	The U.S. Access Board created and established minimum accessible design standards, developed design criteria. Requires transition plan for achieving accessibility.	All federal properties, including the built environment, transportation, telecommunications, medical diagnostic equipment, and IT.	Campus buildings constructed prior to 1977 may relocate programs and services instead of making the building accessible. Anything built after 1977 must adhere to these guidelines.
Fair Housing Amendments Act (FHAA) of 1988	Discrimination includes failure to design and construct new multifamily dwellings that are accessible and usable.	Dwellings of four or more units (residence halls).	Residence halls must have accessible entrances, accessible routes, and electrical features in accessible locations.
Americans with Disabilities Act (ADA) of 1990	The U.S. Access Board developed and provided technical assistance on accessibility guidelines. The most recent are 2010 ADA Standards.	All new construction and alterations to existing structures must remove barriers to access.	Any new campus building or building undergoing any type of reconstruction must follow the accessibility standards.

Keep in mind that being well versed in standards and code is not a necessity—but having a foundational understanding of accessible features is. Recognizing which features have the power to include or exclude is the first step in mitigating those that adversely impact the campus experience.

Universal Design and the Built Environment

Chapter 16 discusses the concept of universal design and universal design for learning (UDL) in detail. It is important to take a moment to emphasize the value that universal design has in inclusive built environments.

The concept of universal design came from famed architect Ron Mace. He proposed that architects should consider disability access from the first design of a building. Mace's universal design concept has changed the way

TABLE 14.2 THE DIFFERENCES BETWEEN TITLE II AND TITLE III OF THE ADA

ADA Title II "Program Accessibility" Standard	ADA Title III "Barrier Removal" Standard
State and local governments must ensure that services, programs, and activities are accessible to people with disabilities.	Places of public accommodation that provide goods and services to people with disabilities must do so on an equal basis with nondisabled people.
Public entities do not have to make each facility accessible if equivalent access to the program is ensured (e.g., relocating a classroom from the second floor to the first).	Private entities must remove all structural and architectural barriers when doing so is "readily achievable."
Any public entity with fifty or more employees should complete a self-evaluation to determine the extent to which programs, services, and activities for students, visitors, and the public are accessible to disabled individuals. Structural changes to provide program access were to be completed no later than July 26, 1995. The DOJ has declined to establish a schedule for ongoing self-assessment as a regulatory requirement, but it does urge public entities to establish their own procedures for ongoing assessment.	There is no requirement to conduct a self-evaluation; however, the DOJ urges establishing procedures for ongoing assessment. What barriers are considered "readily achievable" to remove are determined on a case-by-case basis. The ADA requires barrier removal in historic buildings unless it would threaten or destroy the historic significance of buildings designated as such under the federal, state, or local law. The obligation to engage in barrier removal is an ongoing but not unlimited one. There is no obligation to exceed standards.
The undue burden standard must demonstrate that modifications/accommodations would cause excessive administrative or financial burden.	The undue burden standard is a readily achievable standard that is easily accomplished without much difficulty or expense. Difficult barrier removal now may be readily achievable with small changes and financial planning. The 1991 ADA standards apply to facilities built or altered before March 2012.

we approach the built environment. It gives tools to developers, campus planners, admission counselors, and prospective students around how an IHE can be inclusive without needing to call out a specific ability or disability in the moment. If accessible parking is made available in all campus parking lots, then a prospective student does not need to ask for it ahead of time. If a dining facility is located on the ground floor with electronic door openers, then a vendor does not have to navigate a backdoor drop-off with a utility lift. And if all classroom buildings have a range of desk types, then DSOs do not need to contact the facilities department every time a student has a specific need. Universal design naturally creates a welcoming environment for all without retrofitting spaces or arguing about which building most needs an elevator. It naturally involves a wide range of stakeholders across campus, all working toward greater inclusivity.

Accessibility Advisory Committee

If the IHE does not have a campus-wide think tank for addressing access, we suggest creating one so that the DSO does not shoulder campus accessibility alone. As previously mentioned, stakeholders who have the authority to affect change and advocate for the inclusion of disabled individuals should be the ones leading the charge to expand and design a more accessible campus. Key components of these efforts should include conversations about universal design along with other diversity, equity, inclusion, and justice efforts across campus.

The scope of the committee can be as broad as its membership. Large institutions may have numerous accessibility advisory committees spanning architectural, programmatic, web, communication, and disaster planning access needs. Smaller institutions might have a committee of just a few stakeholders who meet on an ad hoc basis.

Depending on the committee's focus, membership might include those responsible for the planning, building, and maintenance of university facilities; IT; teaching and learning; human resources; public safety; equity, diversity, and access; faculty; and DS. The committee would be incomplete without input from campus community members with disabilities. As primary users of spaces, disabled students are experts in navigating challenging environments. Their lived experiences should serve as the driving force in shaping campus disability initiatives. When designing with accessibility in mind, be sure to incorporate feedback from users with a wide range of disabilities, including cognitive impairments, memory impairments, and hearing and visual disabilities. Consider people who use keyboards, screen readers, captioning, alternative text, service animals, and a variety of mobility devices (wheelchairs, scooters, canes).

Overarching committee goals and objectives might include the following:

- Fostering a campus community that celebrates disability as a valued aspect of diversity
- Facilitating an ethical obligation to design inclusive and socially just campus environments
- Assessing campus barriers to equal access and recommending solutions

- Advising on the prioritization of projects and reviewing progress
- Responding to accessibility needs as they emerge
- Communicating with campus community about accessibility features, barriers, and how to navigate them

The DSP's role in this committee may be in a leadership capacity or simply as a member. In either case, it is likely that participation will intersect with other committee work where access is considered. For example, the DSP may be asked to sit on the planning committee for a new campus building or campus layout change. Participation in capital planning is encouraged, as it offers an opportunity to preemptively advocate for access needs and raise concern about potential barriers.

If an access advisory committee does not yet exist, embrace the opportunity to get one started. It may seem that broadly addressing accessibility on campus is too complex or expensive. It does not have to be. With the right partners who care about access, low-cost incremental changes are possible—while planning and budgeting for substantial ones.

Accessing the Built Environment

In the next section, we cover various areas of the built environment. While the access barriers discussed may not rise to the "necessary to remove" level under minimum accessibility standards, our goal as DSPs is to exceed regulatory compliance. If an institution's mission is guided by a desire to promote inclusivity of all community members, then campus accessibility efforts should be so aligned. Meeting minimum code requirements will not get us there. Aspiring to create a barrier-free and inclusive environment will.

Wayfinding and Signage

The first point of access consideration should be the ease with which a prospective or enrolled student can access the campus. First impressions matter. If students are unable to find the admissions office, accessible parking lots, or the DSO, they may decide it is not worth the hassle. (See Figure 14.1.)

Wayfinding encompasses the many ways in which people orient themselves and navigate spaces, both physical and digital. In a nutshell, wayfinding is assisting people to understand where they are and where they intend to go. As our campuses continue to grow and become increasingly diverse, we are more and more reliant campus maps, mobile applications, and kiosks.

With pocket access to a mobile map readily available, paper maps are becoming a thing of the past. Still, they have a purpose with some demographics. The challenge with paper maps is keeping them updated as campus projects

Wayfinding
Parking lots
Accesible routes
Accesible entrances
Accessible exits
Room identification
Informational signs

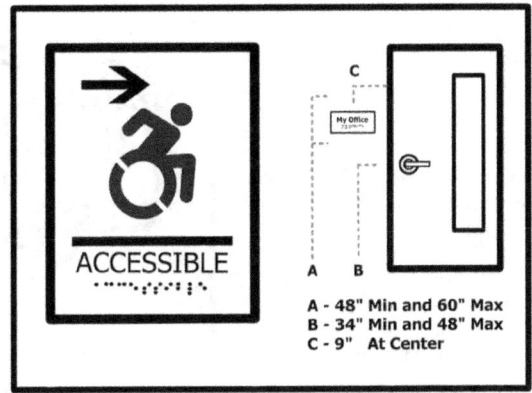

Figure 14.1 ADA Compliant Room Signage

and accessibility features evolve. Mobile applications have become increasingly popular in helping people navigate sprawling campuses and are easier to update on a regular basis.

Wayfinding kiosks are either static or interactive signs in atriums, entryways, and key navigation points around campus. They show "you are here" as a reference point to where someone might want to go. Like mobile maps, interactive digital kiosks have begun to be incorporated by some campuses. According to a systems analyst at Florida International University, kiosks provide for "exceptional customer service and genuine approach to helping develop an amazing customer experience for our students" (Miller 2017).

Signage is an important aspect of a wayfinding system, both indoors and out. It refers to a system of signs that orient people to their current location relative to their desired one. Signage is intended to provide navigational information quickly and accessibly while maintaining branding and aesthetic elements unique to the campus. The goal is to provide directional assistance not only to accessible routes but also away from inaccessible ones. There are many complexities to a sign strategy. To meet design standards, signage should be appropriately formatted for scale, size, color, contrast, position, conciseness, and braille formats.

Transportation and Parking

Transportation at the institution, within the institution, and between campuses are also aspects of the built environment that need consideration. When we discuss transportation, we are including parking on campus. With regards to transportation, the general rule of thumb is that if it is offered to any student, whether in the form of a shuttle, bus, van, or even golf cart, then it must also have an accessible mode of transportation for SWDs. (See Figure 14.2.)

Sufficient accessible parking spaces

Accessible aisles & passenger loading zones

Accesible parking on shortest accessible route to entrances

Accesible transit or paratransit options (when campus provides transportation)

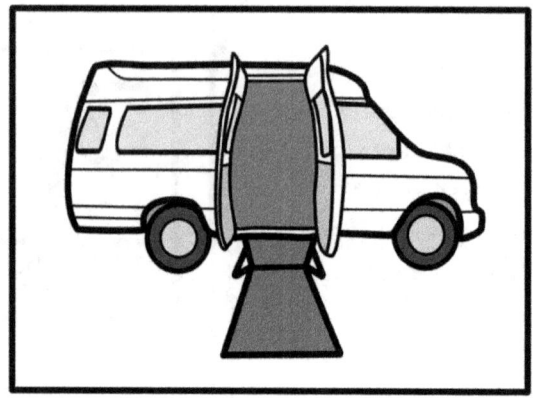

Figure 14.2 Accessible Transportation

An incoming student at an urban university reached out to the DSO and asked for a transportation accommodation to drive them from their residence hall to the academic building where their classes were. The student had a disability that impacted their ability to walk independently. If the institution had had a fleet of vehicles or even offered transportation to any other student on its campus, then the DSO would have been legally required to provide this accommodation. However, because the university did not offer these services to any of its students, it was not and did not provide the accommodation. Instead, the DSO recognized the access barrier the student faced (the campus is in the middle of the city's hilly district) and creatively worked with the student to identify accessible city-wide parking near their residence hall and academic buildings. The DSO also suggested that they consider using a ride-sharing service to help them navigate campus.

However, if the institution does not have a formalized transportation system and instead relies on the local town or city's public transportation system, then it does not need to provide an additional source of accessible transportation. Instead, a DSP should be aware of how the town ensures access to the public and be able to point students to that source of support if requested.

If an institution shuttles students in any way—around campus or to athletic events and field trips—then an accessible form of transportation must be made available. Shuttles equipped with integrated wheelchair lifts offer the most inclusive option.

Some institutions are reevaluating their transportation services to reduce operational costs. Fleet overhead, vehicle maintenance, and driver wages can be expensive. As a cost-effective solution that surreptitiously improves access, institutions are contracting ride-sharing companies to get students from Point A to Point B efficiently and safely. Contracts should include accessible vehicles in the company's fleets.

The proliferation of mobile technology has made transit and alternative transportation options more efficient. Convenience features such as real-time tracking, trip planning, and route visualization take the stress out of navigating campus. While we fully celebrate this more universal approach, user interfaces must be accessible to students with limited mobility and/or vision disabilities.

On-campus parking is another aspect of transportation that should be considered with the built environment. More specifically, "accessible parking spaces must be located on the shortest accessible route of travel to an accessible facility entrance. Where buildings have multiple accessible entrances with adjacent parking, the accessible parking spaces must be dispersed and located closest to the accessible entrances" (U.S. Department of Justice Civil Rights Division 2015). The 2010 ADA standards do not require an IHE to provide the same number of parking spaces as there are placard holders, but they do outline requirements for minimum limits.

Parking spots should be well marked with signs both on the ground and on a sign near the spot. Preferred signage indicating handicap parking should show the person in the wheelchair actively moving, not stagnant (see Figure 14.3). Sarah Hendren and Brian Glenney redesigned the symbol to give agency to the person using the wheelchair—they can determine their own course of path and are not reliant on someone else (Logomyway 2017).

Figure 14.3
Dynamic International Symbol of Access

DSPs should tour their campus on an annual basis to ensure that each parking lot has accessible spaces. Public institutions lacking accessible spaces can call on state transportation agencies to conduct parking audits of their campuses.

Parking-based accommodations may include permission to park in a nonstudent lot and permission to have a car on campus prematurely. Consider students who do not have an accessible parking permit but need access to a parking lot for other reasons—perhaps their point of medical care is not near campus or public transportation. In these situations, we may approve access to a student lot, though the student is responsible for paying for the cost to park there (if there is a cost). Students with accessible parking permits do not need to register with the DSO unless they need access to a nonstudent lot or are not permitted to have a car on campus.

Routes or Paths of Travel

A path of travel includes a continuous, unobstructed way of pedestrian passage through which an area may be approached, entered, and exited that connects the altered area with an exterior approach (sidewalks, streets, parking area), entrance to the facility, and other parts of the facility. (See Figure 14.4.) Features included in path of travel are ramps, unobstructed paths, parking aisles, elevators, and lifts (U.S. Department of Justice Civil Rights Division 2010d). Whenever possible, disabled people should be able to use the same route as others and should not have unusually longer travel times to reach the same destination.

The ADA outlines approach and entry as top-of-list access matters. We agree that getting into a building is important, but one must be able to navigate there first. Providing an interconnected campus—one that connects all

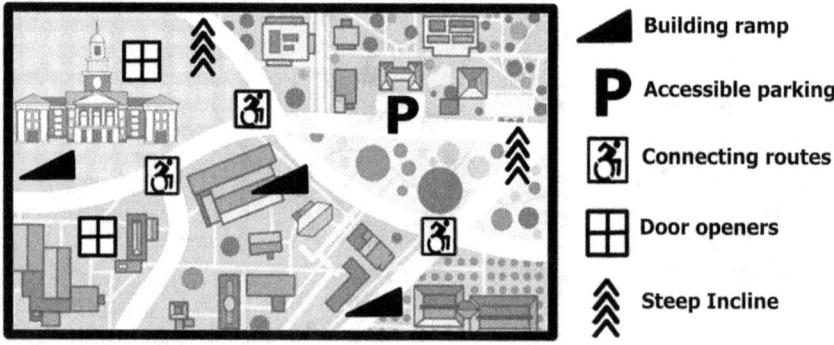

Figure 14.4 Accessible Paths of Travel

Access to the Built Environment / 259

parking spaces, transit stops, and buildings—requires a plan for accessible routes of travel. Having a comprehensive plan for getting around campus will be helpful when unexpected barriers (e.g., weather related) and construction projects develop. This plan will help to inform prioritization of other barriers along the route (e.g., parking, slopes, signage).

The geography and topography of a campus can be challenging. At most IHEs, some degree of natural barrier presents an accessibility challenge. For one of the authors, it is a giant hill in the middle of campus. One creative accessibility solution was to ensure that the buildings on either side of the hill, ones that are ground level and rise to the top of the hill, had elevators.

As DSPs, we are consistently coming up with all sorts of creative solutions to the geographic barriers of our campuses. In the instance of the hill, solutions included relocating classes to more accessible parts of the campus, allowing more time to transition between classes, and providing transportation around the hill. These are all appropriate accommodations.

Buildings and Venues

Once students have arrived on campus, parked, and navigated natural geographic barriers, DSOs are responsible, in part, for ensuring that they can get into the buildings at the institution. (See Figure 14.5.)

The challenge for DSPs is that not all buildings on campus are fully accessible. Some might be for the first floor but not the second or third. Some might not be at all. For existing facilities, the ADA determines accessibility not by meeting architectural standards but by considering whether a program or activity within the building is accessible and usable. If an institution

Clearances for doorways, turning

Elevators/lifts

Doorhandles

Protruding cabinets, handrails, fountains

Accessible furniture

Water fountain height, clearance, usability

Sports stadiums must be accessible

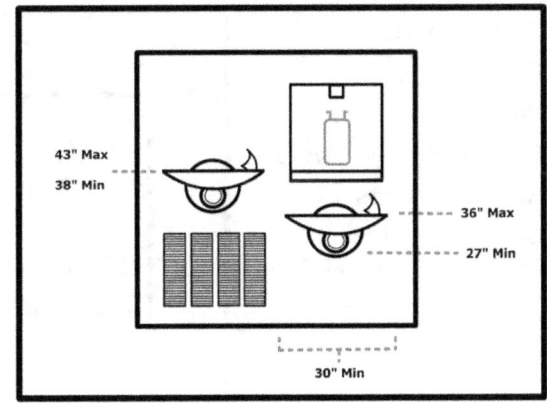

Figure 14.5 ADA Compliant Water Fountain

decides not to make structural changes to an existing facility, it has the option to relocate classes, programs, and activities from inaccessible to accessible facilities. If a student is registered for a class in an inaccessible building or classroom, our job is to work with the registrar to relocate the entire class. Because this task can take some time, we typically provide students who may need relocated classes as an accommodation to register for classes early. If a student needs an accessible residence hall, we work with our colleagues in residence life to relocate the student. Again, the goal is to work with students before they move onto campus, but doing so places the burden on the student to self-identify early and make their request known. As discussed earlier in the book, that is not always feasible.

We also need to be thoughtful about students' nonacademic experiences. Is the dining hall accessible? Are student events held in accessible locations? Does the theater have accessible seating? These are access questions. Through an inclusion lens, we might ask whether the dining hall offers seating for a wide range of stature, body size, and sensory needs. Do student clubs offer a variety of ways to participate? Do ticketing policies allow for accessible seating with companions? As we advocate for architectural barrier removal, let us also explore space and design more universally.

Restrooms

The ADA standards do not address the number of restrooms a facility must have but instead specify which ones are accessible and where they should be located. (See Figure 14.6.) Consideration of these factors include whether the restroom is multiuser or single use; unisex, family, or ungendered; and in a public, private, or residential setting. An audit of one of our campuses ad-

Turning radius
Grab bars
Non-slip floors
Sink height and levers
Accessible exits
Unobstructed floor space beneath fixtures

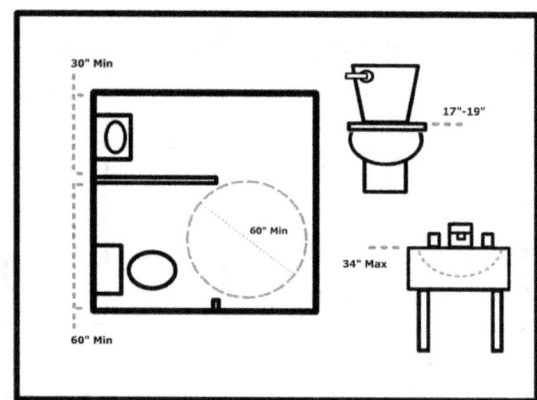

Figure 14.6 ADA Compliant Restroom Design

vised prioritization of at least one accessible restroom in each building, particularly those holding classrooms. Bathroom accessibility looks different for every person. Think of users who have conditions that impact urgency or frequency. For them, restroom proximity is paramount. As a matter of dignity, others may require a single-user bathroom or a stall with a full-length door.

The specifications for restrooms include criteria for clearance, seats, grab bars, mirrors, flushing controls, paper dispensers, receptacles, turning radii, shelves, sinks, and door swing. Accessible restrooms must be labeled with the International Symbol of Accessibility sign. Where a restroom is not ADA compliant, directional signs must indicate the nearest accessible one.

Reporting Barriers

The absence of a barrier reporting system is, in and of itself, a barrier. Access barrier reporting forms have become an industry standard for addressing physical barriers (inoperative elevator, icy pathway, ramp obstruction) and online barriers (uncaptioned video, inaccessible document, broken card reader, missing alternative text). More recently, these forms have included an option to report attitudinal barriers or bias incidents. In some cases, forms may come to the DSO, which is fine, but the DSP needs to raise the issue with the appropriate campus partner instead of assuming full responsibility for it. If the form is not routinely monitored, it should indicate who to contact (and multiple means of doing so) in the event of an emergency or time-sensitive need.

Audits, Self-Evaluations, and Transition Plans

There are legal reasons to conduct a self-evaluation or transition plan, the complexities of which are dizzying. Under certain provisions, Title II requires self-evaluation and, where violations are uncovered, a transition plan for improving campus accessibility needs to be developed. Mandates for self-evaluations may also arise from DOJ complaints. Title III does not require self-evaluation, but if a complaint arises, the DOJ will look more favorably on the case if a good faith effort has been made in addressing the issue. Of course, in the DS world, our goal is to go beyond mere compliance with requirements and endeavor for universally designed spaces.

Launching a self-evaluation is a comprehensive endeavor that typically begins with assessing the campus's accessibility features. Some institutions have the fiscal resources to hire outside firms and vendors to do an accessibility audit of their campus. State schools may be able to rely on state access offices to provide this service for free. Depending on the depth of access analysis the IHE is looking for, this solution usually involves a multiday visit from an access specialist who will walk commonly used routes and evaluate each building's point of access, accessible restrooms, and the accessibility of common student points of interest (the library, financial aid office, dining services, recreation center, etc.). Depending on the scope of work, this evaluation may include the weight of building doors, availability and quality of signage used across campus, and plans for access in inclement weather or emergencies. Accessibility audits are very thorough and result in detailed reports. Many DSPs have used these reports to advance their access needs, though they often have to identify the most pertinent needs due to a lack of campus resources.

Other institutions handle accessibility audits internally. Larger DSOs may rely on one or two staff members to walk the campus and identify access barriers as a summer project. Smaller DSOs may fund a student worker to conduct the audit, though careful training and detailed record keeping are required. And others partner with offices like marketing and communications, human resources, facilities, or public safety to cosponsor the effort, whether with professional employees or student workers. These access audits will be less detailed and official (we should not expect students to be measuring doorways) but can capture the overall access of the campus more easily. Once barriers are identified, next steps include determining the priorities and phasing for corrective action, cost estimates, and funding sources (capital, operational, facilities, grants). These conversations are highly individualized to an institutional setting.

In Summary

Federal laws governing physical accessibility guard against discrimination. They outline minimum compliance standards to ensure program accessibility (Title II) or architectural barrier removal when readily achievable (Title III). As DSPs, our goal is to facilitate a campus climate that does more than comply with the letter of the law, promoting a campus where students are equal members of the community with full rights and privileges of that membership. To achieve an inclusive built environment, we need to move beyond program relocation and accommodation as strategies. While incremental changes are logistically and financially most feasible, institutions should have in place a more comprehensive, strategic, and holistic plan to address physical access. Campus accessibility advisory committees, with disabled students and DSPs as key contributors, are often charged with prioritizing resolutions, responding to emerging needs, and communicating with the campus community about improvements, barriers, and how to navigate them. Campus improvement projects are informed by accessibility audits, which evaluate features such as wayfinding, pathways, building access, and infrastructure.

▸ Reflective Exercise

Three weeks before the semester starts, a student with a mobility impairment reaches out to ask whether their residence hall has an elevator. You conduct an intake and find that while the student can navigate steps, it should be no more than three to four at a time. You call your residence life coordinator to inquire about the student's housing placement and learn that the building does not have an elevator. It does have a ramp to get into the building. You also map out the student's courses and determine that at least two are in inaccessible classrooms. What are the next steps you should take to accommodate the student? Include who you would reach out to and how you would discuss the situation with the student.

▸ Supplemental Job Aids

The following Supplemental Job Aids can be found at https://scholarshare.temple.edu/handle/20.500.12613/8373:

- *Barrier Report Form*
- *Campus Accessibility Map*

15

Access to the Digital Environment

Higher education has changed. Technology touches everything we do, from recruiting and connecting with students to most (if not all) aspects of student life. Perhaps the most drastic changes have allowed us to completely reimagine the ways in which we deliver an educational experience. The technologies we employ—from web ecosystems, social media presence, interactive course content, and cutting-edge applications such as augmented and virtual reality to digital course infrastructure and state-of-the-art academic technology and instructional design—have been nothing short of revolutionary. But new technology must be designed and implemented with careful consideration for how all users will interact with it. In this chapter, we explore the principles of web accessibility and how they apply to higher education, as well as the ways in which they are driving change in our roles as DSPs. Access to the web is a basic human right and, with guidance and advocacy from our offices, our institutions can make access a reality for SWDs.

▶ Guiding Questions

1. Why is digital accessibility important?
2. What is the role of the DSO in ensuring digital accessibility at our institutions?
3. How should I approach this topic if I am not well versed in technology?

4. What content needs to be made accessible?
5. How do we partner with our campuses to move toward accessibility?

Institutions that offer multiple ways to engage with all aspects of the higher education experience increase access to the entire community. We see it in courses when faculty offer students choice in office hour format (online vs. in person). Students can preorder a meal from the dining hall through an app on their phone. Staff create training videos on how to fill out financial aid forms. Technology can make higher education more accessible to more students if used correctly. Throughout this chapter we explore how to ensure that the increasingly digital world our institutions are moving toward is accessible to all who may interact with it.

What Is Digital Accessibility and Why Does It Matter?

Before examining digital access in higher education, it is important to review what accessibility really means. The Job Accommodation Network (JAN) defines accessibility as follows:

> Accessible refers to a site, facility, work environment, service, or program that is easy to approach, enter, operate, participate in, and/or use safely and with dignity by a person with a disability. (JAN, n.d.a)

Within this definition, our role as DSPs is to create spaces at our institutions that are easy for people with disabilities to "approach, enter, operate, participate in, and/or safely use." We do this every day when considering the academic and nonacademic student experiences. We evaluate how to support a student through an exam; we consider the location of their residence hall and assign specific parking locations. These are just a few examples of things we do to ensure that SWDs can participate in our institutions "safely and with dignity."

But what about our websites? If a student with a disability needs access to a form on our bursar's website, who is responsible for getting the form to them in an accessible format? What is the timeline associated with that responsibility? What if a student with a disability wants to reserve tickets to a concert online, but the reservation process is inaccessible? Who do they contact? What happens if all the tickets are taken before they get a chance to ask? If a prospective student is trying to navigate the admissions page but is unable to tab across the screen independent of using a mouse, will they assume our institution is less accessible simply because their first experience online was fraught with barriers?

As more institutions not only put information online but rely on the web to manage daily operations, they must consider access. More specifically, we must consider that

> Websites, tools, and technologies are designed and developed so that people with disabilities can use them. More specifically, people can: perceive, understand, navigate and interact with the web. They can also contribute to the Web. (W3C 2019b)

For some people with disabilities, navigating the web can be difficult if not impossible. A person who is reliant on a screen reader, for example, must be able to navigate through the entire contents of a website smoothly and without encountering any errors. They must be able to determine what is on the web page, where items are in relation to other items on the page, what graphics and images are used, and where they might need to fill out a form if required. Someone with a motor disability may not be able to use their mouse—they must be able to navigate an entire web page using just the keyboard. Someone who relies on closed captioning must be able to engage with a video on our web page without having to ask for captions or a transcript from the creator.

Unlike the individualized work that we do supporting students, websites are open to anyone and available twenty-four hours a day, seven days a week. Accessibility as applied to the web must be proactively considered to meet the needs of all users.

Accessible websites are wonderful examples of universal design. Designing websites with universal access in mind has the potential to benefit a wide range of users, especially as we transition more and more content online. But if universal access does not convince us that website accessibility is the right thing to do, then how about the law? Equal access to anything posted on a website without the need for accommodations is a basic civil right.

What Does the Law Say?

As we have established throughout this book, the ADA is an antidiscrimination law. With the Internet still in its infancy at the ADA's original passage, web accessibility was not a consideration. The Internet's explosive expansion and continuous advancement very quickly outpaced the legislative process. However, the ADA does apply to the web, or, more specifically, inaccessibility of the web, as a means of antidiscrimination protection. From the Justice Department,

Although the language of the ADA does not explicitly mention the Internet, the Department has taken the position that title (II or III) covers Internet Web site access. (U.S. Department of Justice Civil Rights Division 2016b)

The problem of web accessibility in the twenty-first century is tantamount to that of physical access to places of public accommodation. Quite simply, we do business in digital domains. SWDs must be able to access and use all our digital operations and services and benefit from all online opportunities. Inaccessible websites, intranets, forms, infrastructure, course content, LMS, and so on constitute discrimination of SWDs. This fact is self-evident, but it is also broad. We need to investigate the law to further define our obligation.

Unlike physical access—where there is a detailed design guide and construction code—the ADA does not provide well-defined guidelines for making our digital environments accessible. There are, however, some foundational case law and resolution agreements that provide context. It is important to note that the case law in this area is rich. Some of the most prominent cases, the lessons they teach, and their impact on the field are outlined below.

Important Web Accessibility Findings

Kindle/DX—Case Western Reserve University; Reed College; Pace University

Timeline—January 11, 2010; "Dear Colleague" letter issued in June of 2010

Case Overview—Several colleges/universities (named above) partnered with Amazon.com to bring Kindle e-reader technology into the classroom.

Accessibility Barrier—The e-readers had text-to-speech capability for book content. However, menu and navigational controls did not have read-aloud capability, rendering the devices inaccessible to blind users.

Outcome—Three separate resolution agreements. The institutions agreed to not purchase, require, or promote the use of Kindle/DX or similar e-reader devices until the devices were fully accessible or until the institution could provide reasonable accommodations or modifications. A "Dear Colleague" letter was sent to all college and university presidents informing them of the resolutions and urging institutions to take similar steps (Perez and Ali 2010).

Lessons Learned
- The ADA applies to classroom technology.
- Emerging technology must be evaluated for accessibility.
- Emerging technology cannot be adopted unless fully accessible.

"Clickers"—Florida State University
Timeline—2009–2012

Case Overview—Complaint by blind two students regarding inaccessible course technology and content.

Accessibility Barrier—Students were required to use inaccessible LMS for homework and assessments and inaccessible "clickers" for in-class participation; course texts were not available in braille.

Outcome—Settlement agreement. Agreement to take steps to remove accessibility barrier and develop a policy for procurement of accessible technology.

Lessons Learned
- The ADA applies to classroom technology, course content, and LMS.
- Institutions should evaluate technology during the procurement process (Parry, 2012).

Website and Course Content—Penn State
Timeline—2009–2011

Case Overview—Complaint filed by the National Federation of the Blind (NFB) on behalf of students and faculty.

Accessibility Barrier—University website, library website, LMS, course content, classroom technology, on-campus ATMs.

Outcome—Settlement agreement signed in 2011. Agreement includes a fourteen-step plan to address access barriers, which has become known as "The Roadmap" to accessibility. Steps include an accessibility audit; policy statement on accessibility and implementation procedures; procurement policy; website audits and remediation; and LMS, classroom technology, and grievance procedures.

Lessons Learned
- This case is credited as the first sweeping accessibility settlement, raising awareness of accessibility barriers in higher education and the field of DS.
- The fourteen-step settlement agreement has been used as a model for other settlement agreements and, in some cases, adopted voluntarily by colleges and universities.
- Colleges and universities should consider an accessibility audit.
- Institutions should develop an accessible procurement policy.
- Websites are covered under the ADA.
- WCAG 2.0 (WCAG—pronounced like "wick-ag") auxiliary aid standards are being applied as the preferred standards of the DOJ (Pennsylvania State University 2015).

Public Service Announcements—Ohio State University (2010) and Kentucky State University (2012)

Timeline—2010–2012

Case Overview—Complaints filed on behalf of football fans that public announcements were not accessible to Deaf spectators.

Accessibility Barrier—Play-by-play commentating and player introductions.

Outcome—Settlement agreements signed in 2010 and 2012. The agreement was to provide captions on a scoreboard and other screens, including televisions in concourse areas.

Lessons Learned
- Public announcements at college/university athletics events must be captioned.
- The ADA applies to nonacademic opportunities offered by institutions.
- Personal readers, provided by the DSO, may be an appropriate alternative. They must be provided in a timely manner (NAD 2010).

MOOCs and Open Educational Resources—Harvard/MIT EdX

Timeline—2015

Case Overview—Allegations that Open Educational Resources (OERs) hosted by EdX (nonprofit joint venture between Harvard University and Massachusetts Institute of Technology) were not fully accessible. Their content was intended for use in Massive Open Online Courses (MOOCs).

Accessibility Barrier—Navigation, content, and captions for website, mobile application, LMS, and course content were inaccessible to the blind.

Outcome—The institutions must ensure the accessibility of the website, mobile app, and LMS meets WCAG 2.0 auxiliary aid standards; adopt and implement a website accessibility policy; designate a web accessibility coordinator; retain a web accessibility consultant; develop guidelines for content creators; provide training for all web content personnel; and conduct initial and annual accessibility audits.

Lessons Learned
- Captions are required for web content, especially public-facing content.
- The burden of proof for "undue financial hardship" falls to the institution.
- Accessibility training for content creators is essential (U.S. Department of Justice 2015b).

"Mass Filer"—Website Accessibility
Timeline—2015–2021(+)
Case Overview—An educational advocate filed complaints with OCR against thousands of institutions (public schools and colleges/universities) regarding the accessibility of public-facing websites.
Accessibility Barrier—WCAG standards including but not limited to factors such as readable text, alternative text for images, keyboard-only navigation, descriptive links, and closed captions.
Outcome—In March of 2018, the DOJ issued a rule change in its Case Processing Manual "to allow for the automatic dismissal of civil rights complaints" by mass filers that are a continuation of previous complaints (Branson 2018). In November of 2018, the DOJ reversed this rule (Branson 2018). As a result of continued complaints, OCR created a dedicated task force to review complaints.
- Widespread awareness of web accessibility for colleges/universities.
- OCR enforces WCAG standards for colleges and universities.
- OCR assists colleges and universities in reviewing and provides support for remediation of website inaccessibility (Branson 2018).

Digital Accessibility and Our "Campuses"

Our responsibility to SWDs extends to any place a student might engage with while on our campuses (from prospective considerations through alumni status). This is our place of public accommodation. The ADA defines "place of public accommodation" as follows:

> Public accommodation means a facility, operated by a private entity, whose operations affect commerce and fall within one of the following categories—(10) A nursery, elementary, secondary, undergraduate, or post graduate private school, or other place of education. (U.S. Department of Justice Civil Rights Division 2010b)

Today more than ever, IHEs run their day-to-day operations online. It is important to remember that because we operate a place of public accommodation, our targeted audience, or those who might interact with our online domains, is quite large. Table 15.1 offers examples of some of the different online areas a person might need to access based on their relationship with the institution.

The web extends beyond IHEs' websites to course infrastructure, LMS databases, forms, activity calendars, health portals, library databases, and other non–web specific areas. People must be able to use any IHE sponsored app (e.g., transportation or dining apps), access social media platforms, use

TABLE 15.1 POTENTIAL AUDIENCES IMPACTED BY ONLINE ACCESSIBILITY

Audience	Digital Areas to Ensure Are Accessible
Prospective Students	Admissions website and digital application Financial aid website Social media
Enrolled Students	Academic registration pages Intranet/LMS Library equipment (copies, scanners, printers), databases, and systems Social media
Families	Institutional websites Digital forms Social media
Alumni	Social media Engagement and donation pages Career services databases
Faculty	Student record databases/LMS Faculty research websites Academic departmental websites Library databases
Staff	Internal student, course, space, and other databases Institutional overview websites Academic and nonacademic websites
The Public	Institutional websites Websites and sign-up forms for public events Library, museum, and athletic websites Social media

the digital photocopier in the library, participate in a lab simulation, or connect with a faculty or staff member online. The areas of technological advancement in higher education are astounding and show no sign of declining. Given this, what is our role as a DSP in assuring access for SWDs?

The Role of the DSO

Accessibility is the responsibility of the institution. Since accessibility is, first and foremost, tied to nondiscrimination of persons with disabilities, the DSO has a unique stake in the matter. There are a few important distinctions to make. There are three main categories concerning accessibility: (1) public-facing web content, (2) internal, campus-wide accessibility, and (3) accessibility as accommodation.

Public-facing content refers to our institutions' websites; applications; forms; event, marketing, and promotional materials; and so on. Internal content refers to our intranets, LMS platforms, library databases, forms, marketing and promotional materials, course-specific technology, course content, and so on. While both types of content are critical to address, there are accessibility issues that uniquely affect individual students, such as course content. The ideal approach—to ensure the accessibility of all course content—is not always feasible, especially when considering a virtually limitless backlog of content. For individual courses where content is not accessible, it is the responsibility of the DSO to provide reasonable accommodations that achieve accessibility.

DSOs are frequently called on to educate the community and lead initiatives, but they are often underequipped to shoulder the entire burden. Before appropriate workflows can be developed, tasks delegated, and trainings administered, roles and responsibilities must be defined. The information in Tables 15.2 and 15.3 outlines what *is* the responsibility and, equally important, what is *not* the responsibility of the DSO and DSP, other than acting as dedicated accessibility specialists.

By and large, DSOs do not have the resources, bandwidth, technical expertise, or (often) clout to manage campus-wide accessibility. If not case law, best practices from the field dictate that our institutions should have dedicated accessibility staff. Ideally, there is a hierarchy of accessibility staff, including access and accommodations specialists, content remediators, trained course designers and educational technologists, and IT staff, as well as leadership with commensurate authority to create policy and assign funding and other resources. The point is that many of the responsibilities above are shared.

TABLE 15.2　DIGITAL RESPONSIBILITIES OF THE DSO

Responsibilities of the DSO	Specific Responsibilities
Keeping current	Relevant case law, updates from the field, accessibility standards, campus technology, campus resources, continuous training, the work of our colleagues
Awareness and advocacy	Building campus allies, partnering with staff and faculty, addressing barriers, community education, identifying and sharing resources, cochairing a task force
Accessibility initiatives	Proposing/pushing policy, identifying and communicating about barriers, communicating campus obligations to key players
Accommodation policies and processes	Alternative format course materials, captioning, AT, remediation workflows and timeline, course design training, funding accommodations
Accommodation support for SWDs	

TABLE 15.3 DIGITAL RESPONSIBILITIES OF OTHER CAMPUS STAKEHOLDERS

Areas That Are the Responsibility of Others	Specific Responsibilities
Policing college/university-wide accessibility	Website, intranet, portals, LMS, course content, marketing and communications materials, recruitment assets, other IT infrastructure
Identifying/evaluating electronic and information technologies on campus	Library infrastructure, course technology, emerging technology, other IT infrastructure
Ensuring all course content is accessible	LMS, multimedia, course technology, reading material, external content, publisher-provided content, notes, A/V recordings, web conferencing and remote infrastructure
Remediating inaccessible course content	Faculty-created content, publisher-provided content, archival materials, library resources, multimedia, external source materials, open educational resources
Training content creators	Faculty, marketing and communications, social media creators, constant contact originators
Funding accessibility services	Captioning, website implementation, marketing and communications materials, live transcription, remote interpreting, recording transcriptions, electronic and information technology procurement, implementation, and remediation

Accessibility Standards

In the absence of clear and structured guidance, we must look to the experts in the field. "The World Wide Web Consortium (W3C) is an international community where Member organizations, a full-time staff, and the public work together to develop Web standards" (W3C 2008). A facet of the W3C is the Web Accessibility Initiative (WAI), which is responsible for worldwide awareness and advocacy of accessibility for all web users—including, primarily, those with disabilities. According to the mission of the WAI,

> The Web must be accessible to provide equal access and equal opportunity to people with diverse abilities. Indeed, the UN Convention on the Rights of Persons with Disabilities recognizes access to information and communications technologies, including the Web, as a basic human right. (W3C 2008)

One of the WAI's major accomplishments is the publication and maintenance of the WCAG. According to the WAI,

Web Content Accessibility Guidelines (WCAG) is developed through the W3C process in cooperation with individuals and organizations around the world, with a goal of providing a single shared standard for web content accessibility that meets the needs of individuals, organizations, and governments internationally. (W3C 2008)

The WCAG are the standards included in the remediation plans cited in most (if not all) web accessibility litigation, especially concerning higher education. They are also the standards used by OCR when investigating mass filer complaints. While the WCAG include technical standards for complex program features, coding standards, web design, natural information such as text and multimedia, navigational structure, and so on, they have overarching principles that all DSPs should know. Table 15.4 outlines the WCAG.

Predating the WCAG, Section 508 of the Rehabilitation Act (implemented in 2001) sets standards for U.S. federal agencies:

> Section 508 of the Rehabilitation Act of 1973 (29 USC § 794d) requires that when U.S. Federal government agencies develop, procure, or maintain, information and communication technology (ICT), that it is accessible to persons with disabilities. The standards, which have been in place for over 15 years, promote ICT that can be accessed by the public and employees with disabilities. (Level Access 2022)

TABLE 15.4 WCAG GUIDELINES

Standard	Definition	What It Means
Perceivable	Information and user interface components must be presentable to users in ways they can perceive.	Users must be able to perceive the information being presented (it cannot be invisible to all their senses).
Operable	User interface components and navigation must be operable.	Users must be able to operate the interface (the interface cannot require interaction that a user cannot perform).
Understandable	Information and the operation of user interface must be understandable.	Users must be able to understand the information as well as the operation of the user interface (the content or operation cannot be beyond their understanding).
Robust	Content must be robust enough that it can be interpreted reliably by a wide variety of user agents, including AT.	Users must be able to access the content as technologies advance (as technologies and user agents evolve, the content should remain accessible).

Source: W3C 2008

Figures 15.1a and b Accessible Website: (a) Keyboard Navigation, Closed Captions, Visual Focus and (b) High Contrast, Magnification, Visual Focus

In 2018, updated Section 508 guidelines went into effect (General Services Administration 2020). The reauthoring was intended to match the nuances and modern technical competencies included in the WCAG. The updated standards incorporated standards for websites, nonweb electronic documents, operating systems, AT integration, nonsensory disabilities (such as cognitive, language, and learning), and mobile platforms (U.S. Access Board 2019).

While Section 508 does not directly apply to IHEs, they can benefit from it. Specifically, Section 508's Voluntary Product Accessibility Template (VPAT) can provide critical information for our evaluation of electronic and information technology. The VPAT was created to allow electronic and information technology vendors marketing products to federal agencies to provide an up-front evaluation of their product or content, expediting the evaluation process.

Colleges and universities can often use these documents to the same end. In fact, the first step of many successful accessibility evaluation practices is to ask the vendor for a VPAT. It is important to note that we need to evaluate the origin of the VPAT as much as we do its content. As a voluntary template, VPATs are often self-reported. As such, we should take these documents with a grain of salt. However, anecdotally, as awareness of accessibility and pressure from IHEs on vendors grow, more and more are seeking third-party evaluations. The VPAT is becoming a more reliable source and is a cornerstone of many accessible procurement processes. For DSPs, we have boiled some of the highly technical standards down to some common factors in Table 15.5.

Accessibility Testing in Digital Environments

Accessibility testing is an institutional responsibility. It should be done on multiple levels and at multiple junctures. For instance, we evaluate accessibility during the IT discovery and procurement stages; we review course technology, and we remediate content. Sometimes it makes sense for accessibility testing to live within an IT unit. Other times, testing lives within the DSO. A combination of the two seems to work best. Ultimately, it is a campus-to-campus determination.

With the way the field has changed, all DSPs should have some working knowledge of accessibility testing protocol and be able to perform some basic tests. Remember, we are often the front line for access issues. While we often do not possess technical expertise, there are some straightforward principles that anyone with basic computer skills can follow.

Table 15.6 gives examples of beginner tests. The next levels of testing are expert testing and user testing. A user is someone who uses AT, such as magnification or screen reader software, to access content. Having both entry-level users and power users utilize and evaluate the content is a recommend-

TABLE 15.5   COMMON FACTORS TO CONSIDER FOR DIGITAL ACCESSIBILITY

Color Contrast	WCAG recommends a minimum of a 7:1 ratio, where 1:1 is white on white and 21:1 is black on white. High contrast is important for students who cannot perceive the entire color spectrum.
Fonts	Sans serif fonts are typically better, as decorative elements can cause visual confusion. Sans serif fonts are good for students who have dyslexia or other print-based disabilities.
Keyboard Operability	A person should be able to navigate a website or document using only the keyboard. Keyboard-only navigation is necessary for students who cannot find and click a target with a mouse.
Form Fields	Form fields must be labeled with alternative format text identifying the information and format that should be input in the field. Labeled form fields are necessary for students who cannot perceive them.
Alt-Tags	Descriptive text must be provided for images and other figures. Descriptive text should be concise and convey the essential information conveyed by the figure. Alt-tags are necessary for students who cannot perceive the figure.
Captions	Captions must be provided for all video content. Captions should include spoken text and describe sound. Captions are necessary for students who cannot perceive audio and are beneficial for all learners.
Heading Structure	Heading structure, or coded navigation, allows individuals to efficiently navigate a website or document. They allow the user to jump from heading to heading, subheading to subheading; quickly identify links, figures, and form fields; and so on, as opposed to reading left-to-right and top-to-bottom to find the appropriate content. Coded navigation is necessary for students who cannot perceive the visual layout or interface of the content.
Visual Focus	When tabbing through the page, is there a visual indication (such as a highlight or outline) that shows you where your cursor is? Is there visual focus on all clickable links and buttons and for all options in a form field?
Reflow	Reflow is when you magnify your screen until the layout changes (in some cases switching to the mobile view, which typically happens at 200 percent focus or more). Is any content lost or hidden? Does the reading order remain logical?
Descriptive Links	See "Turn Off CSS" in Table 15.6.
Image-Based Text	All text on pages should be selectable.

ed practice. Expert testing can be conducted by internal experts, such as accessibility specialists within IT or a DSO. There are four levels of expert testing to thoroughly evaluate web-based content. Table 15.7 lists potential audiences that might be impacted by online accessibility and the areas that DSPs should prioritize given those audiences.

TABLE 15.6   BASIC TESTS FOR DIGITAL ACCESSIBILITY

Unplug Your Mouse/Turn Off Your Trackpad	Can you access all of the page's content using only your keyboard? Can you navigate in and out of drop-down menus? Are links clickable? Can you select and copy/paste text?
Turn On High Contrast Mode	Is all the content perceivable? Is color-only identification used on the page? Do graphics become less perceivable, or do they convey less information?
Turn Off Images	Can you still identify what the images were conveying (i.e., are alt-tags present)? Were the images used as links? How do the links appear when the image is turned off?
Check for Captions or Transcripts	Do videos and animations have captions? If not, is there dialogue? Do sounds convey meaning?
Click on Field Labels	Are fields labeled? Do labels communicate appropriate format within the field (i.e., MM/DD/YY)?
Turn Off CSS	This one is a little more technical. CSS = Cascading Style Sheet. Disabling the CSS disables the layout and rich formatting elements, leaving the content in a list format. This can be done in the browser or with a web accessibility browser plug-in. Is the same meaning conveyed (i.e., does the visual layout of the page convey essential information)? Are links understandable, or do they just use terms like "click here"? Is there a logical reading order?

Source: Adapted from Groves 2013

TABLE 15.7   FOUR LEVELS OF EXPERT DIGITAL ACCESSIBILITY TESTING

Tool-Guided Evaluation	Using automated testing tools to identify high level errors. (Be mindful of false positives—i.e., an image might be tagged with information that does not convey meaning. The automated checker will only flag images without tags.)
Screening	Use of AT to access site or content to emulate experience of end user. Both experts trained in AT and actual AT users can be employed.
Tool-Based Inspection	Use of specific tools to test individual factors. These can include page structural inspectors, (X)HTML inspectors, color contrast checkers, readability checkers, etc.
Code Review	Best left to the experts . . .

Source: W3C 2019a

Strategies for Making Sure Content Is Accessible

Digital content must be accessible. The vetting, evaluation, creation, and remediation of digital content is a shared responsibility. From a UDL perspective, the ideal scenario is for faculty to create and adopt content that is accessible from the get-go. The institution should provide resources for creating accessible content. These resources can consist of training, tools, and accessible procurement processes.

It is important to remember that accessible content benefits all. It is also important to remember that there are various levels of need for accessible content. Some SWDs have an accommodation-level need for accessibility, and some have an access-level need. Respectively, a student who has a learning disability may need readable text to assist with comprehension, while a student who is blind needs accessible content to perceive the content. DSOs are responsible for providing accessible materials in both cases. Some SWDs may chose not to disclose. It is OK to expect that a student register with the DSO so that accessible materials can be provided, but baked-in accessibility is better.

The common factors listed in Table 15.5 are the main factors to consider when evaluating course content. Some of these require only simple tests. For instance, if text is selectable with a cursor, it is either readable or can be brought into a format that is readable. Fonts can be checked visually, and keyboard-only operation (and logical reading order) can be checked by tabbing through documents and websites. Other factors may involve tool-based inspection.

Programs like Microsoft Office applications and Adobe products have built-in accessibility checkers. These mechanisms can check for the factors listed above, in addition to factors such as headings, tables, and lists. Microsoft mechanisms show user errors and offer suggestions on how to fix them. Adobe mechanisms include tools for remediating accessibility errors. Some errors require additional tools. There are several options available, including free accessibility tools. For instance, W3C maintains a Wiki on accessibility testing and a list of accessibility tools that provide a wealth of information.

Accessibility Policies

Institutional accessibility policies, or policies with access woven into them, are a good way for DSPs to be assured that access is considered broadly, not just on an individual student level through our office. By incorporating access considerations into larger university initiatives, a university signals to its constituents that access is a fundamental component of its mission.

Access may be incorporated in larger campus initiatives in several areas. For the purposes of this book, we focus on three areas that can have significant impact on the larger campus community: (1) procurement, (2) digital accessibility, and (3) captioning.

Procurement

Procurement is the act of purchasing goods or services for the institution. It can range from purchasing hardware (printers, water fountains, and door openers) to software (databases, e-tickets, laptops, and digital lab pipettes). In some institutions, a procurement office oversees the entire purchasing process. In other institutions, individual departments are responsible for handling purchases with little to no oversight by the central administration. Either way, it is a good idea for DSPs to know not only how purchasing works but also who is responsible for major decisions.

Procurement policies require the purchaser to ask for verification of a product's accessibility standards before purchasing the item or agreeing to a contract. These verifications are usually offered in the form of a VPAT.

A procurement policy asks purchasers to do their due diligence when considering a product. Just as institutions ask purchasers to do a cost and data security analysis (if appropriate), an accessibility procurement process requires the same diligence. If the results of the VPAT are less than ideal, or if the vendor cannot verify that the item has been checked for access—and most cannot—it is up to the institution to decide whether to continue with a purchase. Usually, this decision is based on a few different factors: (1) could any other products that are accessible do the job instead and (2) how many people (not just students) will interact with this product?

Firstly, if other products designed to do the same job are accessible, the institution should consider those instead. Common pushback from purchasers will be that it is too expensive to choose the accessible product. As the DOJ has taught us over the years, financial burden is hard to prove and is rarely a reason to choose an inaccessible solution.

Secondly, how many people will interact with the product? If it is a highly specialized item (a firing kiln, for example) that just a few people will engage with, then purchasing the item may be less risky. It is still important that the purchaser work with the DSO to develop a comprehensive accommodation plan, should workarounds be needed.

Digital Accessibility

The term "digital accessibility" can be defined as follows:

> Digital accessibility refers to the inclusive practice of removing barriers that prevent interaction with, or access to websites, digital tools and technologies, by people with disabilities. (Georgetown Law 2022)

Digital accessibility policies should cover all websites and online transactions. At their core, they require website developers and content developers to pay attention to the latest website accessibility standards when creating new sites and content.

Let us pause for a moment and consider the difference between website developers and content developers. Website developers are professionals who design the platform on which our institution's website sits, which includes the mechanics of the site as well as the look and feel. Web content developers are those who post content to a website—a group that probably includes DSPs. When writing a digital accessibility policy, this group will need the most training. Website developers should have some familiarity with the WCAG standards as part of their training. Content developers will most likely be unfamiliar with the guidance around alt-tags, fonts, simplified forms, colors, and other forms of accessibility.

There may be instances where an accessible version of a digital tool is unavailable. If there are two products on the market that do the same thing, but the accessible version is more expensive, an institution cannot choose the cheaper version. However, in the absence of a federal law requiring all digital companies to make their resources accessible, many of the digital tools institutions need will be inaccessible. If there are no accessible options when purchasing a tool, then a statement advising users about where to go to for accommodations must accompany that tool. It is also strongly encouraged that the DSP work to work with the vendor to develop a roadmap to accessibility and obtain support with accommodations and workarounds. Digital accessibility policies should have consistent language that developers and content experts can use for these instances.

Captioning

Captioning should be available to any video file the institution posts on its forward-facing website, on all course materials (including live or prerecorded lectures), at any institutional meeting using an online platform, and at all events. We need to ensure that all participants have access to any content we might create.

Autogenerated captions are an acceptable format of captioning that supports most of our institutional needs. Ideally, they should be checked for accuracy before being posted with an audio or video file. If an audio or video file is going to be posted on a high traffic university website, or if a person with a disability needs captioning as an accommodation, then it is recommended that human-generated captioning be used.

When enacting a captioning policy, there may be immediate concern about the cost, time, and amount of content to be captioned. To help ease the captioning cultural shift, we recommend establishing a timeline as to what should be captioned and what can be grandfathered in as uncaptioned. Ideally, any audio or videos files created before the policy goes into effect should not be captioned unless a person with a disability asks for it as an accommodation. Just like the procurement and digital accessibility policy, a statement accompanying those video files should be placed next to them.

Identifying Stakeholders

There are many challenges to creating, passing, and implementing digital accessibility policies at an institution—everything from being aware of what people are thinking about purchasing to educating hundreds of content developers to shifting how we do business to include captioning. These are not small steps and require key campus partnerships to be successful.

Key campus partners in the digital accessibility world include IT and educational technology departments, media services, marketing and communication departments, the library, and general counsel. As with any stakeholder, when pushing an accessibility agenda, it is important to understand the scope of the person's work, staffing, resources, and any hardships or problems they may be dealing with before adding to their plate. Getting a feel for their day-to-day will let you gauge how much you can ask of them and is an opportunity to creatively infuse your needs into projects they may already be doing.

Passing an institution-wide policy is not easy and will vary in process from institution to institution. Success can be found in starting with a smaller working group of key stakeholders, in which the DSP can share the need for a specific policy by both outlining the law and showcasing its universal impact on our constituents and our operations (always with an eye toward making things easier). As a group, meet and discuss the best way to bring this policy forward. As DSPs, we might lead the group in discussion, form agendas, and keep the group on track, but we should not be the only ones driving the effort. It is too easy to become the sole owner of all things digital accessibility.

Once the group has met to determine what the policy should be and outline a process for implementation, the next step is typically to present the plan to campus administrators who make policy decisions. We recommend partnering with key stakeholders in this effort. Once the policy has passed, the working group should reconvene to determine the process for rolling it out.

In Summary

In an increasingly digital world, accessibility is the new frontier for DS. DSPs are not always technology experts. We are, however, experts in student needs, inclusive practices, the principles of universal design, ensuring equity and opportunity, honoring the rights of our audience, and protecting the interests of our institutions. This is the spirit of accessibility. The successful DSP will create, support, and advocate for accessibility initiatives.

Set the tone. Most people at our institutions are in favor of increasing access for all. What they worry about is the work that doing so might add to their plate and how to balance that work with other institutional priorities. A tone of universal access and collegiality, a cultural shift that aligns with the mission of the institution, resources, and a doable timeline are great ways to demonstrate a commitment to access.

Reflective Exercise

Wendell College—a small, private two-year college—has decided to require all first-year students to take an online new student orientation course prior to coming to campus. Students will not be able to register for courses until they complete this task. The course will include prerecorded video content, interactive campus maps, live chat sessions with faculty, assigned readings and responses, asynchronous group chats, and supplemental content. You have been invited to be a member of the planning committee and have been asked to assist in developing a plan for making the course accessible. What key considerations do you need to take into account given the specific course components? What concerns do you have? What recommendations do you have for the group planning to implement this course?

Supplemental Job Aids

The following Supplemental Job Aids can be found at https://scholarshare.temple.edu/handle/20.500.12613/8373:

- *Example of a Captioning Policy*
- *Statement of Accessibility on All Web Pages and Web-Based Applications*

16

Universal Design as an Access Option

This chapter will explore the concept of universal design and universal design for learning (UDL) as vehicles of access for diverse learners and diverse situations in higher education. UDL is a concept that DSPs have widely and eagerly embraced for years, yet it has been slower to take hold among faculty. We begin with an introduction to universal design as an equalizing concept and move into specific strategies that faculty can employ to offer greater flexibility for students within their courses. UDL also has a place in the nonacademic aspects of higher education as a tool to minimize barriers for students. DSPs are often called on to help solve problems outside of the classroom for students with access needs. This chapter provides DSPs with tools to become UDL advocates across their campuses.

▶ Guiding Questions

1. What is UDL?
2. Why was it harder to infuse UDL into higher education than secondary education?
3. What are some examples of UDL in college courses?
4. How can I support faculty in their UDL adoption?
5. Where else on campus might UDL be a beneficial tool?
6. Who can DS providers turn to for help around UDL in general?

Have you ever had a day when the thought of climbing stairs made you groan? Have you ever pressed an electronic door opener because you were carrying too many things to pull open the door with your hands? Have you ever stood firmly on the moving walkway in airports as other passengers walk by? Have you done these things to create access due to your disability? We can safely argue that we all have at some point in our lives, regardless of ability, done at least one of these things. And if you have too, then you are a consumer of universal design.

UDL is a frequent topic in education. Its basic idea is that education should be designed to be accessible by the greatest number of users from the beginning rather than individually retrofitted to meet each student's individual learning needs. It is simple; it makes sense. It can benefit most learners, yet it has not been fully adopted by educators, especially in higher education. We explore why that is and offer some strategies for expediting the adoption process later in this chapter. First, though, we need to equip you with the tools and rationale as to why UDL is something all DSOs should be promoting.

Universal Design (without the L)

Universal design is an idea that evolved in architecture. Architect Ron Mace used a wheelchair to get around after contracting polio as a child (Woodward, n.d.). Mace designed buildings for individual access, yet at times his own ability to access these buildings was inhibited. At the same time, more and more people wanted to stay in their homes as they aged. Yet homes were inaccessible and became unwelcoming as people aged. Most had stairs; most had bathrooms that could not be retrofitted with bars in the showers or near the toilets. Kitchens had high shelves, and to go outside, people needed to descend steps. As a result, as individuals aged, they needed to move to a more accessible location—usually a nursing home or assisted living facility.

Mace decided to incorporate greater flexibility into the design of a home. He termed the phrase "universal design" as

> the design of products, environments, and communication to be usable by all people, to the greatest extent possible, without adaptation or specialized design. (Institute for Human Centered Design 2022)

Mace's work allowed residents to stay in their homes without having to pay for expensive retrofitting of access tools and, most importantly, without having to ask local agencies, hospitals, and even family members for help. Ultimately, Mace's work was so significant that it was formally introduced in the United States through the 1968 Architectural Barriers Act (Maisel and Ranahan 2017).

Since then, we have seen the concept of universal design make its way beyond our homes and into our everyday lives. Going back to the examples we noted above (elevators, electronic door openers, moving walkways), each was a conscious decision to design a system that makes access to life more flexible. Let us consider a few more examples. Have you ever watched a movie, a class lecture, or a news show with the closed captions turned on? This is an example of universal design. Closed captions are technically an accommodation for one specific group—the deaf and hard of hearing—yet we see them everywhere and use them all the time.

Universal Design for Learning (adding the L)

The concept of universal design makes sense. It is aimed at removing barriers in our day-to-day lives. Barriers also exist in education: students may struggle to read a traditional textbook, sit still behind a desk all day, hold and write legibly with a pencil, or to demonstrate knowledge through a written paper. In higher education, barriers extend to finishing exams on time, capturing all the notes in a class, meeting the attendance requirements of a course, and understanding what was covered in a video lecture. Given these educational access barriers, can the ideas behind universal design be transferred to the classroom? The answer is yes.

Almost forty years after Ron Mace brought the concept of universal design to architecture, the Center for Applied Special Technology (CAST) brought it to education (CAST 2021). CAST added the L, calling the concept universal design for learning. CAST is composed of neuroscientists and educators who, through research, determined that not all students are the same. They do not learn in the same ways; they come to education with different knowledge bases and have different skill sets. Different factors impact their ability to learn at any given time, and they have different support structures at home. Given these vast differences, why are we forcing all these different pegs into the same hole, or rigid, monolithic curriculum? UDL provides a

TABLE 16.1	CAST'S INFORMATION NETWORKS AND SOLUTIONS	
Brain Network	Question	Solution
Recognition	The "what" of learning. How do we gather information?	Present information in multiple ways.
Strategic	The "how" of learning. How do we express our ideas?	Differentiate the ways in which students can express what they know.
Affective	The "why" of learning. How do we motivate learners?	Find a way to connect with student interests. Provide multiple methods of engaging with the material.

framework to design for these differences from the outset (Meyer, Rose, and Gordon 2014). Specifically, CAST incorporated universal design into education through three brain-based information networks and corresponding solutions (CAST 2016) as seen in Table 16.1.

UDL asks educators to design for learner variability ahead of time—before faculty even know their students—by offering students choices in how to recognize, engage with, and report back the information they learn (Tobin and Behling 2018).

Universal Design for Learning in Higher Education

UDL has been embraced slowly in higher education. It is not that faculty do not think it is a good design strategy but more that they do not know about it. We can say confidently, as all of the authors have or are teaching university courses, that faculty are not trained to teach. That does not mean there are not incredible faculty out there doing wonderful, creative, flexible things to meet the needs of diverse learners. It means that many of us never took an education course and thereby may not be aware of UDL unless we happen onto it in another manner.

About a decade after CAST infused UDL into elementary and secondary education, UDL was introduced into college teaching. The U.S. Office of Postsecondary Education offered model demonstration grants to twenty-two different research programs throughout the country. These grants were the catalyst for researchers trying to figure out if UDL might fit the college environment—and if so, how? Each research institution took a different approach to introducing UDL into collegiate environments. Some asked an individual faculty member to redesign their courses with UDL principles in mind. Others brought in keynote speakers and offered workshops designed to give faculty a chance to rethink an assignment or a lecture with guidance. And some institutions formed UDL teams to provide wraparound supports to faculty. The diversity in approaches launched widespread acknowledgment that UDL did indeed belong in higher education.

Disability Service Professionals as Motivators

To DSPs, UDL just makes sense. Why not offer multiple ways to participate in the course? Allowing an extended deadline for an assignment might just be the relief students need. Why not offer a copy of the class notes to everyone in the class? Why not have all course texts be available electronically? These are universal strategies that, if incorporated, automatically reduce the need for specific accommodations. It is important to note that UDL does not eliminate the need for all accommodations (braille readers, ASL interpreters)—but it can drastically reduce the need for many accommodations. To us, UDL represents access without burden on the part of the student. Think of an incoming first-year student who is unaware of our processes or does not want to identify and ask for support. Why should the student have to ask for support or come and find us when many natural supports can be easily built into the curriculum? DSPs have been championing the UDL cause for decades now. The challenges we face are spreading the message widely and actively encouraging implementation.

Key to UDL success and long-lasting impact is creating a UDL campaign that reflects the needs of the key stakeholders of a campus. Tobin and Behling found that each IHE that successfully incorporated UDL into its academic environment did so by acknowledging its mission, finding stakeholders who held the biggest influence, "selling" UDL as a retention tool, and encouraging UDL use in small, bite-sized steps (Tobin and Behling 2018). Each of these aspects will vary from institution to institution, but some commonalities have been identified.

- Reminding institutions of their core values and missions—are there words like "welcoming," "diversity," "inclusive," "academic rigor," etcetera in the values and mission of the institution?
- Identifying stakeholders—which faculty members are popular among students? What are they doing in their courses (we bet that identifying them can uncover UDL strategies they might be doing unknowingly)?
- Partnering with the faculty professional development center—ask a dean to sign a letter of appreciation and acknowledgment for those who work to incorporate UDL into their courses.
- Reminding administrators of the importance of student retention—UDL at its core is a retention tool. Pulling data from previous years, pointing to courses where students get bottlenecked in their academic pursuits, and noting the financial impact of poor retention are all proven successful strategies.
- Making UDL digestible—faculty are busy. They are overwhelmed with teaching, committee work, research, and their own lives. Acknowledge that they have already done UDL work and that they just need to add one more strategy to their courses to engage students even more.

We dig into specific strategies for UDL implementation a bit later in this chapter.

The Plus One Approach

UDL does not mean redesigning each aspect of a course to meet the needs of each learner. While many faculty easily acknowledge the benefits of UDL, they also easily become overwhelmed by all they *could* do. We cannot push a concept without making it digestible. The Plus One approach developed by Behling and Tobin in their text *Reach Everyone Teach Everyone: Universal Design for Learning in Higher Education* answers that need.

UDL is an iterative process. Think of it like building blocks in a child's game. If you add one more strategy to a lecture or assignment or add one more text for students to choose from, then you have automatically increased the flexibility of your course (or the toy you are building). Students can now choose how to interact with course content. We encourage faculty to add just one more strategy and then evaluate it. Did it do what they wanted it to? Is there still a pain point? If so, add one more strategy (one more building block to the tower). Instead of an additional text, add a podcast. Add group work to the lecture; change instructional styles every ten minutes. Now faculty have two additional strategies, increasing the methods of engagement twofold. Plus One should be simple and digestible, not overwhelming.

In higher education, we consider the implementation of UDL in three primary areas: (1) course design, (2) instruction, and (3) assessment. Let us add some Plus One strategies to each of those.

Course Design

Course design is the blueprint of the course. When faculty sit down to plan a course, they must consider the journey their students will go on. Where are the students starting, and where do they need to go to have a mastery of the content? Course designers and instructor development professionals often advise faculty to begin with course goals and learning objectives. These are the fundamentals of any course.

When we think of course design, we are also thinking of the logistics of a course. How will students engage with the course (is it face-to-face, remote, or hybrid)? When will it be taught? When will the faculty be available to meet with students? What texts or resources will be used? What will be the pacing of the course? Each of these questions should be considered with the Plus One model in mind. Table 16.2 offers possible strategies for faculty.

Instructional Methods

Instructional methods vary from course to course and faculty to faculty. Remember, most faculty were not trained to teach. Instead, they rely on their

TABLE 16.2 COURSE DESIGN PLUS ONE STRATEGIES

Course Components	Traditional Method	+ 1 Approach
Goals and objectives	State them	+ diagram how they intersect with each other
Resources	Traditional textbook	+ relevant videos
Communication with students	In-person office hours	+ online office hour
Timeline	A new topic each week	+ add flipped class weeks
Additional policies	List them in the syllabus	+ link to them on the intuitional website
Participation	In class	+ online discussions

own experiences as a student in the classroom—what worked for them—or mirror a colleague they admire. In some cases, they study pedagogical design and rethink their strategies accordingly. Just as faculty were not trained to teach, students were not trained to learn one way. One of the most exciting and yet challenging aspects of working in higher education is that the needs of students change year to year. This is due partly to the diversity of educational experiences students bring from their K–12 years, partly to outside influences (social medial, socioeconomic experiences, and peer groups), and partly to reasons for going to college (from "it is just what you do" to very career focused). The consistently changing background of students means that the way we teach must evolve.

UDL is a wonderful response mechanism for evolving student needs. Today's generation of learners has an attention span of less than eight seconds (Tsuruta 2010). That means that if faculty lecture for the better part of an hour, most of their students will miss the lion's share of the content. Instead, if the class is framed with an essential question, begins with a minilecture (ten minutes), and switches modality a few times throughout, then we can assume that more students will stay engaged longer. Table 16.3 provides some additional Plus One strategies that faculty have used to diversify their instruction.

As stated at the start of this chapter, UDL grew out of the need for accommodations. If one person needs access to closed captioning, we should assume that more people do for a variety of reasons. By offering closed captioning to all, we reduce the need for people with disabilities to ask for support and increase access to content for those who did not know they needed captioning but benefit from it.

Assessment

Assessment is the measurement of a course's learning objectives. It is critical for faculty to remember that they are assessing whether a student has mas-

TABLE 16.3   INSTRUCTIONAL PLUS ONE STRATEGIES

Traditional Method	+ 1 Approach
Lecture throughout class	+ prerecord the most important highlights of class and post them ahead of time for review
Write everything on the board	+ post course slides or outline ahead of class
Serve as the solo instructor	+ bring in guest speakers (in person or online)
Base all learning in the classroom	+ use an LMS to supplement learning
Treat students as passive participants	+ ask students to teach certain aspects of the course (alone or in groups)

tered the goals and objectives of the class, not whether they can write a paper, give a presentation, or take a timed exam. These are difficult concepts for some faculty to separate, as they are used to assessing students one way. Others find it easier to grade multiple choice exams than read papers. But if the form of an assessment is not a learning objective, then faculty should consider adding Plus One strategies to assessment as well.

Too often, students are inadvertently penalized for not being able to perform a certain type of assessment regardless of whether they have a disability. We are sure many of you reading this text have a love-hate relationship with standardized exams. Either you excel at high-pressure, timed exams, or you strongly feel that they do not accurately measure your knowledge or abilities. Many students feel the same way. Students may be excelling on the homework and highly engaged in class discussions only to do poorly on exams or on a paper. If that happens, it is safe to say that the chosen form of assessment does not accurately reflect the abilities of the students. Unfortunately, if faculty do not add UDL strategies to assessments, they risk losing students from their class (dropping out), their academic department (picking a different major), or even the institution itself (especially if a student cannot get past a first-year course).

Adding UDL strategies to assessment is straightforward. It can be as simple as asking students to write a paper but giving them a choice on what that paper is about. Or it can be more intricate, like telling students that they must report out on a topic in a manner that works best for them. By leaving the format open, faculty are inviting students to demonstrate knowledge in a way that highlights their strengths and allowing them to engage in the content in a personalized, meaningful way. Table 16.4 offers more examples of Plus One assessment strategies.

A bonus of diversified assessment is variety in grading. One of the worst things about teaching can be having to grade a stack of papers about the same topic with very little variety at the end of the semester. However, if UDL is added to an assignment, you may end up grading a few papers, some presen-

TABLE 16.4   ASSESSMENT PLUS ONE STRATEGIES

Traditional Method	+ 1 Approach
Exam	+ give students twenty-five questions; ask them to choose twenty to answer
Paper	+ give students a choice of what to write about; scaffold the assignment
Presentation	+ give students the choice of how to present their work (PowerPoint, website, video, poster board)
Group project	+ give students a choice of role within the group (presenter, researcher, recorder)
Lab assignments	+ give students options for how to record their observations (notes, pictures, videos)

A biology professor typically gave three exams during the semester. Given her large class size, she found it easiest to use multiple choice exams. However, when COVID-19 began during the spring 2020 semester, she pivoted her assessment approach. Not trusting that students would not cheat on the exam from home, she offered her students a choice in their final assessment. They could (1) create a video clip describing one of the major processes discussed in class (she gave them four different topics); (2) interview a practicing professional (a doctor, veterinarian, scientist, etc.) about how they reference one of the topics in their day-to-day work; or (3) do a group project detailing one of the topics. She provided the same choice of topics for all the options and one rubric across all three. She reported that her students were much more engaged, likely to ask complicated questions about topics covered, and excited to share their work with their classmates. She plans to continue to add assessment choices within her course moving forward.

tations, a webinar, a Wiki, and a video. We guarantee that within this variety, you will find increased enthusiasm among students about the content they learned throughout the course of the semester.

Pinch Points

It is too easy to get swept up in a pedagogical movement, sit down to rework an entire course, and become quickly overwhelmed. This more than anything is an immediate UDL turnoff. Instead, Behling and Tobin suggest recommending that faculty think back to the last time they taught their course and consider the following questions:

- Where do the students always have questions?
- Where do they always get things wrong on tests or assignments?
- Where do they always ask for explanations in a different way from the one you provide? (Tobin and Behling 2018)

If the course is new, versions of these questions may still apply:

- What aspects of the course are you worried about?
- Is there an assignment that you think will cause confusion?
- Are the required texts easy to find and access?

Answering these questions will identify "pinch points," or points in your course where things have not gone well or might not go well. These are the areas faculty need to start with. How can you add one UDL strategy to a pinch point? Once it is added, it is important to observe and note any changes. Were fewer clarifying questions asked about an assignment? Did more people access the texts? How were the assessment grades? Was there a difference from the last time the class was taught, or if teaching the class for the first time, did it go more smoothly than you thought it would? The Plus One approach makes fixing pinch points easily digestible and not overwhelming.

Additional Strategies for Faculty UDL Adoption

DSPs love UDL. We have been pushing it for years with some luck, though not as much as we might like. The Plus One approach has helped a great deal, but some faculty are still not swayed. In the absence of navigating a difficult situation with a student or being intrinsically motivated, there are a few tricks we have tried with success.

Presenting Inaccessible Course Content

There is nothing more effective than demonstrating to faculty how inaccessible their course is. For some reason, when faculty see the material they have created read incorrectly by a screen reader or watch a DSPs stumble through navigating course documents, they get it. Follow this demonstration with a discussion on the impact of these materials not only on the SWD but on all students. This is the moment to suggest a Plus One strategy.

All UDL workshops should leave room for actually workshopping UDL strategies into course materials. During sessions, you can teach faculty how to determine if their PDF is accessible or not (have them practice on their own content), show the benefits of quality captions, and give a chance to design a Microsoft document with access built in. We have found that if faculty walk away from a presentation having applied what they heard to their own content, they are more likely to embrace UDL and Plus One strategies.

Acknowledging That Faculty Are Already Doing It

We have given many presentations and had even more one-on-one conversations with faculty about UDL, sometimes calling UDL out and other times simply acknowledging their good teaching. Most are already doing UDL. The trick is to help them recognize, celebrate, and build off it. Often, these conversations happen in a vacuum when faculty call the DSO frustrated or concerned about how to support a student. Taking the time to listen, identify the pinch point, and acknowledge the flexibility they have already put in (you can usually find something, even if it is as simple as a topic choice on an assignment) builds trust. Once you have trust, you can gently suggest a Plus One strategy and include the resources or support they may need to implement it. Soon you will have a UDL convert.

During the COVID-19 pandemic, two of the authors did a small research study at their institutions to test their theory that faculty were actively implementing UDL strategies without knowing it. The COVID-19 pandemic forced most faculty to rethink course design, instructional methods, and assessment choices in a matter of days—not the months of planning that they were used to. The research found that faculty were adding Plus One UDL strategies to their courses without necessarily knowing what UDL is. We gathered their UDL strategies into a toolbox designed for faculty by faculty (see Table 16.5). We have found that faculty are more likely to trust fellow colleagues than DSPs, making this resource especially powerful.

Universal Design in Nonacademic Collegiate Activities

At the beginning of this chapter, we introduced the concept of UDL by noting its relationship to the built world around us. While UDL has a place in the way in which we teach students, universal design should also be prominent in the ways in which we welcome students to our institutions. DSPs are used to advocating for buildings to be accessible, whether by asking for a ramp, urging facilities to put in electronic door openers, or reporting broken elevators; there are many universal design opportunities here we cover in Chapter 15. Remember, though, that welcoming a student to our institution extends beyond the physical campus.

If you consider the journey a prospective student takes while considering an IHE, there are many opportunities to build in flexibility with gathering

TABLE 16.5   ACCIDENTAL UDL STRATEGIES AS IDENTIFIED BY FACULTY FOR FACULTY

Directions for using this chart: Choose the question you would like to find a UDL strategy for or the area of your course you are looking to add flexibility to. Follow the path downward for a list of UDL strategies.

What are the most impactful UDL strategies I should use if I just have a few moments?

How do I use technology to increase access and flexibility in my course?

How do I design my course to be flexible no matter the modality?

How do I keep students engaged in my course?

How do I accurately measure my students' knowledge?

Strategy	Few moments	Technology	Modality	Engaged	Measure
Use the LMS modules design system for the course.				x	x
Include general course logistics in multiple places.		x	x	x	
Use scavenger hunts to learn how to navigate the LMS for the course.		x	x	x	
Release your technology requirements before the class begins; encourage students to practice.		x	x	x	
Only use the technology your institution supports. Know who to ask for help.			x	x	
Increase formal office hour options and modalities (including online, in person, going for a walk with students).		x	x	x	
Increase communication with students (weekly roadmaps, course announcements, emails).		x	x	x	
Use the discussion and chat boards as an additional method to engage students.	x	x	x	x	*
Ensure that course documents are accessible.		x	x	x	
Only choose content that is captioned.		x	x	x	
Shorten class times; use extra time for informal office hours.		x	x		
Reduce the number of assignments in the course; focus on those that directly relate to the course learning objectives.	x		x		

(continued)

TABLE 16.5 ACCIDENTAL UDL STRATEGIES AS IDENTIFIED BY FACULTY FOR FACULTY (continued)

Directions for using this chart: Choose the question you would like to find a UDL strategy for or the area of your course you are looking to add flexibility to. Follow the path downward for a list of UDL strategies.

What are the most impactful UDL strategies I should use if I just have a few moments?

How do I use technology to increase access and flexibility in my course?

How do I design my course to be flexible no matter the modality?

How do I keep students engaged in my course?

How do I accurately measure my students' knowledge?

Strategy	Few moments	Technology	Modality	Engagement	Measure
Open the classroom ten minutes early to allow for casual conversation.	x				
Frame each class with an essential question or an outline of what is to be covered.	x				
Begin each class with a roadmap of what will be covered; circle back to that roadmap at the end of class.	x				
Reduce the size of the class by meeting in small groups or teaching the class a few times a week.	x	x	x		
Randomly assign a class notetaker each class; ask them to take notes and post them on the LMS.	x	x	x	x	
Ask students to lead discussions; allow them to sign up for the best time slot for them.	x	x			
Create "critical friend" groups, where students are responsible for checking in on each other and their progress.	x	x			
Allow students to turn off their camera or step out of class from time to time to refocus as needed.		x	x	x	*
Shift the way the content is delivered every fifteen minutes.	x	x	x		
Create podcast lectures that students can access when convenient.		x	x	x	
Post all recorded PowerPoints ahead of class on the LMS.			x	x	
Chunk all PowerPoints recordings into ten-minute chunks.			x	x	
Use prerecorded content from experts in the field; make sure captions are turned on before posting.			x	x	
Bring in guest speakers live via the web conference platform. Record those visits for students who cannot attend live.			x	x	x
Use polling, micro boards, breakout rooms, and other like-minded tools to encourage interactions.	x	x	x	x	*
Provide worksheets for students to use during lectures.	x	x	x		

TABLE 16.5 ACCIDENTAL UDL STRATEGIES AS IDENTIFIED BY FACULTY FOR FACULTY (continued)

Directions for using this chart: Choose the question you would like to find a UDL strategy for or the area of your course you are looking to add flexibility to. Follow the path downward for a list of UDL strategies.

What are the most impactful UDL strategies I should use if I just have a few moments?

How do I use technology to increase access and flexibility in my course?

How do I design my course to be flexible no matter the modality?

How do I keep students engaged in my course?

How do I accurately measure my students' knowledge?

Strategy	Impactful/few moments	Technology	Modality	Engagement	Measure knowledge
Add details to the syllabus about assignments and course topics, including rubrics as links.		x		x	
Post information about assignments and assessments early and in multiple places.		x		x	
Add video explanations to all assignments.			x	x	x
Increase the number of assignments while decreasing and highlighting their point values.	x		x		
Offer optional sessions for students who want to go into more detail in the course.	x	x	x		
Use some class time as work time for students to either log off or to work on assignments and ask for help.	x	x	x	x	*
Encourage students to work in groups to finish assignments.	x	x			
Offer hybrid labs to students.			x	x	x
Offer take home exams and/or open book exams.	x		x		
Add space at the end of each exam for students to share other information as they feel necessary.	x	x			
Scaffold longer assignments and provide feedback throughout.	x	x	x		
Allow students to choose how they complete an assignment; provide a guiding rubric.	x	x	x		
Allow all assignments to be submitted electronically (through the LMS and/or email).				x	x
Allow students to resubmit assignments.				x	
Add flexibility to the late policy for turning in work.				x	
Check in with each student who did poorly after each assessment.	x	x			

Source: Behling, Bibeau, and Pillette 2021

and providing information. IHEs are very cognizant of their website and social media traffic these days, as they are the digital peephole into the university. As we detail in Chapter 16, creating accessible websites with an eye toward flexibility will automatically increase the number of potential students who can actively engage with your institution.

Information Shared Out
All university information should be available in at least two formats—at the very least, online and in paper format. Admissions brochures and maps should be available for those who prefer to hold them and for those who prefer to look at content on their phones. Applications should be available online and in multiple languages. Getting assistance with filling out applications or asking questions should be offered in two forms (phone, email, text message, online chats). Financial aid deadlines should be noted in multiple places. Social media is becoming a go-to for students seeking information on IHEs. Pictures, videos, and podcast interviews with current and former students are all examples of universal design strategies that increase access to an institution.

Once a student enrolls in an institution, the universal design flexibility should continue. Filling out a registration form for classes, getting tickets to a drama show, or entering the housing lottery—all these day-to-day activities should be offered in multiple formats or with multiple entry points. The good news is that many campuses are already doing this work, and students are responding. Email is no longer the preferred method of communication at many institutions; they are trying different things (texting, direct messaging, even calling students). The key is to be flexible and be ready to try new approaches as students change year to year.

Information Gathered
Just as we offer flexibility in how we share information, we should be flexible in how we gather information. This need became very apparent with the COVID-19 pandemic. We could not rely on students accessing a printer to print their papers and hand them in; we could not rely on them having access to Wi-Fi networks, video cameras, or even laptops of their own. We needed to be flexible with how we gathered student information, offering choices as much as possible.

Become a Universal Design for Learning Advocate

As we mentioned at the start of this chapter, DSPs have long been UDL believers and torchbearers. For us, UDL is a method of leveling the playing field for students no matter their learning style, ability, educational background, or personal life. Life is complicated. The COVID-19 pandemic highlighted that in spades. Learning is largely unequal, whether in terms of access to the Internet or a computer, access to time when competing priorities consume bandwidth, educational experiences and readiness, language barriers, or even access barriers.

The challenge we have is gaining buy-in. In today's world, people tend to be running at full speed all the time. Our attention is split between priorities professionally, personally, and within the larger society around us. University staff and faculty are no different: making them aware of UDL is one thing, but getting them to utilize it is another altogether. The idea often resonates and then is quickly added to the pile of good ideas with little time to implement.

There are tangible things a DSP can do to increase awareness and application of UDL on their campus. The steps we suggest include (1) finding stakeholders others will listen to, (2) partnering with those who seem most likely to use UDL strategies, (3) helping to organize a UDL showcase, and (4) practicing what you preach.

Finding Stakeholders

DSPs should not be leading the UDL charge on campus. Tobin and Behling found that faculty respond more readily to other faculty or development offices than student service staff. DSPs should play an active role in getting a team of UDL advocates up and running. Begin by connecting with your instructor development office. Ask how you can support their office to offer a UDL-inspired training or resource. In many instances, a DSP assumes the role of content developer while the instructor development office hosts the training, recruits faculty, and helps run the training. This way, faculty are courted by an office that they see as a resource for them—not for their students.

In the absence of an instructor development office, or with an overwhelmed development office, we suggest finding partners in other areas. One of the easiest ways to identify a UDL stakeholder is through word of mouth. Which faculty are students raving about? Why? Most likely, if you dig just a little, you will discover that they are unknowingly doing UDL work. Likewise, which faculty support your office easily and help spread the word about what you do? Share a cup of coffee with them and discuss the positive impact of UDL, identify UDL practices they already have in place, and ask for their support in spreading the word. Follow their lead but be willing to provide the knowledge content.

Partner with Those Who Seem Least Likely to be Partners

Partnerships should not be limited to faculty. Just as universal design is not limited to academics, partners can be found anywhere. Librarians, instructional technologists, art installers, diversity centers, the registrar, the counseling center, legal, and even students themselves are all usually promoting UDL simply through their day-to-day work.

Librarians are always seeking diverse ways to help students connect with content. Instructional technology is a booming field, especially now that we have proven that education can be done online with good design. Instructional technologists must design multiprong approaches to education to maximize content delivery. Our colleagues in the diversity center are perhaps some of the best partners we can find on campus to promote UDL across an institution. They work each day to create a level playing field for all aspects of a collegiate experience for students. Our diversity office partners understand that no two students come to an institution with the same experiences, abilities, and desires for their time in college.

The registrar and other student service offices (advising, financial aid, study abroad, etc.) can be excellent UDL partners. The goal of many of these offices is to get as much student traffic through the door as possible while ensuring that students who need the offices the most have a clear and simple experience. If forms are available online and in person, information sessions are prerecorded and offered through office hours, and information is emailed and texted, then students have a much higher likelihood of engaging with these offices successfully.

Counseling centers on college campuses are busier than ever. As the student mental health crisis continues to rise (JED 2020), efforts to support students continue to diversify. There are never enough one-on-one appointment times to meet student needs. Instead, counseling centers must offer groups, workshops, mediation practices, walks, animal therapy, and other ways of providing support. Naturally, the way in which they offer these services, combined with their insider knowledge of college stressors, makes them wonderful partners not just in nonacademic UDL work but also in influencing faculty to become UDL adopters. Faculty are very wary of the college mental health crisis and very interested in doing what they can to help alleviate student stress.

A university's legal team can be a good UDL supporter. Legal teams are reading case settlements of institutions that navigated inaccessible or unwelcoming legal battles. Most of us will readily admit that a legal case or an OCR agreement, whether at our institution or one we are familiar with, is a welcome nudge toward universal design adoption. The *Harvard/MIT v. The Na-*

tional Federation for the Deaf (McKenzie 2019), for example, was just the shove that many of us needed to create a university-wide captioning policy. Legal counsel can weigh in on the pros and cons of not doing UDL work and may influence faculty and staff in a way that a DSP cannot.

University administrators are also excellent partners. Whenever you start discussing retention rates, which to some equate to financial dependency, they automatically become interested in what you have to say. Using UDL as a strategy to increase retention rates, especially in first-year courses, is a great way to get administrators to support a larger campus initiative.

Finally, students are wonderful UDL advocates. They are the ones experiencing the paths we have laid out for them. And they are the first to share stories of inaccessibility or inequality compared to their peers. We have seen the powerful impact of a student group upset at a lack of accessible entrance to a building, complaining about unfair assessment practices, or advocating for an allergen-free kitchen for all. Incorporating the student voice into UDL work is a wonderful reminder to those you are trying to convince of why Plus One strategies are here in the first place.

Organize a UDL Showcase

The wonderful thing about universal design and UDL is that they are already happening at your institution. The key to wider appreciation and implementation is showcasing the areas where they are happening. A DSP can help to do this in many ways, though not alone—rely on your stakeholders. Share widely the good work faculty have done, recognize publicly their strong efforts, and highlight the positive impacts on students. The same can be done for student services—show before and after UDL redesigned forms, office promotional materials, and websites. Give offices a chance to spotlight results (i.e., increased foot traffic or online traffic). Make sure that administrators in charge of those offices see this work and recognize it.

Practice What You Preach

DSOs should model universal design and UDL as much as they can. Information about our office should be available in multiple formats (online and on paper) and at multiple intersections of a student's experience with our institution. Students should be able to learn about us at every step of their collegiate way.

Faculty too should be able to learn about us in multiple ways. DSOs should have a dedicated faculty page on their website. Information about accommodation implementation and UDL should be posted there. We should visit department meetings, send out newsletters and syllabus statements, and offer one-on-one meetings as much as possible. By making ourselves available to faculty in different settings and offering content through various means, we are increasing the likelihood that they will engage with us and help students find us.

Just as we offer information in multiple formats and through multiple experiences, we should gather information in a flexible manner. As we stated earlier, there is no reason that students should not be able to send us their documentation electronically. We do not need to physically meet with every student in a room to have an intake or check-in appointment. We can offer flexibility and choice—what works best for students given their schedule (for international students or those who work as well as go to school, coming to campus might not be an option).

Be careful of providing services in just one format. Historically, we have written, printed and asked students to come and pick up their accommodation letters. Why—so we can see the letters Sure, but that practice is neither needed nor reflective of universal design practices. Email accommodation letters to students; let them decide if they would prefer to print them or email them to their professor. Allow students to stop by and book an exam accommodation or to do it online. The same can be said for appointments. Students who need a copy of notes should be able to print it in your office or get it electronically. By doing business with a UDL flare, we are increasing access for students while decreasing burden. This is what UDL is all about.

In Summary

Universal design and UDL are at the core of equity. If we can increase access to the collegiate experiences for all students, fewer will fail, fewer will have to ask for help, and fewer will leave our institutions before they accomplish their goals. Universal design has the power to enhance the experiences of all involved in higher education tremendously. The task for many DSPs is to push the universal design and UDL message forward in a way that broadens the perspectives of faculty and staff as champions of inclusivity.

▶ Reflective Exercise

Staff from both the DSO and the academic tutoring office at a public university have shared similar stories of students complaining about the assessment process in introductory biology and physics courses. Students have reported doing quite well in class discussions, on homework, and in the lab but failing the midterm and final exam, bringing their grades down significantly. After a bit of research, it appears that the midterm and final exams are multiple choice exams, which utilize a scantron answer sheet. The faculty of these courses say that they assess this way because "this is how we always have done it." They also like the ease of grading due to the scantron. What UDL strategies might you suggest to these faculty? How would you go about getting department-wide buy-in to using these strategies?

Supplemental Job Aids

The following Supplemental Job Aids can be found at https://scholarshare.temple.edu/handle/20.500.12613/8373:

- *Best Practices for Ensuring Accessibility in Online Courses: A Checklist*

17

Collaboration across Campus and Beyond

Building effective campus partners can take time and may require a strategy. Understanding your campus culture and how structures work together is critical. This chapter explores identifying natural campus partners, cultivating relationships with them, and bringing them together by focusing on the university's mission and compliance. We also discuss the benefits of building a network outside your institution to help support the DSO's mission.

▶ **Guiding Questions**

1. *How does a DSO actively involve internal partners for collaboration?*
2. *How does a DSO navigate outside partners in supportive collaboration?*
3. *What are some strategies for increasing institutional collaboration?*
4. *How do we identify strategies for working with partners to facilitate cooperation?*

Collaboration has been mentioned in several chapters of this book—and with good reason. SWDs connect all areas of an institution, and the need for access to all areas of the campus is not only essential but mandated by law. Ensuring that students have equitable access to all areas of campus requires collaborative partners. This chapter explores who may be a partner and how to capitalize on partnerships to understand and support equitable access. Collaboration relies on the establishment of partnerships between diverse stakeholders, including various campus support services, administrators, academic departments, and community agencies in a college setting.

As we discussed in earlier chapters, DSOs are diverse. In Chapter 3, an overview of the DSO, we highlighted many differences in where the office is housed and what services are provided at different IHEs. Given that DSOs are unique and seen differently depending on the institution, collaborations within each institution may take on a different feel. Understanding the structure and makeup of your institution is the first step. What works for one institution may be different from what works for another due to makeup, type, and even size. What is not different, however, is how collaboration facilitates inclusion and access for SWDs at an IHE.

Culture and Institutional Landscape

Understanding the institution's landscape and what influences may help or hinder collaboration is the first step for many. Consider whether the institution is unionized, public or private, four years or two, vocational or technical. Is it a residential community or a computer-based institution? Does it have financial security, and what is its political climate? Where does the institution reside—urban, rural, or suburban? Some answers to these questions can be found quickly, while others take years to understand. Considering the institution's unique makeup is the first step in building collaborative partnerships with stakeholders who support the mission of the DSO.

When considering potential partners/collaborators, you may want to take stock of established connections. Students may work with multiple offices that have relationships made to facilitate support for shared students; offices with students in common could be, for example, counseling services, advising, residence life, or TRIO programs. Consider the connection and contacts within those offices. Is there a good working relationship? Have there already been mutually beneficial, successful collaborations?

Change is often slow within education, and IHEs in particular have typically valued tradition over innovation. Sometimes the obstacle to building a successful stakeholder lies in the organizational structure. Identify where a paradigm shift needs to occur to help decrease barriers. It might be as easy as developing a list of offices that share a like mission. Connecting with an office that would not usually work with a DSO is the most powerful way to help shift thinking.

Figure 17.1 Collaboration

Finding Collaborative Partners: Start at the Beginning

How an SWD travels through the college experience may be a way to identify partners. The admissions office is the first official connection to the institution for many students. Disability status does not weigh in on individual student admissions, but familiarizing the DSO with admissions processes and the admissions office with the DSO will help incoming students. Many DSPs meet directly with prospective students during the college search. It is common for the DSO to participate in open houses, accepted student days, or other specialized times when prospective students may visit campus. Having a presence at these events is crucial, as it models the understanding that all students are welcome.

As the National Center for Education Statistics states,

> In 2018–19, the number of students aged 3–21 who receive special education services under the Individuals with Disabilities Education Act (IDEA) was 7.1 million, or 14 percent of all public-school students. Among students receiving special education services, 33 percent had specific learning disabilities. (National Center for Education Statistics 2021b)

According to the National Center for Education Statistics, the population of students who receive special education has grown 11 percent, meaning that students requiring curricular access must be taken into consideration in the admissions process. The collaboration between admissions and the DSO will help admissions counselors explain the office when talking to potential students. As admissions may be the first stop for the student exploring your institution, it stands to reason that this office may well be the first opportunity for connection and collaboration. The increasing numbers of students identifying as having disabilities in K–12 schools may help the relationship between the two offices flourish.

Once the student is admitted, the first-year experience office (FYE) is the next step for many. This office is typically where orientation and first-year initiatives like first-year reading, direction, and other activities are housed. Students often interact with their FYE as soon as they accept admission by joining class pages on social media platforms and browsing websites of admitted students. Understanding the programming of your FYE will build ways for both offices to support accessible education.

The DSO should ask to participate in orientation events. The first step toward participation may be to encourage students who need accommodations for the event to understand how to access them. Training the staff working at orientation on the function of the DSO can help with future questions. The DSO should be present at planned events and speak directly to students during sessions. Doing so allows students with questions about accommodations to learn about the office naturally and without seeking out the DSO. It is also a great way to increase awareness that an office exists to serve SWDs.

Residential students' next step in learning about their new IHE is residence life. Access to the residence hall includes physical space adaptations, specific room types, and residential locations on campus. The makeup of a residence life office lends itself to a partnership around training opportunities. This office often employs graduate assistants along with professional staff. Continual training and meetings may be necessary, as many of the team in residence life naturally cycle through.

For this reason, connecting with the office to participate in onboarding training for professional and graduate levels employees may be an excellent place to start. The offices can connect to build programs for student training at the resident assistant level. The resident assistant is often the person SWDs turn to for answers about your office if they did not connect with you at the orientation stage. Ensuring that resident assistants understand how the DSO works allows for seamless referrals for students seeking services.

Academic advising begins during the orientation experience. Connecting with the advising office each semester to discuss changes to majors and new university requirements is critical. The advising office can help when deciding on appropriate academic accommodations; they know and have firsthand experience with faculty, giving them essential insights into what may be fundamental to the class. As critical parts of the curricular team, advisors can be beneficial when the DSO has questions.

Once a student with a disability is accepted into the institution, their interests determine the offices they interact with. They may be working with athletics, student government, and groups and clubs. The offices that oversee student engagement may be areas to develop partnerships. Collaborating with offices in student engagement on projects and initiatives can enhance the profile of the DSO in other student areas.

SWDs have multiple intersecting identities that connect with different groups, as we saw in Chapter 2. Ensuring the DSO is active in all areas is essential to seamless student access. The diversity, equity, and inclusion office is the expert to lean on when auditing your policies and procedures for inclusivity—another great way to establish collaboration. Establishing a connection and understanding the reporting process helps students first stop at the DSO. The DSO staff will be able to explain the process confidently while supporting the student on their next steps. Understanding how the two offices intersect may come in time or be established during the first meeting.

As stated before, students travel through an institution as they see fit. Collaborating on access, programming, and even training can be a way to ensure equitable access. Identifying needs and working collaboratively to remedy areas of concern facilitates natural partnerships with other campus offices.

Cultivate Partnerships: Ways to Work Together

Once natural partners are determined, what comes next? Cultivating partnerships that mutually benefit both office missions does. Think about the offices that can support DSO initiatives and try to identify a set of stakeholders you had not previously considered. Consider the busy time for prospective collaborators. Would hosting a presentation or training help during this time? It is critical to ensure the other office sees the benefit of collaboration.

Cosponsoring events can also open doors for collaboration. When interacting with other offices, listen for events or projects they might be planning that support access and inclusion. Small talk before meetings can yield information about assignments important to both offices. When an opportunity is identified, reach out to offer to cost share or provide swag and giveaways for the event or project. Consider a minor contribution like catering if the budget does not allow for large-scale sponsorships. The potential significance of the offer to have coffee and cookies for all attending the event should not be overlooked. By sponsoring refreshments, you might be able to spread collaborative participation with a simple sentence on the event poster or a simple sign at the table where the goodies are set up. Simply having the DSO's name on an event brings awareness.

Other ways to connect to essential stakeholders include nominations or placement on important university committees, which can happen by reaching out to committee chairs or asking a supervisor to forward your name. Being present with individuals who represent other levels within the university's organizational chart may be helpful. Participating in university committees can also be valuable when reminding that inclusion is an all-university responsibility. Some committees you consider might seem out of the DSO's focus, but the connection between the office and the other members will be shared by being a member. Working on search committees for important positions is an opportunity to have a say in the hiring process and work with others across the university with a shared goal and outcome. The benefits are layered and may extend the goal of access to those who have not been allies but now understand the mission and their role in supporting it.

Most ISEs participate in the strategic planning process. Writing a new strategic plan can be a five-year process with committees to tackle various aspects of the project. Asking to be a team member can expose you to colleagues from offices that are not typical DSO work partners. More importantly, DSO presence may allow for a focus on inclusive education throughout the planning process. It is much work, but a committee can forge considerable benefits to the university's shared responsibility to diverse learners. Most programs and universities have accrediting bodies that need cyclical reporting to maintain accreditation. This could also be an important area in which to volunteer. Other committees to consider are curriculum and development, institutional review board, diversity and inclusion, and department advisory. Finally, the power of being included on important committees can be beneficial.

A committee that most universities equate with the DSO may be the ADA committee. This committee is critical to the university's compliance, and the expertise of DSO staff within it is crucial. It is a committee many see as an area for DSO members to lead. Leading this committee in ways other than being the chair is significant to pushing the importance of inclusive practices at the university. If a DSO member is nominated, it may be necessary to decline a chairship nomination and select another member, maybe a faculty member who wants to serve as chair. It is often said that faculty learn best by hearing ideas from other faculty members. The institution may be more likely to participate in initiatives coming out of the committee when faculty lead.

Cultivating Relationships with Academic Departments: Working with Faculty

The importance of partnership with faculty cannot be understated. Agreement on and provisions for accommodations often rely on each side understanding its role in providing access for students. We have seen and embarked on several ways to collaborate with faculty with varying success. DSPs' biggest challenge has been faculty concern with time commitment and responsiveness. Faculty can be notoriously unresponsive, especially over breaks and during the summer. No matter how we try to avoid it, after decades of experience in the field, we have come to own it and plan around it. Despite their inability to commit to long-term projects, we have found successful ways to broaden the partnership with faculty beyond conversations around student needs in courses.

Faculty Advisory Board (FAB)

Faculty advisory boards (FABs) are a great low-effort, high-impact collaboration. FABs are designed to educate faculty on what the DSO is doing, gain feedback, and purposefully gain insight into what is happening in the classroom. They can meet as often as once a month (usually a harder sell for busy faculty) or as infrequently as once a year. We have found the sweet spot to be once a semester. Membership can be composed of various faculty—we suggest starting by reaching out to those who have the most contact when supporting students. Some institutions may even get the FAB listed as one of the committees' faculty can volunteer in to fulfill their committee obligations.

FAB meetings are usually structured around updates from the DSO and its work in the classroom. By providing insight into what others are doing and the space to offer suggestions or express a need for more information about a specific issue, the FAB allows a comradery of support to be developed. New initiatives are thoroughly reviewed before being put into play.

Faculty Surveys

Just as a DSO should survey students at the end of the year for feedback on the scope and quality of services, it should survey faculty. Faculty surveys allow for anonymous feedback about the accommodation process. We recommend a combination of quantitative and qualitative questions that gather information on the accommodation experience for faculty and offer an opportunity to share specific feedback and make suggestions.

The FAB is a wonderful avenue to get this survey out. In addition to allowing the DSO to connect with the keeper of the faculty listserv and ask them to distribute the survey, the FAB can add a bit more personalized pressure to the request, helping to increase the response rate. Throughout our years conducting this survey, given the faculty's lack of time, one of the biggest challenges has been choosing when to conduct it. We have found that administering the survey five to six weeks before the end of the spring semester garners the most feedback.

The survey will bring in a wealth of information, even if the response rate is negligible. Some of this information will be incredibly helpful (ideas for streamlining the note-taking accommodation, suggestions for reminding students to connect with faculty, etc.). Others will not be quite so fruitful (requests that the DSO proctor everything, demands for a list of every student who needs accommodations, etc.). We suggest using the results to guide improvement over the summer and as conversation/education prompts when teaching faculty about their roles and responsibilities.

Faculty Website Resources

DSO websites should include a page for faculty resources. When faculty are confused about their role and responsibilities or seeking support around making a document accessible, the website may be one of the first places they search for information (outside of emailing the DSO directly).

We recommend including several things on the DSO website. At minimum, it should have the following resources:

- Faculty roles and responsibilities
- The definition of "disability" under the ADA and a link to the law
- Examples of syllabi statements faculty should use
- A brief synopsis of what the accommodation determination process looks like
- Directions for implementing more complex accommodations (exams, note-taking, interpreters, alternative course materials)
- Contact information for when help is needed

If there is space, we recommend expanding website offerings to include the following:

- A description of what NOT to do as a faculty member (i.e., accommodate in the absence of formal notification from the DSO)
- Direct links to DSO database/exam accommodation management systems
- A referral link to send students to the DSO
- Information on UDL

- Information on how to make course materials accessible
- Testimonials from other faculty members about the DSO

The key to creating an inviting website is to keep it simple. We recommend that such information be included, but it can quickly overwhelm faculty. Use bullets, links, and charts. Stay away from long paragraphs of information. Prioritize what should come first to catch their eye. Consider different modalities (podcasts, links to TED talks, or videos—especially when explaining how to ensure that content is easily accessible). Do not assume that a DSP must create all this content. Instead, rely on others who have developed solid tutorials on UDL implementation or have created charts defining faculty's roles and responsibilities. Finally, ensure the website is shared widely at individual and department-wide faculty meetings.

Build a Network Outside of Your Institution

Focusing on departments and offices that make good partners is essential, as are connections with those outside the institution. AHEAD is an "international, multicultural organization of professionals committed to full participation in higher education for persons with disabilities" (AHEAD n.d.). This organization may be the first stop for those seeking connections outside the institution. AHEAD supports state affiliates where local members can work together in a focused way. Affiliates often hold conferences, membership calls, or training to help new professionals assimilate to the field.

Connecting with DS colleagues in the same position in other institutions can be essential. Ways to connect include hosting a meeting on a subject affecting individuals in the local area. Reaching out to all local DSPs and asking if they want to join in a virtual meeting could be the icebreaker needed to build a network. With technology, the need to leave the office to communicate with one another is no longer the barrier it once was, allowing for more interaction. Hosting or being a part of these meetings will build a local community that advises, supports, and guides you in unfamiliar or unclear areas.

Connections with DSPs who focus on the same things can be meaningful when a question cannot be answered within the institution. Connecting to colleagues doing the same work can help a DSP move initiatives forward, provide ideas that worked for them, or share sample forms. Connecting with other collegiate institutions can feel like a lifeline during hard times.

An example of collaboration with peers within your region can center around building cases for positions. Having a community that understands the culture of an institution can be a helpful resource in building proposals for new positions. Understanding what worked for another college in the same system can be invaluable. Not only will both DSPs share a similar experience, but one can also help the other avoid obstacles. We often use the phrase "don't reinvent the wheel." Using others' experiences can save time and often results in a successful proposal. As stated before, many of our questions are answered with the phrase "it depends." Collaboration between institutions will often fit this phrase. Still, despite differences, the assurance that you are not alone is worth the effort.

How to Market the Collaboration

Once areas for collaboration have been identified and collaborative projects have been successful, one last vital step is to document the success. Making sure a record of success is collected and shared is as important as the relationships themselves. Ideas for spreading successful experiences may lie in the uniqueness of your institution. If there is a way to share important information or celebrate successful projects, take advantage of that. Some universities have internal communications to support the community and share news. Consider putting an article or quick blurb into this internal communication tool. Always give credit to the individuals and offices you worked with. Think about other ways to spread shared information by writing an office newsletter to faculty and cooperating offices, keeping them up to date with initiatives started as well as completed. This can be a great tool to showcase change areas in the office, from staffing to process.

Consider using social media to spread accessible news. This practice has pluses and minuses, but your ISE's culture will indicate whether it is the right way to proceed. If having a DSO social media account is not a good idea, consider Instagram takeovers and tweets sharing meaningful information about the office from university-sanctioned accounts. This allows for a presence without the commitment of an office account. Remember to spread collaborative successes throughout your university, whether through a newsletter, post on social media, or internal communication tools. The idea of inclusion as a shared responsibility is critical to the ease of access for SWDs.

In Summary

At the beginning of this chapter, it was essential to recognize that DSOs are diverse. Their work and methods of facilitating collaboration may vary significantly from institution to institution. What does not change is the need for collaborators and allies both in and out of the institution. Working with SWDs often means interacting with all university areas, as SWDs experience all areas of an institution. Making partners and allies throughout the institution allows for shared responsibility and dedication to the work of inclusion. Collaboration is the way to facilitate the institution's shared commitment to supporting access for all learners. It is also a way to build supportive allies that can help with initiatives critical to the DSO's mission.

▸ Reflective Exercise

The biology department at your university is sponsoring a festival around sustainability. Individuals from your institution as well as guests from the community will be attending. The festival will be held on your campus and sponsor virtual events. You reach out to the committee in charge of the event and ask if you can be a part of the planning. You are on the committee; subcommittees are formed, and you volunteer for the planning group. The event is typically well attended by students, faculty, and community stakeholders and has brought positive attention to your institution in the past. The committee chair has been named and is someone you have worked with in the past. What ideas for collaboration will you bring? How can you situate yourself to support an inclusive environment?

▸ Supplemental Job Aids

The following Supplemental Job Aids can be found at https://scholarshare.temple.edu/handle/20.500.12613/8373:

- *Collaboration Meeting Agenda*

Part VI

Conclusion

18

In Summary

DSPs are unique administrators in the field of higher education. We are simultaneously responsible for access and accommodations, compliance and regulations, and equity and inclusion. We work in support of a student population that is concurrently the most diverse, the most at risk, and by many accounts, the most overlooked. As with the students we serve, no two DSPs have the same background and experience. If you were to ask ten DSPs how they got their start in the field, you would likely get ten different responses. The institutions we serve and the DSOs we operate vary greatly in programming, culture, resources, philosophy, and mission. There are a few things we all have in common, though. We share a calling, and we make access a way of life as much as we do a profession.

We also share the same frustrations. The average DSO is underfunded and understaffed. Not all institutions respond to the call for proactive inclusion of SWDs. Our legal obligations change with every settlement agreement. K–12 institutions are not adequately preparing students and families for the transition to higher education. New accommodation needs and requests are challenging conventions. But, as stated in Chapter 9, DSPs are nothing if not curious, creative, and resourceful, and our network of support from colleagues in the field is rich, diverse, and most of all, collaborative.

If we flip the script, our shared frustrations can become shared opportunities. If we work together, our shared opportunities become shared initiatives. If we stay the course, our marching call for access and inclusion will be heard, and our collaborative efforts will become our shared success. As a field of dedicated, passionate professionals, we can influence a culture of inclusion on our campuses.

Throughout this text, we have explored how DSOs operate, how we enter into the interactive process with good faith efforts, how we must always be watching for compliance updates from the field, and how our ultimate goal is inclusion by design. Below are some key takeaways.

Lessons Learned

Disability Services in Higher Education

"It depends." Perhaps we should have titled the book that . . . No two DSOs in higher education are alike. Despite our institutions' differences in campus size, etc., capital and human resources, professional level and background, DSPs are philosophically united in advancing campus culture and amplifying the conversation about the value of disability diversity. This book is a further effort to bond the field in proven practices through an awareness of the variability in our work and a call to action. Disability, first and foremost, must be recognized as an individualized experience. As DSPs, we must listen to our students' experiences, honor them, and offer inclusive paths that acknowledge the social construct of disability while respecting students' individuality. We must work to educate our higher education communities about disability culture and social justice through a lens of disability as diversity. Throughout this book, we offer strategies for engaging key stakeholders in productive conversations and reflections aimed to create a culture shift of inclusion for all.

Knowing what others are doing or not doing is a powerful tool for a DSP. In this field perhaps more than in others in higher education, we rely on each other across institutional lines. Knowing how other offices run, what resources make the day-to-day manageable, what the staff to student ratio is, or whether to proctor exams not only offers new ideas and strategies but also can be used as leverage when asking for more support. This text offers several resources designed to be customized and used immediately to help a DSP with their day-to-day work.

The Interactive Process

We rely on an interactive process to determine whether a student meets the criteria for having a disability and what accommodations should be made. The importance of the interactive process cannot be understated in our work. Chapter 6 walks through the process for determining eligibility, and all decisions related to accommodations are built around this process.

The determination of an effective or reasonable accommodation for a student is the basis of what we do. This determination is driven by ADA requirements but means interacting with the student and DSP to identify accommodations that might work best for access to the curriculum. Our practices for verifying the request, evaluating the self-report, determining whether it rises to the level of disability, and establishing eligibility must remain consistent for all students requesting accommodations. As DSPs, we want to make sure we are using all the relevant information to support the interactive process. While many types of documentation can be provided by diagnostic and accommodation records, observations, and self-reports, ultimately, the reasonable, good faith efforts and informed judgments of the DSP are central to the process of determining disability. Without the interactive process, we would not have a structure to show our compliance required under the ADA. This book focuses on how one may go about implementing interactive practices. It is important to consider what is fundamental and how the interactive process should work overall. Evaluations can include DSPs, course coordinators, department chairs, deans, and senior level leadership. Again, for consistency, we include some guiding questions in Chapter 7. We illustrate the importance of the interactive process in meeting ADA requirements while providing the students we serve with meaningful accommodations and without fundamentally altering what the course or program is measuring.

Compliance

The heart and soul of this book is rooted in the idea that compliance is the floor, and universal design is what DSPs strive to achieve. However, a huge component of DS work is maintaining compliance. While we prefer to focus on moving the needle beyond compliance and toward true inclusion, meeting compliance standards forms the foundation on which to build DS programs. Knowledge of the laws and regulations that set the parameters for our work, combined with strategic thinking about how to respond and proactively manage potential legal issues, gives DSPs a framework to develop and manage policy, processes, and procedures. Using the law as a basis for all policies, not just those in the DSO, requires accessibility to be considered at all levels of the institution. It also narrows the scope for the actual policies DSOs are responsible for creating and enforcing.

The truth of the matter is that compliance concerns are effective drivers of administrative action that result in more DSP resources and progress. Compliance needs open doors so concepts like universal design can be implemented. Strategically leveraging the opportunities that present themselves through informal, internal complaints or larger, more publicized state or federal proceedings helps us make the case for more resources and innovative programs—and a senior-leadership level response to accessibility and inclusivity.

Utilizing the legal landscape to shape policies and their connected processes and procedures protects the IHE and provides a framework for identifying what needs to be a policy and who should own it. The bottom line is that most administrative decisions are not within our purview, and we need to identify processes and procedures that work with broader institutional policies. We do not want competing or conflicting requirements, so it is best to leave as much policy-oriented work to IHE leadership, advise where appropriate, and develop processes and procedures to provide a channel for the interactive process. The legal and procedural aspects of this work are not always the most exciting and are certainly not the reason why many enter this field, but they are critical to the work and should be a starting point for improving the accessibility of IHEs.

Inclusion by Design

The role of the DSP is wider than most professional positions in higher education. Unlike most roles in higher education, ours extends to the entire student experience, from applying to our institution to eating in the dining halls, parking on campus, attending social events, filling out online forms, and watching courses online. If this feels overwhelming, it should.

Throughout this book, we point to areas of potential access concern and offer guidance around inclusive solutions, including everything from navigating the built campus to asking students to sign up for commencement through an online portal. While it is our job to be aware of potential barriers, it is not our job to fix them all. Instead, we have suggested key collaborators a DSP can educate, partner with, and lean on to take the lead. By creating access allies and promoting the qualities of universal design as a solution for all, we empower others on campus to consider the needs of SWDs in their day-to-day work.

Collaboration is key. Many DSPs are single-person offices. Fewer have one or two staff members, and fewer still have large teams. And yet, even in well-resourced teams, there is always a shortage of expendable time. Collaborating with colleagues on campus—whether faculty, administrators, staff in other departments, or legal counsels—is key to increasing access awareness and, ultimately, to creating a truly inclusive higher education experience.

Parting Words

The authors have a combined seventy years of experience in the field. Do we know it all? No. Do we still wrestle with accommodation determinations?

Yes. Are we waiting for the latest legal settlement to guide how we move forward? Absolutely. Will we ever have all the answers each day we go to work? Probably not.

The field of DS in higher education is malleable and ever changing. This text was designed to give you the blueprint to the field and empower you, as our colleague, to be successful. We thought it might be helpful to share what we wish we had known when we entered the field all those years ago. Our hope is to offer you some advice, no matter where you are in your DSP journey, as you continue to work toward access and inclusion. We look forward to connecting with you and seeking out your advice in this ever-changing field.

What We Wish We Had Known

Kirsten Behling—That intuitions of higher education are welcoming but also places of business. A DSP must be nimble, creative, and able to work within financial, personnel, and professional restrictions in ways that many have never thought of. Higher education is an opportunity for all—students, families, faculty, and those of us in the DS field. As the field grows and the realization that disability is diversity grows, opportunities for built-in inclusion are plentiful. Be patient, consistent, and kind; change will happen.

Eileen Bellemore—If only we had had a crystal ball to forecast that a worldwide pandemic would dramatically and fundamentally disrupt almost every aspect of campus life. Knowing now how a dramatic shift to remote learning would upend quality course delivery, I wish IHEs would have been more aggressive in investing in virtual infrastructure as a strategic asset. What those of us in the DS field have known for a long time is that accessible technology and online learning and engagement have been game changers for educational access. Diversifying how we engage, teach, assess, and support helps to mitigate disability-related barriers and increases options for students to optimize learning and success. Students are afforded more equitable access by UDL-based practices such as video recorded lectures and campus events, virtual office hours, and nontraditional methods of participation (e.g., blogs, chat boards). Adopting similar approaches will expand access to your office and make visitors feel welcome (e.g., videos to help students navigate your services and processes, virtual drop-in hours).

Lisa Bibeau—It is critical that you understand that this field is ever changing. The interpretation of the law changes with each case, and being nimble and dedicated to continue learning is critical to succeeding in the field. We shared the importance of understanding your mission and the restraints of resources. Legal responsibilities may change, and student needs may evolve while your resources stay the same. Being nimble and able to continually pivot to understand the landscape in which you are providing services will be important. I would emphasize the need to build supports throughout campus so that the lift to ensure access is one the institution understands. It is sometimes important for others to advocate for equitable access to build a ground swell that will shape change within your institution.

Andrew Cioffi—People who work and teach in higher education are well intentioned and genuinely want to do right by their students, but accessibility is not always on their radar. It is OK to recognize that accessibility is a campus effort and that we are only as good as the partnerships we create. One hope for this book is to share some of the ways that DSOs can lead that charge.

Bridget McNamee—Accessibility is an institution-wide responsibility even though IHEs want to assign the entirety of the work to one person (maybe two or two and a half people, if you are lucky!). Right off the bat, I wish I had engaged my colleagues as partners in the work instead of staying in the boundaries created by the medical model of disability. It took me years to stop responding to emails from colleagues letting me know that the elevator is broken or that snow needs to be cleared from an area by contacting the appropriate staff. Shifting the response to empowering colleagues to take ownership of the issue and assist in solving the problem creates a culture of collaboration and a sense that accessibility and inclusion are everyone's job. It may be in my title, but the onus is on all of us to ensure an inclusive environment. Accessibility touches everything from building access to how a software program is coded, and we cannot possibly do it all! Our campuses have experts in all these areas—do not hesitate to engage them in accessibility (and remind them that it is part of their job, too).

References

ACICS. 2021. "Accrediting Council for Independent Colleges & Schools." April 2021. http://acics.org.
ADA National Network. 2019. "Guidelines for Writing about People with Disabilities." National Network. https://adata.org/factsheet/ADANN-writing.
———. 2022. "Contact Your Region/ADA Center." National Network. August 2022. https://adata.org/find-your-region.
AHEAD. 2012. "Supporting Accommodation Requests: Guidance on Documentation Practices." Association on Higher Education and Disability. October 2012.
———. 2019. "Supporting Accommodation Requests: Guidance on Documentation Practices." Association on Higher Education and Disability. https://www.ahead.org/professional-resources/accommodations/documentation.
———. 2021a. "AHEAD Professional Standards." Association on Higher Education and Disability. https://www.ahead.org/about-ahead/professional-standards.
———. 2021b. "AHEAD Statement on Language." Association on Higher Education and Disability. https://www.ahead.org/professional-resources/accommodations/statement-on-language.
———. 2021c. "The AHEAD Domain, Program Standards, and Performance Indicators." Association of Higher Education and Disability. https://www.ahead.org/professional-resources/information-services-portal/data-collection-and-management/performance-indicators.
———. n.d. "Mission, Vision and Core Values." Association on Higher Education and Disability. Accessed November 15, 2022. https://www.ahead.org/about-ahead.
AIM Services. 2020. "ABA & ADA: A Timeline of Accessible Architecture & Facility Design." July 20, 2020. Accessed January 31, 2022. www.aimservicesinc.org/news/ada-architecture/.
Alley, Erica. 2012. "Exploring Remote Interpreting." *International Journal of Interpreter Education* 4 (1).

Anderson, Greta. 2019. "Stanford Changes Leave Policies on Mental Illness." Inside Higher Ed. October 8, 2019. https://www.insidehighered.com/news/2019/10/08/stanford-changes-leave-policies-mental-illness.

Arizona State University. 2015. "Terms to Avoid When Writing about Disability." National Center on Disability and Journalism. https://ncdj.org/2015/09/terms-to-avoid-when-writing-about-disability/.

Art Beyond Sight. 2010. "Disability and Inclusion—Social and Medical Models of Disability: Paradigm Change." www.artbeyondsight.org/dic/definition-of-disability-paradigm-change-and-ongoing-conversation/.

ASHA. n.d. "IDEA Part B: Children with Disabilities Enrolled by Their Parents in Private Schools." American Speech-Language-Hearing Association. Accessed January 30, 2022. https://www.asha.org/advocacy/federal/idea/idea-part-b-issue-brief-children-with-disabilities-enrolled-by-their-parents-in-private-schools/.

Behling, K., L. Bibeau, and K. Pillette. 2021. "Accidental UDL: A Silver Lining of the COVID Pandemic." *Thriving in Academe*, 39 (3) (Sept 2021).

Behling, K., and D. Hart. 2008. "Universal Course Design: A Model of Professional Development: Strategies for bringing UCD to a College Campus and Ensuring its Sustainability." In *Universal Design in Post-Secondary Education: From Principles to Practice*, edited by S. Burgstahler. Cambridge, MA: Harvard Education Press.

Bellefeuille, Anne. 2020. "Psychoeducational and Neuropsychological Evaluations Explained." Landmark School. July 17, 2020. https://www.landmarkschool.org/our-school/landmark-360-blog/?id=253264/psychoeducational-and-neuropsychological-evaluations-explained.

Branson, Katie. 2018. "The Department of Education's Office of Civil Rights Reverses Course on Mass-Filer Civil Rights Complaints." EDUCAUSE Review. December 11, 2018. https://er.educause.edu/blogs/2018/12/the-department-of-educations-office-of-civil-rights-reverses-course-on-mass-filer-civil-rights.

Bremer, Christine, Mera Kachgal, and Kris Schoeller. 2003. "Self-Determination: Supporting Successful Transition." University of Minnesota. National Center on Secondary Education and Transition Institute on Community Integration. April 2003. http://www.ncset.org/publications/viewdesc.asp?id=962.

CAST. 2016. "UDL in the ESSA." www.cast.org/news/2016/udl-in-the-essa.

———. 2021. "About Universal Design for Learning." www.cast.org/impact/universal-design-for-learning-udl.

CDC. 2019. "Infographic: Adults with Disabilities: Ethnicity and Race." Disability and Health Promotion. Centers for Disease Control and Prevention. October 25, 2019. https://www.cdc.gov/ncbddd/disabilityandhealth/materials/infographic-disabilities-ethnicity-race.html.

———. 2020. "Infographic: Disability Impacts All of Us." Disability and Health Promotion. https://www.cdc.gov/ncbddd/disabilityandhealth/infographic-disability-impacts-all.html.

Cherry, Kendra. 2019. "How Person Perception Helps Us Form Impressions of Others" Verywell Mind. https://www.verywellmind.com/person-perception-2795900.

CMSA. 2021. "What Is a Case Manager?" Case Management Society of America. https://cmsa.org/who-we-are/what-is-a-case-manager/.

Collaborative for Communication Access Via Captioning. 2012. "What Is CART and FAQ's—Find a CART Captioning Provider." Captioning Activism and Community. September 11, 2012. Accessed January 31, 2022. ccacaptioning.org/faqs-cart/#:~:text=The%20costs%20of%20these%20services.

Cornell University. n.d. "The ADA and Parking." Northeast ADA Center. northeastada.org/resource/the-ada-and-parking.

———. n.d. "Architectural Barriers Act (ABA)." Northeast ADA Center. northeastada.org/resource/architectural-barriers-act-aba.

Daugherty, Daniel. 2017. "The Interaction Flow in Motivational Interviews." Motivational Interview. December 27, 2017. http://motivationalinterview.net/clinical/interaction.html.

DeAngelis, T. 2019. "College Students' Mental Health Is a Higher Priority." *Monitor on Psychology* 50 (11): 80. https://www.apa.org/monitor/2019/12/numbers-college#:~:text=36%25.

Disabled World. 2010. "Definitions of the Models of Disability." Glossary and Definitions. September 10, 2010. https://www.disabled-world.com/definitions/disability-models.php.

ECTA. 2012. "Federal Definitions of Assistive Technology." Early Childhood Technical Assistance Center. ectacenter.org/topics/atech/definitions.asp.

Forber-Pratt, Anjali J., Gabriel J. Merrin, Carlyn O. Mueller, Larry R. Price, and Heather Hensman Kettrey. 2020. "Initial Factor Exploration of Disability Identity." *Rehabilitation Psychology* 65 (1): 1–10. https://doi.org/10.1037/rep0000308.

Freeman, Jonathan B., and Kerri L. Johnson. 2016. "More Than Meets the Eye: Split-Second Social Perception." *Trends in Cognitive Sciences* 20 (5): 362–74. https://doi.org/10.1016/j.tics.2016.03.003.

Gatchalian, Camyl. 2019. "Assistive Technologies in the 21st Century." Pressbooks. Technology and the Curriculum. July 2019. https://techandcurr2019.pressbooks.com/chapter/21st-century-assistive-tech/#:~:text=Today%2C%20the%20use%20of%20mouth.

General Services Administration. 2020. "Section 508 of the Rehabilitation Act of 1973." Section508.gov. July 2020. https://www.section508.gov/manage/laws-and-policies/.

Georgetown Law. n.d. "Digital Accessibility." Accessed January 29, 2022. https://www.law.georgetown.edu/your-life-career/campus-services/information-systems-technology/digital-accessibility/#:~:text=Digital%20accessibility%20refers%20to%20the.

Georgia Tech. n.d. "FAQ's." Office of Disability Services. Accessed February 1, 2022. https://disabilityservices.gatech.edu/resources/faqs.

Global Diversity Practice. 2018. "What Is Diversity & Inclusion?" About Us. December 3, 2018. https://globaldiversitypractice.com/what-is-diversity-inclusion/.

Golden, Claire, and Meghan Tomb. 2016. "What Is a Neuropsychological Evaluation?" Columbia University Department of Psychiatry. Division of Child and Adolescent Psychiatry. https://childadolescentpsych.cumc.columbia.edu/articles/what-neuropsychological-evaluation.

Goodman, Nanette, Michael Morris, Kelvin Boston, and Donna Walton. 2019. "Financial Inequality: Disability, Race and Poverty in America." National Disability Institute. https://www.nationaldisabilityinstitute.org/wp-content/uploads/2019/02/disability-race-poverty-in-america.pdf.

Goyat, Rashmi, Ami Vyas, and Usha Sambamoorthi. 2015. "Racial/Ethnic Disparities in Disability Prevalence." *Journal of Racial and Ethnic Health Disparities* 3 (4): 635–45. https://doi.org/10.1007/s40615-015-0182-z.

Graymore, Dani. 2021. *Service Dogs in Training (SDiT) State Laws*. https://www.servicedogtrainingschool.org/blog/service-dogs-in-training-laws-by-state.

Groves, Karl. 2013. "The 6 Simplest Web Accessibility Tests Anyone Can Do." Karlgroves.com. September 5, 2013. http://www.karlgroves.com/2013/09/05/the-6-simplest-web-accessibility-tests-anyone-can-do/.

Harvard University. 2013. "Provide Captions and Descriptions of Video." Digital Accessibility. https://accessibility.huit.harvard.edu/provide-captions-and-descriptions-video.

Hogan, Andrew J. 2019. "Social and Medical Models of Disability and Mental Health: Evolution and Renewal." *Canadian Medical Association Journal* 191 (1): E16–18. https://doi.org/10.1503/cmaj.181008.

IDEA. 2017. "Sec. 300.320 Definition of individualized education program." Individuals with Disabilities Education Act. https://sites.ed.gov/idea/regs/b/d/300.320.

Ingeno, Lauren. 2013. "Online Accessibility a Faculty Duty." Inside Higher Ed. June 24, 2013. https://www.insidehighered.com/news/2013/06/24/faculty-responsible-making-online-materials-accessible-disabled-students.

Institute for Human Centered Design, n.d. "History." Inclusive Design. Retrieved April 2021. www.humancentereddesign.org/inclusive-design/history.

JAN. n.d.a. "Accessibility." Job Accommodation Network. Accessed January 29, 2022. https://askjan.org/topics/accessi.cfm.

———. n.d.b. "What Does 'Reasonable' Mean?—A Deconstructive Series for ADA Terminology." Job Accommodation Network. Accessed January 28, 2022. https://askjan.org/articles/What-Does-Reasonable-Mean-A-Deconstructive-Series-for-ADA-Terminology.cfm.

JED. 2020. "Survey of College Student Mental Health in 2020." The Jed Foundation. October 22, 2020. www.jedfoundation.org/survey-of-college-student-mental-health-in-2020/.

Kincaid, Jeanne. 2019. "Sinkholes, Potholes, Ice, Rain & Snow: Navigating Rough Roads of Legal Compliance." Lecture presented at the Postsecondary Training Institute, Boston. May 2019.

Kirkwood, Lauren. 2016. "ADA Settlement: UMD to Caption Sports Archive Videos for Deaf Fans." *Maryland Daily Record*, July 29, 2016. thedailyrecord.com/2016/07/29/umd-deaf-fans-lawsuit-settlement/.

Law School Admission Council. 2022. "Common Reasons Why Documentation Is Deemed Insufficient by LSAC." LSAT. https://www.lsac.org/lsat/lsac-policy-accommodations-test-takers-disabilities/common-reasons-why-documentation-deemed.

Level Access. 2022. "What is Section 508 of the Rehabilitation Act?" Section 508 of the Rehabilitation Act. https://www.levelaccess.com/accessibility-regulations/section-508-rehabilitation-act/.

Lhamon, Catherine, and Jocelyn Samuels. 2014. "Memorandum of Understanding between the United States Department of Education, Office for Civil Rights, and the United States Department of Justice, Civil Rights Division." https://www.justice.gov/sites/default/files/crt/legacy/2014/04/28/ED_DOJ_MOU_TitleIX-04-29-2014.pdf.

Logomyway. 2017. "Handicapped Logo and the History behind It." Accessed January 31, 2022. blog.logomyway.com/new-handicapped-logo-and-the-history/.

Lukersmith, Sue, Michael Millington, and Luis Salvador-Carulla. 2016. "What Is Case Management? A Scoping and Mapping Review." *International Journal of Integrated Care* 16 (4): 2. https://doi.org/10.5334/ijic.2477.

Lynch, Kevin. 2020. "Number of Required Accessible Units in Dormitory Suites." Code Red Consultants. April 6, 2020. coderedconsultants.com/insights/number-of-required-accessible-units-in-dormitory-suites/.

Maguire, Angus. 2016. "Equity vs. Equality." Portfolio. http://Madewithangus.com/Portfolio/Equality-Vs-Equity/.

Maisel, Jordana, and Molly Ranahan. 2017. "Beyond Accessibility to Universal Design." Whole Building Design Guide. www.wbdg.org/design-objectives/accessible/beyond-accessibility-universal-design.

Markham, Lauren. 2021. "The Man Who Filed More Than 180 Disability Lawsuits." *New York Times Magazine*, July 21, 2021. https://www.nytimes.com/2021/07/21/magazine/americans-with-disabilities-act.html.

Mason, Micheline, and Richard Reiser. 1994. *Altogether Better (from 'Special Needs' to Equality in Education)*. Hobsons Publishing PLC. http://www.worldofinclusion.com/res/altogether/AltogetherBetter.pdf.

McKenzie, Lindsay. 2019. "Legal Battle Over Captioning Continues." Inside Higher Ed. April 19, 2019. www.insidehighered.com/news/2019/04/08/mit-and-harvard-fail-get-out-video-captioning-court-case.

Medlyn, Maria. 2017. "Intersections between Gender and Disability in a Clinical Setting: The Need for Clinicians' Awareness of the Gendered Effects of Disability." *Morris Undergraduate Journal* 4 (1). https://digitalcommons.morris.umn.edu/cgi/viewcontent.cgi?article=1039&context=horizons.

Meyer, Anne, David H. Rose, and David Gordon. 2014. *Universal Design for Learning: Theory and Practice*. Wakefield, MA: CAST Professional Publishing.

Mid-Atlantic ADA Center. 2012. "Federal, State, and Local Laws: Conflicts or Complements?" *ADA In Focus* 16, no. 3 (Fall).

Miller, Christina. 2017. "Florida International University Installs Outdoor Interactive Kiosks with a Custom Wayfinding Solution." Intermedia Touch. intermediatouch.com/portfolio-posts/florida-international-university-installs-outdoor-interactive-kiosks-with-a-custom-wayfinding-solution-to-guide-and-inform-their-students-and-faculty-members.

Minnesota Guide to Assistive Technology. n.d. "Types of Assistive Technology." mn.gov/admin/at/getting-started/understanding-at/types/.

MIUSA. 2014. "Knowing What Disability Questions to Ask: Sample Accommodations Forms." Mobility International USA. October 24, 2014. https://www.miusa.org/resource/tipsheet/assessmentforms.

Morgan, Paula. 2020. "Invisible Disabilities: Break down the Barriers." *Forbes*, March 20, 2020. https://www.forbes.com/sites/paulamorgan/2020/03/20/invisible-disabilities-break-down-the-barriers/?sh=3392344afa50.

Mueller, C., and A. Forber-Pratt. 2021. "What Is Disability Identity Development, and Why Is That Important?" *Rise to Work* (blog). *TennesseeWorks*, January 21, 2021. https://www.tennesseeworks.org/what-is-disability-identity-development-and-why-is-that-important/.

NABITA. 2020. "Home." National Association for Behavioral Intervention and Threat Assessment. https://www.nabita.org/.

NAD. 2010. "Score for Accessibility: OSU to Provide In-Stadium Captions." National Association of the Deaf. November 23, 2010. https://www.nad.org/2010/11/23/score-for-accessibility-osu-to-provide-in-stadium-captions/.

———. 2019. "Community and Culture—Frequently Asked Questions." National Association of the Deaf. https://www.nad.org/resources/american-sign-language/community-and-culture-frequently-asked-questions/.

———. n.d. "Community and Culture—Frequently Asked Questions." National Association of the Deaf. Accessed January 28, 2022. https://nad.org/issues/american-sign-language/community-and-culture-faq.

National Archives. 2022. "Code of Federal Regulations Section 300.133." Code of Federal Regulations. January 25, 2022. https://www.ecfr.gov/current/title-34/subtitle-B/chapter-III/part-300/subpart-B/subject-group-ECFR3556f7ac2fe0a92/section-300.133.

NCCJ. n.d. "Intersectionality." National Conference for Community and Justice. https://www.nccj.org/intersectionality.

Neurodevelop.com. n.d. "Psychological Versus Neuropsychological Testing." Accessed January 28, 2022. https://www.neurodevelop.com/PsychvsNpsych.

New England ADA Center. 2017. "ADA Checklist for Existing Facilities." https://adachecklist.org/.

Newman, Lynn, Mary Wagner, Anne-Marie Knokey, Camille Marder, Katherine Nagle, Debra Shaver, Xin Wei, and Renee Cameto. 2011. *The Post-High School Outcomes of Young Adults with Disabilities up to 8 Years after High School: A Report from the National Longitudinal Transition Study-2 (NLTS2)*. Menlo Park, CA: SRI International. https://ies.ed.gov/ncser/pubs/20113005/pdf/20113005.pdf.

NVRC. 2021. "University of KY Settles Suit for Captioning of Football Games." Northern Virginia Resource Center for Deaf & Hard of Hearing Persons. February 22, 2012. https://nvrc.org/resources/legislation/.

Open Learn Create. "Language, Definitions and Reflective Learning." Identifying and Responding to Additional Support Needs in ELC. March 2020. https://www.open.edu/openlearncreate/mod/oucontent/view.php?id=148890.

Parry, Marc. 2012. "$150,000 Settlement Reached in Blind Florida State Students' E-Learning Suit." *The Chronical of Higher Education*. https://www.chronicle.com/blogs/wiredcampus/150000-settlement-reached-in-blind-florida-state-students-e-learning-suit.

Pasquini, Laura A. 2016. "Setting the Course: Strategies for Writing Digital and Social Guidelines." *New Directions for Student Services* 2016 (155): 91–104. https://doi.org/10.1002/ss.20185.

Pennsylvania State University. 2015. "Settlement between Penn State University and National Federation of the Blind." Accessibility and Usability at Penn State. January 30, 2015. https://accessibility.psu.edu/nfbpsusettlement/.

People First. n.d. "A History of People First." People First of West Virginia. Accessed January 28, 2022. http://peoplefirstwv.org/old-front/history-of-people-first/.

Perez, Thomas, and Russlynn Ali. 2010. "Joint Department of Justice and Department of Education 'Dear Colleague' Letter on Electronic Book Readers." ADA.gov. U.S. Department of Justice Civil Rights Division. July 29, 2010. https://www.ada.gov/kindle_ltr_eddoj.htm.

PNPI. 2021. "Students with Disabilities in Higher Education." Postsecondary National Policy Institute. https://pnpi.org/wp-content/uploads/2021/10/StudentswithDisabilities_October2021.pdf.

Powell, J. D., J. H. White, and R. K. Robinson. 1987. "Contagious Disease in the Workplace: The School Board of Nassau County v. Arline." *Labor Law Journal* 38 (11): 702–7.

Remington Lighting. 2020. "What Does ADA Compliant Lighting Mean?" ADA-Compliant Lighting. May 14, 2020. remingtonlighting.com/blog/ada-compliant-lighting/.

Roessler, Richard, Stanford E. Rubin, and Phillip D. Rumrill. 2018. *Case Management and Rehabilitation Counseling: Procedures and Techniques*. Austin, TX: Pro-Ed.

Salary.com. 2022. "Educational Sign Language Interpreter Salary in the United States." www.salary.com/research/salary/hiring/educational-sign-language-interpreter-salary.

Scott, Sally. 2018. "The 2018 Biennial AHEAD Survey: Disability Resource Office Structures and Programs." Association on Higher Education and Disability.

Shaefer Lynn, Tanu Thakur, and Michael Meager. 2022. *Neuropsychological Assessment*. Treasure Island, FL: StatPearls.

Smith, Leah. n.d. "#Ableism." Center for Disability Rights. https://cdrnys.org/blog/uncategorized/ableism/.

Smith, Sharon G., Xinjian Zhang, Kathleen C. Basile, Melissa T. Merrick, Jing Wang, Marcie-jo Kresnow, and Jieru Chen. 2018. *The National Intimate Partner and Sexual Violence Survey: 2015 Data Brief—Updated Release*. Atlanta: National Center for Injury Prevention and Control. https://stacks.cdc.gov/view/cdc/60893.

Soken-Huberty, Emmaline. 2020. "What Does Social Justice Mean?" Human Rights Careers. February 13, 2020. https://www.humanrightscareers.com/issues/what-does-social-justice-mean/.

Spacey, John. 2018. "35 Examples of Ability." Simplicable. November 11, 2018. https://simplicable.com/new/ability.

Special Olympics. 2019. "About Spread the Word." Spread the Word. February 7, 2019. https://www.spreadtheword.global/about.

Strangio, Chase. 2021. "A Justice League of Their Own." Interview by Jon Lovett. *Crooked Media*.

Sziron, Monica. 2019. "Higher Education Staff Receive Modest Salary Increases." HigherEdJobs. www.higheredjobs.com/Articles/articleDisplay.cfm?ID=1971.

Think College National Coordinating Center. 2021. *Report on Model Accreditation Standards for Higher Education Programs for Students with Intellectual Disability: Progress on the Path to Education, Employment, and Community Living*. Boston: University of Massachusetts Institute for Community Inclusion. https://thinkcollege.net/sites/default/files/files/resources/TCreport_Accred_full_F3.pdf.

Tobin, Thomas J., and Kirsten Behling. 2018. *Reach Everyone, Teach Everyone: Universal Design for Learning in Higher Education*. Morgantown, WV: West Virginia University Press.

Tsuruta, Aya. 2010. "The Average Millennial's Attention Span—Shorter than Your Goldfish's." Repsly. www.repsly.com/blog/consumer-goods/the-average-millennials-attention-span-shorter-than-your-goldfishs.

Understood for All. 2019. "The Difference between IEPs and 504 Plans." Understood. October 16, 2019. https://www.understood.org/en/school-learning/special-services/504-plan/the-difference-between-ieps-and-504-plans.

United Nations. n.d. "About the Human Rights of Persons with Disabilities." Office of the High Commissioner for Human Rights. Accessed January 28, 2022. https://www.ohchr.org/EN/Issues/Disability/Pages/AboutHumanRightsDisability.aspx.

University of Chicago. 2019. "The Socratic Method." University of Chicago Law School. https://www.law.uchicago.edu/socratic-method.

University of Kansas. "Timeline of the Individuals with Disabilities Education Act (IDEA)." School of Education & Human Sciences. educationonline.ku.edu/community/idea-timeline.

University of Scranton. 2021. "Technical Standards." CLTE. November 2, 2021. https://www.scranton.edu/academics/ctle/disabilities/pages/technical.shtml.

University of Texas at Austin. 2013. "July 26th: ADA Anniversary Day." Division of Diversity and Community Engagement. July 26, 2013. https://diversity.utexas.edu/disability/2013/07/july-26th-ada-anniversary-day/.

———. 2019. "Effective Communication." National Deaf Center. https://www.nationaldeafcenter.org/resource/effective-communication.

———. 2021. "Speech-To-Text Services (STTS)." National Deaf Center. April 21, 2021. www.nationaldeafcenter.org/stts.

University of Washington. 2022. "What Is the United States Department of Education Office for Civil Rights (OCR) and What Do They Do?" Disabilities, Opportunities, Internetworking, and Technology. May 23, 2022. https://www.washington.edu/doit

/what-united-states-department-education-office-civil-rights-ocr-and-what-do-they-do.

U.S. Access Board. 2019. "Home." www.access-board.gov.

———. n.d. "Information and Communication Technology." Accessed January 31, 2022. https://www.access-board.gov/ict.html.

U.S. Department of Education. 1996. "Cabrillo Community College." Case No. 09-96-2150. https://www2.ed.gov/about/offices/list/ocr/docs/investigations/more/09162293-a.pdf.

———. 2018a. "Auxiliary Aids and Services for Postsecondary Students with Disabilities." Office for Civil Rights. September 2018. http://www.ed.gov/about/offices/list/ocr/docs/auxaids.html.

———. 2018b. "Sec. 300.8 Child with a Disability." Individuals with Disabilities Education Act. May 25, 2018. https://sites.ed.gov/idea/regs/b/a/300.8.

———. 2019a. "Frequently Asked Questions." Protecting Student Privacy. https://studentprivacy.ed.gov/frequently-asked-questions.

———. 2019b. "How Many Students in Postsecondary Education Have a Disability?" National Center for Education Statistics. https://nces.ed.gov/fastfacts/display.asp?id=60#:~:text=How%20many%20students%20in%20postsecondary.

———. 2020a. "Questions and Answers on the ADA Amendments Act of 2008 for Students with Disabilities Attending Public Elementary and Secondary Schools." Office for Civil Rights. January 10, 2020. https://www2.ed.gov/about/offices/list/ocr/docs/dcl-504faq-201109.html.

———. 2020b. "A Transition Guide to Postsecondary Education and Employment for Students and Youth with Disabilities (August 2020)." Individuals with Disabilities Education Act. August 2020. https://sites.ed.gov/idea/idea-files/policy-guidance-transition-guide-postsecondary-education-employment-students-youth-disabilities-august-2020/.

———. 2021a. "Family Educational Rights and Privacy Act (FERPA)." March. http://www.ed.gov/policy/gen/guid/fpco/ferpa/index.html.

———. 2021b. "Students with Disabilities." National Center for Education Statistics. May 2021. https://nces.ed.gov/programs/coe/indicator/cgg.

———. 2022a. "Case Processing Manual (CPM)." Office for Civil Rights. https://www2.ed.gov/about/offices/list/ocr/docs/ocrcpm.pdf.

———. 2022b. "How the Office for Civil Rights Handles Complaints." Office for Civil Rights. July 18, 2022. https://www2.ed.gov/about/offices/list/ocr/complaints-how.html.

———. n.d.a. "About IDEA." Individuals with Disabilities Education Act. Accessed January 30, 2022. https://sites.ed.gov/idea/about-idea/.

———. n.d.b. "Free Appropriate Public Education under Section 504." ED.gov. August. http://www.ed.gov/about/offices/list/ocr/docs/edlite-FAPE504.html.

———. n.d.c. "Protecting Students with Disabilities." Office for Civil Rights. January. http://www.ed.gov/about/offices/list/ocr/504faq.html.

———. n.d.d. "34 C.F.R. Part 104." ED.gov. https://www2.ed.gov/policy/rights/reg/ocr/edlite-34cfr104.html.

U.S. Department of Justice. 2012. "Justice Department and Lesley University Sign Agreement to Ensure Meal Plan Is Inclusive of Students with Celiac Disease and Food Allergies." Office of Public Affairs. December 20, 2012. https://www.justice.gov/opa/pr/justice-department-and-lesley-university-sign-agreement-ensure-meal-plan-inclusive-students.

———. 2015a. "Justice Department and University of Nebraska at Kearney Settle Lawsuit over Rights of Students with Psychological Disabilities to Have Assistance Animals in Student Housing." Office of Public Affairs. September 3, 2015. https://www.justice.gov/opa/pr/justice-department-and-university-nebraska-kearney-settle-lawsuit-over-rights-students.

———. 2015b. "United States Reaches Settlement with Provider of Massive Open Online Courses to Make Its Content Accessible to the Disabled." U.S. Attorney's Office District of Massachusetts. April 2, 2015. https://www.justice.gov/usao-ma/pr/united-states-reaches-settlement-provider-massive-open-online-courses-make-its-content.

———. 2016. "Questions and Answers about the Department of Justice's Notice of Proposed Rulemaking to Implement the Americans with Disabilities Act Amendments Act of 2008." ADA.gov. https://www.ada.gov/regs2016/adaaa_qa.html.

———. 2018. "Justice Department Releases Memorandum on Litigation Guidelines for Civil Consent Decrees and Settlement Agreements." Office of Public Affairs. November 8, 2018. https://www.justice.gov/opa/pr/justice-department-releases-memorandum-litigation-guidelines-civil-consent-decrees-and.

U.S. Department of Justice Civil Rights Division. 2010a. "ADA Requirements: Effective Communication." ADA.gov. www.ada.gov/effective-comm.htm.

———. 2010b. "Nondiscrimination on the Basis of Disability in Public Accommodations and Commercial Facilities." ADA.gov. https://www.ada.gov/law-and-regs/design-standards/2010-stds/.

———. 2010c. "2010 ADA Regulations." ADA.gov. https://www.ada.gov/2010_regs.htm.

———. 2010d. "2010 ADA Standards for Accessible Design." ADA.gov. https://www.ada.gov/law-and-regs/design-standards/2010-stds/.

———. 2013. "Americans with Disabilities Act of 1990, As Amended." ADA.gov. https://www.ada.gov/law-and-regs/ada/.

———. 2014. "ADA Technical Assistance Document: Testing Accommodations." ADA.gov. https://www.ada.gov/regs2014/testing_accommodations.pdf.

———. 2015. "ADA Compliance Brief - Restriping Parking Spaces." ADA.gov. https://www.ada.gov/resources/restriping-parking-spaces/.

———. 2016a. "Final Regulatory Assessment, Final Rule—Amendment of ADA Title II and Title III Regulations to Implement ADA Amendments Act of 2008." ADA.gov. October 11, 2016. https://www.ada.gov/regs2016/final_rule_adaaa.html.

———. 2016b. "Part 35 Nondiscrimination on the Basis of Disability in State and Local Government Services." ADA.gov. https://www.ada.gov/law-and-regs/title-ii-2010-regulations/.

———. 2020a. "ADA Requirements: Service Animals." ADA.gov. February 24, 2020. https://www.ada.gov/service_animals_2010.htm.

———. 2020b. "Guide to Disability Rights Laws." ADA.gov. February 2020. https://www.ada.gov/cguide.htm#anchor62335.

———. n.d.a. "How to Report a Civil Rights Violation." Accessed August 8, 2022. https://civilrights.justice.gov/#crt-landing--reporting.

———. n.d.b. "Lesson 2: Factors of Undue Burden." ADA.gov. Accessed January 28, 2022. https://www.ada.gov/reachingout/l2factors.html.

U.S. Equal Employment Opportunity Commission. 2011. "Questions and Answers on the Final Rule Implementing the ADA Amendments Act of 2008." March 25, 2011. http://www.eeoc.gov/laws/regulations/ada_qa_final_rule.cfm.

Utah State University. 2020. "Captions, Transcripts, and Audio Descriptions." WebAIM. July 1, 2020. https://webaim.org/techniques/captions/.

Viennet, Romane, and Beatriz Pont. 2017. "Education Policy Implementation: A Literature Review and Proposed Framework." OECD Education Working Papers, No. 162, ERIC, OECD. https://eric.ed.gov/?id=ED581629.

Villarreal, Mary Ann. 2022. "Students Notice Diversity. That's a Good First Step (Opinion)." Inside Higher Ed. January 6, 2022. https://www.insidehighered.com/views/2022/01/06/after-increasing-campus-diversity-work-foster-belonging-opinion.

Vivanti, Giacomo. 2019. "Ask the Editor: What Is the Most Appropriate Way to Talk about Individuals with a Diagnosis of Autism?" *Journal of Autism and Developmental Disorders* 50 (November): 691–93. https://doi.org/10.1007/s10803-019-04280-x.

Wells, Catlin. 2021. Letter to Bridget McNamee. March 23, 2021.

The Welsh Centre for Language Planning. 2011. "Developing Policies, Protocols, and Procedures." https://www.iaith.cymru/uploads/general-uploads/policies_and_procedures_jan_13___2_.pdf.

WHO. 2021. "Disability and Health." World Health Organization. November 24, 2021. https://www.who.int/news-room/fact-sheets/detail/disability-and-health#:~:text=Over%201%20billion%20people%20are.

Wilson, David. 2016. "Responding to Risk through Behavioral Intervention." *Journal of Campus Behavioral Intervention* 6 (4): 2–5. https://www.brianvanbrunt.com/_files/ugd/b64c59_265f06180de141299468b0aea3285e59.pdf.

Woodward, Stephanie. n.d. "Ronald Mace and His Impact on Universal Design." Accessed January 28, 2022. https://cdrnys.org/blog/advocacy/ronald-mace-and-his-impact-on-universal-design/.

Workplace Fairness. 2022. "Disability Discrimination." https://www.workplacefairness.org/disability-discrimination#:~:text=The%20most%20common%20types%20of.

Wright, Peter W. D., and Pamela Darr Wright. 2018. "Transition: Summary of Performance (SOP)." Wrightslaw. December 10, 2018. https://www.wrightslaw.com/info/trans.sop.htm.

W3C. 2008. "World Wide Web Consortium (W3C)." https://www.w3.org/.

———. 2019a. "Accessibility Testing." WC3 Wiki. May 20, 2019. http://www.w3.org/wiki/Accessibility_testing.

———. 2019b. "Introduction to Web Accessibility." Web Accessibility Initiative (WAI). https://www.w3.org/WAI/fundamentals/accessibility-intro/.

Zeisler, Andy. 2016. "College Guide for Students with Disabilities." Best Colleges. March 28, 2016. https://www.bestcolleges.com/resources/students-with-disabilities/.

Index

Ability, 3, 4, 5, 12, 14–18, 21–22, 25–26, 28–29, 31, 38, 53, 59, 62, 69, 71, 81, 87, 90, 94, 100, 105, 107, 118, 124–125, 127, 131, 144, 148, 156, 159, 178–179, 195, 211, 219, 227, 233, 235, 237, 252, 256, 285–286, 299
Abroad accommodations, 122, 152, 153, 155
Academic accommodations, 4, 13, 23, 38, 59–60, 83, 88, 94, 104, 108, 119, 127, 130, 132–133, 139, 189, 198, 234, 235, 307
Accessibility advisory committee, 253, 263
Accessibility testing, 164, 276, 278–279
Accommodation Letters, 51, 69, 114, 136, 139, 302
Accommodations: differences between high school and college, 83, 88–89
ADA checklist for existing facilities, 250
ADA Standards for Accessible Design, 251
Administrative Assistant, 40, 62
Advisory Board, 66, 310
AHEAD, 9, 20, 56, 62, 74, 94, 99, 101, 102, 108, 110, 112, 139, 182, 183, 204, 208, 229, 232–233, 238, 252, 287, 291, 296, 312
Alt-text, 164
American Sign Language (ASL), 19, 26, 58–59, 145, 168, 175–177, 206–207, 288
Americans with Disabilities Act (ADA), 3–5, 7, 11, 13, 20–21, 28–31, 34, 36, 39–42, 46–47, 53, 63, 80, 82–83, 86, 90, 95–100, 103–104, 112, 117, 119–120, 126, 129, 134, 147–148, 152–153, 158, 161, 164, 166, 172, 188, 190, 213, 219–220, 223, 233–234, 240, 243–245, 250–252, 255, 257–261, 266–270, 309, 311, 319, 323, 325–330
Americans with Disabilities Act Amendments Act (ADAAA), 4, 34, 39, 82, 96–100, 104, 112, 219, 233, 240, 244
Architectural Barriers Act (ABA), 251
Assessment, 43, 83, 90, 107–108, 111, 113–114, 122–123, 126, 128, 130, 134, 182, 187, 211, 291–293, 297, 301–302
Assistance Animal, 8, 155, 228–229, 237, 331
Assistive Listening Device, 88
Assistive Technology (AT), 14, 60, 63, 65, 84, 91, 93, 99, 145, 156–161, 164–165, 169, 170–182, 193, 204, 207, 272, 274, 276, 278
Assistive Technology (AT) labs, 54
Attendance, 8, 67, 86, 123, 145–146, 151, 153–155, 211–212, 214, 234–235, 237, 240, 286
Audit, 238, 260, 262
Auxiliary Aid, 6, 4, 8, 91, 104, 138, 140, 143, 145, 156, 158–159, 161, 164–165, 169, 172–174, 176–177, 183, 234, 269

Auxiliary programs, 203
Auxiliary Service, 167–169

Barrier removal, 6, 154, 252, 262
Barrier reporting, 261
Benchmarking, 63
Blind/Low Vision, 12, 19, 21, 27, 91, 98–99, 145, 147, 158, 162–164, 169, 178, 225–226, 267–268, 279
Braille, 29, 40, 59, 60, 73, 145, 158–159, 162–164, 171, 175–176, 178, 205, 255, 268, 288
Budget, 41, 50, 54, 56–65, 69–70, 153, 208, 218, 241, 254
Built environment, 6, 249–251, 253, 255, 257, 259, 263

Captions, 59, 156–157, 165, 167, 266, 269, 277, 278, 281, 286, 296, 326
CART, 58–59
CAST, 286–287
CCTV, 175
Centralization, 44
Closed Caption, 158
Collaboration, 6, 8, 36, 181–182, 197, 227, 240, 304–305, 307, 309–314, 320, 322
College completion rates, 5
Commencement, 28, 320
Compensation, 56–60, 70
Content experts, 119, 121–122
Contingency, 150–151, 154
Convocation, 37, 60, 65, 169

Database, 60, 66–67, 69, 71–72, 184, 196, 204, 208, 270–271, 280, 311
Decentralization, 44
Department of Justice (DOJ), 4, 12–13, 98–99, 126, 130, 148, 161–162, 218–219, 223–234, 257–258, 267, 270
Digital Environment, 6–8, 264–267, 269, 271, 273, 276–277, 279, 281, 283
Dining accommodations, 15, 43, 60, 65, 101, 119, 127, 132, 139–140, 142, 149, 154, 162, 237, 250, 252, 260, 262, 265, 270, 320
Disability, 3–29, 31, 34, 36, 38–39, 40–41, 43–44, 46–48, 50–51, 54–55, 57, 62, 65, 67–68, 70, 73, 79–89, 91–114, 116–117, 119–120, 122, 125, 127–130, 132, 134, 136, 137, 139, 140, 142–143, 146–148, 151–154, 157–159, 162, 169, 173–174, 176, 180, 183, 187, 189–193, 196–198, 200–201, 203–205, 208, 209, 211–212, 217, 219, 220, 225, 235, 238, 243, 251–253, 256, 265–266, 279, 281–282, 285, 287, 306, 308, 311, 318–319, 321
Disability disclosure, 235
Disability language conventions, 5
DSSHE, 9

Eligibility, 6–7, 18, 22, 25, 65, 81–85, 87, 90, 94–95, 98, 102–105, 107, 109, 111–112, 115, 122, 125, 127, 128–129, 136, 138–139, 152, 177, 183, 190, 201, 237, 318–319; categories, 68, 81–82, 109
Emerging technology, 178, 267
Emotional Support Animal (ESA), 8, 146–148, 155, 228
Experiential learning accommodations, 7, 118, 123, 142, 150, 154

Faculty Advisory Board (FAB), 310
Fair Housing Act (FHA), 128, 147–148, 223
Family Education Rights and Privacy Act (FERPA), 86
Fee-for-service, 34, 47–48, 56
504 Plan, 85, 86, 110, 111
FM, 136, 166
Free and Appropriate Public Education (FAPE), 81, 85
Fundamental alteration, 88, 125, 131, 134, 138, 146, 210, 211
Fundamental requirement, 200, 202, 210

Good faith efforts, 114, 119, 127, 139, 318–319
Grant(s), 12, 15, 22, 27, 52, 56, 61, 94, 102–104, 110, 116, 119–120, 122, 126–129, 131, 141, 156, 174, 176–177, 200, 203, 219, 233, 245, 262, 287
Grant Writer, 61
Grievance, 41, 68, 103–104, 132–133, 137, 183, 213, 233, 237, 240, 242–243, 245, 268

Higher Education Opportunities Act (HEOA), 91–92
Housing accommodations, 26, 43, 60, 65, 72, 110, 119, 127–128, 132, 134, 139, 142, 145–148, 154, 189, 193, 195, 223, 228, 232–233, 237, 242–243, 251, 263, 298, 331

Individualized Education Program (IEP), 67, 79, 81–86, 90–98, 101–102, 109–111, 114, 190

Individuals with Disabilities Education Act (IDEA), 22, 25, 31, 39, 44, 46–47, 51, 55, 62, 69, 80–90, 96, 103, 112, 117, 190, 306
Intake, 32, 40–41, 46, 48, 51, 62, 64–67, 74, 102–106, 111, 114, 119, 126, 139–140, 148, 155, 173–174, 176, 181–182, 184–188, 190–192, 194–195, 197–198, 235, 263, 302
Intellectual disability, 18, 98
Intellectual property, 204, 207, 236
Interactive process, 6, 8, 77, 80, 94–95, 99, 102–104, 106–108, 111, 113–114, 118–119, 121–122, 125, 127, 132–133, 136, 138–140, 152–153, 176, 180, 185, 188, 195, 202, 211, 232–234, 238–240, 242, 244, 318–320
International symbol of accessibility, 257, 260
Interpreters, 41–42, 57–59, 72, 158, 165, 168, 180, 187, 236, 288, 311
Inward facing website, 55

Learning management system (LMS), 27, 56, 204–206, 267–271, 273, 291, 295–297
Legal standards, 250

Mace, Ron, 251, 285–286
Map, 53, 175, 234, 244, 254–255, 263, 283, 298
Massive Open Online Courses (MOOCs), 269
Merit, 68

Noncompensation, 56, 58–60, 70
Note takers, 57, 63, 72, 154, 158, 174
Note taking assistance, 203

Office of Civil Rights (OCR), 34, 82, 85, 211, 217–223, 225–227, 229, 233, 235, 270, 274, 300
Onboarding, 64–65, 75, 233, 307
Orientation, 14, 16, 35, 48, 55, 65, 72–74, 91, 151, 153, 171, 187, 233, 283, 307
Outward facing web site, 73

Parking accommodations, 15, 149–150, 154, 168, 250, 252, 254–255, 257–259, 265, 320, 331
Paths of travel, 258
Pinch points, 292–293
Plus-One strategies, 289–292, 294, 301
Private school, 83–84, 270

Proctoring, 42, 51–54, 58, 63–64, 74, 133, 173, 208–209
Procurement, 149, 179, 240–241, 268, 273, 276, 279–280, 282
Program accessibility, 252, 262
Public facing content/website, 218, 223, 269, 271

Ratios, 40, 60, 63, 277, 318
Relocation, 40, 130, 145, 151, 154, 262
Resident Assistants (RA), 307
Resolution agreements, 217, 232, 267
Restrooms, 250, 260, 262
Roadmap, 6, 8, 49–50, 268, 281, 295–296
Routes of travel, 250, 259

Section 504, 4–5, 82–86, 90, 110–111, 134, 152, 204, 219–220, 330
Section 508, 274, 276, 325–326
Self-determination, 88, 90–91, 191, 324
Self-evaluation, 252, 261–262
Service animal, 142, 146–149, 220, 233, 253, 331
Signage, 29, 149, 164, 170, 254–255, 257, 259, 262
Stakeholders, VII, 6, 39, 64, 66, 79, 130, 195, 239–240, 242, 244, 253, 273, 282, 288, 299, 301, 305, 308–309, 314, 318
STEM, 59
Sticky keys, 165
Summary of Performance (SOP), 82, 101, 332

Teaching Assistant (TA), 73, 136, 209
Telecommunications Device for the Deaf (TTY), 158
Testing accommodations, 52, 60, 84, 101, 109, 116, 143–144, 164, 202, 207, 276–279, 331
Text-to-Speech, 27, 54, 59, 144, 154, 165, 170, 173–176, 206, 267
Think College, 92, 329
Transition plan, 79–82, 88, 90–91, 251, 261
Transportation accommodation, 4, 15, 43, 45, 65, 119, 130, 142, 147, 149, 150–151, 154, 172, 187, 193, 236, 251, 255–258, 270
Transportation parking, 147, 149–151, 154, 168, 236, 250, 252, 254–259, 265, 320, 325, 331

Undue burden, 60, 88, 103, 113, 129–131, 252, 331
Unions (student, faculty), 38, 57–58, 230, 305
Universal Design (UD), 7–8, 15, 28, 42–43, 157, 206, 217, 238, 240–241, 251, 253, 266, 282, 284–286, 294, 298, 300, 302, 319–320, 324, 326–327, 329, 332
Universal Design for Learning (UDL), 286–289, 301–302

Video remote, 158
Voluntary Product Accessibility Templates (VPAT), 276, 280

Wayfinding, 29, 164, 170
Web accessibility, 7, 218, 240, 264, 266–267, 269–270, 273–274, 278, 325, 332
Web Content Accessibility Guidelines (WCAG), 268–270, 273–274, 276–277, 281

Kirsten T. Behling is the Associate Dean of the Student Accessibility and Academic Resource (StAAR) Center at Tufts University. She is the coauthor of *Reach Everyone, Teach Everyone: Universal Design for Learning in Higher Education*.

Eileen H. Bellemore is a Senior Specialist and clinician at the Association of American Medical Colleges. She formerly led disability services offices at several small private colleges.

Lisa B. Bibeau is the Assistant Dean for Student Success and Disability Services as well as Adjunct Professor in the Health Care Studies Program at Salem State University.

Andrew S. Cioffi is the Director of Disability Services at Suffolk University and Adjunct Professor of Disability Services in Higher Education.

Bridget A. McNamee is an Accommodations Advisor in corporate human resources. She was the former Associate Director of Accessibility Services at Wentworth Institute of Technology.

www.ingramcontent.com/pod-product-compliance
Lightning Source LLC
Chambersburg PA
CBHW050134240426
43673CB00043B/1668